Digital Media Strategies of the Far-Right in Europe and the United States

Digital Media Strategies of the Far-Right in Europe and the United States

Edited by
Patricia Anne Simpson and Helga Druxes

LEXINGTON BOOKS
Lanham • Boulder • New York • London

Published by Lexington Books
An imprint of The Rowman & Littlefield Publishing Group, Inc.
4501 Forbes Boulevard, Suite 200, Lanham, Maryland 20706
www.rowman.com

Unit A, Whitacre Mews, 26-34 Stannary Street, London SE11 4AB

British Library Cataloguing in Publication Information Available

Library of Congress Cataloging-in-Publication Data Available
The hardback edition of this book was previously catalogued by the Library of Congress as follows:

Digital media strategies of the far right in Europe and the United States / edited by Patricia Anne
Simpson and Helga Druxes.
pages cm.
Includes bibliographical references and index.
1. Right wing extremists--Europe. 2. Right wing extremists--United States. 3. Digital media--Politi-
cal aspects--Europe. 4. Digital media--Political aspects--United States. 5. Internet--Political aspects--
Europe. 6. Internet--Political aspects--United States. I. Simpson, Patricia Anne, 1958- editor of compilation, author. II. Druxes, Helga, 1959- editor of compilation, author.
HN380.Z9R3284 2015
302.23'1094--dc23
                                        2015000943

ISBN: 978-0-7391-9881-0 (cloth)
ISBN: 978-0-7391-9883-4 (pbk.)
ISBN: 978-0-7391-9882-7 (electronic)

Contents

Acknowledgments

The editors wish to thank Montana State University and Williams College for providing assistance for the research that led to the publication of this volume. Simpson began the project during a sabbatical leave in 2011. Helga Druxes would like to acknowledge Williams College for its generous leave policy and research support. We would like to thank our students at both institutions for opportunities to engage in rigorous intellectual exchange, and our editor Lindsey Porambo at Lexington Books for her support and guidance through the stages of production. We are also grateful to two anonymous readers whose responses to our original proposal helped shape the final volume.

Colleagues have been a vital source of support and perspective as well. Simpson would like to thank the staff at the Archiv der Jugendkulturen in Berlin for providing unique and crucial research opportunities. Further, colleagues in European Studies and American Studies at MSU and elsewhere have been invaluable sources of support, especially Michael Rauhut, Mark Yoffe, and Susan Kollin. Druxes would like to thank colleagues at Williams for their support: Magnus Bernhardsson, Thomas A. Kohut, Gail Newman, Kashia Pieprzak, Jana Sawicki, and Olga Shevchenko. In Germany, Druxes would like to thank Dunja Brill, Alexander Häusler, Christoph Schultheis, Olaf Sundermeyer, Claudia Wein, Karin Yesilada, and Andreas Zick for their interest and helpful suggestions.

This volume would not have been possible without the stalwart support and forbearance of our families, especially the constant encouragement of Alex Mihailovic, who stepped in with a second piece when a contributor had to withdraw, and of Theo Lipfert, who assisted with technical and graphic design issues. Finally, we would like to express our gratitude to the contributors for their energy, commitment, and intellectual generosity.

Introduction

Patricia Anne Simpson and Helga Druxes

Whether at the margins or in the mainstream of global media, right-wing movements and their proponents continue to make a variety of headlines, from astonishing political victories in some of Europe's weakening democratic states, to choreographed terrorist acts. The Internet in the age of Web 2.0 has become, among other things, an instrument of communication and community; a malleable tool easily wielded by seemingly invisible hands. As the authors of *Viral Hate: Containing Its Spread On the Internet* observe, "The ways in which the Internet is being used to disseminate and promote hateful and violent beliefs and attitudes are astounding, varied, and continually multiplying."[1] A common response to the existence of and events authored or sponsored by radical right-wing activists frequently involves a sense of dismayed shock about the vitriol and persistence of the extremist groups that provide a range of agents with ideological and social infrastructure. Increasingly, new rightist groups network with each other; some advocate violence, while others maneuver their ideological positions closer to mainstream politics. Striking is the relationship between the German fascist past and the contemporary international mobilization of its racial hatred, symbols, and rhetoric. With the leverage of digital reproducibility, historical messages of hate are finding new recipients with breathtaking speed and scope. While some scholars note that the actual membership in extremist groups may be declining, the spread of xenophobic rhetoric strengthens a perception of disenfranchisement among local populations and offers these groups an easy target to blame for the effects of globalization and economic crises—conferring more political agency on groups whose numbers may indeed be small, but whose voices can be amplified to reach a receptive global audience.

The arrival of Web 2.0 social networking has accelerated the formation of new radical right groups, facilitated violent actionism, and enhanced the groups' ability to forge virtual cross-linkages.[2] In Europe, for example, populist right-wing activists organized around an anti-immigration agenda are becoming more vocal and increasingly mainstream, providing pushback against the increase in migration flows from North Africa and Eastern Europe and countering support for integration with a categorical rejection of multiculturalism. The rapid growth in popularity of right extremist groups in response to transnational economic crises underscores the importance of examining in detail the language and political mobilization strategies of the New Right, a European characterization of the movements. Moreover, established Right Parties like Marine Le Pen's National Front in France and Geert Wilders's Freedom Party in the Netherlands also actively cooperate to obtain European Parliament funding that increases their sphere of influence and their potentially populist appeal. Whether they opportunistically exploit democratic structures or position themselves on the radical fringe, New Right groups now share a pragmatic approach to mainstreaming their message in order to shift popular support away from liberal or centrist positions and towards rightist goals and beliefs. In the United States, anti-immigration sentiment continues to provide a rallying point for political and personal agendas that connect the rhetoric of borders with national, racial, and security issues.

Immigration remains one crucial issue that unites the platforms of right-wing movements in the United States and Europe, but it also forges unsettling connections between extremism and mainstream politics in the public sphere. In the United States, anti-immigration discourse has long been a staple of right-wing media fare and the politics it feeds: the 2014 controversy about young Latin American refugees underscores the increasingly populist appeal of this ticket. A headline in *U.S. News*, for example, reads: "Anti-Immigrant Hate Coming From Everyday Americans." The article stresses that protests to reroute busloads of immigrants do not represent hate groups or radicals. Quoting a report from Southern Poverty Law Center (SPLC), the journalist Lauren Fox notes that "'nativist extremist' groups have actually been in decline," due in part to the achievement of short-term goals to pass anti-immigration legislation.[3] This issue creates common ground between the "average" and the extreme. The National Socialist Movement in the United States, which was founded in 1974 and grew under the leadership of Jeff Schoep, currently claims fifty-five units across the country and remains, despite setbacks, one of the larger neo-Nazi groups, with an explicit stance that is pro-European American and adamantly against illegal immigration.[4] Anxiety about shifting demographics in the United States and elsewhere has resulted in the cooptation of discourses about diversity and multiculturalism—the assertion of whiteness as a racial category now subject to discrimination. The website stormfront.org, for example, proclaims on the entry page: "*We are the voice of the new, embattled White minority!*"[5]

Alongside the nativist, racist, and anti-immigration politics, anti-Semitism still features prominently in the rhetoric and media strategies of the American far right. While the Anti-Defamation League was able to report a decline in anti-Semitic attacks in the United States during 2013, high-profile acts of violence persist with high frequency. We have the example of the alleged gunman in the Kansas attacks on three people at two Jewish facilities in April 2014. Frazier Glenn Cross, a former KKK leader, was known for his racist and anti-Semitic views and posted frequently on online forums. The historical legacy of such violent hate groups as the KKK is evident in this tragic and senseless killing. The discourses connect the racism and anti-Semitism of the American radical right with the National Alliance, the Aryan Nations, and some aspects of the Christian Identity movement.

Anti-Semitism is also resurgent in Europe. As Jochen Bittner, an editor for the German weekly *Die Zeit*, observes in an opinion piece: "The new anti-Semitism does not originate solely with the typical white-supremacist neo-Nazi; instead, the ugly truth that many in Europe don't want to confront is that much of the anti-Jewish animus originates with European people of Muslim background."[6] This "ugly truth" is inflected elsewhere in Europe. For example, in Hungary Viktor Orban's Jobbik Party advocated placing Jews in camps and deporting them. It was also in evidence during virulent anti-Semitic demonstrations in Paris, the killings of three people at the Jewish Museum in Brussels, Belgium, on 24 May 2014—on the eve of the European Parliament elections, and persistent incidents of anti-Semitic graffiti in Alsace and Germany. These targeted Jewish tombstones, as well as Jewish German Holocaust victims' memorial markers, the so-called *Stolpersteine* (tripping stones) in Berlin neighborhoods.[7] While these acts vary greatly in their severity, they need to be considered as part of a spectrum of transatlantic anti-Semitism. The contributions in this volume focus on the far-right "web" both in the literal and figurative senses. With emphasis on transnational right wing activism, movements, and political parties, the essays explore the ways in which members of extremist groups use the media, popular music, sports events, political rallies, but also Facebook, YouTube, blogs, flash mobs, and other means of mechanical and digital reproduction to form virtual and face-to-face communities for the purpose of disseminating their political message.

This volume represent a collective effort to examine and understand these issues, informed by the conviction that an interdisciplinary and transnational approach can allow productive comparison of media strategies in Europe and the United States. There are points of convergence between the two largest producers and consumers of white supremacist politics and practices.[8] At the outset, we acknowledge that definitions of far-right politics differ; individual authors take the variations in definitional and disciplinary language into account in their respective analyses. With a focus on enacting ideologies on the far-right, on sometimes violent pro-national and anti-immigrant stances, and on the skillful creation and manipulation of virtual communities, the contributions in this volume foreground the cultural shibboleths that are exchanged among far-right supporters on the Internet, which serve to generate a sense of group belonging and the illusion of power far greater than the known numbers of neo-Nazis in any one country, for example, might suggest. Moreover, with attention to transatlantic right-wing causes and movements and their use of digital media, the essays exert pressure on the similarities among the various national agents, while accommodating differences in the virtual and sometimes violent identities created and nurtured online.

The contributors represent a variety of academic disciplines and professions, including the social sciences and humanities, professional journalists and data analysts, philosophers and cultural critics. With a range of research agendas, the resulting essays are informed by a variety of historical contexts and theories that engage issues of communication strategies, extremist positions defined trans-locally, and some degree of organized political persuasion and/or affiliation in international consumer societies. Thanks to the low cost, speed, and ease of producing a virtual life-world, even a small group can generate the illusion of a critical mass in response to social crises and foment terrorist youth actionism.[9] In other words, the global expanse of Web 2.0 exceeds anything theorized by Jürgen Habermas's theory of the bourgeois public sphere, which emerged from the context of European print media.[10] Nor can Jean Baudrillard's later concept of "hyperreality," cogently summarized by Mark Poster as "the new linguistic condition of society, rendering impotent theories that still rely on materialist reductionism or rationalist referentiality," fully encompass the performative aspects of Internet communication.[11] For members of right-wing organizations and their recruits, the lure of a largely uncensored virtual domain creates greater potential for violent posturing and experimentation with more extreme alternative identities and alter egos. Further, there is evidence that virtual online communities create opportunities for offline contact as well at music festivals, soccer games, street protests, or flash mobs.

Our work emerged from an urgent need to understand the role of media in political radicalism. The persistence, in some cases resurgence, of the right wing and its transnational appeal motivated our further exploration of the relationships between online ideologies and right-wing agency. There is no doubt that the Internet can facilitate any form of activist and/or terrorist ideologies, but our focus on the radical right stems from a historical interest in the legacy of National Socialism. In the United States, Pete Simi and Robert Futrell's *American Swastika: Inside the White Power Movement's Hidden Spaces of Hate* (2010) provides both an overview of and insight into the strategies and practices of white power communities, including their creation of "hidden spaces," emphasis on family, cultivation of commitment through music, ritual, paraphernalia, symbolism, and the use digital media. Their concentration on the "critical use of cyberspace as an Aryan free space" informs our approach.[12] Their scholarship gained greater importance retrospectively after the publication of their op-ed in *The New York Times*, "The Sound of Hate," in which they make the connection between Wade Michael Page's participation in the hate music scene and his violent action: the murder of six Sikhs at a Wisconsin temple.[13] Simi and Futrell's scholarly work takes an ethnographic approach to the multiple articulations of right-wing activism and activists, lending insight into the "Aryan free spaces" in which white power radicals can nurture and sustain racist ideologies, recruit members, and live their daily lives.[14] The focus on Aryan identity links radical racialist politics and their proponents in the United States with more mainstream identity movements in the European arena. Political scientist and specialist on right-wing extremism Thomas Grumke states succinctly that: "Pan-Aryanism, the ideological basis for this network, is essentially a modern anti-modern ideology. [. . .] Transnationally co-operating right-wing extremists are [. . .] fundamental enemies of pluralism, parliamentary democracy and its representatives. This identity-oriented resistance is de facto the globalization of hatred and in Western and Eastern Europe alike a battle for the parliaments and civil society."[15] The seductive power of merging "hidden spaces" with publicity as a recruitment strategy relies on the creation of a compelling virtual life world in which supporters can feel embedded, in contrast to more stringent hate speech controls in the real-world public sphere.[16] One example of this strategy the German far-right cell the National Socialist Underground (NSU), members of which murdered nine small business owners of Greek, Turkish or Turkish German descent. They took photos of some of their victims with their cell phones in order to include these on a confessional DVD, which their surviving accomplice Beate Zschäpe sent to news media after Uwe Mundlos's and Uwe Böhnhardt's decade-long rampage ended in a suicide pact. Excerpts from the killer video were also posted on youtube.de and introduced by the popular children's cartoon character Pink Panther. Moreover, explicit references to their murder spree were retroactively discovered in far-right music tracks, suggesting that members of the far-right scene had some awareness of these acts of racial cleansing.[17] Once the NSU-murders became officially known, the far-right chat room *thiazi.net* registered over 1,500 posts from supporters.[18] These instances show the far-right perpetrators' acute awareness of social media as a forum in which such acts can elicit approval, and possibly find imitators. In this regard, attracting new recruits is a motivating factor.[19]

There appears to be a correlation between the increasing trafficking of far-right beliefs through the blogosphere and the rise in acts of criminal violence. German politically motivated crime statistics for the year 2013 may serve as a case in point. In May 2014, the German *Bundesnachrichtendienst,* the equivalent of the United States' FBI, reported for the past year an increase in physical attacks as part of far-right criminal activity, listing 16,557 right extreme criminal offenses from a total of 22,129 acts of politically motivated crime. Regarding Internet use, the 2013 interior ministry report recognizes "shorter and shorter intervals until radicalization," which often occurs with activists "helping themselves to a few prefab argument blocks out of the Internet offerings."[20] On the local level, far-right parties can mobilize voters in economically depressed regions by doing grassroots work: acting as social caretakers, helping the unemployed fill out paperwork, organizing youth soccer leagues, generally doing social work with the elderly and the young where such official services were lacking. Moreover, the far right strategically infiltrates citizens' initiatives, initially adopting those concerns, then occupying leadership positions and revealing more of their own agenda, a strategy that has worked for them in Germany, France, Belgium, and many other European countries.[21] By contrast, some violent far-right actors like the NSU or Anders Behring Breivik adhere to a mantra of "deeds instead of words," and operate as small units or individuals backed by a loose network of supporters. Even right-wing supporters who have no known history of violence are enthusiastic collectors of military paraphernalia, weapons, unlicensed guns, and explosives.[22] The NSU started out disaffected by German unification and the economic upheaval in their working-class suburb with petty theft, then anti-Semitic graffiti, graduating to placing home-made bombs in suitcases at public sites in the town of Jena, which led police investigators to a rented garage full of explosives. Even after the trio went underground, Böhnhardt and Mundlos used mixed forms of violence: setting of a nail bomb attack on a street with many ethnic businesses, executing Turkish, Greek, and Turkish German storekeepers with shots to the head. The DVD that they manufactured contained graphic shots of victims taken during the attacks, combined with satirical commentary. Their choice to document their deeds in this way shows a shift from earnest written tracts to the genre of (albeit cynical) "edutainment."

Internet blogs and opinion sites feed a sense of populist outrage against a diffuse array of contemporary changes in the homeland: the building of mosques in Germany, the burqa or the headscarf, the erosion of the welfare state, climate change, gay people—in short any indicators of a liberalism or multiculturalism, or economic resource tightening, always deflecting responsibility for these phenomena onto culturally "foreign" immigrants with supposedly non-western values that resist or reject any assimilation. The journalists Toralf Staud and Johannes Radke describe the right populist website *Politically Incorrect,* online since 2004, as a paradigmatic tool for creating an active online community, which then foments right populist moral outrage in the comment pages of liberal news sites: it gets 60,000 hits per day and has spawned regular discussion groups in more than fifty cities in Germany, as well as in Austria, Switzerland, and the Czech Republic.[23] This site positions itself as pro-American and pro-Israeli; its authors, Staudt and Radke assert, "aggressively posture as martyrs, who finally speak out frankly against the opinion terror of political correctness."[24] Such rhetoric validates a sense of belonging to a new partisan fighter elite in the culture wars, a self-understanding whose historical lineage reaches back to the anti-Semitic tirades of Treitschke in the late nineteenth century, and was revived in the 1950s by conservative nationalists like Carl Schmitt and Arnold Gehlen.[25] The ideologues of the New Right share a sense of being an elite brigade of Culture War crusaders for Christian and family values, a position they share with the Christian Identity movement in the United States, in the face of cultural decline triggered by globalization, Islam, and "weak" democracies. Such an enthusiastic embrace of new technologies may seem counterintuitive in light of the anti-modernism of the New Right, however, social media and the Internet facilitate a virtual enhancement of the pedestrian everyday by allowing online commentators and content producers to feel more included, and therefore more agentive.[26]

In this volume, we devote particular attention to the effects of the Internet as a virtual sphere that enhances experimentation with radical, sometimes violent stances with the potential to foment outrage around perceived "hot button" national and transnational issues that deepen the real divide between a "identity" and "difference."

CHAPTER OVERVIEW

The volume is divided into three sections. In the first, "Extremisms and the Internet," four chapters provide a general overview of Internet practices adopted by the extreme right in the United States, Norway, and Russia. In "Swastikas in Cyberspace: How Hate Went Online," Chip Berlet and Carol Mason investigate ways the ultra right in the United States was able to transition from print to digital media. Their research focuses on the influential activism of one individual, the German American immigrant George P. Dietz (1928–2007), who positioned himself as a publisher and distributor of neo-Nazi material. His acquired expertise with computers enabled him to bring hate online. According to Berlet and Mason, his goal was to launch an online network of right-wing activists who had been using ham radio to communicate across the country, and he did initiate the first electronic bulletin board system utilized by the American far right. Dietz was able to disseminate anti-Semitic and racist publications internationally, generate publications using print media, such as *The Liberty Bell* and *White Power Report,* and bring "hate online" with the Liberty Bell Network in order to thwart the supposed Jewish monopoly of media. Drawing from primary archival materials, Berlet and Mason examine the impact of Dietz's work across the United States and abroad, demonstrating how new technologies were deployed in the service of popularizing revisionist history on the far right.

In the next essay, "The Lone Wolf Comes from Somewhere, Too," Øyvind Strømmen and Kjetil Stormark assess the motivations and narratives of "lone wolf" terrorists and compare their use of the media. With a focus on Anders Behring Breivik, the perpetrator of the 22 July 2011 attacks in Norway, the authors analyze the implications of his online presence, his anti-Muslim ideology, and ultimately his failed attempt to gain the widespread influence he sought with his manifesto. Prior to his deadly shooting spree against young liberal Norwegians, Breivik published a lengthy manifesto on the Internet. Journalists Strømmen and Stormark observe that Breivik was a lone wolf, but they also make connections between his ideology and that of other right-wing extremists. Drawing on specific aspects of the Breivik case and other examples of lone-wolf terrorism, the authors elaborate on what this can tell us about the phenomenon and attempt to determine how Internet use can make a difference in comparison with earlier cases of this type of terrorist activity.

In "Mobilizing on the Fringe: Domestic Extremists and Antisocial Networking," Kyle Christensen, Arian Spahiu, Bret Wilson, and Robert D. Duval examine extremist political movements that have proliferated on the Web in recent years, thanks to the advent of minimal publication costs and almost universal access. Whether White Supremacist, neo-Nazi, anti-abortion, black separatist, radical Christian—all have found a home (and voice) on the Internet. This chapter explores the Internet base of extremism in the United States through an analysis of network structures and linkages. The authors examine a moderately large networked set of linkages among several hundred web-based extremist groups. Using social network analysis (SNA), the authors' intent is to facilitate our understanding of why some political extremists adopt violent strategies and of the ways by which the propensity for violence is moderated and enhanced by network characteristics.

In "Hijacking Authority: Academic Neo-Aryanism and Internet Expertise," Alexandar Mihailovic considers two purported experts who occupy the fringes of right-wing intelligentsia in the United States and Russia. Identifying their common project of establishing "neo-Aryan" origins for their respective nationalist authoritarian projects, Mihailovic analyzes the online presence of Kevin MacDonald and Aleksandr Dugin. These two figures present themselves as academic experts, and disseminate their respective and occasionally overlapping extremist "expertise" via Internet sites. Their successful "self-credentialization" shares an appeal to larger political communities that rely on and respond to largely nonrational modes of discourse.

In the next section, "Far-Right Politics and Internet Identities," five essays focus on the intersection among politics, media strategies, and extremist "citizenships" in the EU, and more specifically in Germany, Hungary, Sweden, and France. Glen M. E. Duerr's "Identity, Tradition, Sovereignty: The Transnational Linkages of Radical Nationalist Political Parties in the European Union" looks critically at the legacy of even short-lived extremist parties and their influence on the contemporary European context. From January to November 2007, a new political party: Identity, Tradition, Sovereignty (ITS), was active in the European Parliament (EP) and participated politically alongside all other political groupings. The major difference, according to Duerr, is that ITS was a political group which shared ground with more radical political viewpoints, often characterized as far-right or extreme. There are limitations to the transnational outreach to other far-right political parties given that ITS disbanded just ten months after it had been established. Duerr's essay follows the trail of influence from ITS to two subsequent political groupings: the Alliance of European National Movements and the European National Front have become political alternatives for right-wing supporters, thereby illustrating the emergence of transnational political linkages in Europe for these groups.

The ideology of far-right individuals and groups, such as those Duerr discusses, is mirrored in attenuated form by some within the mainstream in European politics. In a 2011 survey, for example, one in ten Germans supported a call for a strong leader, although in the 25 May 2014 European Parliament Elections, the German winners on the right were the Alternative für Deutschland (Alternative for Germany, hereafter AfD), the Euroskeptics with 7 percent, but not the far-right Nationaldemokratische Partei Deutschlands (National Democratic Party of Germany, NPD), which only received one mandate. What the far right and moderate right have in common is an isolationist anti-European and anti-globalization message. Marine Le Pen's French far-right party (Front National) won 25 percent of the votes, and in regional elections, the FN took over the town halls of eleven cities. What tempts the disparate parties on the right-wing spectrum to make transnational alliances is their desire to create a subversive coalition block within the European Parliament, for which a minimum of seven parties are needed. Potential voters are now transnationally agitated with such content, as the emergence of new far-right movements such as the French Génération Identitaire (GI), the British National Front, and the Greek Golden Dawn demonstrate. Cynically, the GI claims to be "100 percent anti-racist" to attract young supporters even as they do promote a racist nationalist agenda.

In Helga Druxes's "Manipulating the Media: The German New Right's Virtual and Violent Identities," the author examines the legacy of National Socialism and extreme right-wing terrorism. Xenophobes of the New Right have shifted their target from race to culture. They have become adept at promoting a more toned-down form of casual racism via nationalist language couched in terms more acceptable to the mainstream. Within the New Right, its leaders have created a round robin of cash awards and fraudulent prizes for journalistic excellence. They have also sponsored neo-Folk concerts with darkly romantic nationalist themes, created an online chat room targeting high school students, and various online publishing ventures. These sites and events promote strategies lifted from gifted 1968 leftist radicals such as Rudi Dutschke and Ulrike Meinhof, creating a convergence of extreme left tactics with extreme right views. Through their virtual life-world, the far right generates the illusion of a critical mass of responses to social crises and foment terrorist youth actionism. The NSU murder series of Turkish, Greek and Turkish German business owners need to be seen as a real-life consequence of such propaganda.

In Domonkos Sik's contribution, "The Imitated Public Sphere: The Case of Hungary's Far Right," the author examines the impact of exclusion from the mainstream public sphere on far-right communities, which seek alternative ways to create their own public sphere. The blogosphere, easily accessed and maintained, plays a key role. Far-right blogs have an exceptional influence on the readers' interpretation of the world and their identity construction. Relying on Habermas's communicative action theory (1981), Sik explores the impact of Hungarian far-right blogs, which emerge as a form of pseudo-communication. He examines data about blog participants and the formations of their identities in an effort to understand their motivations. The results of his investigation have implications for anti-radical social policies as well. Sik concludes that preventing radicalism cannot be solely based on cognitive persuasion; instead it must include an attempt to eliminate the need for a simulated public sphere as an outlet for alienated individuals.

In Lara Mazurski's "Right-Wing Campaign Strategies in Sweden," the exploration of far-right politics and media use continues through the lens of Judith Butler's concept of "excitable speech." When the Sverigedemokraterna (Sweden Democrats, SD) unveiled their campaign advertisement for the 2010 parliamentary election, they scapegoated immigrants through a series of images that posited a link between immigration and Sweden's domestic budget crisis. While the advertisement associated immigration and Islam with the economic failings of Swedish society, the SD also energized new forms of representation, a new embodiment of Swedish identity and, additionally, of conceptualizations of "the Other." On the surface, the controversial campaign ad identified economic concerns and moral corruption with immigration, women, and Islam. The subsequent act of censorship garnered considerable media coverage and the SD claimed it was being unlawfully persecuted. The extremist campaign strategy, despite (or because of) the censoring of the ad, ultimately gained the Party further publicity.

Fabian Virchow's "The Identitarian Movement: What Kind of Identity? Is it Really a Movement?" focuses our attention on the development of far-right media strategies in France and their influence in Europe. On 20 October 2012, a group of people occupied a mosque in the French city Poitiers, holding a banner with the words "Génération Identitaire." The group claims not to be racist, yet the main messages are anti-immigrant, anti-Muslim, and opposed to the idea of ethno-pluralism. Virchow's contribution investigates the origins, formation, and performance of a new kind of movement that makes use of unorthodox acts of political propaganda; and one that integrates popular cultural symbols and icons into their performances, while referring to racist identitarian ideology. Attracted by the dynamic self-presentation, some more traditional German neo-Nazi groups are trying to capture the essence of the new movement. This essay also includes a closer look at the concept of "identity" as used by the growing number of activists who are organizing around this idea.

In the final section, "Homophobia, Race, and Radicalism," the essays examine the contexts in which extremist politics and beliefs are performed to enforce exclusionary, nationalist, and racialist identities in Greece, Russia, the United States, and Germany. In his magisterial work *Distinction* (1979), Pierre Bourdieu showed that taste is not a subjective category, but rather a grid of cultural practices meant to maintain an elite's cultural capital and to generate distinctions among social classes and groups. Right-wing populists fashion themselves and their followers into elite groups—"tastemakers" of a sort—by claiming ownership of specific cultural shibboleths, in some cases copying and adapting strategies, symbols, and dress codes from historical precursors, deploying Celtic crosses, Nazi references, even referencing the radical left playbook of the 1968 generation in Western Europe. Further, the ideological expressions of "taste" emanating from the far right avail themselves of what Carol Mason has identified as "the powerful role of narrative," specifically in pro-life politics,[27] but the model can be extended to accommodate other inflections of right-wing extremism. Those narratives, mediated digitally, now reach a global audience. This enhanced communicative capacity urges a closer examination of the verbal and visual encoding of ideological narratives from the far right.

In this section's first essay, Alexandra Koronaiou, Evangelos Lagos, and Alexandros Sakellariou explore "Singing for Race and Nation: Fascism and Racism in Greek Youth Music." As the authors observe, Greece has faced an incredible rise of the extreme (nationalist/fascist/racist) right, its peak being the electoral success of the neo-Nazi party "Golden Dawn" in the 2012 national elections, i.e., during a period of severe economical and socio-political crisis. The high percentage of youth vote that "Golden Dawn" gleaned reveals the unexpected appeal of extreme right identity and culture to Greek youth. This chapter focuses on the presence of a nationalist, fascist, and racist position in youth music culture through an investigation of the Greek extreme-right music scene and its Internet activity. The authors analyze the content of the lyrics of relevant songs and the ideological texts that accompany them in extreme-right (and especially on Golden Dawn's) websites and social media pages. They provide an overview and an understanding of the Greek nationalist, fascist, and racist musical identity within Greek youth culture, thereby contributing as well to an understanding of the construction of contemporary youth political identities.

In Alexandar Mihailovic's "'The Order of the Vanquished Dragon': The Performance of Archaistic Homophobia by the Union of Orthodox Banner Bearers in Putin's Russia," the focus shifts to recent events in Russia. The distinctly Russian far-right understanding of liberalism as a form of Russophobic misogyny—directed at feminized symbols of Russian national identity—has recently also entered into the internet language of the public actions of homophobic antidemocratic groups. A curious feature of such groups is their eclectic theatricality. The archaizing tendency among such groups is particularly evident in their performance of collective prophylaxes against the "foreign threat" of homosexuality. Several of these youth groups have staged what can be plausibly understood as their own versions of performance art, in which the values and publications of LBGT culture are ritualistically defiled on the public square of the Internet, if not on actual public squares.

In "Pure Hate: The Political Aesthetic of Prussian Blue," Patricia Anne Simpson focuses on the career trajectory of twins Lynx Vaughan Gaede and Lamb Lennon Gaede, who enjoyed a brief period of intense, transnational popularity while they performed as the white supremacist band Prussian Blue (2003–2007). To the outside eye, it appears that the blond, blue-eyed girls were pressed into politics and service by their mother, April Gaede, who home-schooled them, promoted them, and shaped their politics in her image, according to the principles of the National Alliance—though in early interviews, they deny this. Sometimes referred to as the "Olsen-Twins of the neo-Nazi scene," the twins' musical performances and recordings resonated from the Western part of the United States to the former Eastern states of the Federal Republic of Germany. Featuring songs such as "Sacrifice," a tribute to Rudolf Hess, the girls toured sympathetic venues as the newest and freshest faces of hate music, referred to by fans as "racial music" and white power. The resonance between German and U.S. white power scenes, exemplified by "Prussian Blue," shares a political element as well. As they matured, the twins distanced themselves from the music scene and the politics of white nationalism. In response, their mother April Gaede has turned her attention to the founding of "Pioneer Little Europe" (Kalispell, MT), promoting and facilitating white dating, and supporting anti-choice "pro-life" organizations locally and nationally—establishing spaces where whiteness can be a way of life. The interplay among the aesthetics, politics, and performance of hate is the focus of this chapter.

In Justin D. García's "The New 'Great White Hope?': White Natioinalist Discourses of Mexican Boxer Sául 'Canelo' Álvarez," the author considers the career and media image of Sául "Canelo" Álvarez, a current twenty-one-year-old middleweight boxing champion from Guadalara, Mexico. Álvarez has emerged as a promising young star of professional boxing today and, as García observes, a source of ethnic and cultural pride for both Mexican and Mexican American/Chicano boxing fans. Despite his obvious origins, however, white supremacists have been using the Internet and online blogs and message boards through the website Stormfront.org in an attempt to appropriate Álvarez as one of their own, a fellow "Caucasian" whose athletic accomplishments serve to corroborate his alleged white superiority. In both the United States and Europe, white supremacists have targeted non-European immigrants rhetorically and physically, rendering their appropriation of Álvarez all the more ironic: the Mexican pugilist has reddish hair and a fair complexion—indications to numerous commentators on Stormfront.org that Álvarez is more "Aryan" than Mexican. García explores the social discourses on the Internet surrounding Sául Álvarez, thereby illuminating an intersection of sports, race, social media, and nationalism in the promotion of white supremacist ideologies in the early twenty-first century.

We close the volume with a contribution from the writer, actress, activist, and former East German citizen, Freya Klier, who recounts from personal experience her knowledge of "The Roots of East German Xenophobia." Since the 1990s, sociologist Jan Schedler has been tracing the rise of a "groupuscular right," of flexible, loosely organized clubs (*Kameradschaften*) whose membership fluctuates over time, and who draw young people in through "pre-political" leisure activities rather than requiring adherence to a set of right extremist beliefs. They organize themselves according to the radical left playbook of the Red Army faction, which relies on decentralization, democratization and participation.[28] The significant advantages over a traditional party model, however, are flexible nodality, speedy actionism, and a low entry threshold. This model was followed by a small, terror cell from former East Germany that went on a unprecedented xenophobic killing spree all over Germany between 2000–2007. In April 2013, Beate Zschäpe, the last surviving member of the right-wing extremist terror cell National Socialist Underground, or NSU, went on trial in Munich. Along with her, four neo-Nazi supporters were to be tried. 1,200 witnesses were deposed since Zschäpe's arrest, more than 6,000 documents were amassed and entered into evidence. This trial constitutes an enduring history lesson for posterity. In this concluding essay, Klier shares a personal and political commentary on the past and present of German fascist politics, German-German racism and neo-Nazism, and the imperative to understand the intersection between the local and global in a continued struggle to honor human rights in an integrating Europe.

In many ways, the inaugural debate about the political instrumentalization of new technological developments launched in response to the spread of European fascism pertains today. Walter Benjamin famously and erroneously asserted an exclusively left-wing agenda of mechanical reproducibility, while Theodor Adorno advanced an opposing argument, highlighting instead the ability of the same innovations to reproduce fascist identities. Media technologies alone have no political agency: constituents from any point on the political spectrum can empower themselves and expand their virtual sphere of influence. The effects are homogenizing, relying on what Adorno described as follows with regard to propaganda: "constant reiteration and scarcity of ideas are indispensable ingredients of the entire technique."[29] These provide the ground of fascist personalities. With regard to the authoritarian personality traits, Adorno writes:

> It cannot be doubted that the critique of psychological types expresses a truly humane impulse, directed against that kind of subsumption of individuals under pre-established classes which has been consummated in Nazi Germany, where the labeling of live human beings, independently of their specific qualities, resulted in decisions about their life and death.[30]

If we reach across disciplinary, geographic, and historical boundaries, we can better identify in Adorno's words the strategy employed by many contemporary far-right prophets of apocalypse and persecution.

NOTES

1. Abraham H. Foxman and Christopher Wolf, *Viral Hate: Containing Its Spread on the Internet* (New York: Palgrave Macmillan, 2013), 11.

2. Michael Whine, "Trans-European Trends in Right-Wing Extremism," in Andrea Mammone, Emmanuel Godin, and Brian Jenkins, eds., *Mapping the Extreme Right in Contemporary Europe* (London: Routledge, 2012). The author, a British consultant on defense and security to the European Jewish Congress, argues that far right violence "is real and growing and does not involve large numbers, only isolated individuals and small cells. This is emerging as a clearly defined trans-European threat" (330). However, we show that the support networks that enable and finance these violent cells, as is currently emerging in the German NSU-murder trial, may comprise several hundred people. For example, under the motto "One for all, all for one," over 500 neo-Nazis recently traveled from all over Germany to attend a far right music fundraiser in East Brandenburg for Ralf Wohlleben, one of the four neo-Nazis standing trial in Munich.

3. Lauren Fox, "Anti-Immigrant Hate Coming From Everyday Americans," *U.S. News and World Report*, 24 July 2014, http://www.usnews.com/news/articles/2014/07/24/anti-immigrant-hate-coming-from-everyday-americans, accessed 6 October 2014.

4. See http://www.nsm88.org, accessed 8 October 2014.

5. https://www.stormfront.org/forum/, accessed 8 October 2014. Emphasis in the original.

6. Jochen Bittner, "What's Behind Germany's New Anti-Semitism," *The New York Times*, 16 September 2014, http://www.nytimes.com/2014/09/17/opinion/jochen-bittner-whats-be-

hind-germanys-new-anti-semitism.html?smprod=nytcore-ipad&smid=nytcore-ipad-share&_r=0, accessed 10 October 2014.

7. The website of the German anti-racist Amadeu Antonio foundation lists 30 graffiti incidents or other forms of defacement on public buildings or monuments for 2013: https://www.amadeu-antonio-stiftung.de/die-stiftung-aktiv/themen/gegen-as/antisemitismus-heute/chronik-antisemitischer-vorfaelle-1/chronik-antisemitischer-vorfaelle-2013/, accessed 17 June 2014.

8. See also Andrea Mammone, Emmanuel Godin and Brian Jenkins, *Mapping the Extreme Right in Contemporary Europe From Local to Transnational* (London: Routledge, 2012). This is part one of a projected two-volume study of right-wing extremism in Europe, based on essays originally published in *Journal of Contemporary European Studies* 2008 and 2009. We endorse the argument that local expressions of far right nationalism can at the same time participate in a global extremist discourse. Several contributions point out cross-national parallels in neo-Nazi party organizations. But none extend these linkages to a desire for pan-European nationalism. See also Sabine von Mering and Timothy McCarty, eds., *Right-Wing Radicalism Today: Perspectives from Europe and the US* (London and New York: Routledge, 2013), which emphasizes the growing internationalization of radical right-wing groups, especially in Europe.

9. W. Lance Bennett, "Changing Citizenship in the Digital Age," *Civic Life Online: Learning How Digital Media Can Engage Youth*, edited by W. Lance Bennett. The John D. and Catherine T. MacArthur Foundation Series on Digital Media and Learning (Cambridge, MA: The MIT Press, 2008), 1–24.

10. Jürgen Habermas, *The Structural Transformation of the Public Sphere: An Inquiry into a Category of Bourgeois Society*, translated by Thomas Burger (Cambridge, MA: MIT Press, 1991).

11. Mark Poster, "Introduction," *Jean Baudrillard: Selected Writings*, edited by Mark Poster (Palo Alto: Standford University Press, 2001), 2.

12. Simi and Futrell, *American Swastika: Inside the White Power Movement's Hidden Spaces of Hate* (Lanham, MD: Rowman & Littlefield, 2010), 83.

13. Robert Futrell and Pete Simi, "The Sound of Hate," *The New York Times*, 8 August 2012, http://www.nytimes.com/2012/08/09/opinion/the-sikh-temple-killers-music-of-hate.html?_r=0, accessed 15 October 2012.

14. Simi and Futrell, *American Swastika*, ix.

15. Thomas Grumke, "Globalized Anti-Globalists: The Ideological Basis of the Internationalization of Right-Wing Extremism," in Uwe Backes and Patrick Moreau, eds. *The Extreme Right in Europe* (Göttingen: Vandenhoeck and Ruprecht, 2012), 330.

16. See Manuela Caiani and Linda Parenti, *European and American Extreme Right Groups and the Internet* (Burlington, VT: Ashgate, 2013). This volume analyzes right-wing web blogs for the period 2004–2009; and Uwe Backes and Patrick Moreau, eds. *The Extreme Right in Europe: Current Trends and Perspectives* (Göttingen: Vandenhoeck and Ruprecht, 2012), which devotes roughly half to the 2009 elections and to established far-right political parties, and two chapters address cultural trends.

17. Simone Rafael, "Neues zur NSU: Nazi-Bands singen seit Jahren über die NSU," 17 November 2011, http://www.taz.de/Studie-zu-Neonazis-im-Netz/!97117/, accessed 17 June 2014.

18. Young people are often recruited on the Internet through eye-catching hot button issues like child molestation, or animal abuse, or requests to help local flood victims, with the far-right context initially veiled. Stefan Glaser, the director of the German online platform *Jugendschutz.net*, notes in a 2012 interview that: "users are passed on to right-wing pages through links or 'like' buttons. This is often how one enters into the scene. [. . .]." He also mentions that in 2012, the number of far-right twitter accounts doubled, and that in 2011, his organization traced 3,700 videos, profiles or blog posts. Elisabeth Gamperl, "Sanfter Einstieg über Likes und Links: Studie zu Neo-Nazis im Netz," *taz*, 11 July 2012, http://www.taz.de/Studie-zu-Neonazis-im-Netz/!97117/, accessed 12 July 2012.

19. Stefan Glaser, "Rechtsextremismus im Social Web—Entwicklungen und Gegenstrategien," *BIK Netz* (Berlin: Bildungsministerium für Familie, Frauen und Jugend, 2012), https://

www.biknetz.de/fileadmin/Dokumente/Oeffentlichkeit_herstellen/Themen/Aufsaetze/Aufsatz_S._Glaser__final.pdf, accessed 26 June 2014.
20. https://www.amadeu-antonio-stiftung.de?
21. Astrid Geisler and Christoph Schultheis, *Heile Welten: Rechter Alltag in Deutschland* (München: Hanser, 2011), 15–34.
22. See *Verfassungsschutzbericht 2013*, 74.
23. Toralf Staudt and Johannes Radke, *Neue Nazis: Jenseits der NPD: Populisten, Autonome Nationalisten und der Terror von rechts* (Köln: Kiepenheuer und Witsch, 2012), 175–78.
24. See *Neue Nazis*, 176.
25. See Volker Weiß, "Partisanen im Diskurs," *Deutschlands Neue Rechte: Angriff der Eliten - Von Spengler bis Sarrazin* (Paderborn: Schöningh, 2011), 89–106.
20. See Volker Weiß, 131. Weiß argues that the Sarrazin debate taught far-right groups the strategic importance of the immigration issue for mainstreaming their own eugenics and nationalist beliefs and thus gaining broader popular support.
26. See Volker Weiß, 131. Weiß argues that the Sarrazin debate taught far-right groups the strategic importance of the immigration issue for mainstreaming their own eugenics and nationalist beliefs and thus gaining broader popular support.
27. Carol Mason, *Killing for Life: The Apocalyptic Narratives of Pro-Life Politics* (Ithaca: Cornell University Press, 2002), 8.
28. Jan Schedler, "'Modernisierte Antimoderne': Entwicklung des Neonazismus 1990–2010," Jan Schedler and Alexander Häusler, eds. *Autonome Nationalisten: Neonazismus in Bewegung* (Wiesbaden: VS Verlag für Sozialwissenschaften, 2011), 29–33.
29. Theodor Adorno, "Freudian Theory and the Pattern of Fascist Propaganda" (1951). http://www.sacw.net/article2899.html, accessed 26 March 2014.
30. Theodor Adorno, "Types and Syndromes," Chapter XIX of *The Authoritarian Personality*, T. W. Adorno, Else Frenkel-Brunswik, Daniel J. Levinson, R. Nevitt Sanford. Studies in Prejudice, Max Horkheimer and Samuel H. Flowerman, eds. (New York: Harper & Row, 1950), 745–46.

REFERENCES

Adorno, Theodor. "Freudian Theory and the Pattern of Fascist Propaganda (1951). http://www.sacw.net/article2899.html, accessed 26 March 2014.
Adorno, Theodor. "Types and Syndromes," Chapter XIX of *The Authoritarian Personality*, T. W. Adorno, Else Frenkel-Brunswik, Daniel J. Levinson, R. Nevitt Sanford. Studies in Prejudice, Max Horkheimer and Samuel H. Flowerman, eds. New York: Harper & Row, 1950. 745–46.
Amadeu Antonio Foundation: https://www.amadeu-antonio-stiftung.de/die-stiftung-aktiv/themen/gegen-as/antisemitismus-heute/chronik-antisemitischer-vorfaelle-1/chronik-antisemitischer-vorfaelle-2013/. Accessed 17 June 2014.
Backes, Uwe and Patrick Moreau, eds. *The Extreme Right in Europe: Current Trends and Perspectives*. Göttingen: Vandenhoeck and Ruprecht, 2012.
Bennett, W. Lance. "Changing Citizenship in the Digital Age." In *Civic Life Online: Learning How Digital Media Can Engage Youth*, edited by W. Lance Bennett. The John D. and Catherine T. MacArthur Foundation Series on Digital Media and Learning. Cambridge, MA: The MIT Press, 2008. 1–24
Bittner, Jochen. "What's Behind Germany's New Anti-Semitism." *The New York Times*, 16 September 2014, http://www.nytimes.com/2014/09/17/opinion/jochen-bittner-whats-behind-germanys-new-anti-semitism.html?smprod=nytcore-ipad&smid=nytcore-ipad-share&_r=0, accessed 10 October 2014
Caiani, Manuela and Linda Parenti. *European and American Extreme Right Groups and the Internet*. Burlington, VT: Ashgate, 2013.
Fox, Lauren. "Anti-Immigrant Hate Coming From Everyday Americans." *U.S. News and World Report*, 24 July 2014, http://www.usnews.com/news/articles/2014/07/24/anti-immigrant-hate-coming-from-everyday-americans, accessed 6 October 2014.

Foxman, Abraham H. and Christopher Wolf. *Viral Hate: Containing Its Spread on the Internet.* New York: Palgrave Macmillan, 2013.

Futrell, Robert and Pete Simi. "The Sound of Hate," *The New York Times*, 8 August 2012, http://www.nytimes.com/2012/08/09/opinion/the-sikh-temple-killers-music-of-hate.html?_r=0. Accessed 15 October 2012.

Gamperl, Elisabeth. "Sanfter Einstieg über Likes und Links: Studie zu Neo-Nazis im Netz." *taz*, 11 July 2012, http://www.taz.de/Studie-zu-Neonazis-im-Netz/!97117/. Accessed 12 July 2012.

Geisler, Astrid and Christoph Schultheis. *Heile Welten: Rechter Alltag in Deutschland* München: Hanser, 2011.

Glaser, Stefan. "Rechtsextremismus im Social Web—Entwicklungen und Gegenstrategien," *BIK Netz* (Berlin: Bildungsministerium für Familie, Frauen und Jugend, 2012. https://www.biknetz.de/fileadmin/Dokumente/Oeffentlichkeit_herstellen/Themen/Aufsaetze/Aufsatz_S._Glaser__final.pdf. Accessed 26 June 2014.

Grumke, Thomas "Globalized Anti-Globalists: The Ideological Basis of the Internationalization of Right-Wing Extremism." In Uwe Backes and Patrick Moreau, eds. *The Extreme Right in Europe*. Göttingen: Vandenhoeck and Ruprecht, 2012. 323–32.

Habermas, Jürgen. *The Structural Transformation of the Public Sphere: An Inquiry into a Category of Bourgeois Society*. Translated by Thomas Burger. Cambridge, MA: MIT Press, 1991.

Mammone, Andrea, Emmanuel Godin and Brian Jenkins, *Mapping the Extreme Right in Contemporary Europe From Local to Transnational*. London: Routledge, 2012.

Mason, Carol. *Killing for Life: The Apocalyptic Narratives of Pro-Life Politics*. Ithaca: Cornell University Press, 2002.

Mering, Sabine von and Timothy McCarty, eds., *Right-Wing Radicalism Today: Perspectives from Europe and the US*. London and New York: Routledge, 2013.

Poster, Mark. "Introduction." *Jean Baudrillard: Selected Writings*. Edited by Mark Poster. Palo Alto: Stanford University Press, 2001. 1–8.

Rafael, Simone. "Neues zur NSU: Nazi-Bands singen seit Jahren über die NSU." 17 November 2011, http://www.taz.de/Studie-zu-Neonazis-im-Netz/!97117/. Accessed 17 June 2014.

Schedler, Jan. "'Modernisierte Antimoderne': Entwicklung des Neonazismus 1990- 2010." In Jan Schedler and Alexander Häusler, eds. *Autonome Nationalisten: Neonazismus in Bewegung*. Wiesbaden: VS Verlag für Sozialwissenschaften, 2011. 29–33.

Simi, Pete. and Robert Futrell, *American Swastika: Inside the White Power Movement's Hidden Spaces of Hate*. Lanham, MD: Rowman & Littlefield, 2010.

Staudt, Toralf and Johannes Radke, *Neue Nazis: Jenseits der NPD: Populisten, Autonome Nationalisten und der Terror von rechts*. Köln: Kiepenheuer und Witsch, 2012.

Weiß, Volker. "Partisanen im Diskurs." *Deutschlands Neue Rechte: Angriff der Eliten – Von Spengler bis Sarrazin*. Paderborn: Schöningh, 2011. 89–106.

Whine, Michael. "Trans-European Trends in Right-Wing Extremism." In Andrea Mammone, Emmanuel Godin, and Brian Jenkins, eds. *Mapping the Extreme Right in Contemporary Europe*. London: Routledge, 2012. 485–513.

I

Extremisms and the Internet

Chapter One

Swastikas in Cyberspace

How Hate Went Online

Chip Berlet and Carol Mason

The rhetorical work of right-wing organizations and their media strategies have elicited much scholarship and historical analyses over the years as conservatism became an increasing influence on U.S. politics in the second half of the twentieth century. As researchers who have written about right-wing movements before studying conservatism became trendy,[1] we reject the faux neutrality of descriptive histories of the rise of the right. Recognizing the effect that language has on society, we hold that right-wing rhetorical strategies, cultural narratives, and media deployments function to undermine participatory democracies, respect for diversity, and economic justice. We consider it a matter of social justice not only to document right-wing strategies but also to examine how they work to the detriment of society. In this essay, we examine the ultra right's move from print to digital media in the United States, recognizing the virulent white supremacism that motivated the transition.[2]

A variety of scholars have documented the rise of the U.S. right in terms of media and technological innovation. The Ku Klux Klan in the 1920s was organized in part through a network of newspapers,[3] while Catholic Anti-Semite Father Coughlin took to the airwaves when radio was in its infancy (until his religious superiors pulled his plug).[4] Stories of evangelical Christian and anticommunist broadcasting have brought to light just how important harnessing new technologies was for the ascendency of conservatism and the Christian Right in America starting in the 1970s.[5] After early skepticism in academia, several scholars now persuasively argue that online information systems can and do assist social movement mobilization and growth.[6] Research in the social sciences has shown that rhetoric in media can influ-

21

ence ideas and actions in the general public[7] and in specific social movements including the Ultra-Right,[8] whose views were deemed too extreme for public airwaves and the mainstream press. For such outsiders, prior to the 1980s, the preferred media included underground and alternative magazines and newspapers, newsletters, and "ham" radio.[9] Evidence of the content of these media is scant and primarily exists as ephemera in library archives or personal collections.[10] Consequently, the story of how ultra-rightwing agitators adopted new online technologies in the U.S. is less well known, and it begins with a man named George Dietz.

A much-overlooked yet internationally influential immigrant from Germany, George P. Dietz (1928–2007) arrived in the U.S. at the age of twenty-nine in 1957. Dietz became an American citizen in 1962 while living in New Jersey; he then relocated in 1971 to Roane County, West Virginia, where he worked as a real estate broker and set up a print shop.[11] This essay examines the context in which Dietz ran his international operation of neo-Nazi publications, the way he set up the first online communication among white supremacists in the U.S., and the influence he had on other ultra-right organizers who went digital.

FROM AMERICAN OPINION TO WHITE POWER

In May 1974, George Dietz joined the John Birch Society and opened an American Opinion Bookstore, which featured John Birch Society material, in Reedy, West Virginia.[12] At the time, about an hour away in the state capital of Charleston, an important conflict over school curriculum was brewing in Kanawha County.[13] Several historians have identified the Kanawha County textbook controversy of 1974–1975 as a significant part of the shift to conservatism in U.S. politics and as an early indicator of the rise of the Christian Right in the late 1970s or the more recent Tea Party movements.[14] Dietz's role in this controversy highlights how ultra-right forces were affected by the conflict, in which protesters opposed the implementation of a multiracial language arts curriculum in public schools. Protesters objected to the selected textbooks for a variety of reasons, only some of which were overtly racist. Dietz's print shop produced a steady stream of advertisements and flyers (more than 200,000 by one estimate) that textbook protesters used early in the controversy to garner mass opposition to the school board.[15] Dietz also published a magazine, the *Liberty Bell*, which fanned the flames of the curriculum dispute and became a precursor of white supremacist online activity. The *Liberty Bell* at first was in accordance with John Birch Society rhetoric, but became more blatantly attuned to Dietz's neo-Nazi outlook, which was promoted internationally in print and online.[16]

During the textbook controversy, Dietz's *Liberty Bell* showcased stock arguments from the John Birch Society regarding the general failure of American education, attributing it to a communist conspiracy to turn children against parents and society by indoctrinating them with militant multiracial literature, situational ethics, and psychological conditioning. These accusations fed a class-based, populist sentiment that the elitist and overly liberal school board was tyrannically institutionalizing a curriculum without parental approval. Therefore, while thousands of parents rallied against what they saw as lack of representation and input, those who were also Liberty Bell readers were privy to the inside information that, purportedly, the motivation behind the "tyranny" was "to convert the great American republic into a helpless branch of their One World-Socialist society."[17] Essays and commentary linked the local textbook controversy to a supposed national crisis of education, repeating themes about impending policies that would give "learning technicians" the go-ahead to drug students, and then psychologically manipulate them to engage in acts of depravity and eventually into outright anarchy. To learn more, *Liberty Bell* readers could buy John Birch Society literature with titles such as Forced Bussing: Government Control of Our Children , New Education: The Radicals are After Your Children, Public Schools: They're Destroying Our Children and The NEA: Dictatorship of the Educariat. These booklets and other publications (books such as Toward Soviet America, The Child Seducers, The Romance of Education, and a special "Parents Save Your Children" packet) were available at George Dietz's American Opinion Bookstore on Main Street in Reedy. Or, with postage paid, Dietz would send the materials by mail.

One essay printed in *Liberty Bell*, which did not appear to have a tie-in to materials for sale at Dietz's bookstore, stood out as vibrantly proud of the white, Christian, Appalachian heritage that supposedly created America. "A Message to All True Sons of Appalachia" attacked pro-textbook clergy as persecutors of the "blood line of the children of Appalachia, the sons and daughters of the 'Covenanteers' of the Highlands of Scotland . . . , disparaged by our enemies as WASPS (White Anglo-Saxon Protestants)."[18] The piece uniquely discussed the textbook controversy in terms that are not regurgitated Birch conspiracies but, instead, laid out a whole history of battling against "tyrants," creating a coherent narrative that begins with the "godly Germans" and "our Scotch-Irish fathers" being "persecuted and harassed" because they have throughout history refused to worship any other God but Christ.[19] "A Message to All True Sons" was unique in its situating the 1974 textbook conflict explicitly in terms of region, religion, *and* race.

Given this view of the textbook controversy, readers of the *Liberty Bell* could determine whom to trust and whom not to trust, based on their authenticity as heirs to the Scotch-Irish or Germanic bloodline, what constituted the "true sons of Appalachia." It was thus made clear that someone like the evangelical preacher Charles Quigley was trustworthy because "the fact that his name is Charles CAMERON Quigley tells from what people he sprang." Someone like an Episcopal reverend such as James Lewis, who supported the new multiracial curriculum, was worthy of nothing but disdain: "we don't want and don't need Lewis' of any color around here!"[20] This particular racialization of the actors in the textbook conflict was a different articulation from John Birch Society rhetoric. Unlike the John Birch Society which, historically speaking, "helped to transform earlier, more blatant, biological forms of ethnocentric White racism and Christian nationalist antisemitism into less obvious cultural forms," the *Liberty Bell* promoted a racism based on biology, heredity, and blood.[21] "A Message to All True Sons of Appalachia" was infused with the biologically determinist idea that "blood will tell."[22]

And so the pages of the *Liberty Bell* indicated an interesting tension between at least two kinds of right-wing visions of the textbook controversy: one in which racial politics—be they school integration by busing or multiracial textbooks—were a matter of competing cultures; and one in which they were a matter of biological difference. It would not be long after the publication of "A Message to All True Sons" that Dietz would reveal the kind of right-wing politics to which he and the *Liberty Bell* were more devoted.

As the textbook controversy progressed and ultimately died down through the spring and summer of 1975, the *Liberty Bell* denounced Robert Welch, president of the John Birch Society and relinquished its brand of anticommunism in favor of an overt, biologically based anti-Semitic politics. By August 1975, Dietz officially broke with the John Birch Society because, according to him, it did not share his view that Jews were the puppeteers of the communist threat. Reports from the John Birch Society president painted a different picture, suggesting that the organization had thrown Dietz out for his "unAmerican" views—reports which Dietz called "reverberations of a belch by Robert Welch."[23] Ever the businessman, Dietz wrote a letter to John Birch Society headquarters in Belmont, Massachusetts, requesting the remainder of dues he paid for membership for himself, his wife, Elsbeth (Betty), and his children, Rainer (Ray) and Barbara.[24] In response, J. B. S.'s director of field activities wrote back, making clear "that an American Opinion [Bookstore] franchise no longer exists" in Reedy, that J. B. S. material was copyrighted, and that Dietz was no longer authorized to use the organization's name or profit from the reprinting and sale of its publications. Given the fact that Dietz had only joined the John Birch Society in May 1974, when the textbook controversy was just starting to heat up, the John Birch Society officials had cause to wonder if profiteering was a motivation for joining. It is unlikely that ideological consistency was the impetus because Dietz's politics were to the right of the JBS. Born in Kassel, Germany, in 1928, Dietz was a member of the Hitler Youth during the Third Reich.[25] A review of archival materials offers little to suggest he ever wavered from his upbringing.

The aftermath of the textbook controversy saw George Dietz launch bolder neo-Nazi programs locally, nationally, and internationally. "I met you at the Charleston Textbook Rally in November 1974," a correspondent wrote to Dietz, who published the letter in his overtly neo-Nazi journal, *White Power Report*. "I have received your publications since then," the fan noted, signing off with a "Heil Hitler!"[26] By 1977, Dietz was showing *Triumph of the Will*, Leni Riefenstahl's unforgettable and visually stunning, though morally repulsive, Nazi propaganda film to select audiences in Reedy.[27] In May 1977, Simon Wiesenthal (who was known for tracking down and exposing Nazis in hiding) announced that Dietz was linked to the "Patriotic Legal Fund" of Marietta, Georgia, which collected "money from some 80 neo-Nazi and neo-Fascist groups in the U.S. and Canada to help former Nazi butchers avoid detection and prosecution."[28] Dietz's publishing efforts now included printing "60 publications in five languages that are used in propaganda campaigns in the U.S., South America, Europe and South Africa," not to mention Germany, where Nazi literature had been outlawed.[29] In July 1978, on the occasion of the death of his father, Heinrich Dietz, who was pictured in his Nazi uniform in that month's issue of *White Power Report*, George Dietz traveled to Germany for the funeral.[30] That same issue of *White Power Report* gave explicit instructions for "what the white man must do to escape execution," and argued that "underground or conspiratorial mode of resistance is the only practical course of action" for the time being.[31] The *Report* encouraged readers to create "new, independent, secret organizational units"; to "develop a reservoir of 'sleepers'—whites with 'clean,' non-activist backgrounds" for the purposes of infiltrating "police, security agencies, armed forces"; to "learn how to live double, even triple lives"; to rest assured that "those who die for the white race in no matter what manner or circumstance should rest assured that they have died for the greatest cause ever"; and to awaken white racial consciousness by undermining "the Jewish propaganda onslaught against the white man's survival."[32] Clearly Dietz's print media production aimed to do that.

In addition to buying annual subscriptions and bulk copies of periodicals he edited, Dietz encouraged readers to build a personal library appropriate for "patriots." Liberty Bell Publications' mail order service included U.S. Army training manuals (including "Booby Traps," "Chemistry of Powder and Explosives," "Explosives and Demolitions," and "Unconventional Warfare Devices"), writings by leading National Socialists and anti-Semites (including, of course, works by Adolf Hitler as well as Henry Ford, Revilo P. Oliver, Francis Parker Yockey, and George Lincoln Rockwell), classics of Western white literature (works by Nietzsche, and Pound), and pantheistic legends ("Gods and Myths of Northern Europe"), and all manner of racist and anti-Semitic materials (such as "Proud to be a Racist," "The Hoax of the Twentieth Century," and the classic hoax publication Protocols of the Learned Elders of Zion , in French as well as in English). Historic speeches, German marches, and battle songs were available on cassette tapes. Dietz did not stop there; he moved on to a new medium.

Ten years after the *Liberty Bell* was first published, George Dietz reported to its subscribers that he had been "working, for the past two weeks, until 4-5 o'clock in the morning, trying to learn 'computerese' so that so that Yours Truly may talk to that monster in ITS language and on ITS terms."[33] One advantage to learning computer skills was security: "from now on, there will be in our offices no more written records, or any of the bulky address plates we have been using in the past, which are prone to 'inspection' by 'undesirables,' and everything will be safely stored on 'disposable' disks."[34] Another advantage was expanding communication among white supremacists, an upgrading perhaps of "The Liberty Net," a ham radio network that "as far back as the early '70s, before [personal] computer technology was developed," brought right-wing thinkers into conversation with one another three nights a week.[35] With computer skills mastered, Dietz initiated the first white supremacist electronic bulletin board system (or BBS).[36] Called Liberty Bell Network, and run using an Apple IIe personal computer, Dietz in 1983 launched a new era of white supremacist organizing in cyberspace.[37] Dietz saw the new bulletin board system as a way to thwart the Jews. Reportedly, Dietz exclaimed with delight to his colleague, "Boy, are the Yids going to scream when they learn about this!"[38] A selling point for the early network was its being the "only computer bulletin board system and uncontrolled information medium in the United States of America dedicated to the dissemination of historical facts—not fiction!"[39] Not surprisingly, some of the first postings on the BBS were electronic versions of Liberty Bell articles.[40]

ARYAN CYBERSPACE AFTER DIETZ

Shortly after the launching of his BBS, Dietz "helped Louis Beam to establish the Aryan Liberty Network with computers in Texas, North Carolina, Illinois, Michigan and Idaho."[41] Known for his influential discussions of independent paramilitary cells and their capacity for "leaderless resistance,"[42] Beam no doubt saw computer communication networks as instrumental for the type of decentralized action he was promoting in response to government crackdowns on right-wing organizing.[43] Beam's "Aryan Liberty Net" went online sometime in the spring of 1984 and quickly surpassed Dietz's Liberty Bell as the preferred online communication for white supremacists.[44] As the leader of various Texas Ku Klux Klan (KKK) factions that worked closely with Richard Butler, who presided over an Aryan Nations Christian Identity compound in Idaho,[45] Beam may have discussed the idea of a computer network as early as July 1983 at a meeting at Aryan Nations.[46] He also announced the launch of Aryan Liberty Net in an undated Spring 1984 issue of the *Inter-Klan Newsletter & Survival Alert* published from the Aryan nations compound in Hayden Lake, Idaho. In an article "Computers and the American Patriot," Beam wrote: "It may very well be that American know-how has provided the technology which will allow those who love this country to save it from an ill-deserved fate."[47] Later, an article titled "Announcing Aryan Nations/Ku Klux Klan Computer Net" heralded "a special electronic code access available only to Aryan Nations/ Ku Klux Klan officers and selected individuals is being implemented."[48] The article continued: "At last, those who love God and their Race and strive to serve their Nation will be utilizing some of the advanced technology available heretofore only to those in the ZOG (Zionist Occupational Government) government and others who have sought the destruction of the Aryan people."

Next to come online (in late 1984 or early 1985) was the White Aryan Resistance BBS in Fallbrook, California, under the auspices of Tom Metzger. Metzger announced the "W.A.R. Computer Terminal" in *War '85*, the newspaper of his White Aryan Resistance.[49] It originally ran on a Commodore 64 with a 300 bits per second (bps) modem.[50] At the time this speed was cutting-edge technology. Today pocket-sized 4G smart phones deliver content at up to 9,600,000 bps.

One of the first messages sent out by Metzger was directed at "any Aryan patriot in America who so desires" to arrange for local cable access channel broadcast of Metzger's new cable TV program "The World as We See It," later renamed "Race and Reason."[51] During this same period, there were over one dozen call-in telephone hot lines with recorded messages containing racist and antisemitic material.[52] Thus white supremacists were using all available technology to proliferate their hateful ideas, which continued to spread online, hence across national borders.

Around August 1984, a one-page flyer circulated in Canada, announcing remote access (through the Aryan Liberty Net) to racist material otherwise banned under Canadian laws against hate speech.[53] The white supremacist U.S.-based BBSs allowed people in Canada and in European countries, where distribution of bigoted literature is often restricted by law, to gain access to these race-hate texts through their computer. This was a major goal of the early racist BBS operators.[54] Metzger bragged that his system had "ended Canadian Censorship."[55] "Already White Aryan comrades of the North have destroyed the free speech blackout to our Canadian comrades," wrote Metzger.[56]

In early 1985, Aryan Nations Liberty Net consisted of the Aryan Nations BBS in Hayden Lake, Idaho, a KKK BBS's with two additional phone lines in Dallas, Texas, and a KKK BBS in the Raleigh/Durham area of North Carolina.[57] These systems were generally built around relatively inexpensive (for the period) Apple or Radio Shack computers running standard BBS software. The Aryan Liberty Net was an actual network, while Metzger's War Information Network computer and Dietz's Liberty Bell Network computer, were single units despite being called networks.[58] In June of 1985, this distinction was evident in a message that announced the new conglomeration: "Finally, we are all going to be linked together at one point in time. Imagine if you will, all of the great minds of the patriotic Christian movement linked together and joined into one computer. All the years of combined experience available to the movement. Now imagine any patriot in the country being able to call up and access those minds, to deal with the problems and issues that affect him. You are on line with the Aryan Nations brain trust. It is here to serve the folk." Clearly excited by the possibilities of unprecedented electronic outreach, these wired white supremacists signed off with the tagline, "Aryan Nation liberty net (an Aryan communications system). Please call again! One Nation—One race—One God."

By May of 1986, the Aryan Liberty Net had systems operating in Idaho, Dallas and Houston in Texas, North Carolina, and Chicago, and was listing the WAR site in California as an affiliate.[59] By the end of 1986, Metzger's *War* newspaper was listing these, minus the original site in Idaho, but with additional BBS's in Wisconsin and Arkansas.[60] Other bigoted BBSs began appearing, carrying racist, antisemitic, and homophobic material well into the mid 1990s. Racist Skinheads started to use BBS's to spread their messages.[61] By 1989 Metzger's BBS was running a "multiuser 286-based AT clone with a 40MB hard disk running FidoNet software. The developer of FidoNet, Bay-area resident Tom Jennings, regrets the group's use of his software. "I don't like them using FidoNet . . . but I suppose it's inevitable."[62] Using FidoNet software allowed the material on Metzger's BBS to be echoed on numerous other BBS sites.

At various times other BBS's with racist material popped up, including The Aryan Resistance Information Exchange Service in Tennessee; the Cyber Space Minutemen in Illinois (which carried material from the KKK and National Alliance); the Transponder BBS in Pittsburgh (with National Alliance material); the Aryan Resistance Center in Sacramento, CA; and Our Nation BBS outside Los Angeles.[63] In the early 1990s, before a graphic interface produced the World Wide Web, hate online was often posted to early Internet USENET news groups, a system of message-based topical conferences. There was vigorous debate over policy within the USENET community, often by critics of hate, but also among far right activists.[64] Neonazi skinheads dominated one online skin conference, but their views were attacked by anti-racist skins.[65]

A few bigots also managed to post messages in discussion groups on the commercial services such as America Online (AOL), Compuserve, and Prodigy, although the rhetoric was often muted or coded. A common tactic on both online services and the Internet was to suggest the purchase by mail-order of specific anti-government or conspiracist books and pamphlets with innocuous-sounding titles. When those items arrived in the mail they were often accompanied with a list of other materials with white supremacist or antisemitic themes.

As technology advanced, national commercial and non-profit online systems and the Internet began supplanting the bulletin board systems. By the mid-1990s many BBS's had disappeared or moved onto the Internet. The advent of direct computer networking and increased access to the Internet meant that online hate could proliferate even more.[66] As the graphic interface for the early Internet evolved into the World Wide Web, a few sporadic web pages carrying racist, antisemitic, or other bigoted material began to appear. In May 1995, for example, Don Black set up the neo-Nazi Stormfront site, the first major website by a national race hate organization.[67] It remains online today, and a handful of its participants have gone on to carry out acts of terrorism and murder.[68] White supremacists like Don Black and his Internet associates carried forward George Dietz's vision of swastikas in cyberspace.

CONCLUSION

George Dietz has left an infamous legacy. He was unapologetic in his allegiance to Hitler's vision of the world. He admonished those who masked or coded their white supremacism and anti-Semitism. "I and my associates live and breathe National Socialism every waking moment (and sometimes sleeping, for that matter) of our lives. We do not doubt ourselves, nor do we wish to hide the fact that we are on the White Man's side. Those who shrink from wearing the Swastika today," wrote Dietz in 1976, "will next shrink from wearing their White skins."[69] With this loyalty to fascism, Dietz cultivated and distributed an American Nazi worldview worldwide across an array of media. Beginning with the *Liberty Bell* magazine, he left the conspiracism of the John Birch Society behind to fan the flames of a revolutionary right-wing movement that went far beyond conservatism. Translating his print media into an electronic bulletin board format, Dietz was the first to open cyberspace up to white supremacist organizing.

Ironically, Dietz promoted allegiance to "White skins" online where no one could—until technology incorporated cameras into personal computers—see skin color. With this new dimension of personal anonymity, cyberspace was initially theorized as a liberating arena in which one could escape the social confines of race or gender, and the physical constraints of corporeal being. Cultural historians of the Internet know that William Gibson's novel *Neuromancer,* introduced "cyberspace" in 1984 in terms of a "consensual hallucination."[70] While 1980s authors and artists like Gibson offered a radical vision of a new online world in which identity was mutable and inessential, George Dietz and other white supremacists at the same time were using computers to promote their own consensual hallucination of Jewish persecution of "the white man" and to plan a triumphant fascism in which identity was paramount and essentialist. Racists' efforts to translate print media into digital documents, to circumvent national prohibitions on anti-Semitic materials, and to inspire rightwing revolutionaries envisioned the Internet—and beyond—as an unsafe, unfree place to be without "White skin."

AUTHORS' NOTE

A collection of expanded online resources compiled by the authors can be found at http://www.buildingracialjustice.us/jump/online-neonazis.html.

NOTES

1. Alan Brinkley, "The Problem of American Conservatism," *American Historical Review* 99 (April 1994): 409–29. This article heralded a call for historians to take conservatism seriously, eventuating in a mainstream academic field of study.
2. We use the term "ultra right" to refer to social movements and groups that reject the mainstream political parties and democratic electoral consensus and move beyond reform to exclusionary ideas of proper citizenship and in some cases insurgency. For more distinctions, see Ann Burlein, *Lift High the Cross: Where White Supremacy and the Christian Right Converge* (Durham, NC: Duke University Press, 2002); and Martin Durham, *The Christian Right, the Far Right and the Boundaries of American Conservatism* (Manchester, England: Manchester Univ. Press, 2000).
3. Rory McVeigh, The Rise of the Ku Klux Klan: Right-Wing Movements and National Politics (Minneapolis: University of Minnesota Press, 2009).
4. Warren, Donald I. Radio Priest: Charles Coughlin, the Father of Hate Radio (New York: Free Press, 1996).
5. Some representative studies include: Sara Diamond, *Roads to Dominion: Right Wing Movements and Political Power in the United States* (New York: Guilford Press, 1995); Heather Hendershot, *What's Fair on the Air: Cold War Right-wing Broadcasting and the Public Interest* (Chicago, Ill.; London: University of Chicago Press, 2011); Linda Kintz and Julia Lesage, eds., *Media, Culture, and the Religious Right* (Minneapolis: University of Minnesota Press, 1998); Claire Snyder-Hall and Cynthia Burack, *Right-Wing Populism and the Media* (New York: Routledge, 2014).
6. Jennifer Earl and Katrina Kimport, *Digitally Enabled Social Change: Activism in the Internet Age* (Cambridge, MA: MIT Press, 2011); Castells, Manuel, *Networks of Outrage and Hope: Social Movements in the Internet Age* (Cambridge: Polity Press, 2013).
7. The following list is illustrative: Edward L. Bernays, *Crystallizing Public Opinion* (New York: Liveright, 1923); Edward L. Bernays, *Propaganda* (New York: Liveright, 1928); Gordon W. Allport, "Demagogy," in *Conspiracy: The Fear of Subversion in American History*, eds. Richard O. Curry and Thomas M. Brown (New York, NY: Holt, Rinehart and Winston:

1972), 263–76; Maurice Charland, "Constitutive Rhetoric: The Case of the *Peuple Québécois*, *Quarterly Journal of Speech* 73:2 (1987): 133–50; Patricia Ewick and Susan S. Silbey, "Subversive Stories and Hegemonic Tales: Toward a Sociology of Narrative," *Law & Society Review* 29:2 (1995) 197–226; Jack Levin, *The Violence of Hate: Confronting Racism, Anti-Semitism, and Other Forms of Bigotry* (Boston: Allyn and Bacon, 2002); Mark Frohardt and Jonathan Temin, *Use and Abuse of Media in Vulnerable Societies*, Special Report 110, (Washington, DC: United States Institute of Peace, October 2003), online at http://www.usip.org/sites/default/files/sr110.pdf.

8. These examples focus on right-wing rhetoric: Robert Altemeyer, *Enemies of Freedom: Understanding Right-Wing Authoritarianism* (San Francisco: Jossey-Bass, 1988); Robert Altemeyer, *The Authoritarian Specter* (Cambridge, MA: Harvard University Press, 1996); David Neiwert, *The Eliminationists: How Hate Talk Radicalized the American Right* (Sausalito, CA: PoliPointPress, 2009); Chip Berlet, "Heroes Know Which Villains to Kill: How Coded Rhetoric Incites Scripted Violence," in *Doublespeak: Rhetoric of the Far-Right Since 1945*, eds. Matthew Feldman and Paul Jackson (Stuttgart: ibidem-Verlag, 2014), 303–30.

9. Ham radio operators use a special set of shortwave radio frequencies to contact and hold conversations with multiple others who are using the same frequency at the same time.

10. Chip Berlet, "The Write Stuff: U.S. Serial Print Culture from Conservatives out to Neonazis," *Library Trends*, 56:3, Special Issue: Alternative Print Culture: Social History and Libraries, 2008 (Winter): 570–600.

11. "George P. Dietz, 79." The Hur Herald, 1 May 2007; online at http://www.hurherald.com/obits.php?=23225.

12. This section contains analysis previously published in Carol Mason, *Reading Appalachia from Left to Right: Conservatives and the Kanawha County Textbook Controversy.* (Ithaca, NY: Cornell University Press, 2009): 69–78.

13. American Opinion Bookstores carried the flagship periodical publication of the J. B. S. which also was named *American Opinion*.

14. James Moffett, *Storm in the Mountains: A Case Study of Censorship, Conflict, and Consciousness* (Carbondale, IL: Southern Illinois University Press, 1989); Lisa McGirr, "A History of the Conservative Movement from the Bottom Up," *The Journal of Policy History* 14:3 (2002): 331–39; William Martin, *With God on Our Side: The Rise of the Religious Right in America* (New York: Broadway Books, 2005); Mason, *Reading Appalachia from Left to Right;* Carol Mason, "From Textbooks to Tea Parties: An Appalachian Antecedent of Anti-Obama Rebellion," *West Virginia History, New Series* 5:2 (Fall 2011): 1–26; Rick Perlstein, *The Invisible Bridge: The Fall of Nixon and the Rise of Reagan* (New York: Simon and Schuster, 2014).

15. "The Kanawha Fight is About More than Textbooks," *World Magazine* (22 February 1975); reprinted as "Red Joke of the Month!" Liberty Bell 2:8 (April 1975): 17–19. See also National Education Association, Teacher Rights Division, Inquiry Report: Kanawha County West Virginia A Textbook Study in Cultural Conflict (Washington, DC, 1975), 48.

16. For background on neo-Nazi and neo-Fascist subcultures in the U.S, see Betty A Dobratz and Stephanie L. Shanks-Meile, *The White Separatist Movement in the United States: "White Power, White Pride!"* (Baltimore, Maryland: John Hopkins University Press, 2000); Chip Berlet and Stanislav Vysotsky, "Overview of U.S. White Supremacist Groups," in *Journal of Political and Military Sociology*, 34:1, special Issue on the White Power Movement in the United States, eds. Betty A. Dobratz and Lisa K. Walsner (Summer 2006): 11–48; Ernest Hearst, Chip Berlet, and Jack Porter, *Encyclopaedia Judaica*, 2nd ed., vol. 15 of 22, *s.v.* "Neo-Nazism," eds. Michael Berenbaum and Fred Skolnik (Detroit: Macmillan Reference USA/Thomson Gale, 2007), 74–82.

17. Dr. Joseph Sheppe, "Textbook Protest in W. VA." Liberty Bell (December 1974): 5.

18. Glenn C. Roberts, "A Message to All True Sons of Appalachia." *Liberty Bell* (December 1974): 6.

19. Roberts, "A Message."

20. Roberts, "A Message," 8.

21. Chip Berlet and Matthew N. Lyons, *Right–Wing Populism in America: Too Close for Comfort* (New York: Guilford Press), 183.

22. Roberts, "A Message," 8.

23. "Reverberations of a Belch by Robert Welch," Liberty Bell (November 1976): 17–18.

24. Dietz reproduced the correspondence with the John Birch Society, Liberty Bell (November 1976): 20–21; Tim Miller, "The Electronic Fringe," The Magazine , reprinted in Liberty Bell (July 1985), refers to George Dietz's wife as "Betty."

25. White Power Report (December 1976): 34.

26. White Power Report (January 1977): 36.

27. White Power Report (January 1977): 51.

28. Marcia Kramer, "Two Groups Accused of Funding Nazis," *Daily News*, 15 May1977; reprinted in White Power Report (July 1977). Evidence of Dietz's desire to defend those under suspicion of Nazi war crimes by the Office of Special Investigation of the Justice Department: "The O.S.I. Witch Hunt" seeks "contributions for the legal defense of Dr. Rudolph," a man accused of Nazi crimes, "and others already similarly harassed by OSI may be mailed to: OLDTIMER'S DEFENSE FUND, Inc., P. O. Box 1000, Huntsville, AL 35801." Supplement to Liberty Bell (October 1986).

29. Supplement (October 1986).

30. *White Power Report* (July 1978): 54.

31. *White Power Report* (July 1978): 57.

32. "Break Out of Your Death Cell, White Man!" *White Power Report* (July 1978): 55-60.

33. George Dietz letter to Joseph Dilys, 10 August 1983, (Wilcox Collection of Contemporary Political Movements, Spencer Research Library, University of Kansas).

34. Dietz letter to Dilys.

35. Wesley McCune, "Extremists are linked by a computer network," *Group Research Report* 25:3 (March 1986): 10 (People for the American Way Library).

36. A BBS is run on a single personal computer connected to a phone line through a modem connecting device allowing one visitor at a time to access a selection of text material being made available for online reading.

37. Portions of this and the following section were first presented as a paper, "When Hate Went Online," by author Berlet at the Northeast Sociological Association Spring Conference, April 2001.

38. *National Socialist Vanguard Report* 10: 4, October/December 1992): 3 (People for the American Way Library).

39. Berlet, "When Hate Went Online."

40. Author Berlet signed in, copied, and reposted to anti-racist activists the first responses to the BBS.

41. *National Socialist Vanguard Report* 10:4 (October/December 1992): 3, (People for the American Way Library).

42. Beam is often wrongly credited with developing the concept of "Leaderless Resistance," however Beam in his newsletter properly credited another newsletter editor, former U.S. intelligence operative, Col. Ulius Louis Amoss, who first wrote of the idea in the mid 1950s as part of an anticommunist Cold War strategy in Eastern Europe. See for details Chip Berlet, "The Write Stuff: U.S. Serial Print Culture from Conservatives out to Neonazis,*" Library Trends*, 56:3, Special Issue: Alternative Print Culture: Social History and Libraries, (Winter 2008).

43. Ann Burlein, *Lift High the Cross*, 91.

44. It appears that notices for Dietz's online system were sometimes referred to as the Liberty Bell network and sometimes the Info. International network.

45. For background on this period, see James, Corcoran, *Bitter Harvest: The Birth of Paramilitary Terrorism in the Heartland*, rev., (New York: Viking Penguin, ([1990] 1995); and James Aho, *The Politics of Righteousness: Idaho Christian Patriotism* (Seattle: University of Washington Press, 1990).

46. Jessica Eve Stern, "The Covenant, the Sword, and the Arm of the Lord," in *Toxic Terror: Assessing Terrorist Use of Chemical and Biological Weapons,* ed. Jonathan B. Tucker (Cambridge, MA: MIT Press with the Belfer Center for Science and International Affairs, Harvard University, 2000), 139–57.

47. Louis Beam, "Announcing Aryan Nations/Ku Klux Klan Computer Net," *Inter-Klan Newsletter & Survival Alert*, undated, circa summer 1984, pages not numbered.

48. Louis Beam, "Computers and the American Patriot," *Inter-Klan Newsletter & Survival Alert*, undated, circa summer 1984, pages not numbered.

49. Tom Metzger, "W. A. R. Computer Terminal," *War '85*, 4:1, no date (perhaps early 1985).

50. Peter Sills [pseud.], "Dark Contagion: Bigotry and Violence Online," *PC Computing*, December 1989, 144–49.

51. Downloaded from Aryan Liberty Net in 1985 by author Berlet; text printout on file at Political Research Associates library.

52. See various issues of *WAR* in 1984–1986.

53. Wayne King, "Computer Network Links Rightist Groups and Offers 'Enemy' List," *New York Times*, 15 February 1985, A17; Ric Bohy, "Hate Mail Sent via Computer: White Supremacists are Now Linked by Electronic Network," *Detroit News*, 28 April 1985, 1, 20.

54. David Lowe, *Computerized Networks of Hate: An ADL Fact Finding Report* (New York: Anti-Defamation League, 1985), 2.

55. Lowe, *Computerized Networks*, 2.

56. Metzger,"W.A.R. Computer Terminal."

57. Locations for some BBS's listed throughout this chapter are approximate, based on the nearest major city for each telephone area code.

58. Chip Berlet, "KKK/Aryan Racist Computer Networks," memo (Chicago: Midwest Research, 5 January 1985), on file at PRA.

59. List downloaded by author Berlet from Liberty Net in May 1986.

60. Boxed list, in *WAR '86 5:5* 1986, no date, (probably late October or early November based on dates in articles), 16. Dated as received 5 December 1986 by the Library at the State Historical Society of Wisconsin.

61. Sills, "Dark Contagion."

62. Sills, "Dark Contagion," 146.

63. Chip Berlet, "KKK/Aryan Racist Computer Networks," memo, 5 January 1985 and "What We Are Proposing," memo, 18 May 1985, both on file at PRA library.

64. Author Berlet's monitoring. On generic differences and struggles within rightist groups, see Betty Dobratz and Stephanie Shanks-Meile, "Conflict in the White Supremacist/Racialist Movement in the United States," *International Journal of Group Tensions* 25:1 (1995): 57–75.

65. Author Berlet's monitoring. In the U.S. many skinheads are culturally identified youth rebels who are not explicitly racist, and in some cases are actively anti-racist; Mark S. Hamm, *American Skinheads: The Criminology and Control of Hate Crime* (Westport, CT: Praeger, 1994).

66. For a detailed look at early bigotry on the Internet, see Devin Burghart, "Annotated list of race hate BBS's and Internet sites," unpublished memo, on file at PRA library; Devin Burghart, "Cyberh@te: A Reappraisal," *The Dignity Report* (Coalition for Human Dignity), Fall 1996, 2–16; Wayne Madsen, "The Battle for Cyberspace: Spooks v. Civil Liberties and Social Unrest," *CovertAction Quarterly*, Winter 1996–1997; Todd J. Schroer, "White Racialists, Computers, and the Internet" paper presented at the annual meeting of the American Sociological Association, Toronto, 1997; Todd J. Schroer, "Issue and Identity Framing within the White Racialist Movement: Internet Dynamics," in *The Politics of Social Inequality,* (Research in Political Sociology, Vol. 9), eds. Betty A. Dobratz, Lisa K. Walder, and Timothy Buzzell, 2001: 117–63; Les Back, Michael Keith, and John Solomos, "Racism on the Internet: Mapping Neo-Fascist Subcultures in Cyberspace," in *Nation and Race: The Developing Euro-American Racist Subculture*, eds. Jeffrey Kaplan and Tore Bjørgo (Boston: Northeastern University Press, 1998): 73–101; Val Burris, Emery Smith, and Ann Strahm, "White Supremacist Networks on the Internet," *Sociological Focus* 33:2, May 2000: 215–35; For information on Europe, see Louise Bernstein, "Hate on the Internet," *Searchlight*, March 1996, 12–15.

67. Stormfront website, http://www.stormfront.org.

68. Heidi Beirich, "White Homicide Worldwide," *Intelligence Report* (Southern Poverty Law Center), Summer 2014, 154, online at http://www.splcenter.org/get-informed/intelligence-report/browse-all-issues/2014/summer/White-Homicide-Worldwide.

69. *White Power Report* (December 1976): 34.
70. William Gibson, *Neuromancer* (New York: Ace Books, 1984): 51.

REFERENCES

Aho, James. *The Politics of Righteousness: Idaho Christian Patriotism*. Seattle: University of Washington Press, 1990.

Allport, Gordon W. "Demagogy." In *Conspiracy: The Fear of Subversion in American History*. Edited by Richard O. Curry and Thomas M. Brown. New York, NY: Holt, Rinehart and Winston: 1972. 263–76.

Altemeyer, Robert. *Enemies of Freedom: Understanding Right-Wing Authoritarianism*. San Francisco: Jossey-Bass, 1988.

———. *The Authoritarian Specter*. Cambridge, MA: Harvard University Press, 1996.

Back, Les, Michael Keith, and John Solomos, "Racism on the Internet: Mapping Neo- Fascist Subcultures in Cyberspace." In *Nation and Race: The Developing Euro-American Racist Subculture*. Edited by Jeffrey Kaplan and Tore Bjørgo. Boston: Northeastern University Press, 1998. 73–101.

Beam, Louis. "Announcing Aryan Nations/Ku Klux Klan Computer Net." *Inter-Klan Newsletter & Survival Alert*. No date, circa summer 1984. No pagination.

———. "Computers and the American Patriot." *Inter-Klan Newsletter & Survival Alert*. No date, circa summer 1984. No pagination.

Beirich, Heidi. "White Homicide Worldwide." *Intelligence Report*. Southern Poverty Law Center. Summer 2014, 154. Online at http://www.splcenter.org/get- informed/intelligence-report/browse-all-issues/2014/summer/White-Homicide- Worldwide.

Berlet, Chip. "Heroes Know Which Villains to Kill: How Coded Rhetoric Incites Scripted Violence." In *Doublespeak: Rhetoric of the Far-Right Since 1945*. Edited by Matthew Feldman and Paul Jackson. Stuttgart: ibidem-Verlag, 2014. 303–30.

———. "The Write Stuff: U.S. Serial Print Culture from Conservatives out to Neonazis." *Library Trends*, 56:3, Special Issue: Alternative Print Culture: Social History and Libraries, 2008 (Winter): 570–600.

———. "When Hate Went Online." Paper at the Northeast Sociological Association Spring Conference, April 2001.

———. "KKK/Aryan Racist Computer Networks." Memo (Chicago: Midwest Research, 5 January 1985). On file at Political Research Associates Library.

———. "What We Are Proposing." Memo, 18 May 1985. On file at Political Research Associates Library.

———. and Stanislav Vysotsky, "Overview of U.S. White Supremacist Groups." In *Journal of Political and Military Sociology,* 34:1. Special Issue on the White Power Movement in the United States. Edited by Betty A. Dobratz and Lisa K. Walsner (Summer 2006): 11– 48.

———. and Matthew N. Lyons, *Right–Wing Populism in America: Too Close for Comfort*. New York: Guilford Press.

Bernays, Edward L. *Crystallizing Public Opinion*. New York: Liveright, 1923.

———. *Propaganda*. New York: Liveright, 1928.

Bernstein, Louise. "Hate on the Internet." *Searchlight*, March 1996, 12–15.

Bohy, Ric. "Hate Mail Sent via Computer: White Supremacists are Now Linked by Electronic Network." *Detroit News*, 28 April 1985, 1, 20.

Brinkley, Alan. "The Problem of American Conservatism," *American Historical Review* 99 (April 1994): 409–29.

Burghart, Devin. "Annotated list of race hate BBS's and Internet sites." Unpublished memo, on file at PRA library.

———. "Cyberh@te: A Reappraisal," *The Dignity Report* (Coalition for Human Dignity), Fall 1996, 2–16.

Burlein, Ann. *Lift High the Cross: Where White Supremacy and the Christian Right Converge*. Durham, NC: Duke University Press, 2002.

Burris, Val, Emery Smith, and Ann Strahm. "White Supremacist Networks on the Internet." *Sociological Focus* 33:2, May 2000: 215–35.

Castells, Manuel. *Networks of Outrage and Hope: Social Movements in the Internet Age.* Cambridge: Polity Press, 2013.

Charland, Maurice. "Constitutive Rhetoric: The Case of the *Peuple Québécois, Quarterly Journal of Speech* 73:2 (1987): 133–50.

Corcoran, James. *Bitter Harvest: The Birth of Paramilitary Terrorism in the Heartland*, rev., New York: Viking Penguin, ([1990] 1995).

Diamond, Sara. *Roads to Dominion: Right Wing Movements and Political Power in the United States.* New York: Guilford Press, 1995.

Dietz, George. Letter to Joseph Dilys, 10 August 1983. Wilcox Collection of Contemporary Political Movements, Spencer Research Library, University of Kansas.

Dobratz, Betty A. and Stephanie L. Shanks-Meile, *The White Separatist Movement in the United States: "White Power, White Pride!"* Baltimore, Maryland: John Hopkins University Press, 2000.

———. and Stephanie Shanks-Meile. "Conflict in the White Supremacist/Racialist Movement in the United States." *International Journal of Group Tensions* 25:1 (1995): 57–75.

Durham, Martin. *The Christian Right, the Far Right and the Boundaries of American Conservatism.* Manchester, England: Manchester University Press, 2000.

Earl, Jennifer, and Katrina Kimport. *Digitally Enabled Social Change: Activism in the Internet Age.* Cambridge, MA: MIT Press, 2011.

Ewick, Patricia and Susan S. Silbey. "Subversive Stories and Hegemonic Tales: Toward a Sociology of Narrative." *Law & Society Review* 29:2 (1995) 197–226.

Frohardt, Mark and Jonathan Temin. *Use and Abuse of Media in Vulnerable Societies*, Special Report 110, (Washington, DC: United States Institute of Peace, October 2003). online at http://www.usip.org/sites/default/files/sr110.pdf.

"George P. Dietz, 79." The Hur Herald, 1 May 2007. Online at http://www.hurherald.com/obits.php?=23225.

Hamm, Mark S. *American Skinheads: The Criminology and Control of Hate Crime.* Westport, CT: Praeger, 1994.

Hearst, Ernest, Chip Berlet, and Jack Porter. *Encyclopaedia Judaica,* 2nd ed., vol. 15 of 22, *s.v.* "Neo-Nazism." Edited by Michael Berenbaum and Fred Skolnik. Detroit: Macmillan Reference USA/Thomson Gale, 2007. 74–82.

Hendershot, Heather. *What's Fair on the Air: Cold War Right-wing Broadcasting and the Public Interest.* Chicago, Ill.; London: University of Chicago Press, 2011.

King, Wayne "Computer Network Links Rightist Groups and Offers 'Enemy' List." *New York Times*, 15 February 1985, A17.

Kintz, Linda and Julia Lesage, eds. *Media, Culture, and the Religious Right.* Minneapolis: University of Minnesota Press, 1998.

Kramer, Marcia. "Two Groups Accused of Funding Nazis." *Daily News*, 15 May 1977; reprinted in White Power Report (July 1977).

Levin, Jack. *The Violence of Hate: Confronting Racism, Anti-Semitism, and Other Forms of Bigotry.* Boston: Allyn and Bacon, 2002.

Lowe, David. *Computerized Networks of Hate: An ADL Fact Finding Report.* New York: Anti-Defamation League, 1985. 2.

Martin, William. *With God on Our Side: The Rise of the Religious Right in America.* New York: Broadway Books, 2005.

Madsen, Wayne. "The Battle for Cyberspace: Spooks v. Civil Liberties and Social Unrest." *CovertAction Quarterly*, Winter 1996–1997.

Mason, Carol. *Reading Appalachia from Left to Right: Conservatives and the Kanawha County Textbook Controversy.* Ithaca, NY: Cornell University Press, 2009.

———. "From Textbooks to Tea Parties: An Appalachian Antecedent of Anti-Obama Rebellion," *West Virginia History, New Series* 5:2 (Fall 2011): 1–26.

McCune, Wesley. "Extremists are linked by a computer network." *Group Research Report* 25:3 (March 1986): 10. People for the American Way Library.

McGirr, Lisa. "A History of the Conservative Movement from the Bottom Up." *The Journal of Policy History* 14:3 (2002): 331–39.

McVeigh, Rory. *The Rise of the Ku Klux Klan: Right-Wing Movements and National Politics.* Minneapolis: University of Minnesota Press, 2009.

Metzger, Tom. "W.A.R. Computer Terminal," *War '85*, 4:1. No date, (perhaps early 1985).

Miller, Tim. "The Electronic Fringe." The Magazine, reprinted in Liberty Bell (July 1985).

Moffett, James. *Storm in the Mountains: A Case Study of Censorship, Conflict, and* Consciousness. Carbondale, IL: Southern Illinois University Press, 1989.

National Education Association, Teacher Rights Division. Inquiry Report: Kanawha County West Virginia A Textbook Study in Cultural Conflict (Washington, DC, 1975), 48.

National Socialist Vanguard Report 10: 4, October/December 1992): 3 (People for the American Way Library).

Neiwert, David. *The Eliminationists: How Hate Talk Radicalized the American Right* Sausalito, CA: PoliPointPress, 2009.

Perlstein, Rick. *The Invisible Bridge: The Fall of Nixon and the Rise of Reagan.* New York: Simon and Schuster, 2014.

"Reverberations of a Belch by Robert Welch," Liberty Bell (November 1976): 17–18.

Roberts, Glenn C. "A Message to All True Sons of Appalachia." *Liberty Bell* (December 1974): 6.

Schroer, Todd J. "Issue and Identity Framing within the White Racialist Movement: Internet Dynamics." In *The Politics of Social Inequality,* (Research in Political Sociology, vol. 9). Edited by Betty A. Dobratz, Lisa K. Walder, and Timothy Buzzell, 2001: 117–63.

———. "White Racialists, Computers, and the Internet." Paper presented at the annual meeting of the American Sociological Association, Toronto, 1997.

Sheppe, Joseph, Dr. "Textbook Protest in W. VA." Liberty Bell (December 1974): 5.

Sills, Peter [pseud.]. "Dark Contagion: Bigotry and Violence Online." *PC Computing*, December 1989. 144–49.

Snyder-Hall, Claire and Cynthia Burack. *Right-Wing Populism and the Media.* New York: Routledge, 2014.

Stern, Jessica Eve. "The Covenant, the Sword, and the Arm of the Lord." In *Toxic Terror: Assessing Terrorist Use of Chemical and Biological Weapons,* ed. Jonathan B. Tucker. Cambridge, MA: MIT Press with the Belfer Center for Science and International Affairs, Harvard University, 2000. 139–57.

Stormfront website, http://www.stormfront.org.

"The Kanawha Fight is About More than Textbooks." *World Magazine* (22 February 1975); reprinted as "Red Joke of the Month!" Liberty Bell 2:8 (April 1975): 17–19.

WAR, boxed list, in *WAR '86 5:5* 1986, no specific date, (probably late October or early November based on dates in articles). Dated as received 5 December 1986 by the Library at the State Historical Society of Wisconsin.

Warren, Donald I. Radio Priest: Charles Coughlin, the Father of Hate Radio. New York: Free Press, 1996.

White Power Report. White Power Publications, Liverpool, WV. Housed in Wilcox Collection of Contemporary Political Movements, Kenneth Spencer Research Library, University of Kansas.

Chapter Two

The Lone Wolf Comes From Somewhere, Too

Øyvind Strømmen and Kjetil Stormark

"We have to know history to understand our contemporary times, and to be able to shape the future," Eskil Pedersen, the leader of the Labour Youth (AUF), said. It was 22 July 2011. He was uncovering a memorial plaque at Utøya, honoring members of the organization—the youth wing of Norway's social democratic Labour Party—who were killed during the Spanish Civil War, fighting the forces of right-wing authoritarian general Franco.

"Gunnar Skjeseth from Kabelvåg, Martin Schei from Førde, Torbjørn Engebretsen from Lørenskog and Odd Olsen from Trondheim died fighting for democracy and justice," Pedersen added. "They understood the consequences of the rise of fascism, many years prior to Hitler sending his soldiers to occupy Norway."

A press release on the speech was shared through the Twitter profile of AUF, titled "Remembering those who died." It was almost 10:30 in the morning. It was raining.[1]

It rained in Oslo, too. About one and a half hour after the press release from the Labour Youth, Anders Behring Breivik parked a silvery Fiat Doblo at the parking lot at Hammersborg torg, a square in central Oslo. CCTV recorded the thirty-two-year-old man as he walked toward the center, through the government quarters. He was carrying an umbrella. At Stortorvet—another square, just a few hundred meters away—he entered a taxi, and asked to be driven to Skøyen. He was going home to his mother.

Until recently, he lived there. He still has a room there, a bed, a black office chair, a PC, a couple of posters on the wall. Below the posters, there is a safe, where he has been storing ammunition. Breivik has spent much time in this room; behind the computer screen, playing computer games, surfing the Internet, reading, taking part in debates, planning terrorism.

Since that day in July 2011, many stories have been told about Breivik. Some of them are about insanity. Some of them are about the relationship between Breivik and his mother, about a troubled childhood. Some of them have been about politics, about extremism, about hatred.[2] Breivik had his own story he wanted to tell. He had set up a Twitter account, posting only one tweet, misquoting John Stuart Mill: "One person with a belief is equal to the force of 100,000 who have only interests."[3]

Breivik had also registered a new Facebook account, which contained pictures of himself, meant for publication in the media. Here he stated that he was a "Christian" and a "Conservative." Before he left his mother's apartment that day, he also sent an email. He had hoped to send it to more than eight thousand email addresses he had gathered over a long period, the addresses of "European patriots." However, his email provider had a built-in spam filter and a daily limit of one thousand emails. The list of recipients was therefore amputated.

"Western European patriot," he wrote, "I'm hereby sending you my new compendium." He then outlined that it covered the "ongoing Islamicization of Western Europe," the "current state of the Western European Resistance Movements," "solutions," and "strategies":

> I humbly ask you to re-distribute the book to as many patriotic minded individuals as you can. I am 100% certain that the distribution of this compendium to a large portion of European patriots will contribute to ensure our victory in the end. Because within these three books lie the tools required to win the ongoing Western European cultural war, the war against the anti-European hate ideology known as multiculturalism.
>
> [. . .] Time is of the essence. We have only a few decades to consolidate a sufficient level of resistance before our major cities are completely demographically overwhelmed by Muslims. Ensuring the successful distribution of this compendium to as many Europeans as humanly possible will significantly contribute to our success. It may be the only way to avoid our present and future dhimmitude (enslavement) under Islamic majority rule in our own countries.[4]

The email reveals at least two things. It reveals that Breivik thought highly of himself. It also reveals quite a bit about the political ideas that motivated him.

THE TERROR ATTACKS AND THEIR AFTERMATH

About an hour after leaving his mother's apartment, Breivik parked the rented, white Volkswagen Crafter outside the main entrance of the so-called H-block in Oslo's government quarters, holding the Prime Ministers Office as well as the Ministry of Justice. He then exited the large van, wearing a fake police uniform and a helmet with a thick glass visor, and walked away, toward his escape car at Hammersborg torg. Exactly at 15.25.22, a massive bomb went off.

It did not take long before the news reached social media. After only 23 seconds, one Norwegian Twitter user, the writer Gunnar R. Tjomlid, wrote: "Holy crap. Did Oslo just explode?" In the next couple of minutes, similar messages followed: "Oh my God! Bomb in Oslo?"; "Everyone says it's a bomb. Could it be an accident?"; "Heard explosion far away in the Oslo fjord—windows rattled."

Social media soon went into overdrive. Even while Norwegian Twitter users largely reacted by calling for calm and with outright anger when rumours spread about Muslims being targeted "in retaliation," not everybody reacted equally responsible. Anti-Muslim and radical right-wing blogs also picked up the news from the Norwegian capital.

At *jihadwatch*—one of the most influential websites in the so-called counterjihadist blogosphere—the site published several articles. "No one is claiming responsibility and no one is being blamed at this point, but the news wires are citing the terror charges against Mullah Krekar last week and other jihad-related incidents as possible causes," the editor, Robert Spencer, wrote in the first of several articles.[5] *Jihadwatch* readers, however, were in little doubt about who to blame: "Islam IS terrorism"; "End multi-culturalism now!"; "Well, they wanted the Moslem imports, now they got them, jihad bombs and all"; "Islam! Guilty"; "The fruits of unasked-for, undesirable, self-hating and self destructive multiculturalism"; "Muslims living in the West should be locked up in internment camps." Islam was also described as parasitical. And as a cancer.

Meanwhile Breivik traveled on to Utøya, to the summer camp of the Labour Youth, and started shooting people, most of them under the age of 18. At six in the evening, trying to catch his breath in the midst of his shooting rampage, he called the police.

- The police emergency line.
- Yeah, hello, my name is commander Anders Behring Breivik, of the Norwegian anti-Communist resistance movement.
- Yes?
- I am at Utøya at the moment. I wish to surrender.
- Ok, what number are you calling from?
- I am calling from a mobile.
- You are calling from your mobile?
- Yes. It's not mine, someone else . . .
- Someone else, what was your name? Hello. . . ? Hello. . . ?[6]

The connection was cut off before Breivik and the acting chief of staff of the local police district were able to negotiate terms of his surrender. Breivik sounded slightly mentally unstable, a person the police under other circumstances would have treated with a high degree of skepticism. Twenty-six minutes later Breivik called again, this time stating he was the commander of an organization called Knights Templar of Europe, a part of the resistance movement against "the Islamicization of Europe and the Islamicization of Norway." Whether or not Breivik had real intentions to surrender or just wanted to delay the police response, giving him sufficient time to complete his attack, is still unclear.[7]

At about the same time, in the comments on the blog *Gates of Vienna*— another key counterjihadist blog—nobody really expected the events in Oslo to be anything but an Islamist terror attack. One man, calling himself "PatrickHenry," wrote:

> My Norwegian cousins, you had better heed our advice this time . . . it's time to begin MASS DEPORTATIONS of your "cultural enrichers," unless this is the "enrichment" you have sought! Send them all back to the the cesspools from which they came. If you don't start now, it will be much worse next time. How many more Norwegians must be slaughtered before you stop stewing? Act!
> [. . .] It's high time to initiate "cultural purification" and restore Norway to it's historical roots. I'd hate to think you'll allow your elected "leaders" to kowtow to you[r] "cultural destroyers" any further. Send them home, NOW, before it's too late. There are no moderates in their midst, only murderers or their enablers, be they liberal multicultis or your "cultural invaders." They just declared war upon your peaceful country, now you must ACT!
> If you elect one more liberal, you're all INSANE![8]

His comment was not merely an impassioned call for ethnic cleansing. It was—unknowingly—a summary of much of the content in Breivik's "compendium." The phone-book sized manifesto, an often confused cut-and-paste work, largely boils down to these ideas: Europe is threatened by Muslims, an alien, invasive force. Liberal politicians are to blame. Purification is necessary. It's war. One needs to act.

PROFILING THE LONE WOLF

In her book *Hunting the American Terrorist,* former FBI investigator Kathleen M. Puckett provides a closer look at ten American solo terrorists, amongst them Ted Kaczynski, the Unabomber. All the ten solo terrorists in Puckett's study are men, like almost all solo terrorists.[9] Toward the end of the book, Puckett describes what she calls "paranoid personalities," individuals "characterised by enduring patterns of distrust and suspicion [. . .].

[This] leads them to believe things are connected, but in a dangerous and malevolent way." The human mind, Puckett notes, is built to make meaningful connections between different elements of life, but paranoid personalities go far beyond that. She refers specifically to conspiracy theorists. Conspiracy theories are often part and parcel of extremist ideology, and extremist groups are built up around hatred toward others, suspicion, political paranoia.

But what about the solo terrorists? Puckett finds some striking similarities between them. Many of them were reserved individuals, even as children. They had few friends. They were seen as socially awkward, in particular in relation to women. Nine of them also had another thing in common: They had tried to become part of established, political groups; attempts that largely failed. Puckett writes:

> Consider an essentially paranoid personality who can't successfully affiliate—for reasons having to do with his own psychological makeup and social difficulties—with the group whose ideology he shares. Just because he fails in joining the group doesn't end his desire—his need—to do so.
> Being part of a group, besides making him feel good, would give him power and importance outside of himself. He could claim the stature of the group, and he would *matter*. [10]

When group identity does not turn out, such an individual may very well choose to connect to the one thing that cannot refuse him, *ideology* itself. He becomes the "true believer." He becomes the one who—unlike the rest—actually does something.

James Clayton Vaughn, Jr., had a troublesome family background. His family was poor. His father was a violent alcoholic. As a teenager, James was silent and withdrawn. Then he became a believer in so-called British Israelism, a belief that Western Europeans—Britons in particular—are the true descendants of the Lost Tribes of Israel; and thus the true Chosen People. In 1968, when he was eighteen, Vaughn joined the National Socialist White People's Party. He married, but his marriage quickly failed. A second marriage also ended badly, but resulted in a daughter.

Vaughn became a neo-Nazi activist, took part in violent demonstrations and can also be spotted on a photography taken outside the White House, where he went—wearing a Nazi uniform—to demonstrate against the visit of Israeli prime minister Golda Meir. Gradually, however, he started considering other members of the movement as unreliable and not sufficiently violent. He wanted a race war, and to "cleanse" America of Jews and Blacks. Others seemingly only wanted to talk. [11]

In 1974, Vaughn moved to Atlanta, where he joined the National States Rights Party (NSRP), a racist organization combining two different expressions of right-wing extremism: On one hand they entertained an enthusiasm for German Nazism, on the other hand the group actively glorified the Confederate States of America. The NSRP leader, Jesse Benjamin Stoner, was a glowing extremist, who dreamt of the extermination of American Jews: "The only thing I find wrong with Hitler [is] that he didn't exterminate all those six million Jews he's credited with." The NSRP was linked to several violent attacks, amongst them the bombing of an Atlanta synagogue in 1958.

Vaughn also listened to and became a fan of the radio programs of William Pierce, a leading right-wing extremist who is also noted as the author of the *Turner Diaries,* a novel about a coming, giant racial war. For a while, Vaughn also joined a branch of the Ku Klux Klan, but in 1976 he had reached his conclusion: The Klan was nothing but a joke. [12] That same year he changed his name to Joseph Paul Franklin, in honour of the infamous Nazi leader Paul Joseph Goebbels, and of the American revolutionary leader Benjamin Franklin. [13]

In 1977, Vaughn—now named Franklin—started his terror campaign as a solo terrorist. Using a bomb, he targeted the home of Morris Amitay, a Jewish lawyer in AIPAC. Miraculously, only the family dog was killed in the attack. A few days later Franklin carried out another bomb attack. This time he targeted a synagogue in Chattanooga, Tennessee. Once again, only pure luck ensured nobody was killed: A meeting in the synagogue that evening had been cut short, since few people had shown up. The timed bomb went off after everyone had gone home. In August 1977, Franklin eventually succeded in killing someone for the first time, when he shot down and murdered a mixed couple, Alphonse Manning and Toni Schwenn. In October, he hid outside a mosque in St. Louis, Missouri, and started shooting when members of the congregation came out of the building. Several people were injured. Gerald Gordon was killed.

In the three years to follow, Franklin carried out a number of attacks, while he moved from state to state, using different names. It is believed that he killed as many as twenty people. According to Franklin himself, one of those targeted was the porn magnate Larry Flynt, who survived the shooting, but was paralyzed. In 1980, Franklin was at last arrested. [14] In November 2013, he was executed in Missouri.

BREIVIK VS. FRANKLIN

There are certain similarities in the stories of Breivik and Franklin. The first pair of court-appointed psychiatrists in Breivik's case concluded that he was a paranoid schizophrenic. An expert witness for the defense in Franklin's case gave him the same diagnosis. Both of them tried to involve themselves in more established groups. Breivik registered at the international neo-Nazi web forum *Stormfront.org* and tried to appeal for a fight against Islam there. He was also an active commenter on the Norwegian web site *document.no*, a site with a strongly sceptical focus on immigration in general and on Muslim immigration in particular. He went to a meeting arranged by "Friends of Document," and also contacted the editor, trying to convince him that he should establish the web site as a regular paper-based newspaper; outlining somewhat grandiose and unrealistic plans involving himself and the Norwegian populist party Fremskrittspartiet—a party he had himself left years earlier.

Breivik also contacted the Norwegian blogger Fjordman, a central ideologist to the international "counterjihad" blogosphere. He hoped that he too would come to the meeting in Friends of Document. Fjordman—later revealed to be Peder Nøstvold Jensen—kept a low profile and was not interested. The day after the meeting, Breivik did however write back to Jensen, complaining that there hadn't been "much action."[15]

"[Editor] Hans [Rustad] and a couple of others are afraid to consolidate in an effective manner," Breivik wrote. "They're afraid they'll contribute to creating a kind of 'monster' they will lose control over at a later stage." He complained that *document.no* was hesitant to pursue his newspaper concept, and that the site did not want to establish contact with what he called "other, established culturally conservative organizations." In his email to Fjordman, Breivik seems disenchanted with *document.no*. He says that he does not write much there, since he is only censored, anyway. He says that he's planning a roundtrip in Europe to hold talks about the book he is working on, *2083*. It's a strategy-oriented book, he writes, a book about how "modern culturally conservative movements can be consolidated." He writes about civil war.

His language is peculiar, his Norwegian laden with English words and terminology. At the same time, Breivik shows familiarity with the texts of Fjordman. He inquires whether Fjordman has attempted to get his *Defeating Eurabia*, a self-published anti-Muslim screed, published also through an American or European "dissident publisher." Breivik declares that he feels no conservative intellectual in Northern Europe has "done so much for so little" as Fjordman. He would love to meet him, he writes, to have a couple of beers.[16]

Interrogated by the police after the dramatic events on 22 July 2011, Fjordman said that he did not remember that he had any contact with Breivik when Breivik's name first became public. The blogger later said that he found Breivik's emails boring. They never met to drink a few beers.[17] While Breivik—unlike Franklin—did not only seek out extremist organizations, they both attempted to become recognized by larger groups, and failed. Fjordman was disinterested in Breivik.

A combination of social awkwardness and failed attempts to join a wider movement seems to be a key feature of a number of solo terrorists. Franklin saw the Nazi groups he had joined as failures. Hence he initiated his own personal race war. Buford Furrow, who attacked a Jewish center in Los Angeles in 1999 was a former member of the right-wing extremist Aryan Nations organization, but became disillusioned, and decided to "wake up America" on his own. David Copeland, the UK solo terrorist behind three nail bomb attacks in London in 1999 was a former member of the British National Party and the National Socialist Movement. Benjamin Daniel Smith, the perpetrator of a three day shooting rampage in Illinois and Indiana in 1999—targeting blacks, Jews, and Asians—had been a follower of the white supremacist group World Church of the Creator. The Swedish serial shooter Peter Mangs was active within conspiracy theory circles and commented on the Swedish nativist web site *Politiskt Inkorrekt.*

Breivik, like many other solo terrorists, did not receive the recognition he sought within established movements and organizations. Instead he, too, started perceiving himself as the true believer, as the one who actually turns ideas into action. In the trial against him, Breivik stated: "It is one hundred per cent certain that there will be a war between nationalists and internationalists in Europe. We, the first militant nationalists, are the first drops of water who realized that a large storm is coming."[18]

If we are to understand why Breivik became a solo terrorist, it is necessary to investigate and analyze his personal history, the way Puckett maps the personal histories of the American solo terrorists she writes about. As the Norwegian author Audhild Skoglund points out in her book *Sinte hvite menn* (Angry white men), there is not necessarily a contradiction between the mental state of solo terrorists and their ideology. Society often has a tendency to view people either as mentally stable, and thus capable of having an ideology, or as mentally unstable and thus incapable of the same. Skoglund argues that solo terrorists—at least to a certain degree—can rather be indicative of sentiments of hatred found in a culture, or in specific subcultures.[19] In other words, while Franklin might very well have been a paranoid schizophrenic, his choice of targets made ideologically sense. While Breivik certainly suffers from personality disorders, none of his attacks were random. They were not natural disasters. Breivik did not come out of the blue.

THE MEDIA STRATEGY

Both the targeting process as well as the level of casualties Breivik felt he needed to inflict on the Norwegian society in what he called "the operation" was heavily influenced by his overall media strategy. Breivik was convinced he needed to kill a large enough number of people to be able to attract satisfactory, international media attention. And the media attention was necessary to get his message out to a bigger audience.[20] His original plan was to build three terror bombs, something Breivik failed to achieve.[21] But by killing seventy-seven people, of whom sixty-nine were gunned down at point blank or drowned trying to escape Breivik's bullets at the Utøya youth summer camp, he nevertheless succeded in both setting a grim world record in the world of lone killers as well as attracting the instant attention of the global media community. Breivik only regretted that he was unable to reach an even higher body count, according to statements he made during the trial hearings in 2012.[22]

The next phase for Breivik was the marketing of his ideology and his manifesto, whereas the trial was identified by Breivik to be the key marketing plattform. On one hand Breivik has often said he expected to be tortured and killed by the police when they arrested him after his shooting spree at Utøya.[23] After surviving his arrest, he has nevertheless stated on several occasions, that the trial was the perfect opportunity for him to get his message out to the European population.[24] His attempts to use the trial for marketing purposes were, however, severely limited by the court judges imposing strict limitations on the broadcasting of live images and audio when Anders Behring Breivik was given the opportunity to speak in the trial against him.

Breivik has said he—in the build-up to the terror attacks in 2011—made several attempts to use the established media to get his message out, but that he was censored and eventually gave up.[25] He considered editors and senior reporters of the established media to be traitors, cooperating with the Labour Party in selling out the Norwegian society to multicultural and Muslim domination.[26] Breivik even went as far as carrying out surveillance operations against the Norwegian Broadcasting Company's (NRK) news department in Oslo, as well as against a national, annual congress of investigative reporters in Norway. The purpose was to gather information for the benefit of target development. Breivik considered attacking media organizations directly.[27] Instead, Breivik chose to attack the Labour Party government and their youth politicians at the summer camp at Utøya Island.

A significant part of Breivik's original plan was to capture former Norwegian prime minister and WHO secretary general Gro Harlem Brundtland and/ or the AUF youth labour leader Eskil Pedersen and film their execution(s).[28] However, Breivik forgot the video camera in the car before entering the ferry to the Utøya Island.[29] Neither was he able to catch any high profile politicians during his massacre at the island. Heavily influenced by jihadists and salafist terrorists, Breivik admitted during the court proceedings, he intended to behead Brundtland and other high profile leaders, and to post the recording on YouTube. Every detail of the attacks had been thought through, but Breivik failed to implement many of his plans when carrying out the terror attacks.[30]

In his efforts to maximize the media impact, Breivik also considered carrying out attacks against nuclear power plants as well as using weapons of mass destruction (WMD), meaning biological, chemical, or radiological compounds. He went to great lengths in researching these alternative attack plans, which he outlines in his manifesto. Ultimately Breivik lacked the money, the time, or the knowledge to carry out such attacks. But Breivik went to great lengths building a list of potential targets and a rudimentary users manual.[31]

After his arrest and subsequent conviction, Breivik received thousands of letters, many from individuals and groups sharing some or many of his political beliefs. From his solitary confinement within the high-level security regime in the two prisons taking turn in housing the most dangerous convict in Norway, Breivik is actively trying to set up and organize an international political movement. But his efforts are again seriously hampered, this time by aggressively enforced restrictions on his ability to communicate freely with the outside world. Every letter and message that can be interpreted as efforts to instigate further violence, is effectively stopped and censored by the Norwegian prison authority (Kriminalomsorgen).

In a letter to one of the authors, dated 21 February 2014, Breivik writes: "Over the last two years I have received more than three thousand letters of support and I am about to establish a good contact base in all of the thirteen Nordic countries. The problem, however, is that all letters to these contacts have been stopped and censored."

From his prison cell, Breivik claims to have written two books, of which the second is called "The Nordic Federation." At the same time he has made several, futile attempts to establish a Norwegian fascist party. Breivik still signs his letters of protest, regularly sent to news organizations, scientists, researchers and government entities in Norway with "Anders Behring Breivik—The Norwegian Fascist Party (under construction)."[32]

In the manifesto "2083—A European declaration of independence" Breivik outlined a detailed set of rules and a hierachy of what kind of resistance movement he wanted to form. Whether he believes himself to already be a member of such an organization—the Knights Templar of Europe—or whether it was an elaborate lie in order to try to get the blueprint out to "other patriots," as previously discussed, is yet to be determined. Breivik has, nevertheless, succeeded in establishing himself as a living martyr and legend in the dark recesses of extreme right politics in Europe. He also wants to be an ideological and practical leader, at which he—at least so far—has not succeeded.

SOURCES OF INFLUENCE

After the terror attacks of 22 July, two questions are obvious. Is there anything within Norwegian society promoting the kind of extremism that influenced Breivik to commit his atrocious acts? And from where did he get his ideas?

The first question is truly difficult to answer, since the answer of the second question will show that Breivik was not a "Norwegian" terrorist, in the ideological sense of the word. The ideology—or rather ideologies—that inspired him—or his perception of the world, were shaped through the websites he frequently read. These websites are heavily influenced by what you could call an international "movement" and/or ideology. This international movement has surely found some adherents in Norway, but not in a dominant fashion.

In his phone book sized manifesto Breivik points to three writers and attributes them to be the primary contributors to the ideological "school" he himself claims to belong to, the "School of Vienna"—possibly a term Breivik has come up with himself. These three writers are Fjordman, the *Jihadwatch* editor Robert Spencer, and the author Bat Ye'or. He also mentioned three specific web sites, *Gates of Vienna, Brussels Journal* , and *The Green Arrow*. [33] What all six have in common—with a partial, and interesting exception in *The Green Arrow*—is their connection to the so-called counterjihadist movement.

When Breivik carried out his attacks, he primarily tried to reach an international audience. His "compendium" or manifesto is in English. His Twitter message, and the Facebook page he set up shortly before the attacks were also in English. His YouTube propaganda video was in the same language.

Let us dwell for a short moment upon *The Green Arrow,* the exception. Unlike the other sites mentioned, it does not exist anymore, although an archive is currently available, and a new site has come in its place—the *British Resistance.* While anti-Muslim views are equally central to *The Green Arrow* and on *British Resistance* as to the other sites mentioned, one difference is clear: *The Green Arrow/British Resistance* is considerably closer to a more traditional form of right-wing extremism. Here, anti-Semitism thrives and the focus on race theories is more obvious. In short, *The Green Arrow* is closer to the point-of-view Breivik has taken while in prison, where he has expressed clearer support for traditional neo-Nazi ideas than in his so-called manifesto and claimed the use of "double psychology" in order to (indirectly) inflict damage to the "anti-Nordicist/ethnocentrist wing within the counter-jihad," including "Fjordman and his Jewish network." His motivation was that he wanted to provoke his "fellow patriots" to act as a result of increased "suppression" of them after his terror attack on their behalf. Thus far he has failed.

More questions still need to be asked:

Are Breivik's claims to be a member of a modern-day Knights Templar, a terrorist group, completely fictitious—or is it possible that he as at least met with others sharing a similar extremist ideology, also offline? Breivik stated that he took part in a founding meeting of the organization in London in April 2002.[34] The court found no basis for these claims, even if the police found evidence suggesting Breivik was in fact in London at the time. The Norwegian police has not been able to determine what Breivik actually did in London during his stay there in April 2002.

And did Breivik have mentors, co-conspirators or at least confide in anyone about his plans? Breivik himself has claimed to have had two mentors. Their true identity, if they ever existed, has not been determined. One mentor, according to Breivik, was a former Serbian war "hero" or "criminal," depending on your perspective.[35]

One former member of the Norwegian anti-Muslim movement claims there has been contact between Breivik and a named third person, indicating possible violence against "traitors" on social media prior to 22 July. Unsubstantiated rumours like these started developing soon after the terror attacks. A Norwegian blogger with sources inside extreme anti-Muslim groups claims he himself heard from a person who was in contact with Breivik before 22 July that "something" would happen. Again hearsay, but a part of the Norwegian public debate after 22 July.

The story of Martin Rustad is somewhat more specific. Toward the end of the last decade, Rustad was one of Breivik's Internet friends. "We were all brainwashed," Rustad later said. They talked about establishing an anti-Muslim organization. "He wanted to organize, to reach the people, to wake them up. In private message, he did not seem opposed to the idea of a civil war," Rustad later told the Norwegian daily *Dagbladet.* According to him, Breivik mentioned a "renovation project."[36] Breivik spoke about both Knights Templar and murders while drunk on the town, without anyone seemingly taking it seriously. It is not unlikely that Breivik told someone whom he wanted to impress, at least about his manifesto. Several witnesses has stated to the police that Breivik told them he was working on a book and that he would soon become famous.[37] The police investigation has, however, found no indication of anybody else being directly involved in the planning and execution of Breivik's terror attacks. The group of Knights Templar that Breivik claimed to belong to, is—the police believe—pure fantasy.[38]

If the police are correct, it would hardly be unique as far as solo terrorists go. The Austrian right-wing extremist and solo terrorist Franz Fuchs, who carried out a bombing campaign between 1993 and 1997, killing four and injuring fifteen, claimed to belong to a Bajuwarische Befreiungsarmee (Bavarian Liberation Army). Ted Kaczynski, the Unabomber, claimed to lead a group called Freedom Club.[39] The American Eric Rudolph, most known for his terror attack during the Olympics in Atlanta in 1996, claimed to belong to the Army of God. There are few indications that the first two ever existed. The latter does exist, even though it is more an idea than an actual group.

CONCLUSION

We know that Breivik did have contact with many people who had ideas similar to his own. He himself claimed to have had more than six hundred members of the English Defence League as Facebook friends, and to have spoken directly with dozens of members and leaders. He even claims to have provided them with ideological material and having suggested rhetorical talking points and strategies to them.[40] All of this appears as yet another example of Breivik's wish to position himself in an important role. As described above, Breivik, like other solo terrorists, went from being a failure within organized groups to seeing himself as the "true believer," the one that went from talk to action. He also appears to have constructed a terrorist organization, a modern-day order of Knights Templar; complete with the self-made uniform he wanted to wear in court, and the constructed "military" decorations described in his so-called manifesto.

Breivik did, however, have actual contact with a number of EDL members. Sources within the EDL has claimed that Breivik took part in a demonstration in London in support of the Dutch radical right-wing politician Geert Wilders.[41] The email addresses he gathered, and to whom he sent his manifesto, also tell us that he went to great lengths in finding potential contacts across Europe. His mailing list included Italian and French neo-fascists, British members of the English Defence League and the British National Party, central members in the now defunct far-right Swedish party Nationaldemokraterna, Norwegians involved in online anti-Muslim groups, several politicians in the radical right-wing Belgian party Vlaams Belang, both anti-Semitic and anti-Muslim bloggers and others. While there are also individuals on his email list that seem to have landed there for no good reason at all, his choice of email recipients shows who Breivik hoped to speak to and/or influence, and therefore also reveals from whom and where he sought inspiration.

For obvious reasons, however, both parties such as the Vlaams Belang and most counterjihadist bloggers want nothing to do with Breivik, even as he shares many of their anti-Muslim ideas. Even for those counterjihadist writers who fantasize about a coming civil war, and there are quite a few, the *actual* violence of Breivik is difficult to accept; in particular the mass murder at Utøya.

Furthermore, it is dangerous to be identified by the intelligence community as someone who was in touch with Anders Behring Breivik prior to the terror attacks in the summer of 2011. Thus, the support Breivik later has found for his actions have been on the periphery of the counterjihadist movement, as well as from more traditional neo-Nazi circles—particularly in former Soviet countries. This might explain his changed focus in prison, where Breivik has started expressing support to Norwegian neo-Nazis such as Tore

Tvedt, Erik Blücher and Nicolay Kvisler, and to the former metal musician, self-declared Odinist and anti-Semitic writer Varg Vikernes, in the past convicted of church fires and murder in Norway, and recently convicted of hate speech in France.

In 1989, William Pierce, author of the *Turner Diaries,* published a new book, called *Hunter.* The book's main character is a man who kills interracial couples in an attempt to forment a race war. It was dedicated to Joseph Paul Franklin. David Copeland, the London nailbomber, has received support in neo-Nazi circles too; a sticker was made in the name of the neo-Nazi group Combat 18, stating "Stand by David Copeland—leaderless resistance works." And Breivik, too, has found support. Sometimes it has been expressed by members of anti-Muslim groups such as the EDL, othertimes it has shown up on the fringes of such movements, for example when the two young Britons John Roddy and Tobias Ruth, who were arrested in January 2013 after daubing racist graffiti on an Islamic Center in Torbay and sending threatening messages to mosques around the United Kingdom. The two men drew inspiration from Breivik and had performed an initation ceremony during which they branded each other on the arm with a cross.

Sometimes the support is expressed by individuals that are obviously disturbed, such as the sixteen-year-old British school boy who allegedly plotted a "new Columbine"—targeting his former school in Loughborough, Leicestershire—while also declaring himself a Commander of the Knights Templar. Sometimes it shows up in neo-Nazi circles, sometimes in bizarre extreme right-wing groups barely existing outside the Internet.

What all of this tells us is that Breivik—the lone wolf—was not entirely lonely. He was not, as the Norwegian author Roy Jacobsen claimed in Danish *Weekendavisen* in October 2011, "the loneliest man in the world."[42] The lone wolf comes from somewhere, too—and the next one mixing his own ideology of hatred, might very well bring both the all too widespread anti-Muslim ideas and Breivik's call to action into his own lethal mix.

NOTES

1.   AUF, "Til minne om de som falt," *auf.no,* 22 juli 2011. Online at http://auf.no/-/bulletin/show/671900_til-minne-om-de-som-falt?ref=checkpoint. All translations, unless otherwise noted, are our own.

2.   See Åsne Seierstad, *En av oss, en fortelling om Norge,* (Oslo: Kagge Forlag, 2013); Aage Borchgrevink, *En norsk tragedie* (Oslo: Gyldendal, 2012); and Marit Christensen, *Moren* (Oslo: Aschehoug, 2013). Recently his father, Jens Breivik—who had only limited contact with his son—also wrote a book on their relationship and how he experienced the terror attacks, see Jens Breivik, *Min skyld?* (Oslo: Juritzen Forlag, 2014).

3.   The exact quote from John Stuart Mill: "One person with a belief, is a social power equal to ninety-nine who have only interests." (*In Consideration of Representative Government*, London: 1861). The quote is to be found in "Chapter I: To What Extent Forms of Government are a Matter of Choice."

4. E-mail sent by Anders Behring Breivik, 22 July 2011, 14:08. Also see Kjetil Stormark, *Massemorderens private e-poster* (Oslo, Spartacus Forlag, 2012).

5. Robert Spencer, "Huge blast hits Oslo government buildings, at least one person dead," *jihadwatch.org,* 22 July 2011. Online at http://www.jihadwatch.org/2011/07/huge-blast-hits-oslo-government-buildings-at-least-one-person-dead.html.

6. Jens Christian Nørve, "Breivik fortsatte skytingen etter denne telefonen fra Utøya," TV2.no, 22 November 2011. Online at http://www.tv2.no/a/3642681.

7. Kjetil Stormark, *Da terroren rammet Norge. 189 minutter som rystet verden* (Oslo: Kagge Forlag, 2011).

8. Baron Bodissey [Edward S. May], "Terror Attack in Central Oslo," *Gates of Vienna*, 22 July 2011. http://gatesofvienna.blogspot.no/2011/07/terror-attack-in-central-oslo.html.

9. In a comprehensive overview by Ramon Spaaij, only two of eighty-eight solo terrorists listed are women: the anti-abortion extremist Rachelle Shannon and the British Islamist Roshonara Chodury. See Ramon Spaaij, *Understanding Lone Wolf Terrorism* (Dordrecht, London and New York: Springer, 2012), 13.

10. Kathleen M. Puckett and Terry D. Turchie, *Hunting the American terrorist. The FBI's war on homegrown terror* (New York: History Publishing Company, 2007), Kindle locations 3128–3168.

11. Mel Ayton, *Dark Soul of the South. The Life and Crimes of Racist Killer Joseph Paul Franklin* (Washington: Potomac Books, 2011), 31–34.

12. Ayton, *Dark Soul*, 37.

13. Ayton, *Dark Soul*, 38–39.

14. Ayton, *Dark Soul*, 42–72.

15. Email sent from Breivik to Fjordman, 11 December 2009.

16. Breivik email to Fjordman, 11 December 2009.

17. Report from police interrogation of Peder Nøstvold Jensen (Fjordman), Oslo police district, 4 August 2011.

18. From Anders Behring Breivik's statement in Oslo district court, 17 April 2012.

19. Audhild Skoglund, *Sinte hvite menn* (Oslo: Humanist Forlag, 2013), 22.

20. Police interrogation of Anders Behring Breivik, 10 August 2011, and Anders Behring Breivik's statement in Oslo district court, 19 April 2012. In his manifesto "2083—A European Declaration of Independence," 833. Breivik wrote: "In order to successfully penetrate the cultural Marxist/multiculturalist media censorship we are forced to employ significantly more brutal and breath taking operations which will result in casualties. In order for the attack to gain an influential effect, assassinations and the use of weapons of mass destruction must be embraced." On page 954, he continued: "If the WMD acquirement phase fails, go with a basic shock operation." And on page 1363, Breivik added: "there have been more than a hundred successful operations from armed nationalist movements in Europe the last decade. But the main problem is that a great majority of these operations are not "spectacular" enough to break media censorship." The page numbers vary in different online versions of the manifesto. The page number referenced above refers to the file available on the publicintelligence.net.

21. Anders Behring Breivik's statement in Oslo district court, 20 April 2012.

22. Anders Behring Breivik's statement in Oslo district court, 19 April 2012. In his statement, Breivik said his aim was to kill all of the participants at the AUF Labour Youth summer camp at Utøya. Anders Behring Breivik repeated this claim in his statement in Oslo district court, 23 April 2012.

23. Police interrogation of Anders Behring Breivik, 10 August 2011, as well as Anders Behring Breivik's statement in Oslo district court, 23 April 2012. Breivik also stated to the arresting officers on 22 July 2011 that he expected to be executed after the terror attack on the island.

24. Anders Behring Breivik's statement in Oslo district court, 24 April 2012. Breivik described himself as a "salesman trying to convey his own ideas to the public."

25. Anders Behring Breivik's opening statement in Oslo district court, 17 April 2012, as well as his statement to the court on 20 April 2012. Breivik also made numerous references to media censorship in his manifesto "2083—A European Declaration of Independence," 54, 304,

352, 386, 416, 538, 805, 831, 1363. The page numbers vary in different online versions. These page numbers refer to file available on publicintelligence.net.

26. Anders Behring Breivik's statement in Oslo district court, 20 April 2012. In his statement, Breivik claimed he would not have carried out the terror attacks if the media had respected democratic values and done a proper job reporting on racial tension in Europe. In his manifesto, "2083—A European Declaration of Independence," 938, Breivik categorized the following professional groups as "category B traitors": Journalists, editors, teachers, lecturers, university professors, various school/university board members, publicists, radio commentators, writers of fiction, cartoonists, and artists/celebrities etc. "Category A traitors" were described as "Political leaders (NGO leaders included), media leaders (chief editors), Cultural leaders, Industry leaders" and "any current Heads of State,, ministers/senators, directors and leaders of certain organisations/boards."

27. Anders Behring Breivik, "2083—A European Declaration of Independence," 953. The page numbers vary in different online versions. This page number refers to the file available on publicintelligence.net.

28. Anders Behring Breivik's statement in Oslo district court, 23 April 2012.

29. Breivik statement, 23 April 2012.

30. Anders Behring Breivik, "2083—A European Declaration of Independence," 952, where Breivik stated that: "There are annual gatherings for journalists in all Western European countries. These gatherings are considered THE MOST attractive targets for large scale shock attacks due to the amount and quality of category B traitors." Breivik has said, both in police interrogations as well as in later court statements, that he carried out surveillance operastions against e.g., the Norwegian Broadcasting Corporation (NRK) as well as the Norwegian newspaper Aftenposten and the annual SKUP conference for investigative reporting in Norway. See also *nrk.no*, "- Breivik spanet på NRK-ansatte," 4 February 2012. Online: http://www.nrk.no/ norge/_-breivik-spanet-pa-nrk-ansatte-1.7982353.

31. Anders Behring Breivik, "2083—A European Declaration of Independence," 959–72 and 985–88.

32. Letters from Anders Behring Breivik to Norwegian authorities, the media and research institutions, dated 10 March 2014 and 18 August 2014. In the last letter, Breivik categorizes himself as the "party secretary and parliamentary candidate of The Norwegian Fascist Party and the Nordic League."

33. Anders Behring Breivik, "2083—A European Declaration of Independence," 1237.

34. Anders Behring Breivik, "2083—A European Declaration of Independence," 1379.

35. Anders Behring Breivik, "2083—A European Declaration of Independence," 1379–1380, 1415.

36. Torgeir P. Krokfjord, "Slik var de private nettsamtalene med Breivik," *dagbladet.no,* 9 April 2012. Online at http://www.dagbladet.no/2012/04/09/nyheter/anders_behring_breivik/ terrorangrepet/utenriks/islamkritikk/20667914/.

37. TV 2 Documentary, 9 January 2014: "The tale of the stepmother." Just weeks before the 2011 terror attacks, Breivik stated to his stepmother that he would become a famous author. See also Jens Christian Nørve/Asbjørn Olsen, tv2.no, "- Utrolig at han ikke avslørte seg selv," 9 January 2014.

38. "Knights Templar Europe." Analysis of evidence gathered in the police investigation of the 2011 terror attacks, Oslo Police District/National Criminal Investigation Service. The document has not been made available to the media, but the conclusions from the documents was submitted to Oslo district court during the trial against Anders Behring Breivik in April-June 2012.

39. Spaaij, *Understanding Lone Wolf Terrorism,* 18.

40. Maren Næss Olsen, "En massemorders univers," *Morgenbladet,* 29 July 2011. Online at http://morgenbladet.no/samfunn/2011/en_massemorders_univers?quicktabs_mest_lest_mest_ kommentert=1#.Uqc4Jqwju1E.

41. Mark Hughes and Gordon Rayner, "Norway killer Anders Behring Breivik had extensive links to English Defence League," *Daily Telegraph,* 25 July 2011. Online at http:// www.telegraph.co.uk/news/worldnews/europe/norway/8661139/Norway-killer-Anders-Behring-Breivik-had-extensive-links-to-English-Defence-League.html.

42. Hans Mortensen, "Nej, det er ikke kommet et andet Norge," *Weekendavisen,* 21 October 2011. Quoted from the online version of the article, which is no longer available.

REFERENCES

AUF.no, "Til minne om de som falt," *auf.no,* 22 juli 2011. Online: http://auf.no/-/bulletin/show/671900_til-minne-om-de-som-falt?ref=checkpoint.

Ayton, Mel. *Dark Soul of the South. The Life and Crimes of Racist Killer Joseph Paul Franklin.* Washington: Potomac Books, 2011.

Bodissey, Baron. "Terror Attack in Central Oslo." Gates of Vienna, 22 July 2011. Online: http://gatesofvienna.blogspot.no/2011/07/terror-attack-in-central-oslo.html.

Borchgrevink, Aage. *En norsk tragedie.* Oslo: Gyldendal, 2012.

Breivik, Anders Behring. "2083—A European declaration of independence" (manifesto), 2011.

Breivik, Anders Behring. Letters sent from prison.

Breivik, Anders Behring. Emails.

Breivik, Anders Behring. Police interrogations.

Breivik, Anders Behring. Social media profiles.

Breivik, Anders Behring. Statements made in court.

Breivik, Jens. *Min skyld?* Oslo: Juritzen Forlag, 2014.

Christensen, Marit. *Moren.* Oslo: Aschehoug, 2013.

Hughes, Mark and Gordon Rayner. "Norway killer Anders Behring Breivik had extensive links to English Defence League." *Daily Telegraph,* 25 July 2011. Online: http://www.telegraph.co.uk/news/worldnews/europe/norway/8661139/Norway-killer-Anders-Behring-Breivik-had-extensive-links-to-English-Defence-League.html.

"Knights Templar Europe." Analysis of evidence gathered in the police investigation of the 2011 terror attacks, Oslo Police District/National Criminal Investigation Service, 2012.

Krokfjord, Torgeir P. "Slik var de private nettsamtalene med Breivik." *dagbladet.no.* 9 April 2012. Online: http://www.dagbladet.no/2012/04/09/nyheter/anders_behring_breivik/terrorrangrepet/utenriks/islamkritikk/20667914/.

Mill, John Stuart. *In Consideration of Representative Government.* London: Parker, Son, and Bourn, 1861. Accessed through Project Gutenberg on 9 October 2014.

Mortensen, Hans. "Nej, det er ikke kommet et andet Norge," *Weekendavisen.* 21 October 2011 Quoted from the online version of the article, which is no longer available.

Nrk.no, "Breivik spanet på NRK-ansatte." 4 February 2012. Online: http://www.nrk.no/norge/_-breivik-spanet-pa-nrk-ansatte-1.7982353.

Nørve, Jens Christian and Olsen, Asbjørn, tv2.no, "Utrolig at han ikke avslørte seg selv." 9 January 2014. Online: http://www.tv2.no/a/5209653.

Nørve, Jens Christian and Olsen, Asbjørn, TV 2, Documentary, "The tale of the stepmother." 9 January 2014.

Nørve, Jesn Christian. "Breivik fortsatte skytingen etter denne telefonen fra Utøya." TV2.no, 22 November 2011. Online: http://www.tv2.no/a/3642681.

Olsen, Maren Næss. "En massemorders univers." *Morgenbladet.* 29 July 2011. Online: http://morgenbladet.no/samfunn/2011/en_massemorders_univers?quicktabs_mest_lest_mest_kommentert=1#.Uqc4Jqwju1E.

Oslo Police District, Interrogation of Peder Nøstvold Jensen (Fjordman). 4 August 2011.

Puckett, Kathleen M. and Terry D. Turchie, *Hunting the American terrorist. The FBI's war on homegrown terror.* New York: History Publishing Company, 2007. Kindle locations 3128–3168.

Seierstad, Åsne. *En av oss, en fortelling om Norge.* Oslo: Kagge Forlag, 2013.

Skoglund, Audhild. *Sinte hvite menn.* Oslo: Humanist Forlag, 2013.

Spaaij, Ramon. *Understanding Lone Wolf Terrorism.* Dordrecht, London and New York: Springer, 2012.

Spencer, Robert. "Huge blast hits Oslo government buildings, at least one person dead." *jihadwatch.org.* 22 July 2011. Online: http://www.jihadwatch.org/2011/07/huge-blast-hits-oslo-government-buildings-at-least-one-person-dead.html.

Stormark, Kjetil. *Massemorderens private e-poster.* Oslo, Spartacus Forlag, 2012.
Stormark, Kjetil. *Da terroren rammet Norge. 189 minutter som rystet verden.* Oslo: Kagge Forlag, 2011.
Strømmen, Øyvind. *Det mørke nettet.* Oslo: Cappelen Damm, 2011.
Strømmen, Øyvind. *I hatets fotspor.* Oslo: Cappelen Damm, 2014.

Chapter Three

Mobilizing on the Fringe

Domestic Extremists and Antisocial Networking

Kyle Christensen, Arian Spahiu, Bret Wilson,
and Robert D. Duval

On 13 April 2014, seventy-three-year-old former Ku Klux Klan (KKK) Grand Dragon Frazier Glenn Miller walked into the Jewish Community Center of Greater Kansas City in Overland Park, Kansas, and shot and killed three people, including fourteen-year-old Eagle Scout Reid Underwood.[1] Miller, who also goes by the names Frazier Glenn Cross, F. Glenn Miller, and the online name *Rounder*, has been an active KKK member and white supremacist for decades. Founder of both the Carolina Knights of the Ku Klux Klan and the White Patriot Party, Miller has been a visible presence in the extremist culture for many years. In 1987 Miller pleaded guilty to, and served three years in prison for, among other things, conspiring to assassinate Southern Poverty Law Center founder Morris Dees. Active in many ways in the KKK/white supremacist movement throughout this period, Miller became the archetypal Internet extremist. Using the screen name *Rounder*, Miller posted over 12,000 comments on multiple websites, most particularly in the Vanguard News Network (SPLC 2014). No longer needing robes and sheets, racist organizations, hate groups, neo-Nazi's, and others have found that the Internet offers them such cover and communications assets: a new age of political extremism has arrived.

History will pass down its verdict on Frazier Glenn Miller, and he will likely be seen as a political extremist of some note. Miller represents the most violent fringes of extremist culture, providing us with the culmination of his immersion in violence and hatred. Yet what is important to retain from Miller's violent spree is not that he is the exception, as much as he is the end-product of a cultural meme of hatred. Miller's aiming of his anti-Semitic hatred at innocent individuals at the Jewish Community Center likely signifies the violent end of his public career as an extremist. After decades of targeting Jews in speech, his shift to violent action produces a shooting spree that kills three Christians, and no Jews, providing a violently ironic counterpoint to his disjointed and misanthropic logic.

Miller's actions, and the reactions to it, provide a violent resonance with Scott Roeder's murder of George Tiller at the Reformation Lutheran Church in Wichita, Kansas, on 31 May 2009.[2] Dr. Tiller's murder was a focused attack upon a specific target, a doctor who provided midterm abortions at a clinic. While most reactions to the Tiller shooting generally condemned the murder, a noticeable lack of concern for the crime came from a few anti-abortion advocates, some even approving of Dr. Tiller's death, if not the manner in which he died.[3] Roeder, a former "sovereign citizen" member of the Montana Freemen, was following in the footsteps of one Shelley Shannon, who sixteen years earlier had shot Dr. Tiller five times. Shannon's prior attempt was praised by the *Army of God* website, an anti–abortion extremist group that also publishes the writings of Eric Robert Rudolph, the Alabama abortion clinic bomber who eluded law-enforcement in the North Carolina mountains for more than five years. The *Army of God* praised Shannon's attempt on Tiller's life, essentially classifying her actions as heroic.[4]

Scott Roeder and Frazier Glenn Miller committed the extreme act of murder and used it similarly to implement their personal viewpoints. But theirs represent focused or targeted acts of violence by a lone individual who is backed by a group that expresses approval of violence as an acceptable means of political action. They have support in the extremist communities, but their actions are largely idiosyncratic; or they result from severe personality pathologies. Society cannot readily protect itself against the lone gunman, but fortunately these events have been relatively rare. Still, networked extremism remains a disturbing development in the study of social movements. Frazier Glenn Miller's extensive involvement with extremist organizations coupled with increasing social media usage underscores a growing concern about the potential impact of networked antisocial movements. The birth of online politics has given rise to many new mechanisms and avenues for political activity and political engagement. In a relatively short period of time the Internet has evolved from an esoteric new technology to the predominant form of media for almost every group and organization engaged in politics today.

This chapter examines a particular class of political organizations: domestic political extremist groups, and we focus here on those we would characterize as right-wing extremism. More specifically, this study examines a sample of extremist group web sites in order to analyze the interrelationships between the type of extremism espoused, the techniques used for group mobilization, and violent or antisocial behavior. To corroborate this argument, we survey right-wing extremists' online landscape, selecting a range of extremist organizations, collecting data from a broad segment of their online activities, and attempting to describe relationships among the diverse groups out there. Right-wing extremists, as we demonstrate, encourage and engage in what for us constitutes essentially violent political behavior directed at individuals and racial and ethnic groups.

BACKGROUND: DOMESTIC EXTREMISM AND THE WEB

Conventional participation on the Internet has garnered a great deal of political interest and support in political science. Research by several scholars has shown increased use of the Internet for both information gathering[5] and mobilization.[6] Many of the same attributes associated with computer skill, one of the strongest predictors of online participation, such as education and wealth are also highly correlated with traditional forms of political participation.[7] However, a striking indicator is that younger individuals tend to prefer this medium, which may work to challenge the way in which scholars view it. The Internet greatly reduces individual costs associated with participation and provides easily accessible networks for issues of interest, thus allowing individuals to participate in new and dynamic ways.

The selection of the Internet as a medium for engagement by activist organizations is rooted in several key environmental factors. First, the individual is able to maintain some degree of anonymity that might not otherwise be present in day-to-day interactions. Research on Internet based activity has shown that individuals engage in information seeking activities that they otherwise would not have engaged in when they believe they are anonymous.[8] Information seeking activities may range from gathering information otherwise deemed embarrassing to engaging in forms of socially deviant behavior. This should not be surprising, as a long history exists in which situational factors that mask individual identity have previously shown the dehumanizing impact of anonymity.[9] Additionally, the ability to effectively stop or hinder these activities is greatly limited by widely available tools that encrypt data or obscure the web address of individuals engaged in deviant or antisocial online behavior.

Second, the Internet provides a valuable tool for rallying existing membership and engaging individuals. Researchers[10] note that individuals who seek out membership in Internet groups tend to have constrained or stigmatized identities. The anonymity provided by the medium provides the perfect environment for building social capital[11] and experiencing fuller membership in a broader community.[12] The elimination of spatial distance afforded by the Internet results in a concomitant reduction in social distance as individuals coalesce into groups or online communities. The use of the Internet as a recruitment tool for these movements allows activist organizations to prosper on a level they previously would never have thought possible. The Internet has allowed extremists to move far afield from the days of public confrontation and protest as the primary means for getting one's message out, obviating the need for extreme public confrontation such as the National Socialist Party of America's attempt to march in Skokie, Illinois, in 1977.

Third, the use of the Internet provides for a diffuse organizational structure. Cunningham notes the impact of FBI infiltrations of domestic groups during the 1960s and 1970s.[13] This government activity caused many groups to seek an organizational medium resilient to such destabilization. The Internet and "lone wolf" or diffuse activity of members as individuals or cells provides this protection and makes it extremely difficult for law enforcement to protect society from activist organizations that engage in criminal behavior.

The ability to participate in an online environment allows activist organizations to build organizational strength and resources necessary to perpetuate their positions. Research into the activities of activist organizations on the Internet has largely been conducted by computer scientists and sociologists who approach the topic with different techniques. Work by computer scientists has yielded a variety of interesting results including the ability to find unique clusters based on web linkage data and levels of technical sophistication by groups that rival or exceed traditional government websites.[14] These examples provide excellent taxonomic coverage and a rich technical discussion of the subjects under study, but are fundamentally constrained by limited or poorly conducted analysis of both the web content and the site's orientation toward political behavior. In essence, work in computer science provides an excellent tool for surveying a broad array of sites quickly with effective analysis of key structural aspects of web data, but sole reliance on these techniques leaves crucial substantive questions unanswered.

The political behavior and sociological literatures are replete with studies that focus on particular areas of political activism. Studies exploring the dynamics of domestic extremist groups in this literature have focused primarily upon content analysis[15] and on descriptive studies of web use.[16] These studies tend to rely on qualitative coding for content analysis coupled with descriptive statistics concerning various site features. However, the quality of this work makes it very useful. For example, Adams and Roscigno note differences between the Ku Klux Klan and neo-Nazi groups using textual analysis to identify key themes in the groups' respective political orientations.[17] The methods employed in these studies are time consuming and exceedingly difficult to implement as the sample size of a study increases. However, the depth of the information about the groups cannot be matched by current automated taxonomic methods.

From the previous overview it is evident that there are serious deficiencies in both computer aided and human coded perspectives. An effective marriage of these methods of analysis is necessary to provide a comprehensive study of activist organizations and their linkages. We therefore seek to advance the study of political extremism through the following steps:

- An examination of the structural attributes of the websites in question.
- A network analysis of the interrelationships between extremist groups.
- A re-examination of the behavioral characteristics of the sites in light of our understanding of both the site attributes and relational structure.

This analysis is guided by the desire to understand the evolution of online participation in its unhealthier manifestations—by which we mean right-wing extremism and violence. One need go no farther than to look at the *Army of God* website and the already noted promotion of Shelly Shannon and abortion clinic bomber Eric Robert Rudolph. Shannon's nearly successful earlier attempt on Dr. George Tiller's life finds palpable approval in the pages. A copy of the *Army of God* manual was found buried in her yard, further demonstrating that there is some level of connection between the political views of extremist groups and the behavior of individuals of similar political orientation. Similarly, James von Brunn, the individual who shot the guard at the Holocaust Museum in Washington DC in June 2009, and his *Holy Western Empire* web site appear in our linkage data, collected just prior to the shooting.

POLITICAL NETWORKS AND POLITICAL EXTREMISM

The development of methods and tools for network analysis has brought about a paradigm shift in the way we examine data concerning extremist groups, terrorist organizations, and violent non-state actors in general. Relational data such as individual contacts, group membership, financial transactions, telephone calls, and website links all provide information about social structure for the study of political extremism, violence, transnational crime, and terrorism. And indeed, the examination of the social structure of terrorist networks has emerged as a prominent field of study in recent years.[18]

The primary application of social network analysis (SNA) to the study of violent actors or groups is to identify their social structure, ascertaining which actors are central, and who belongs to what "cliques" or subgroups.[19] These data are then used to generate a variety of actor and graph specific statistics. Similarly, these data may also be used to identify and examine subgroup characteristics as well. An analyst may choose to represent multiple aspects of social structure quickly and effectively using tools such as multidimensional scaling or clustering techniques to classify groups of actors, potentially identifying cells and less compliant groups within larger networks or movements. This affords the analyst a powerful means for visualization and discovery of new information. Such information is at the heart of both military and law enforcement tactical intelligence and Reed makes a strong case that the incorporation of network analysis into the Intelligence Preparation of the Battlefield is a crucial step for modern warfare.[20] The assessment of strengths, weaknesses, and tactics requires an understanding of the interrelationships between the units and assets of the opposition, and thus become a relevant approach when we turn to addressing potential domestic threats.

While we are concerned with violent extremists in a cross-national setting, it is useful to note that there are many types,[21] and that network analysis has been used to reveal significant findings about a number of them: terrorist organizations,[22] militias,[23] warlords and cartels,[24] insurgencies,[25] gangs,[26] and organized crime.[27]

In examining domestic extremists, we encounter an even richer diversity, due to the broad ideological components that political extremism affords. In our work we have started with a basic classification of domestic groups into the following categories: Klan or KKK groups, Neo-Nazis, White Nationalists, White Nationalists—Anti-Immigration Extremists, Militia Movements, Christian Identity, Radical Traditionalist Catholics, Skinheads, Neo-Confederates, Anti-Semitic groups, Anti-Semitic—Holocaust Denial, Minority groups—Black Nationalist, Black Separatists, Jewish Extremists, Latino Separatists, Muslim Extremists, and single issue groups such as: Environmental, Tax Resister, Anti-Abortion, and Animal Rights extremists. This list is not exhaustive. These groups share beliefs, opinions or goals that are generally perceived as extreme because they are held by relatively few individuals across the political spectrum, and our concern in examining them is to understand what leads from extreme opinion to extreme action, or violence. And these types of actors relate to each other through contacts, meetings, activities, training, financial transactions, authority relationships, and many other structural relationships. All represent social systems that have close kinship, tribal or regional proximity affiliations that foster the growth of network structures. In addition, their violent nature means that they are usually clandestine, and thus must trade organizational effectiveness for operational security.[28] This results in the reliance on pre-existing social networks, and constrains both operational detection on the part of state actors, and recruitment on the part of the extremist group.

Central to our current analysis of right-wing extremism is the ability to ascertain organizational structure and identify avenues of recruitment. As we increase our ethnographic base for analyses such as these, our understanding of the components of recruitment and organizational structure will grow as well.[29] Understanding recruitment into violent international organizations is likely to have significant bearing on recruitment of domestic extremists as well. The expansion of the use of the Internet has become the major path for messaging and mobilization, with any and all groups finding a means to get out their message. The power to persuade is no longer hampered by significant publication costs.

One of the more visible groups studying network analysis and a range of violent actors is the Dark Web Portal at the University of Arizona.[30] This large-scale open source project has produced a considerable body of work about the use of the Internet by extremist groups and terrorist organizations, both international and domestic. The Dark Web project points to the utility of network analysis in ascertaining community structures or groupings. Analysis of linkages between sites has produced network clustering that matches substantive expertise with substantial understanding of the topic. When the organizational structure of movements can be modeled on data that can be updated readily and frequently, we can move beyond our previous sole reliance on post hoc analysis and move to real time monitoring. The Dark Web project has done extensive examination of extremists on the Web, with network analyses focusing on network extraction, group identification and clustering, subgroup detection and the discovery of network interaction patterns.[31]

Network analysis of violent actors has been conducted over many diverse types of networks. Reed's analysis of trust networks involved immediate and extended family ties as well as friendships and bodyguards to establish the network of individuals around Saddam Hussein. This network was merged with strategy and goals mapping which utilized information from financial transactions and insurgency operations.[32] Ultimately these mappings led to the inference that members of the Iraqi insurgency built upon their trust ties, as described by their network connectivity, leading ultimately to U.S. operations that resulted in Hussein's capture.

Networks are also of interest because of their novel methods for engaging calls for action. Recent attention has been focused on swarming behavior, where networks of resisters or protesters are mobilized on very short time scales via mobile phones and other electronic communications devices. The "Battle in Seattle" protest at the WTO in 1999 was a precursor to swarming as a tactic in social protests.[33] Such swarming behaviors and the rise of the microblogs such as Twitter make this an important area of SNA that needs to expand and be monitored for extremist and terrorist utilization. 2011 saw an inordinate expansion of flash mobs and swarming from the "Arab Spring" to the London riots. The use of social media has erupted as a factor in mobilizing individuals for political or anarchist behavior. Indeed, the flash mob has apparently emerged as a tactic for crime in the summer of 2011 in Germantown, Maryland, with the robbery of a 7-11 convenience store by an estimated thirty people within approximately one minute.

Increasingly, network analysis suggests that network reach is a key factor.[34] Researchers have also begun identifying international relationships between extreme right groups using network analysis of social media platforms such as Twitter.[35] Social media platforms have made it easier for extreme right groups to establish international relationships with like-minded groups in other parts of the world. In addition, social media platforms are often utilized to re-direct users to external websites, which has made socializing across geopolitical boundaries easier.

RECENT DEVELOPMENTS IN NETWORK ANALYSIS

SNA provides a useful medium for exploring the behavior of actors in a variety of environments. Current research concerning the study of violent non-state actors and their use of the Internet has been focused on two key areas of study. The first major area of literature is rooted in sociology and has been particularly focused on content analysis and ethnographic research.[36] These studies typically provide excellent analyses of segments of the domestic extremist groups, but are limited by the inability to link these groups effectively. There has also been considerable work in the computer science literature devoted to the taxonomic study of Internet extremist groups based on content analysis.

There are several applications of social network analysis that study violent non-state actors engaging in activities on the Internet. First, social network analysis has been used effectively to assist in assigning roles for individuals engaged in online discussion forums.[37] Similarly, social network analysis was used to detect and monitor activities of individuals who commented on jihadist videos placed on YouTube.[38] These two studies provide clear examples of network analysis being used to classify and link behavior of individuals within a defined space on the Internet showing how individuals or groups spread extremist messages and which individuals may be receptive to potential inducements.

Another excellent example of social network analysis being used to study extremist behavior on the Internet was conducted by Zhou, Chen, and colleagues at the University of Arizona.[39] This group focused their work on a semi-automated collection of websites in which collection software, referred to as a spider, traced linkage data. These sites were then coded and classified using the clustering techniques of SNA. This study shows the unique applications of both automated and human interactions to analyze data in order to produce complex but easily understandable sets of visualizations and clusters.

It is increasingly important to study extremist groups' use of the Internet because they employ it as a medium for communication, recruitment, and resource mobilization. Social network analysis serves as a key tool that can enable researchers to quickly visualize networked structures and identify clusters based on characteristics or ties among suspect persons or groups. Social network analysis has the ability to define and classify group boundaries and further analyze individual activity using Web 2.0 features such as social networking or media sites. This aspect of the methodology may provide critical support in combating online propaganda and recruitment activities.

Networks, as diffuse structures, grow unpredictably, and heal after damage.[40] Alternate communication routes are established through existing sets of actors, and new actors are recruited to provide additional pathways, not merely as replacements for nodes that have been removed. Networks are resilient due to the differentiation that emerges from confrontation and the need to adapt to operational conditions.[41] The robustness of network structures lies in the interconnectedness of the nodes. Rigidly hierarchical structures are vulnerable; diffuse networks are robust. Hierarchical structures have specialized paths that represent the only communications channels between the nodes, providing a formalized chain of command. In networks, additional connections provide redundancy through alternate paths, control is diffuse, and information channels are robust. The result is that violent extremist groups have evolved networks rather than organized military organizations because their flexible command structures make them hardier than conventional force structures. These networks are organizationally resilient and adapt both organizational structure and operational tactics based upon their environment.[42] Similarly, the analysis of the content of extremist websites shows that persistence of content was more likely for group identity, whereas group goals were more likely to change overtime.[43]

As a result, SNA identifies who is important, and where network vulnerabilities lie. Selected properties of networks become of great interest when we assemble the structures from the available relational data. We are interested in properties such as centrality, with particular interest in "closeness" and "betweenness." Nodes with greater closeness are connected to more individuals. They are rapid disseminators of information and other communications. Nodes with greater "betweenness" are the linkages between subgroups that otherwise may have little contact with each other. They are essential to communicate with different areas of the network and act as boundary spanners bringing ideas and innovation to both subgroups to whom they connect. Often these two assessments result in different tactics and different targeting strategies in a counterterrorism context. In fact, research on disrupting terrorist networks suggests that while removal of emerging leaders is a desirable second-best strategy, random node removal is the best strategy for network destabilization.[44, 45]

Law enforcement efforts are clearly aided by the ability to look for vulnerabilities in the organizational structure of violent groups and their members. And in a complementary fashion, network analysis is providing valuable support for counterterrorism by identifying vulnerabilities in critical infrastructure. Network analysis of target vulnerability of gas pipelines, electricity grids, and water supplies, for example, provides useful complementary information that while not describing the behavior of violent non-state actors, may well provide insight into their targets, given an understanding of motivations and past behaviors.[46]

SAMPLING

The selection of an appropriate sample of websites from the Internet is particularly difficult because such sites can appear and disappear during the time of study. In order to find an appropriate sample of extremist organizations a convenience sampling method was used based on the Southern Poverty Law Center's Hate Watch[47] and a few existing studies.[48] This method produced an initial sample of about 150 traditional domestic extremist websites. Additional work was done to expand the sample to include more sites using similar convenience methods and "respondent driven" or "snowball" sampling. Collectively, the initial sample consists of 493 target domestic activist organizations across the political spectrum we identified as having websites.

The decision to move away from traditional group studies was made for several reasons. First, scholars who study domestic extremism note that the membership may shift between groups, thus implying a more fluid social construction than existing heuristics provide. Second, the power of the social network is in the relational nature of the data. Arbitrarily excluding cases greatly diminishes the explanatory power provided by a network perspective. Finally, it is crucial to explore comparisons between groups of different types to determine what strategies are being used online for resource mobilization and recruitment.

DATA COLLECTION

In order to develop an analytically informative social network of active extremist groups, a set of website linkage data had to be collected along with some site attribute data. From the initial 493 sites we found that only 319 of them were active at the time of data collection at the site URLs we had identified. We collected attribute data on all sites that remain online at the time of the survey. The information we collected on each site consisted of:

- the name and website of the organization.

- what was the type of organization (white supremacists, KKK, neo-Nazi, etc.).
- what was the nature of authorship for the site (single versus multiple authors).
- what was the audience they wished to appeal to.
- what was their target of political intent.
- whether they sought to engage the political system, however they saw it.
- what type of online resources did they use to mobilize people.
- what means of online communications did they employ.
- what was their "knowledge capital" (did they attempt to construct logical or supported arguments for their positions).
- whether there were clear gender roles within the organization.
- whether they attempted to engage youth in the organization.
- whether they advocate or tolerate the use of violence.

We believe this set of variables will give us substantial insight into right-wing extremist groups' approach to political mobilization and political action.

Next, a retrieval of web data using *WGet* was conducted. *WGet* is a GNU open source collaborative software project that can be used as a web spider for recursive web retrieval.[49] Recursive retrieval options allow the researcher to download the contents of a website and all the sites which link from that site, which can be an extremely fast method for collecting social networks, provided the researcher has the technical means to extract the necessary linkage data from raw files. This retrieval consisted of a depth of 2 linkages in which all sites one link from the host URL were also crawled. All file types except large media files were also retrieved for subsequent analysis. *WGet* is also useful if the researcher intends to view websites offline.

Table 3.1.   Acceptance of the Use of Violence on the part of Extremist Groups

Acceptance of Violence	Frequency (n=319)
Totally Pacifist	23 (7.2%)
Preference for Peace	11 (3.5%)
Indifference toward Violence	76 (23.8%)
Preference for Action	131 (41.1%)
Full Support of Violent Action	47 (14.7%)
Cannot Determine	31 (9.7%)

As noted, we are interested in ascertaining the degree of violence of these extremist groups based upon their acceptance of, or statements about, violence contained in their websites. When you cast the net as broadly as we have by putting all types of political extremists in the same basket, we should expect that there are differences among their approach to political activity. Table 3.1 provides the distribution of the acceptance of violence, which has a slight skew toward action, which should not be a surprise for a set of groups we label as extremist. About 15 percent have a full acceptance of violence as a useful mechanism to support their ends, and another 41 percent strongly support political action. Peaceful protest would fall into this latter category. Only slightly over 10 percent seem to explicitly prefer non-violence and lawful activity.

Table 3.2 gives us a breakdown of the types of extremist organizations in our sample along with their average score on the five-point acceptance of violence scale. The results are interesting. The reader should note that because of the convenience sample nature of this set we cannot make assumptions about the relative number of organizations. In other words, animal rights groups are not necessarily the second most prevalent type of extremist group out there. The larger numbers in each group give us more confidence about our assessment of that group's characteristics but the relative proportion of the types of groups is less certain.[50]

Table 3.2.   A Breakdown of Domestic Extremist Groups in Sample

Type of group	Number in sample	Average Violence Score
Animal rights	61	3.41
Anti-immigration extremists	9	4.00
Anti-Semitic	9	3.55
Anti-Semitic- Holocaust Denial	9	3.22
Christian identity	25	3.04
Environmental	43	3.40
Jewish extremists	4	4.00
KKK	10	4.20
Militias	5	4.40
Muslim Extremists	6	3.67
Neo-Nazi	11	4.36
Radical traditionalists Catholic	5	3.40
Skinheads	7	4.29
White Nationalists	75	3.65
Other	9	3.79
Total	319	3.52

In our sample the right-wing extremists, the Militias, neo-Nazis, and Skinheads voice the most acceptance of violence. Note that in our coding, approval of the violence of others is sufficient for a score of five on the five-point scale. It does not necessarily mean the organization is advocating that its members engage in violence. At the opposite end of the scale the Christian identity and anti-Semitic sites that focus on denial of the Holocaust received the lowest scores.

Since concern for the violence of these groups motivates our research, we will return to a closer examination shortly. At this point we can simply say that there is substantial variation in the acceptance of violence on the part of these different types of groups. And of note, no category has a majority of groups that advocate non-violence.

Table 3.3. Extremist Groups: A Breakdown of Authorship by Type of Extremism

Type of group	Number in sample	Single Author or likely Single Author	Small Group	Multi- Authored	Unable to Ascertain
Animal rights	64	25	4	5	30
Anti-immigration extremists	9	8	0	0	1
Anti-Semitic	9	9	0	0	0
Anti-Semitic-Holocaust Denial	10	9	0	0	1
Christian identity	26	23	0	1	2
Environmental	43	30	4	2	7
Jewish extremists	4	3	0	0	1
KKK	12	10	0	0	2
Militias	5	3	0	0	2
Muslim Extremists	6	4	0	1	1
Neo-Nazi	14	10	3	1	0
Radical traditionalists Catholic	5	5	0	0	0
Skinheads	7	5	0	1	1
White Nationalists	96	75	5	7	1
Other	8	6	0	1	1
Total	318	225	16	19	49

As we further examine the characteristics of these extremist groups some interesting points begin to emerge. The breakdown of authorship provided in Table 3.3 gives us one such interesting insight. We are generally led to believe, based upon the language that is used to describe extremists groups and their websites that these sites tend to represent groups of individuals. And the naming of these "organizations" fosters this impression. For instance, the knowledge that there are Ku Klux Klan groups out there suggests to us that each KKK website implies a group. Based upon examination of our sample, almost 90 percent of the sites appear to be the work of a single author. We, too, are guilty of the assumption that each website represents a group of individuals. It appears this is not necessarily the case. Only nineteen of the 319 sites appear to actually be large groups, and only 16 were clearly small groups.[51] It may well be that our heightened apprehension about groups on the web is in fact based largely upon a moderate number of individuals who use the Internet for personal soapboxes.

The target audience variable breakdown in Table 3.4 provides no unusual findings. Typically websites appear to seek a target audience of anyone who will listen. Fully 70 percent seem to be addressing the general public, while about 30 percent seem to assume selective audience characteristics.

The target of intent variable does indicate an orientation toward targeting specific groups, with 69 percent focusing their animosity, rage, frustration, or hatred toward a specific group. In addition, the government is a noticeable additional target (24 percent). And 6 percent of the groups appear not to like anyone.

We expected to see some variation in gender roles across the websites. For the most part, this was not the case. Only nine sites total (3 percent) even addressed the issue of gender roles. And four of them were largely egalitarian in their orientation. This was counter to our expectations.

Knowledge capital drew our interest with 53 percent of these groups or pages attempting to provide some level of support, with 23 percent of them even attempting some form of scholarly argument. Yet about half of them were simply exercising free speech without the discomfort of logical thought.

As with our expectations about gender roles, we anticipated some differential targeting of youth in the websites' marketing. In fact, we found that very few groups specifically targeted youth. Over 95 percent simply did not have any orientation toward youth, suggesting that recruitment is not approached as a form of educational indoctrination.

Perhaps the most interesting variable among attributes is the political engagement score. About a third are indifferent toward the political system, another 33 percent actively distrust the government, and approximately 15 percent strongly believe in engaging the political system. Most interestingly there appear to be very few moderates. Political engagement has a rather rare characteristic for a political variable—a tri-modal distribution.

Table 3.4.   Domestic Extremist Website Characteristics

Variable	Category	Frequency (Percent)

Authorship	Likely single individual.	134 (42.0%)
	Obvious single individual.	92 (28.8%)
	Small group.	16 (5.0%)
	Large open contributions or multi authored site	19 (6.0%)
	Unable to Ascertain	58 (18.2%)
Target audience	General Public	93 (29.2%)
	Specific Societal Group	226 (70.9%)
Target of Intent	General Public	18 (5.7%)
	Government	63 (19.8%)
	Government – Federal	13 (4.1%)
	Specific Group	222 (69.8%)
	(Corps)/Gov/ People	1 (0.3%)
	Multiple	1 (0.3%)
Knowledge capital	Scholarly Knowledge	72 (22.6%)
	Supported Positions	97 (30.4%)
	Unsupported Positions	107 (33.5%)
	Unable to Ascertain	43 (13.5%)
Gender roles	Highly Differentiated Roles	2 (0.6%)
	Differentiated Gender Norms	3 (1.0%)
	No Position on Gender Norms	308 (97.2%)
	Egalitarian Gender Norms	3 (1.0%)
	Highly Egalitarian Roles	1 (0.3%)
Engagement of youth	Focuses on Youth Engagement	2 (0.6%)
	Youth Engaged Frequently	5 (1.6%)
	Youth Targeted Selectively	3 (0.9%)
	Youths Not Targeted	1 (0.3%)
	No Attitude	304 (95.3%)
	Unable to Ascertain	4 (1.3%)
Political engagement	Strongly believes in Engaging the System	46 (14.4%)
	Moderately Believes in Engaging System	1 (0.3%)
	Indifference Toward System	106 (33.3%)
	Moderately Distrusts Government	19 (6.0%)
	Strongly Distrusts the Government	106 (33.3%)
	Cannot Determine	41 (12.9%)

Two additional variables provide a little richer view of these groups: the resource mobilization mechanisms and the communication mechanisms. These were counts of the number of communications mechanisms employed (email, postal address, phone, FAX, RSS, forums and chat, social networking media, etc.) and the means by which they try to mobilize individuals to the cause (meeting space, money, time, etc.). Clearly the websites demonstrate that people can mobilize time and money, with meeting space being available for perhaps 20 percent of the groups. More sophisticated mobilization mechanisms such as political allies, media relations, and good law enforcement contacts are scarce for these groups as they clearly operate on the fringe of society. The empirical data does confirm what we anticipate about domestic extremist groups.

The communication mechanisms provide a little more information in that most groups tend to rely upon standard e-mail, regular post, and telephone for contacts. About 10 percent of the sites have chat rooms or forums. Interestingly, in the summer of 2009 very few of these groups had turned to Web 2.0 technologies to reach a larger audience. We observed no apparent Facebook, Twitter, or other social media. This has likely changed substantially in the last few years. Publicly visible Internet use in 2009 was limited to instant messaging and about 10 percent, mostly larger groups, were using RSS to get out their information via newsfeed.

For both the resource mobilization and communication variables we created a composite score by simply summing the number of each type of resource mobilization or communication mechanism that they used. More active groups would likely utilize more resources and engage in more communication mechanisms.

THE USE OF VIOLENCE

This research leads us to ask whether we can explain any of the observed variation in extremist groups' acceptance of violence based upon these characteristics. While we do anticipate that different groups have differential preferences for violence, as Table 4.2 affirmed, we are also interested in whether group characteristics, apart from their ideological or political orientation, contribute to an overall predisposition toward violence. We have several hypotheses that we will test.

- H1: the more an extremist group engages the political system the less likely it is to advocate violence.
- H2: the greater the knowledge capital of an extremist group less likely it is to advocate violence.

- H3: the more resource mobilization mechanisms available to the extremist group the less likely it is to advocate violence.
- H4: the more communication mechanisms employed by the group the less likely it is to advocate violence.
- H5: the greater the gender role differentiation the greater the prevalence for violence.
- H6: the greater the orientation toward youth the greater the prevalence for violence.
- H7: different types of extremist groups will also vary in their preference for violence.

In order to test these hypotheses we estimate a statistical ordered logit model which predicts a website's acceptance of violence score based upon the attribute variables as hypothesized. The communications and resource mobilization variables are counts of the mechanisms employed, the knowledge capital, political engagement, youth orientation, and gender role variables are all ordinal scales, as is the dependent variable acceptance of violence. Dichotomous group identity variables are used to examine differences across the types of groups. The ordered logit model is provided in Table 3.5.

The use of violence attribute model is enlightening. The more a group expresses the desirability of engaging the political system, the less it uses language that seems accepting of violent means to whatever ends the group advocates. The strong z score demonstrates that violence and beliefs in political efficacy appear strongly related. The other variable of note is knowledge capital. Groups who articulated verbal arguments for their position, whether logical, well-grounded or not, seemed less likely to opt for violence. And the dummy variables for group type showed that once we control for the other website attributes, only the neo-Nazis seemed significantly more prone to violence, while only the Christian identity groups seemed significantly less likely to accept or advocate violence. Clearly the group's perceptions about its ability to engage the political system and its means to do so influence its predilection for violence. The more isolated a group perceives itself to be, the more alienated it becomes, with some groups becoming sufficiently politically estranged to advocate violence.

This interest and concern with isolation that is indicated strongly by the political engagement variable suggests to us that the relationships among the groups will be an important aspect to consider. In order to do so we will turn to limited social network analysis of the link structures among these domestic extremists.

Table 3.5. Ordered Logit on Use of Violence

Variables	Full Model (n=196) Coef. (z score)	Trimmed Model (n=196) Coef. (z score)	Network Model (n=104) Coef. (z score)
Gender Roles	0.3000 (0.89)	-0.3029 (0.91)	-
Knowledge Capital	-0.3997* (-3.7)	-0.4003* (3.75)	-.2724* (-1.85)
Political Engagement	-0.6384* (8.18)	-0.6314* (8.18)	-.5828* (-4.90)
Communications	0.1191 (1.47)	0.1277 (1.63)	.0698 (0.62)
Resource Mobilization	-0.0537 (0.54)	-0.0553 (0.56)	-.1056 (-.76)
Authorship	0.2459 (1.57)	0.2327 (1.5)	-.0891 (0.40)
Gov as Target	-0.1296 (0.56)	-0.1359 (0.59)	-.2106 (-0.60)
Fed Gov as Target	0.3656 (0.93)	0.3824 (0.98)	-.7654 (-1.20)
Youth	0.5044 (1.37)	0.5051 (1.41)	.8080 (1.64)
Animals	0.2831 (0.92)	0.2422 (0.8)	-
Neo-Nazis	1.0657* (2.64)	1.0458* (2.62)	1.0591 (1.79)
Skinheads	0.5596 (1.03)	0.5331 (0.99)	.0062 (0.01
Christian Identity	-0.557* (1.96)	-0.5969* (2.15)	-.6729 (-1.95)
Environmentalists	0.2904 (1.15)	0.2559 (1.04)	-.1963 (-.021)
Jews	1.1406 (1.7)	1.1080 (1.66)	-
Muslims	-0.0060 (0.01)	-	-
Militias	0.3558 (0.53)	-	1.2361 (1.38)
Catholics	0.4050 (0.7)	-	.6344 (0.74)

Anti-Semitic	0.0977	-	-
	(0.23)		
Closeness Centrality	-	-	-.0741
			(-1.02)
Number of obs	196	196	104
LR M^2(19)	119.48	118.7	49.08
Pseudo R^2	0.2276	0.2261	.1877

SOCIAL NETWORK ANALYSIS

The collection of link data from domestic extremist groups provides a unique chance to examine their structure in a relational or social setting. This allows the researcher to explore the linkages between types of groups within a network while recognizing the broader connections between defined groups.

Of the 319 websites active at the time of the sample, 84 had to be excluded from the network analysis, as they are isolates; they have no linkages to other extremist websites. This is an interesting observation in and of itself. Fully 25 percent have virtually no interaction with any of the other organizations in the sample. This leaves us with a network comprised of 235 nodes. Even with this reduced number of sites, network visualization is problematic, for even moderately sized social networks produce a "fur ball" or massive graph that is impossible to visually interpret, thus requiring the use of egocentric networks to explore cases of interest. However, valuable information can be observed from network characteristics, most notably a number of centrality measures. Measures of centrality are valuable because they provide a quick and efficient measure of the importance of actors or nodes in the network by counting the number of linkages (degree centrality), their proximity to other actors (closeness centrality), the presence of a key actor based on location between actors (betweenness centrality), and the overall importance of an actor to a network (Eigenvector centrality). These characteristics provide a set of key measures for comparing key actors within a network.

For example, the domestic extremist organizations in the sample that figure most prominently in terms of degree centrality are highlighted in Table 3.6. This attribute is commonly selected for discussion purposes, and in this data it mirrors many of the other measures of centrality fairly well. White Nationalists and Christian Identity groups tend to be the most interactive or connected types of sites, given their prominence in this table.

Table 3.6. Top 10 Extremist Sites in Sample by Degree Centrality

Site (Name)	Type	Degree Centrality	Closeness	Betweenness	Eigenvector
Christianparty.net (The Christian Party)	Christian Identity	43.966	27.619	32.355	42.627
Kelticklankirk.com (Keltic Klan Kirk)	KKK/Christian Identity	31.034	25.439	21.816	23.366
thebirdman.org (The Birdman)	White Nationalists	31.034	25.635	10.101	37.653
davidduke.com (David Duke)	White Nationalists	28.448	25.806	10.605	37.462
anu.org (American Nationalist Union)	Single Issue-Anti Government	25.000	24.919	8.665	27.531
adelaideinstitute.org (Adelaide Institute)	Anti-Semitic / Holocaust Denial	24.569	25.135	5.841	33.651
nspcanada.nfshost.com (The National-Socialist Party of Canada)	Neo-Nazi	17.672	23.364	3.855	22.158
conspiracypenpal.com (Conspiracy Pen Pal)	White Nationalists	16.379	25.217	2.616	28.355
fpp.co.uk (Focal Point)	Neo-Nazi	15.517	24.707	3.031	26.651
churchoftrueisrael.com (Church of the True Israel)	White Nationalists	14.224	24.498	3.143	17.215

Our quick examination of this sample of sites prompts us to make the point that many of these sites facilitate extensive communications forums and provide media support for their respective movements. Indeed, among the sites in the full sample, *Virginia Dare* and *Stormfront* are organized largely as web forums. Sites such as the *Institute for Historical Review* and the *Adelaide Institute* serve the function of trying to legitimize their movement via the development of intellectually styled materials on topics of ranging from race to the proper role of the government. Interestingly, the content on these sites ranges substantially across sites as well. *American Renaissance* and the *Bird Man* both represent more moderate forms of intolerance on their sites, as does the forum site *Virginia Dare*. Finally, topical issues such as immigration are reflected in the popularity of the *American Border Patrol* site. Extensive descriptive analysis of extremists' sites is both interesting and enlightening but our purpose here has been to look at these extremist sites as a means of mobilization, and a quick examination of how that mobilization and recruitment ties into their approach toward violence. As such we are more interested in looking at the degree to which a site is centrally placed and at factors that indicate its predisposition toward violence. Our essential hypothesis is: sites that receive peer recognition will tend to be less advocating or accepting of violence.[52]

Having produced these network centrality scores for all of these sites in the sample network, we included them as an independent variable within the ordered logit model of acceptance of violence described earlier. Because of the isolates, and missing values on some variables, our sample size is reduced to only 109, which indicates a bit of reduction in statistical power. The essential hypothesis we have is that network centrality will lead a site to be less prone to support violence. The earlier hypotheses on political engagement suggest that sites that receive recognition from others of like mind will feel less prone to engage in more antisocial behavior. The centrality score in the ordered logit model does indicate in the direction hypothesized, but the strength of the relationship is well below the threshold for statistical significance. And the concern for the reduction in statistical power does play out as most coefficients have weaker t-tests. There are no surprises in the model, and there is the expected attenuation of the strength of the inferential tests.

The conclusions that can be drawn from this set of sites are limited but useful. First, the data represent a broad political spectrum in terms of content and substance. Second, the data on these sites contain strong similarities in terms of technical structure and content formats. This knowledge certainly helps inform subsequent research into the content and substance of these networks. Third, the linkages between these sites show the fluid nature of group membership and the role of key information sites for legitimizing activities across groups.

This social network analysis, tantalizing as it is, rather than enlightening, moves us only part way toward our goal. We wish to enhance our understanding of these groups by exploring their content as well their structure and attributes. Social network analysis indeed suggests that it can provide a series of powerful analytic tools. But what this model does not incorporate adequately are the network effects. To the extent that these groups are essentially individuals operating in an isolated or estranged environment, they are more likely to be violent. We believe, and see hints here, that integration into a social network, even a social network of fellow extremists, reduces the propensity to act violently. This effect is probably greater on smaller groups or individuals than it is on large groups. And in general we expect the larger groups to be less violently oriented.

In order to test this hypothesis we would need to actually incorporate network effects into the attribute model. Only recently have tools been developed to do this, such as, exponential random graph models (ERGMs). ERGMs provide the means of examining network structure by allowing models of behavior to include network effects in ways that go somewhat beyond the simple inclusion of centrality scores in linear or logit models.

CONCLUSION

Clearly our discussion is preliminary. Expansion of this preliminary analysis is imperative for future research if we wish to be able to demonstrate that attributes can influence behavior by accounting or controlling for network structure. A number of developments will greatly enhance their use in both academia and the analytic community. Expansion of our data set, and inclusion of further data is strongly recommended by this pilot study. The ability to process high volumes of content to strengthen the assessment of several of the key variables is highly desirable (use of violence, political engagement, target of intent, etc.)

There is cause to believe that our characterization of domestic extremist activity warrants substantially closer examination. This is not to say that concern for these groups is over-rated. We do not believe that is the inference at all, but rather that the environment is not fully what it seems to be. And it is subject to change. The impact of perceptions of political engagement suggests to us that groups that have a specific policy focus, and are more engaged with the political process, will be less violent, or act and react with reduced levels of anti-social behavior.

It is perhaps improbable to think that such analysis, even enhanced with Social Network Analysis and text analysis, might have prevented George Tiller's murder in 2009, or the 2014 Overland Park, Kansas, shootings at the Jewish Community Center. But quite possibly, a well-informed law enforcement agency might have been able to see an upswing in the acceptance of violence or even its intent, and given the Wichita clinic a heads-up. If we learn to understand violent extremist behaviors and the network of groups who live on its fringe, it may assist us in doing something to deter it or intervene earlier in the path to violence that some of these groups and/or individuals seem to follow.

NOTES

1. This research has been supported by a WV EPSCoR grant from the West Virginia Higher Education Policy Commission.

2. George R. Tiller News, *The New York Times*, 2011, accessed 18 August 2011, http://topics.nytimes.com/topics/reference/timestopics/people/t/george_r_tiller/index.html?scp=1-spot&sq=George percent20Tiller percent20&st=cse.

3. Scott Roeder News, *The New York Times*, 2011, accessed 18 August 2011, http://topics.nytimes.com/top/reference/timestopics/people/r/scott_roeder/index.html?scp=1-spot&sq=Scott percent20Roeder&st=cse.

4. Joe Stumpe and Monica Davey, "Abortion Doctor Shot to Death in Kansas Church," *The New York Times,* 31 May 2009, accessed 18 August 2011, http://www.nytimes.com/2009/06/01/us/01tiller.html?adxnnl=1&ref=georgertiller&adxnnlx=1313691804-ZzAw7cOQjuCM-891F4YrB0g.

5. Jason MacDonald and Caroline Tolbert (2008), "Something Rich and Strange: Participation, Engagement and the Tempest of Online Politics," in *Civic Engagement in a Network Society*, edited by Kaifeng Yang and Erik Bergrud (New York: Information Age Publishing 2008).

6. Brian Krueger, "Assessing the Potential of Internet Political Participation in the United States: A Resource Approach," *American Politics Research* 30 (2002): 476–98; Samuel Best and Brian Krueger, "Analyzing the Representativeness of Internet Political Participation," *Political Behavior* 27 (2005): 183–215.

7. Brian Krueger, "A Comparison of Conventional and Internet Political Mobilization," *American Politics Research* 34 (2006): 759–76.

8. Adam Joinson and Phil Banyard, "Psychological Aspects of Information Seeking on the Internet," *Aslib Proceedings 54* (2002): 95–102; Yaman Akdeniz, "Anonymity, Democracy, and Cyberspace," *Social Research* 69 (2002): 223–37.

9. Craig Haney, Curtis Banks and Philip Zimbardo, "Interpersonal Dynamics in a Simulated Prison," *International Journal of Criminology and Penology* 1 (1973): 69–97.

10. John Bargh and Katelyn McKenna, "The Internet and Social Life," *Annual Review of Psychology* 55 (2004): 573–90; and Katelyn McKenna and John Bargh, "Causes and Consequences of Social Interaction on the Internet: A Conceptual Framework," *Media Psychology* 1 (1999): 249–69.

11. Robert Putnam, *Bowling Alone: The Collapse and Revival of American Community* (New York: Simon & Schuster, 1995).

12. Bruce Bimber, "Information and Political Engagement in America: The Search for Effects of Information Technology at the Individual Level," *Political Research Quarterly* 54 (2001): 53–67; Bargh and McKenna, "The Internet and Social Life"; and McKenna and Bargh, "Causes and Consequences," 261–65.

13. David Cunningham, "The Patterning of Repression: FBI Counterintelligence and the New Left," *Social Forces* 82 (2003): 209–40.

14. Yilu Zhou, et al., "U.S. Domestic Extremist Groups on the Web: Link and Content Analysis," *IEEE Intelligent Systems, Special Issue on Artificial Intelligence for National and Homeland Security* (September/October, 2005): 44–51.

15. Josh Adams and Vincent J. Roscigno, "White Supremacists, Oppositional Culture and the World Wide Web," *Social Forces* 84 (2005): 759–78; Phyllis B. Gerstenfeld, Diana R.

Grant and Chau-Pu Chiang, "Hate Online: A Content Analysis of Extremist Internet Sites," *Analysis of Social Issues and Public Policy* 3 (2003): 29–44.

16. Joseph Schafer, "Spinning the Web of Hate: Web-Based Hate Propagation By Extremist Organizations," *Journal of Criminal Justice and Popular Culture* 9 (2002): 69–88.

17. Adams and Roscigno, "White Supremacists."

18. Marc Sageman, *Understanding Terror Networks* (Philadelphia: University of Pennsylvania Press, 2004); Marc Sageman, *Leaderless Jihad: Terror Networks in the Twenty-First Century* (Philadelphia: University of Pennsylvania Press, 2008).

19. Brian Reed, *Formalizing the Informal: a Network Analysis of an Insurgency* (University of Maryland, College Park, 2006), accessed 18 August 2011, http://drum.lib.umd.edu/handle/1903/3759.

20. Brian Reed, "A Social Network Approach to Understanding an Insurgency," *Parameters* (Summer 2007): 19–30.

21. Phil Williams, "Violent Non-state Actors and National and International Security," *International Relations and Security Network*, 25 November 2008, accessed 18 August 2011, http://www.isn.ethz.ch/isn/Digital-Library/Publications.

22. Sageman, *Understanding*.

23. Zhou, et al., "U.S. Domestic Extremist Groups."

24. Milward and Raab, "Dark networks."

25. Reed, *Formalizing the Informal*.

26. Hsinchun Chen, et al., "Crime Data Mining: An Overview and Case Studies," *ACM International Conference Proceedings Series,* Volume 130 (2003), accessed 20 August 2014, http://ieeexplore.ieee.org/stamp/stamp.jsp?tp=&arnumber=1297301.

27. Luigi Ferrara, Christian Mårtenson, Pontus Svenson, Per Svensson, Justo Hidalgo, Anastasio Molano, and Anders L. Madsen, "Integrating Data Sources and Network Analysis Tools to Support the Fight Against Organized Crime," *Intelligence and Security Informatics Lecture Notes in Computer Science* Volume 5075 (2008): 171–82.

28. Clinton R. Clark, Jeffrey D. Weir, Richard F. Deckro, and Marcus B. Perry, *Modeling and Analysis of Clandestine Networks* (Air Force Institute of Technology, Wright-Patterson AFB, OH, 2005), accessed 18 August 2014, http://oai.dtic.mil/oai/oai?verb=getRecord&metadataPrefix=html&identifier=ADA444968.

29. Fred Renzi, "Networks: Terra Incognita and the Case for Ethnographic Intelligence," *Military Review* (September-October, 2006): 16–22; Maura. Conway and Lisa McInerney, "Jihadi Video & Auto-Radicalisation: Evidence from an Exploratory YouTube Study," in *Intelligence and Security Informatics: European Conference, EuroISI 2008 Proceedings,* D. Ortiz-Arrovyo et al., eds., (Heidelberg: Spring Berlin, 2008).

30. Hsinchun Chen, et al., "The Dark Web Portal: Collecting and Analyzing the Presence of Domestic and International Terrorist Groups on the Web," *Proceedings of the 7th International Conference on Intelligent Transportation Systems (ITSC)*, (Washington, 2004).

31. Chen, "Crime Data Mining."

32. Reed, *Formalizing the Informal*.

33. David Ronfeldt and John Arquilla, "Networks, Netwars, and the Fight for the Future," *First Monday,* Vol. 6. Number 10 (1 October, 2001).

34. The "Small World" or "Six Degrees of Separation" descriptions of the networked society may be too large to be useful for network detection. Initial research on ordinary citizens in the U.S. suggests that two to three steps is frequently all that is required to uncover the essential network structure, or link across it, regardless of the social network. See J. Surface, "Six Degrees of Bin Laden: The FBI's Use of Link Analysis for Counterterrorism Investigations," National Defense Intelligence College, (2007) for the extension to counterterrorism.

35. D. O'Callaghan, D. Green, M. Conway, J. Carthy, and P. Cunningham, "An Analysis of Interactions Within and Between Extreme Right Communities in Social Media," in *Ubiquitous Social Media Analysis*, eds. Martin Atzmueller, et al., Springer. 8329 (2013): 88–107.

36. Kathleen Blee, "Ethnographies of the Far Right," *Journal of Contemporary Ethnography* 36 (2007): 119–27; Chip Berlet. "Christian Identity: Apocalyptic Style, Political Religion, Palingenesis and Neo-Fascism," *Totalitarian Movements and Political Religion* 5 (2004): 459–506; Adams and Roscigno, "White Supremacists"; Gerstenfeld et al., "Hate Online."

37. Howard Wesler, et al., "Visualizing the Signatures of Social Roles in Online Discussion Groups," *Journal of Social Structure* Volume 8 (2007), accessed 22 August 2014, http://www.cmu.edu/joss/content/articles/volume8/Welser/.
38. Conway and McInerney, "Jihadi Video."
39. Zhou et al. "U.S. Domestic Extremist Groups."
40. Cunningham, "The Patterning of Repression."
41. Jörg Raab and H. Brinton Milward, "Dark networks as problems," *Journal of Public Administration Research and Theory* 13 (2003): 413–39.
42. H. Brinton, Milward and Jörg Raab, "Dark networks as organizational problems: Elements of a theory," *International Public Management Journal* 9 (2006): 333–60.
43. Michael McCluskey, "Website Content Persistence and Change: Longitudinal Analysis of Pro-White Group Identity," *Journal of Information Science* Vol. 39, No. 2 (2013): 188–97.
44. Kathleen Carley, Ju-Sung Lee and David Krackhardt, "Destabilizing Networks," *Connections*, 24 (2002): 79–92.
45. Note that our use of "removal" does not imply assassination, although we recognize that in some quarters that might be inferred. In addition, our own work on a novel centrality measure, Laplacian centrality, contributes to this literature, although in the context of this article it is somewhat less 'central' to our discussion. See Qi, Xingqin, Robert D. Duval, Kyle Christensen, Edgar Fuller, Arian Spahiu, Qin Wu, Yezhou Wu, Wenliang Tang, and Cunquan Zhang. "Terrorist Networks, Network Energy and Node Removal: A New Measure of Centrality Based on Laplacian Energy," *Social Networking* 2, January 2013. Accessed on 23 August 2014 http://www.scirp.org/journal/PaperInformation.aspx?PaperID=27402.
46. George E. Apostolakis and Douglas M. Lemon, "A screening methodology for the identification and ranking of infrastructure vulnerabilities due to terrorism," *Risk Analysis* 25 (2005): 361–76.
47. Southern Policy Law Center, "Frazier Glenn Miller," retrieved on 22 April 2014, http://www.splcenter.org/get percent20informed/intelligence percent20files/profiles/Glenn percent20Miller
48. Raymond A. Franklin, *The Hate Directory*, accessed 15 August 2009, http://www.hatedirectory.com/; Gerstenfeld, Grant, and Chiang, "Hate Online"; Joseph Schafer, "Spinning the Web of Hate: Web–Based Hate Propagation By Extremist Organizations," *Journal of Criminal Justice and Popular Culture 9 (2002)*: 69–88.
49. Free Software Foundation, *GNU Wget*, Retrieved 15 July 2007 from http://www.gnu.org/software/wget/.
50. We are beginning a new round of data collection in 2014-2015 that will give us a more accurate estimate of the relative proportion of groups out there.
51. Our coding decision rules coded any site that listed two or more individual names or email addresses as a "small group," and if the website ran a blog or forum that was in use, it was treated as a large or multi-authored site.
52. It is anecdotally interesting that Frazier Glenn Miller's site, the *Vanguard News Network*, has a rather low 5.1 degree centrality. That score indicates that it is not isolated, but also not particularly prominent or active within the White Nationalist component of the overall network.

REFERENCES

Adams, Josh., and Vincent J. Roscigno. "White Supremacists, Oppositional Culture and the World Wide Web." *Social Forces*, 84 (2005): 759–78.
Akdeniz, Yaman. "Anonymity, Democracy, and Cyberspace." *Social Research* 69 (2002): 223–37.
Apostolakis, George E., and Douglas M. Lemon. "A screening methodology for the identification and ranking of infrastructure vulnerabilities due to terrorism." *Risk Analysis* 25 (2005): 361–76.
Bargh, John, and Katelyn McKenna. "The Internet and Social Life." *Annual Review of Psychology* 55 (2004): 573–90.

Berlet, Chip. "Christian Identity: Apocalyptic Style, Political Religion, Palingenesis and Neo-Fascism." *Totalitarian Movements and Political Religion* 5 (2004): 459–506.

Best, Samuel, and Brian Krueger. "Analyzing the Representativeness of Internet Political Participation." *Political Behavior* 27 (2005): 183–215.

Bimber, Bruce. "Information and Political Engagement in America: The Search for Effects of Information Technology at the Individual Level." *Political Research Quarterly* 54 (2001): 53–67.

Blee, Kathleen. "Ethnographies of the Far Right." *Journal of Contemporary Ethnography* 36 (2007): 119–27.

Carley, Kathleen, Ju-Sung Lee, and David Krackhardt. "Destabilizing Networks." *Connections* 24 (2002): 79–92.

Chen, Hsinchun, Wingyan Chung, Yi Qin, Michael Chau, Jennifer Jie Xu, Gang Wang, Rong Zheng, and Homa Atabakhsh. "Crime Data Mining: An Overview and Case Studies." *ACM International Conference Proceedings Series,* Volume 130 (2003).

Clark Clinton R., Jeffrey D. Weir, Richard F. Deckro, and Marcus B. Perry. *Modeling and Analysis of Clandestine Networks.* Air Force Institute of Technology, Wright-Patterson AFB, OH, 2005. Accessed 18 August 2014. http://oai.dtic.mil/oai/oai?verb=getRecord& metadataPrefix=html&identifier=ADA444968.

Conway, Maura. and Lisa McInerney. "Jihadi Video & Auto-Radicalisation: Evidence from an Exploratory YouTube Study." In *Intelligence and Security Informatics: European Conference, EuroISI 2008 Proceedings.* D. Ortiz-Arrovyo, H. Larsen, D. Zeng, D. Hicks, and G. Wagner, eds. Heidelberg: Spring Berlin, 2008.

Cunningham, David. "The Patterning of Repression: FBI Counterintelligence and the New Left." *Social Forces* 82 (2003): 209–40.

Ferrara, Luigi, Christian Mårtenson, Pontus Svenson, Per Svensson, Justo Hidalgo, Anastasio Molano, and Anders L. Madsen. "Integrating Data Sources and Network Analysis Tools to Support the Fight Against Organized Crime." *Intelligence and Security Informatics Lecture Notes in Computer Science* Volume 5075 (2008): 171–82.

Franklin, Raymond A. *The Hate Directory.* Accessed 15 August 2009. http://www.hatedirectory.com/.

Free Software Foundation. *GNU Wget.* Retrieved 15 July 2007. http://www.gnu.org/software/wget/.

George R. Tiller News - *The New York Times.* Accessed 18 August 2011. http://topics.nytimes.com/topics/reference/timestopics/people/t/george_r_tiller/index.html?scp=1-spot&sq=George percent20Tiller percent20&st=cse.

Gerstenfeld, Phyllis B., Diana R. Grant, and Chau-Pu Chiang. "Hate Online: A Content Analysis of Extremist Internet Sites." *Analysis of Social Issues and Public Policy* 3 (2003): 29–44.

Haney, Craig, Curtis Banks, and Philip Zimbardo. "Interpersonal Dynamics in a Simulated Prison." *International Journal of Criminology and Penology* 1 (1973): 69–97.

Joinson, Adam and Phil Banyard. "Psychological Aspects of Information Seeking on the Internet." *Aslib Proceedings* 54 (2) (2002): 95–102.

Krueger, Brian. "A Comparison of Conventional and Internet Political Mobilization." *American Politics Research* 34 (2006): 759–76.

Krueger, Brian. "Assessing the Potential of Internet Political Participation in the United States: A Resource Approach." *American Politics Research* 30 (2002): 476–98.

———. "A Comparison of Conventional and Internet Political Mobilization." *American Politics Research* 34 (November 2006): 759–76.

McKenna, Katelyn and John Bargh. "Causes and Consequences of Social Interaction on the Internet: A Conceptual Framework." *Media Psychology* 1 (1999): 249–69.

MacDonald, Jason, and Caroline Tolbert. "Something Rich and Strange: Participation, Engagement and the Tempest of Online Politics." In *Civic Engagement in a Network Society.* edited by Kaifeng Yang and Erik Bergrud. New York: Information Age Publishing, 2008.

McCluskey, Michael. "Website Content Persistence and Change: Longitudinal Analysis of Pro-White Group Identity." *Journal of Information Science* 39 (2013): 188–97.

Milward, H. Brinton, and Jörg Raab "Dark networks as organizational problems: Elements of a theory." *International Public Management Journal* 9 (2006): 333–60.

————. "Dark Networks as Problems Revisited: Adaptation and Transformation of Islamic Terror Organizations since 9/11." Paper presented at the 8th Public Management Research Conference at the School of Policy, Planning and Development at University of Southern California, Los Angeles, September 29-October 1, 2005.

Scott Roeder News - *The New York Times* (2011). Accessed 18 August 2011. http://topics.nytimes.com/top/reference/timestopics/people/r/scott_roeder/index.html?scp=1-spot& sq=Scott percent20Roeder&st=cse.

Niksic, Hrvoje. Wget Software. N.D. Retrieved from http://www.gnu.org/software/wget/ on 15 July 2007.

O'Callaghan, D., D. Green, M. Conway, J. Carthy, and P. Cunningham. "An Analysis of Interactions Within and Between Extreme Right Communities in Social Media." In *Ubiquitous Social Media Analysis*. Edited by Martin Atzmueller, Alvin Chin, Denis Helic, and Andreas Hotho. Springer. 8329 (2013): 88–107.

Putnam, Robert. *Bowling Alone: The Collapse and Revival of American Community.* New York: Simon & Schuster, 1995.

Qi, Xingqin, Robert D. Duval, Kyle Christensen, Edgar Fuller, Arian Spahiu, Qin Wu, Yezhou Wu, Wenliang Tang, and Cunquan Zhang. "Terrorist Networks, Network Energy and Node Removal: A New Measure of Centrality Based on Laplacian Energy." *Social Networking* 2 (January 2013). Accessed 23 August 2014. http://www.scirp.org/journal/PaperInformation. aspx?PaperID=27402.

Qin, Jialun, Yilu Zhou, Edna Reid, Guanpi Lai, and Hsinchun Chen. "Analyzing Terror Campaigns on the Internet: Technical Sophistication, Content Richness, and Web Interactivity." *International Journal of Human-Computer Studies* 65 (2007): 71–84.

Qin, Jialun, Yilu Zhou, Guanpi Lai, Edna Reid, Marc Sageman, and Hsinchun Chen "The Dark Web Portal: Collecting and Analyzing the Presence of Domestic and International Terrorist Groups on the Web." *Intelligence and Security Informatics Lecture Notes in Computer Science* 3495 (2005): 623–24. Accessed 23 August 2014. http://link.springer.com/chapter/ 10.1007 percent2F11427995_78.

Raab, Jörg and H. Brinton Milward. "Dark networks as problems." *Journal of Public Administration Research and Theory* 13 (2003): 413–39.

Reed, Brian. *Formalizing the Informal: a Network Analysis of an Insurgency.* University of Maryland, College Park, 2006. Accessed 18 August 2011, http://drum.lib.umd.edu/handle/ 1903/3759.

Reed, Brian. "A Social Network Approach to Understanding an Insurgency." *Parameters* (Summer, 2007): 19–30.

Renzi, Fred. "Networks: Terra Incognita and the Case for Ethnographic Intelligence." *Military Review* 86 (September-October 2006): 16–22.

Ronfeldt, David, and John Arquilla. "Networks, Netwars, and the Fight for the Future." *First Monday* 6 (1 October 2001).

Sageman, Marc. *Understanding Terror Networks.* Philadelphia: University of Pennsylvania Press, 2004.

Sageman, Marc. *Leaderless Jihad: Terror Networks in the Twenty-First Century.* Philadelphia: University of Pennsylvania Press, 2008.

Schafer, Joseph. "Spinning the Web of Hate: Web–Based Hate Propagation By Extremist Organizations." *Journal of Criminal Justice and Popular Culture 9 (2002)*: 69–88.

Southern Policy Law Center. "Frazier Glenn Miller." Accessed 22 April 2014 from http:// www.splcenter.org/get percent20informed/intelligence percent20files/profiles/Glenn percent20Miller

Stephen, Timothy. "Concept Analysis of Gender, Feminist, and Women's Studies Research in the Communication Literature." *Communication Monographs 67* (2000): 193–214.

Stumpe, Joe, and Monica Davey. "Abortion Doctor Shot to Death in Kansas Church." *The New York Times.* May 31, 2009. Accessed 18 August 2011. http://www.nytimes.com/2009/06/01/ us/01tiller.html?adxnnl=1&ref=georgertiller&adxnnlx=1313691804- ZzAw7cOQjuCM891F4YrB0g. Accessed 18 August 2011.

Surface, J. (2007). "Six Degrees of Bin Laden: The FBI's Use of Link Analysis for Counterterrorism Investigations." National Defense Intelligence College, 2007.

Wesler, Howard T., Eric Gleave, Danyel Fisher, and Mark Smith. "Visualizing the Signatures of Social Roles in Online Discussion Groups." *Journal of Social Structure* Volume 8 (2007). Accessed 23 August 2014 http://www.cmu.edu/joss/content/articles/volume8/Welser/.

Williams, Phil. "Violent Non-state Actors and National and International Security." *International Relations and Security Network*. 25 (November 2008). Accessed 23 March 2014 from http://www.isn.ethz.ch/isn/Digital-Library/Publications.

Zhou, Yilu, Edna Reid, Jialun Qin, Guanpi Lai, and Hsinchun Chen. "U.S. Domestic Extremist Groups on the Web: Link and Content Analysis." *IEEE Intelligent Systems, Special Issue on Artificial Intelligence for National and Homeland Security*, September/October. (2005): 44–51.

Chapter Four

Hijacking Authority

Academic Neo-Aryanism and Internet Expertise

Alexandar Mihailovic

The academic and journalistic careers of Kevin MacDonald, a tenured professor in the department of psychology at California State University in Long
Beach, and Aleksandr Dugin, a Professor of Sociology at Moscow State
University, would not seem to have much in common. The highly specific
language of Dugin's pronouncements about the need for a neo-Bolshevik
Russian empire continues to reverberate in President Vladimir Putin's
speeches and in the tendentious narratives provided by the Kremlin's media
empire, whereas MacDonald, anchored within the fringe of American conservatism, seems to be a figure with scant potential for crossing over into a
more expansive notoriety and influence. Retiring from his academic position
in 2014, MacDonald's political activity remains within the narrow ambit of
his non-peer reviewed publications and the white identity journal *The Occidental Quarterly,* to which he was appointed as editor in 2007. Since 2011,
he has served on the board of Directors of the anti-immigrant and white
nationalist American Freedom Party, which is also known as American Third
Position.[1]

Yet a consideration of MacDonald and Dugin as parallel figures is war-
ranted, and for several different reasons. MacDonald and Dugin portray
themselves as supporters of nationalist authoritarianism who are also posses-
sors of weighty cultural capital within traditional academic institutions: Mac-
Donald in his capacity as a tenured professor at one of the largest state-
funded university systems in the United States, and Dugin as a full professor
at the Russian university that has served as one of the most important sources
for the replenishing of political elites. Since the time of his tenuring in 1994,
MacDonald has carefully cultivated the persona of someone who serves as an

organic link between the informational pathways of legitimate scholarship on the one hand, and anti-Semitic Christian identity movements and fringe activism on the other. He is the "academic expert" whose work is most often cited by the right-wing website Stormfront.

In a deliberate attempt to appeal to the ideological eclecticism of the New Right in Russia—with its attempts at forcing a seemingly unlikely synthesis of pre-Soviet Russian nationalism, neo-Stalinist isolationism, Leninist statism, and the energy resource agendas of plutocratic constituencies—Aleksandr Dugin has shrewdly parceled out his Internet presence across a range of websites, each of which is meant to appeal to a specific niche in the political marketplace, such as Russian Orthodoxy, Eurasianism, fascism, anti-globalism, or occultism. MacDonald freely distributes most of his amateur scholarship on Jewish culture from his personal web page and the website of the *Occidental Observer*. MacDonald and Dugin are intent upon the construction of self-validating scholarly subcultures that have a strong diegetic component with specific appeal to non-rationalist modes of discourse, while intersecting with larger communities of political action.

PSYCHOLOGIST AS HISTORIOGRAPHER: THE EVOLUTION OF KEVIN MACDONALD

Kevin MacDonald's three books on Judaism as an evolutionary strategy were originally published in the late nineties by Praeger, a largely respected academic imprint that specializes in research within the social sciences. MacDonald's monographs fell under the rubric of the Praeger series "Human Evolution, Behavior and Intelligence," other publications in which included the work of racialist social scientists such as Richard Lynn, Arthur R. Jensen, Michael E. Levin, and J. Phillipe Rushton. MacDonald's first book about Judaism, *A People That Shall Dwell Alone: Judaism as a Group Evolutionary Strategy,* was published in 1994; the second and third, *Separation and Its Discontents: Toward an Evolutionary Theory of Anti-Semitism* and *The Culture of Critique: An Evolutionary Analysis of Jewish Involvement in Twentieth-Century Intellectual and Political Movements,* in 1998. The editor of the series in which MacDonald's book appeared was Seymour W. Itzkoff, now a Professor Emeritus of Psychology at Smith College. In 1996, Itzkoff had run afoul of the administration at Smith for accepting a grant from the Pioneer Fund, which subsequently retracted the award when the discussion of the openly racialist research agendas of both Itzkoff and the foundation became more publicly known.[2] Notwithstanding the broad research consensus of the series contributors, Itzkoff had grave reservations about the second two volumes of MacDonald's work, asking him for further revisions before final publication.[3]

When MacDonald published the last two of his volumes, the erosion of the academic respectability of Praeger's series "Human Evolution, Behavior and Intelligence"—and the perception of it as a cluster of publications that bypassed any rigorous peer-reviewing outside of its coterie of researchers— had already begun, and was accelerated by the unfolding critical discussion of Charles Murray's and Richard J. Herrnstein's 1994 *The Bell Curve*.[4] In support of their conclusions about the racial inheritability of intelligence and the pointlessness of educational reforms in the American public school system, Murray and Herrnstein extensively cite many of the researchers who had contributed to the Praeger series, singling out Rushton's work (controversial for its assertion of an inverse relation in humans between intelligence and the size of genitalia) for particular praise.[5] By 2002, Praeger had ceased to print MacDonald's books. MacDonald subsequently undertook to have them published by the non-academic print-on-demand companies Author-House and iUniverse.

One of the first things that a reader notices about MacDonald's books about Judaism is their considerable redundancy of argumentation. In its assumption of a uniform cultural self-image among Jews over a period of thousands of years, much of MacDonald's writing brings to mind Richard Hofstadter's acute observation about "higher paranoid scholarship" as competing with the culturally destructive forces that it seeks to uncloak: "it believes that is up against an enemy who is as infallibly rational as he is totally evil, an it seeks to match its imputed total competence with its own, leaving nothing unexplained and comprehending all of reality in one overreaching, consistent theory."[6] A highly representative passage of *The Culture of Critique* positions Jacques Derrida as just another foot soldier in the Jewish campaign against gentile culture: "Derrida's Jewish political agenda is identical to that of the Frankfurt School [. . .]. As with the Frankfurt School, [in Derrida's view] the radical skepticism of the deconstructivist movement is in the service of preventing the development of hegemonic, universalist ideologies and other foundations of gentile group allegiance in the name of *tout autre,* i.e., the 'wholly other.'" Macdonald concludes his discussion of Derrida with a statement that manifests his larger style of argumentation, of assertion enhanced by repetitious phrasing and circular reasoning. This rhetorical approach can be understood as a moment in which MacDonald's bland tone of sociological exposition falters, giving us a glimpse of the obsessive binary ideation that lies at the heart of his conception of Judaism: "[t]hus in the end, Derrida develops yet another in the age-old conceptions of Judaism as a morally superior group [*sic*] while ideologies of sameness and universality that might underlie ideologies [*sic*] of social homogeneity and group consciousness among European gentiles are deconstructed and rendered as morally inferior."[7]

In spite of such crude and reductionist writing, the reviews of MacDonald's books that appeared in mainstream academic journals were surprisingly lenient. In a highly critical yet temperate response to *A People Who Shall Dwell Alone* in *The Journal for the Scientific Study of Religion,* Eugen Schoenfeld takes particular issue with MacDonald's use of the term "evolutionary strategy" to describe Jewish practices of endogamy, cultural separatism and (what he perceives to be an unrelenting) chauvinism from the fall of the last temple to the present day: "The author proposes that his study investigates Judaism as a group evolutionary strategy. Strategy implies, at least to me, a rational goal-oriented behavior. If this is the case, then who made the decisions that led to Jewish exclusivist social norms?"[8] It is a pity that Schoenfeld did not further explore the considerable problems (from the multiple perspectives of the disciplines of biology, cultural studies, and historiography) that beset MacDonald's use of this odd formulation. Evolution is a process, not a social practice: it unfolds over multiple generations of a species undergoing natural selection and adaptation to changing physical environments. In what sense can an animal—much less a human, a group of humans, or a culture—be said to implement strategies for the survival of their species? MacDonald's handling of this formulation is highly reminiscent of Ayn Rand's equally meretricious and opaque concept of "rational self-interest," only here it seems to be transferred from the level of the individual's consciousness and experience to that of a group, if not a species. But there are other problems with this way of thinking about adaptive self-defense in a cultural setting. Very often, MacDonald argues for a subconscious solidarity among Jews across wide spans of time and place, which suggests an adherence to the semi-mystical and discredited notion of collective racial memory that was most famously propounded by Carl Jung. "Many of the Jews involved in the [progressive] movements [. . .] may sincerely believe that these movements are really divorced from specifically Jewish interests or are in the best interests of other groups as well as Jews [but] the best deceivers are those who are self-deceived."[9] It should go without saying that MacDonald's conception of racial memory—as both an instinctual reflex for collective self-defense, and a cognitive engine that takes into account past victories and mistakes before drawing up a calculus for future actions—has a strong Lamarckian component that makes it incompatible with any branch of evolutionary science. Furthermore, assuming that the concept of evolutionary strategies has integrity as an analytical tool, how can we speak of a person of group of people who lived prior to the 1859 publication of *The Origin of Species* as possessing an awareness of it? MacDonald's writing about Judaism is riddled with logical inconsistencies, anachronisms, and methodological fallacies that speak to the serious difficulty of transplanting paradigms from a sub-field of the natural sciences into a historiographical context.

But perhaps the central problem with MacDonald's writing about Judaism is that it has very little to do with any branch of psychology or historiography, and is more deeply informed by the anti-Semitism that is specific to American nativism. MacDonald is particularly exercised by what he sees as the undue influence of Jewish lobbyists on the escalating generosity of American immigration policy, which culminated in the 1965 Immigration and Nationality Act. What was the purpose behind this push for the liberalization of immigration laws, promoted by "Jewish" (as MacDonald is wont to remind us) activists such as the New York Senator Jacob Javits? The more or less articulated ideal, according to MacDonald, was to foster an "ethnic and religious pluralism"; the concealed, and more passionately felt agenda, was to disperse "political and cultural influence among the various ethnic and religious groups," in order to make it "difficult or impossible to develop unified, cohesive groups of gentiles united in their opposition to Judaism."[10] Here MacDonald is merely repackaging the demi-scholarship and pleonastic sermonizing of writers such as Roger Pearson, an editor from the early days of the racialist academic journal *Mankind Quarterly* who once wrote that "Jewish influence" would result in "race-mixing, dysgenic and Communist activities [. . .] aimed at the destruction of all potential rivals to the Jewish community, in their [*sic*] apparent eagerness to obtain world power" and dominion "over a vast, sub-normal mass of sub-humanity."[11] Years later, both MacDonald and the future authors of *The Bell Curve* would contribute articles to *Mankind Quarterly.* As Jean Baudrillard might say, MacDonald and his racialist colleagues strive to produce a simulacrum of a community of disinterested and scrupulous researchers, authors whose works fill the shelves of a virtual library.

In MacDonald's series of books about Judaism—to call it a trilogy seems ennobling, and therefore wrong—another typical point at which the mask of scholarly rectitude and punctiliousness dislodges from the historical narrative occurs in his discussion of the cultural forces that facilitated the rise of National Socialism. MacDonald does not acknowledge the extensive testimony of Jews in Germany who passionately identified with gentile German high culture, a tragic generation whose experience was documented by writers as different as Joachim Fest and Gershom Scholem. More poignant and interesting to MacDonald is the anguish and panic, in the nineteenth century, of German gentiles such as Richard Wagner,[12] who drew conclusions about Jewish enmity to Christian values. In *Separation and Its Discontents,* MacDonald writes feelingly of the responses in *Mein Kampf* and the publications of Houston Chamberlain to the demographic and institutional threats posed by Jewish culture in Germany.[13] MacDonald uses these and other *loci classici* of anti-Semitism (such as the inflammatory publications of Henry Ford) as primary historical texts—as *engagé* chronicles of events and circumstances—positioning them as biased, yet nonetheless thoughtful, witnesses to a time of upheaval and cultural dissolution.

Less obvious to many readers, yet more significant in giving a patina of respectability, is MacDonald's lengthy bibliography, which cites a wide range of scholarly studies in the social sciences together with other, lesser known, publications. MacDonald often cites legitimate sources in close prox- imity with others that are nothing more than rabble-rousing political pamph- lets or egregious and discredited examples of racialist pseudo-science, such as the work of Fritz Lenz (a geneticist who actively worked within the Third Reich),[14] the Russian anti-Semitic propagandist Igor Shafarevich, and the fringe American anti-immigration agitator Peter Brimelow. Hypertextual conflation and fusion is a diegetic practice that is highly characteristic of MacDonald's writing. In a discussion that serves as a conceptual bridge to the chapter "The Frankfurt School and Pathologization," Macdonald simplis- tically argues that all of Sigmund Freud's work is animated by a diabolical philo-Semitism and hatred of gentile culture, deliberately ignoring the siz- able body of scholarship that documents Freud's exceedingly complicated and often conflicted relation both to Judaism and his own Jewishness. From there, it's a spritely skip and a hop to the malign tendentiousness of the Frankfurt School, and its project to undermine and dismantle Christianity in the West. MacDonald is keen to acknowledge individual agency to the voices of National Socialists and their fellow travellers, but loathe to do the same for their contemporaries on the other side of the ideological divide. What enables MacDonald to avoid any reference to the primary debates and controversies surrounding particular subject areas is the way in which he embeds his writ- ing into a distinct bibliographical database, one that is propped up by a clique of researchers who engage in a practice of logrolling peer-review.

To be sure, this practice is hardly new—or, for that matter, unique—to the precincts of the far-right academy in the United States. As early as 1964, Hofstadter argued that "[t]he entire American right wing movement [. . .] is a parade of experts, study groups, monographs, footnotes and bibliogra- phies."[15] It is important to bear in mind that MacDonald and his colleagues at *The Occidental Observer* and his numerous supporters on websites such as Stormfront are interested, above all, in constructing an informational hub that mimics the administrative structures of institutions of higher learning, while also relativizing the notion of objective criteria for research. Much of what MacDonald himself authors on the Internet resembles a virtual university. Any place of instruction requires, of course, a library, and MacDonald is particularly interested in constructing an archive of knowledge whose author- ity is bolstered by the intellectual cachet of the scholarly monograph. Here we should bear in mind similar efforts among the conservative intellectuals during the mid-nineties. Discussing in 1998 his promotion of Murray and Herrnstein's *The Bell Curve,* Michael Joyce characterized his work as President of the conservative Lynde and Harry Bradley Foundation in Milwaukee as an endeavor to create a book-based network of alternate forms of knowledge and information:

> We have the conviction that most of the other media are derivative from books. Books are the way that authors put forth more substantial, more coherent arguments. It follows that if you want to have influence on the world of ideas, books are where you want to put your money. It is what we are most proud of, of all the things we've done here. [16]

On the site that represents the largest resource for MacDonald's writing (www.kevinmacdonald.net), a click on the link "Essays on Jews and Other Diaspora Peoples" leads to a page that makes eye-catching use of multiple typesets and formatting styles for the listing of his Praeger publications, and his two collections published by the Occidental Quarterly. The same Internet domain—which uses the word 'book' nine times, in reference to MacDonald's five monographs—can be accessed from other points of MacDonald's site, and has the address rubric with the word "books."[17]

The distinctive configuration of this bibliography page brings us to the realization that MacDonald essentially wrote his books on Judaism in the style of a large hypertext. The appeal of these books for MacDonald's audience is that they simulate the experience of browsing in an extensively cross-referenced library. MacDonald adopts a historiographical organization to his books, while suggesting that history itself—the distinctiveness of its multiple stages—is irrelevant during a time of Manichaean struggle between cultures. On what one researcher recently called "America's most popular online hate site,"[18] over 1,250 discussion threads reference MacDonald and his publications about the racial aspects of evolutionary psychology. In one representative posting, a "sustaining member" of Stormfront writes that: "I grew up a liberal who accepted without question the Jewish (false) history of the Third Reich and Adolf Hitler, but beginning with Kevin MacDonald's *Culture of Critique,* I was gradually led to the truth."[19] The postings about MacDonald on Stormfront are overwhelmingly positive, and often refer to him by his professional title of Doctor. References to MacDonald's work occur over a wide swath of subject matter in Stormfront, including such seemingly unrelated threads such as "Russia and Ukraine/Maidan," "Aspergers Test," and "WHY [*sic*] do normal average Americans hate Nazis?" One hundred and eight threads on Stormfront foreground MacDonald not just as a passing reference, but as a dedicated tag in their subject matters. More threads are devoted to him than to any other right-wing "scholarly" researcher. MacDonald had forfeited much of his academic respectability in 2000, when he volunteered to testify on behalf of the anti-Semitic non-academic historian David Irving's libel suit in the UK against the Emory University professor

Deborah Lipstadt. On Stormfront, only twenty discussions are devoted to David Irving. The multiple hypertextual points of entry into (and from) Mac-Donald's work undoubtedly accounts for much of its appeal to Stormfront users: no fewer than 488 discussion threads re-post the address of MacDonald's virtual library site.

In designing the interlocking series of domains of his work—with links that shunt the user from his California State University faculty page on to his cluster of essays on *The Occidental Quarterly,* his blog on the white nationalist and anti-immigration site VDare, and back to his personal web page—MacDonald displays a shrewd awareness of the self-validating possibilities of content redundancy in cyberspace.[20] In the end, however, the design flourishes of this Internet archipelago cannot offset the traditional alliances of American far-right thought that inform MacDonald's work. MacDonald hews quite faithfully to the platform of the American Third Position party. Unlike the National Front in France and United Kingdom Independence Party (UKIP), American Third Position is avowedly paleo-conservative, and makes no attempt to modernize its positions by hybridizing them with anti-globalism and the thinking of "classical" liberals such as Raymond Aron or John Stuart Mill. Indeed, MacDonald abandoned all pretense to a detached scholarly mien well before he retired from California State at Long Beach. In 2012, David Duke interviewed MacDonald on his white supremacist radio program. Shortly after Duke's introduction of him as "one of the intellects and academics I respect most in the world," MacDonald gets down to business with the assertion that "[Jewish] people hate us [and have] this sense of persecution going back to the Middle Ages, of Christianity as the fount of all evil." Perhaps sensing the usefulness of such inflammatory statements on a program devoted to fundraising for Duke's organization, MacDonald goes on to say that such animosity is "absolutely fundamental to Jewish identity," and that the prospect of "white people" becoming "a minority, is something that they just can hardly wait to have it happen. It's absolute paradise for them [. . .]. Jewish identity is hating Christianity."[21] Together with his more recent essays asserting the existence of a Neolithic-era Northern European phenotype that possessed the genetic behavioral markers for altruism and individualism—which he asserts to be absent from Semitic and African peoples[22] — MacDonald's scholarly neo-Aryanism had come full circle with anti-immigrant traditions of American racist populism, which responded to the wave of Irish immigration that followed the potato famine with one of its earliest militant articulations. Jews and others outside of the ancient ambit of the ur-homeland of European identity in the North were all descendants of cultures that privileged the clan over the nuclear family, the tribe over the individual. Seen from the perspective of such dubious and untested assumptions, it can hardly come as a surprise that MacDonald perceives Jews as lacking the faculty for morally autonomous judgment that he claims Nordic Europeans possess as a part of their genetic identity.

THE EURASIANISM OF ALEKSANDR DUGIN: ACADEMIC DISCOURSE AS GRAND NARRATIVE

In contrast with MacDonald's clear-cut ultramondane ways of thinking about—or rather, against—cultural and racial diversity, the work of Aleksandr Dugin presents a daunting set of evaluative challenges. The volume of Dugin's publications has been prodigious. At the time of this writing, Dugin has published as many books as his forty-seven years. The eclecticism of his expository style—alternating between the scholarly, the lyrically portentous, the pedantic and the plainspoken incendiary—is as bewildering as the eccentricity of his political philosophy. While withholding at the moment detailed judgment about the success of Dugin's project of attaining a higher synthesis of intellectual traditions as different as Jungian occultism, racial essentialism, and nineteenth- and twentieth-century glorifications of state (such as Bonapartism, Konstantin Pobedonostsev's passionate advocacy for the tsarist empire as a modern bureaucratic institution, and the work of the early Nazi political theorist Carl Schmitt), we should take note of the scholar Andreas Umland's observation about the tactical significance of Dugin casting a wide net to gather those who had become bitter or bruised in the wake of the Soviet collapse.[23] A turning point in Dugin's career was his 1998 stint as an advisor to Gennady Seleznev, the Speaker within the State Duma or lower house of Parliament. Dugin's often absurd post-modern pastiches and millenarian thundering about the onslaught of geo-political end times would seem to be embarrassments in someone who has positioned himself to be a mentor without portfolio to policy makers in the Kremlin. In a possible effort to curry favor, in 2001 Dugin applauded Putin's economic policy and "new course of power," as "moving ever more clearly in the direction of a Eurasian policy."[24] In 2008, Dugin was chosen to serve as the Director of the newly created Center for Conservative Studies, within Moscow State University. Certainly Dugin's appointment at a high position within the flagship institution of the federal educational system—combined with the modesty of his academic training, and the unprofessional character of his publications— suggests that he occupies an unparalleled ideological authority within the Russian academy that is not commensurate with his actual achievements as a researcher.[25] But what is the core of Dugin's politically ascendant philosophy?

The most immediate response to this question would be that it represents an updating of the movement of Eurasianism, which conceptualizes Russia as a dynamic cultural and historical synthesis of Europe and Asia. Dugin takes special efforts to distinguish his Eurasianism from its more famous and influential twentieth-century articulations, in the works of Lev Gumilev and the expatriate philologist Nikolai Trubetskoy. Dugin is intent upon building a system of political interpretation of global events. According to him, the contemporary world is dominated by a Huntingtonian clash of civilizations, between maritime powers (which Dugin also calls "Atlanticist" and "thalassocratic") and land-based, or "tellurocratic" ones.[26] A union of Russia and several different Asian countries would represent the cultural values of tellurocracy, in opposing the movement toward neo-liberal globalization that is at the center of the constellation of maritime powers that is guided by the United States. As Dugin himself acknowledges, his rhetoric of anti-globalization is open to creative amplification, if not revision. Dugin regards his opposition to Atlanticist imperialism as a testing ground for the formation of new or unusual political alliances. Two things come to mind when reading his writing against a backdrop of newly fungible global capital. First, his conception of ideological convergences and coalitions has a strong theoretical—if not dialectical—feel to it, as if he is proceeding less from observed actual alliances and more from the theoretical constructs and the projection of archetypes into the future. The sociological category of groupuscles seems tailor-made for his approach. Second, this notion of a reshuffling of powerful countries into new supranational economic and political "zones" is shrewdly pitched at a politically diverse audience.

But what is most radically new about Dugin's Eurasianism—what diverges most fundamentally from the work of Gumilev and Trubetskoy, who articulated the values of Eurasian identity as forming only in the Mongol period of Russian history—is his stated belief in the existence of what may be termed a "proto-Eurasian" land and people, of the Siberian Arctic territories as the cradle of an Aryan civilization that represents the spiritual ancestor of Russian culture's more recent synthesis between Europe and Asia. In this regard, it is important to note that Dugin began his career as a political writer at the point where MacDonald had, in effect, ended his: with a speculative consideration of the ancestral Aryan homeland. Cross-pollinating early forms of Eurasianism with the fraudulent archeological theories of the Nazi-sponsored philologist Herman Wirth, Dugin gives the name of "Arktogaya" to this ancient civilization, and at a very early point in his career as a pamphlet writer (already in 1989, prior to the Soviet collapse) dubbed his conception of Asian Aryanism as the Hyperborean theory. One of the most curious aspects of Dugin's idiosyncratic theory is its willingness to entertain the possibility that race is more a cultural construct than (as MacDonald and his supporters would insist) a bio-genetic reality.

Yet it needs to be said that Dugin's soft-focus on race is less an attempt to make his ideas more palatable to an educated Russian mainstream (which, even in its most socially conservative elements, remains wary of theories developed in the Third Reich) than a strategy of modulated equivocation, aimed at appealing to supporters of Putin's assertive foreign policy as well as those on the far right and skinhead fringe within Russia. As Dugin explains, the original Nordic race of Arktogaya had a religious system that was preeminently metaphysical. They were the people of the transcendent subject, followers of an Apollonian cult of the Sun. Opposed to them both culturally and racially were the swarthier people of the South, who in their religious systems celebrated the reified or fetishized object, and their kinship with the animal world. Dugin insists that the differences between these ancient religious systems are the direct result of an intractable racial (and therefore genetic) divide in the Neolithic era between the Northern people of the Subject and the Southern people of the Object.[27] Yet he also points out two factors that mitigate the importance of race. First, the Tower of Babel-like mixing of languages and peoples that followed the Neolithic period renders racial identity for most people in the present as something of an imponderable. Second, the original Aryans were remarkable more for their cultural practices of embarking upon passionate metaphysical missions, than they were for their specific genetic make-up. In other words, the Aryans represent an ideal, which all of us—our racial backgrounds notwithstanding—are capable of following. The new Aryans are a class, rather than a race, of people. As Dugin writes in *The Russian Thing: Sketches of a National Philosophy*—a collection presented in a style meant to suggest Nazi publications, with the title printed in gold-colored Fraktur-style Cyrillic letters upon a black binding—"[w]e are not a Russian nation; we are a Russian class."[28]

Unlike MacDonald and his cohorts, Dugin assigns only secondary importance to racial identity because he sees no particular connection between it and the maintenance of cultural integrity. Among other things, Dugin's nationalism is distinctive for having only a muted element of anti-Semitism, which has furthermore all but disappeared in his writing over the last six years. Already in 2001, in *The Russian Thing,* Dugin states that: "the Semitic socialist, revolutionary, communist and gnostic are much closer to us than ethnically Russian capitalists."[29] In fact, Dugin is not at all opposed to the idea of a multicultural polity. In a pivotal essay from 1995, titled *The Goals and Tasks of Our Revolution,* Dugin articulates a conception of Russian culture as a multi-ethnic category: "The New Nation can become understood both as a general, supra-ethnic category, as a union of all nations and all social strata within the New State."[30] The political scientist Marlène Laruelle, one of the most serious researchers on Dugin, takes particular note of his "doctrinal consistency" of Dugin's writing, and the persistence of his interest in a concept of "blind and determinist destiny" among geopolitical entities.[31] More often than not, those entities are empires, territories with distinct centers and sprawling conurbations of other cultures. Yet for Dugin such territories are as often states of mind as they are actual nation states.

One can certainly be an advocate for an empire that has long ceased to exist. But Dugin considers projects of political nostalgia—the resurrection of previous forms of governance and specific "lost" traditions—to be often impractical, if not deluded. Strictly speaking, Dugin is more interested in the full convergence of Eurasia with the Hyperborean ideal of the "metaphysical" Aryans, than in that of Eurasia with contemporary Russia. Dugin is a utopian: he believes that the most significant form of advocacy is for the pure ideal, the quixotic agitation for the empire that has never historically existed. Hence his agitation for a "Eurasian" empire which, although roughly coterminous with the political tergiversations of Russia from the era of Ivan the Terrible to the present, cannot be said to be exclusively east Slavic in its character.

The influence of Dugin's peculiar distillation of rightist ideologies—most of them pointedly not Russian in provenance[32]—is sometimes evident in recent policy statements from the Kremlin. In a 29 August 2014 question-and-answer session with a patriotic youth group, about Russian support for independence in the Donbas region, Putin made a lengthy statement about "[o]ur interests concentrated in the Arctic" that was almost baffling in its unrelatedness to the Ukrainian crisis: "And of course we should pay more attention to issues of development of the Arctic and the strengthening of our position."[33] Putin's odd linking of the disputes about national sovereignty in the South with the uncontested borders of the far north can, of course, be understood primarily in emotive and symbolic terms, as an evocation of Russia's Northern military bases and untapped natural resources as points of national pride. Yet his wording here is largely a paraphrase of statements from a chapter of Dugin's textbook on geopolitics, which continues to be used in the Russian military academies. In *The Foundations of Geopolitics,* Dugin asserts that the "Russian [far] North" is nothing less than a "transcription" of the cyclically repeating manifestation of the idea of Eurasia, which in the present day takes the complex form of being strategically important for Russia's military identity, being rich in mineral resources, and for being the homeland of those autochthonous cultures that "preserve the memory of the cosmic proportions."[34]

The oracular tone of this last statement—seemingly out of place in a political science textbook, yet so characteristic of Dugin's expository style of punctuating the unfolding of timelines with quasi-mystical pronouncements—draws our attention once again to the variegated content of his ideas. While Dugin has largely evacuated references to the "Hyperborean theory" from more recent policy-oriented publications such as his *The Foundations of Geopolitics,* they can still be found in abundance in the texts that he posts on his multiple websites. Furthermore, many of Dugin's more pragmatic essays since 2008, about the balancing of Eurasianist aspirations with the demands of *realpolitik,* are written in a way that invites readers to clarify

certain enigmatic concepts by consulting the author's diverse Internet resources on www.arcto.ru, www.arctogaia.com, www.dugin.ru, and his daily
updated pages on Facebook and vKontakte. In sharp distinction to MacDonald's strategy of using multiple domains as nodes on a feedback loop for self-
certification, Dugin has virtually no links connecting his various personal
websites. The Hyperborean theory continues to be the concealed theater director that organizes most of the interactions and affinities that we see enacted on the main stage of Dugin's writing. We need not argue for the
absurdity of Dugin's views about the existence of a proto-Eurasian Nordic
race, whose mantle Russia has inherited in the form of specific folkways and
ancient linguistic paradigms. Like MacDonald, Dugin ignores what serious
and mainstream scholarship has said about many of the subjects that interest
him, which of course does not prevent him from borrowing some of their
methodologies without proper acknowledgement. In his structural analysis of
national mythologies, Dugin draws heavily on the interpretive approaches of
the Soviet school of Semiotics, without ever referencing the pioneering work
of scholars such as Eleazar Meletinsky and Yuri Lotman—possibly, one
suspects, because they were Jewish. Yet the "scholarly" turn in Dugin's
publications, the point at which he began to use footnotes with references to
academic publications, can be dated with some precision: with the publication, in 1996, of his slim monograph *The Mysteries of Eurasia.* What motivated Dugin to change the tone of his writing, to assume (like MacDonald)
the stance of what he understood to be professorial dispassion, counterbal-
anced (as we shall see) by the occasional eruption of heated advocacy? And
why has Dugin fashioned a disaggregate, rather than centripetal, structure to
his profile on the Internet?

In order to answer these questions, and to come to an understanding of
Dugin's own Internet strategies in contradistinction to MacDonald's, we
need to contemplate a pivotal yet largely unexamined event in his career
from almost twenty years ago. In the fall of 1995, the jazz and pop keyboard
player Sergei Kurekhin persuaded Dugin (who at that time was, as David
Remnick memorably puts it, "as marginal as a Lyndon LaRouche follower
with a card table and stack of leaflets"[35]) to establish residency in St. Petersburg, in order to run for a local seat in the Duma, as a candidate from Eduard
Limonov's fascist National Bolshevik Party (NBP). Kurekhin was a highly
eccentric figure, a notorious lover of media pranks and an impresario of
musical and theatrical "happenings" that he named "Pop Mechanics." In
these performances, mute actors dressed in a dizzying array of period costumes—much like a wordless version of Monty Python, but with the additional *épatage* of donning the garb of Soviet military and law enforcement
personnel—shared the same stage with sauntering geese and the often punk-
dancing, thrashing figure of Kurekhin himself. Each "Pop Mechanics" performance was accompanied by clamorous music that suggested a fusion of

Frank Zappa, King Crimson, and Miles Davis's experimental compositions from the early seventies. Kurekhin organized a "Pop-Mechanics" concert in support of Dugin's election campaign, and participated in a series of discussions with prospective voters. In the end, Dugin performed dismally in the election, netting less than 1 percent of the vote.[36] One video from that time has the two men sitting awkwardly next to each other on a political talk show, with Kurekhin inappropriately staring directly at the camera, smirking and occasionally interrupting Dugin's earnest statements with chortling repetitions of the campaign's pithy (if portentously biblical) Russian slogan about the need for transparency (*"Tainoe stanet iavnym* [That Which is Secret Will be Revealed]").[37] In more ways than one, Dugin's interaction with Kurekhin proved to be an instructive embarrassment, a fact that Dugin himself has acknowledged in at least one rueful yet thoughtful statement about the campaign: "Kurekhin was interested in . . . Eurasianism very ironically, with internal irony, if you will. But that irony was not obvious to those who surrounded him, because in that society the topic was taboo."[38]

I would argue that the episode of Kurekhin's abortive and mostly tongue-in-cheek campaign—together with Dugin's stinging experience of humiliation, in what quickly became a media-driven theatre of cruelty—motivated Dugin to cultivate a rebarbative style of intellectual gravitas in his published work and public appearances, rendering them into attention-grabbing spectacles of the educational experience. Two years later, Dugin would write in a eulogistic vein about Kurekhin (who died in 1996), describing "Pop Mechanics" as a relentlessly cruel—and one might say imperialistic—art of vanquishing the self, of performers willingly becoming manikins in a strange cultish rite organized by the magus figure of the artist. "It's in Kurekhin's work—particularly in his colossal, totalistic, mass-oriented 'Pop Mechanics'—that we see the impressive striving to bring together *absolutely everything* [author's emphasis], everything that is seized together."[39] Dugin concludes his discussion of Kurekhin's esthetics of subjugative violence by asserting that it is only natural that someone who was interested in the British occultist Aleister Crowley's uncompromising binary ethic of submission or destruction would also be drawn to the political doctrine of Eurasianism.[40] In the provocative musical and dramaturgical dissonances of Kurekhin's theatricalized concerts, Dugin came to recognize the principle of an anarchist *Gesamtkunstwerk,* where the barrier between act and word, audience and spectacle, is regularly blasted away by performers who sacrifice their egos to an art of total experience.

CONCLUSION

In several respects, Macdonald's self-advertising as a contrarian scholar is quite similar to the public practices of right-wing academics in Russia such as Dugin and the mathematician (and later, anti-Semitic propagandist) Igor Shafarevich. Much in the vein of Antonio Gramsci's conception of the organic intellectual and Edward Said's ideal of the public intellectual as an uncredentialized amateur, both MacDonald and Dugin present themselves as erudite generalists who write in order to give voice to the concerns of a disenfranchised community. But Macdonald and Dugin's preoccupation with the authority of cultural legacies and the imagined communities of a transnational pan-Aryanism ultimately runs against the grain of Gramsci's and Said's interest in the figure of the oppositional intellectual, because of the ways in which they construct academic identities with the goal of taking on the mantle of "conventional" authority. Both men have made the bulk of their political writing widely available on the Internet, where they have gained a reputation of being academic experts that far right groups in the United States and Russia can refer to as authorities. MacDonald's and Dugin's use of social media as a venue for self-credentialization is the ultimate expression of this circular pathway for the creation of academic reputation.

Yet there are crucial differences between the personae of the two men. In his 2009 manifesto *The Fourth Political Theory*, Dugin emphasizes the ideal of a collaborative relation between teacher and student: "[i]t is essential to expand the target audience by *simplifying the form of the Eurasian message* [. . .] *The simplification has to come from you.*"[41] By creating groups and sites for political consumers that he later abandons without actively disavowing, Dugin at the very least projects an Internet profile that is more dynamic and participatory than MacDonald's. A prime example of this strategy of identity subterfuge is the Dugin-created group "Eurasian Artists [*sic*] Association, est. 2013," which Dugin coyly lists on his Facebook page as having once worked at.[42] Dugin wants his audience to decode his creations, to lose themselves in a search for connections and generalizations that seem not to be emanating from Dugin himself. Among the varied panoply of his websites, there is only one direct link, from his vKontakte page to his Facebook page. At the time of this writing, Dugin's vKontakte page has 14,579 subscribers, and his Facebook page 19,423. Dugin is vividly aware of both his "audience" and his (virtual) lecture hall, concepts that are felicitously joined together in the same Russian word (*auditoriia*). The lecture halls that Dugin uses—the spaces for the dissemination of what he knows, and what he encourages his subscribers to re-post—are the various Internet domains that he has created. MacDonald and Dugin ultimately believe that academic authority is a fiction, a status they forge through a form of writing in order to attract a general audience that subsequently testifies to their status as teachers and scholars, thereby retroactively conferring upon each of them a status of virtual professor in fields for which they had no credentials. Both men have created Internet profiles as figures of authority that stand at the pinnacle of academic subcultures. Dugin models his conception of the teacher scholar after Kurekhin's definition of artist as avant-garde demiurge, rendering the figure of the Internet professor into a kind of performance artist without walls. In Dugin's online self-presentation as a professor in the trenches of the current Russian-Ukrainian conflict, we see elements of Kurekhin's glorification of violent performativity, particularly the notion that the artist is someone who is ready to put himself at risk. In the dispatch from Donbas in July 2014 that resulted in the suspension of his academic position, Dugin, a "professor of MGU (Moscow State University)," demanded that the supporters of the Maidan movement for Ukrainian independence be "killed, killed, killed"![43] As he ominously wrote in his 2002 *The Philosophy of Traditionalism,* the "New University" needs to teach us an "eschatological humanism."[44] While the title of professor becomes, for both MacDonald and Dugin, the equivalent of a military rank, it is Dugin who more substantially undertakes the task of constructing an alternate system of learning, as the training ground for real war.

NOTES

1. http://american3rdposition.com/?p=7796. Unless indicated otherwise, all Internet sources for this article were accessed on 20 September 2014.

2. For a discussion of the controversy at Smith surrounding the Pioneer Fund's grant to Itzkoff, see Robert M. O'Neill, *Free Speech in the College Community* (Bloomington, IN: Indiana University Press, 1997), 174–78. The website for the Institute for the Study of Academic Racism, located at Ferris University, has a page that documents Itzkoff's racialist research (http://www.ferris.edu/htmls/othersrv/ISAR/bibliography/Itzkoff.htm).

3. Commenting on MacDonald's *The Culture of Critique* to *Slate* writer Julie Shulevitz, Itzkoff stated that: "I said to the people at Greenwood that these [sections] would destroy his book—they were so beyond the pale in terms of factuality. But I couldn't censor or ask that he rewrite everything." Julie Shulevitz, "On Fighting Bad Ideas." http://www.slate.com/articles/news_and_politics/culturebox/2000/01/on_fighting_bad_ideas.html.

4. At the final stages of copy-editing this article, I discovered Ian Frederick Finseth's blog essay "Racist Publishing," http://www.commonwealinstitute.org/archive/racist-publishing, accessed 6 October 2014. Finseth's argument about the insularity and cronyism of the Praeger series runs parallel to mine, albeit without reference to MacDonald's Internet strategies. I disagree with Finseth's assessment of MacDonald as a "borderline case." I would argue that a racialist agenda is evident in much of MacDonald's research about evolutionary psychology, even outside of his publications about Judaism. See MacDonald's article "Parent-Child Play: An Evolutionary Perspective," in the edited collection *Parent-Child Play: Descriptions and Implications* (Albany, NY: State University of New York Press, 1993), 113–43, especially pages 122, 124, and 128.

5. In his Acknowledgments for the final volume in his trilogy, MacDonald thanks Rushton and Frank Salter for their comments on his manuscript. In 1999, Salter wrote a glowingly positive and exculpatory review of MacDonald's third volume for Praeger, an act that raises questions about conflict of interest given Salter's involvement in the book's preparation for publication (Salter, "Is MacDonald a Scholar?" *Human Ethology Bulletin* 15:3 [September

2000]: 16–22). See especially the penultimate paragraph of Salter's review, with its disingenu-ous assertion that "[u]nfortunately for those who rebel at his empirical claims, these are mostly not MacDonald's assertions but the expert opinions of leaders in various scholarly and scientif-ic fields" (21). At the time he wrote the review, Salter was a research associate at the Max Planck Institute.

6. Hofstadter, "The Paranoid Style in American Politics," in *The Paranoid Style in American Politics, and Other Essays* (New York: Alfred A. Knopf, 1965), 36–37.

7. Kevin MacDonald, *The Culture of Critique: An Evolutionary Analysis of Jewish In-volvement in Twentieth-Century Intellectual and Political Movements* (Westport, CT: Praeger; 2nd edition, 1st Books Library, 2002), 201, 203.

8. Eugen Schoenfeld, Review of Kevin MacDonald's *A People That Shall Dwell Alone: Judaism as a Group Evolutionary Strategy*, in *Journal for the Scientific Study of Religion* 34:3 (September 1995): 408–10, here 409.

9. MacDonald, *The Culture of Critique*, 241–42.

10. MacDonald, *The Culture of Critique*, 245.

11. William H. Tucker, *The Funding of Scientific Racism: Wickliffe Draper and the Pio-neer Fund* (Urbana, IL: University of Illinois Press, 2002), 174.

12. Kevin MacDonald, *A People That Shall Dwell Alone: Judaism as a Group Evolutionary Strategy* (Westport, CT: Praeger Publishers, 1994; 2nd edition, 1st Books Library, 2002), 35, 50–51, 80. As is often the case, MacDonald quotes the incendiary anti-Semitism of Wagner and others as if they were essentially empirical observations, and not intemperate expressions of bigotry.

13. Kevin MacDonald, *Separation and Its Discontents: Toward an Evolutionary Theory of Anti-Semitism* (Westport, CT: Praeger Publishers, 1998; 2nd edition, 1st Books Library, 2003), 147–50.

14. About the unqualified respect for Lenz's work among American racialists such as Berkeley's Arthur Jensen, see Tucker, *The Funding of Scientific Racism*, 155–56.

15. Hofstadter, "The Paranoid Style in American Politics," 37.

16. Quoted in Eric Alterman, *What Liberal Media? The Truth About Bias and the News* (New York: Basic Books, 2003), 85–86

17. http://www.kevinmacdonald.net/books.htm.

18. Seth Stephens-Dawidowitz, "The Data of Hate." *The New York Times.* 13 August 2014: SR4.

19. Posted on 12 July 2014, by TCA, on the thread "Dr. Carl Jung's Diagnosis of Adolf Hitler" https://www.stormfront.org/forum/t1046318/#post12223800, accessed 12 August 2014.

20. The list of MacDonald's cross-referenced web pages:http://www.kevinmacdonald.net/, http://www.kevinmacdonald.net/Blog.htm, http://www.theoccidentalobserver.net/author/kmac/, http://www.csulb.edu/~kmacd/index.html, http://www.vdare.com/users/kevin-macdonald.

MacDonald's columns at the *Occidental Observer* are also automatically linked at the *Daily Stormer* website (http://www.dailystormer.com), and MacDonald regularly links his Facebook page to them (https://www.facebook.com/kevin.macdonald.77770?fref=ts).

21. "Cal. State University Professor Endorses, Fund-Raises for David Duke." Posted 1 July 2012 on "JHate: A Blog About Anti-Semitism." http://jhate.wordpress.com/2012/07/01/cal-state-university-professor-endorses-fund-raises-for-david-duke/, accessed 12 August 2014. Tuchman's article contains a link to the audio recording for MacDonald's interview with Duke (http://mediaarchives.gsradio.net/dduke/030512.mp3). Accessed 26 September 2014.

22. See MacDonald's essay "What Makes Western Culture Unique?," in his collection *Cultural Insurrections: Essays on Western Civilization, Jewish Influence and Anti-Semitism* (Atlanta, GA: The Occidental Press, 2007), 271–99, here 275–78.

23. Andreas Umland, "Kulturhegemoniale Strategien der russischen extremen Rechten. Die Verbindung mit faschistischer Ideologie und metapolitischer Taktik im ‚Neoeurasismus' des Aleksandr Dugin," *Österreichische Zeitschrift für Politikwissenschaft.* 33:4 (2004): 437–54. Umland discusses Dugin's "double strategy" of courting both the extreme right and mainstream Russian conservative audience (442).

24. Aleksandr Dugin, "Evraziiskaia ekonomika," in *Osnovy evraziistva* (Moscow: "Arkto-geia-tsentr," 2002), 626–37, here 636.

25. For an overview of Dugin's academic appointment, see Umland, "Dugin i MGU: pravoradikal'nyi ideolog kak professor vedushschego VUZa Rossii" (Dugin and Moscow State University: A Far-Right Ideologue as a Professor in Russia's Leading Institution of Higher Learning"), *Forum vostochnoevropeiskoi istorii I kul'tury* 1 (2013): 482–87. http://www1.ku-eichstaett.de/ZIMOS/forum/inhaltruss19.html.

26. Marlène Laruelle, *Russian Eurasianism: An Ideology of Empire,* translated by Mischa Gabowitsch (Baltimore, MD: The Johns Hopkins University Press, 2008), 116–17.

27. Dugin, *Giperboreiskaia teoriia* (Moscow: "Arktogeia," 1993), 73, 97–98; *Filosofiia traditsii* (Moscow: "Arktogeia-tsentr" 2002), 195; *Misteriia Evrazii* (Moscow: "Arktogeia," 1996), 125.

28. Dugin, *Russkaia veshch', V. 1* (Arktogeia," 2001), 482.

29. Dugin, *Russkaia veshch', V. 1,* 483.

30. Dugin, *Tseli i zadachi nashei Revoliutsii* (Moscow: Fravarti, 1995), 20.

31. Laruelle, *Russian Eurasianism,* 114.

32. Laruelle, *Russian Eurasianism,* 121–24.

33. http://www.theguardian.com/world/2014/aug/29/putin-ukraine-forces-nazis-arctic. For the Russian text of Putin's statement see: http://www.rg.ru/2014/08/29/arktika-site-anons.html and https://www.youtube.com/watch?v=ksg5x6kD_d8.For the Russian text of Putin's statement see : http://www.rg.ru/2014/08/29/arktika-site-anons.html and https://www.youtube.com/watch?v=ksg5x6kD_d8.

34. Dugin, *Osnovy* geopolitiki (Moscow: "Arktogeia," 1997), 309–10, 311–13.

35. David Remnick, "Letter From Moscow: Watching the Eclipse," *The New Yorker* (11 & 18 August 2914): 52–65, here 62.

36. Laruelle, *Russian Eurasianism,* 109.

37. "Tainoe stanet iavnym. Dugin i Kurekhin. 1995 god. Efir pered vyborami v Gos. Dumu": https://www.youtube.com/watch?v=tqGjyMGhdqU.

38. Quoted in Aleksei Yurchak, "A Parasite From Outer Space: How Sergei Kurekhin Proved that Lenin Was a Mushroom," *Slavic Review* 70:2 (Summer 2011): 307–33, here 330.

39. Dugin, *Tamplery proletariata,* (Moscow: "Arktogeia," 1997), 278.

40. Dugin, *Tamplery proletariata,* 274–75.

41. Aleksandr Dugin, *Chetvertaia politicheskaia teoriia* (Moscow: "Amfora," 2009), 278.

42. https://www.facebook.com/EurasianArtistsAssociation/timeline.

43. http://newsru.com/russia/16jun2014/dugin.html.

44. Dugin, *Filosofiia traditsionalizma,* (Moscow: "Arktogeia," 2004), 11.

REFERENCES

Alterman, Eric. *What Liberal Media? The Truth About Bias and the News.* New York: Basic Books, 2003.

Dugin, Aleksandr. *Chetvertaia politicheskaia teoriia (The Fourth Political Theory).* Moscow: "Amfora." 2009.

Dugin, Aleksandr. "Evraziiskaia ekonomika (Eurasian Economics)." In: *Osnovy evraziistva (The Foundations of Eurasianism).* Moscow: "Arktogeia-tsentr" 2002: 626–37.

Dugin, Aleksandr. *Filosofiia politiki (The Philosophy of Politics).* Moscow: "Arktogeia," 2004.

Dugin, Aleksandr. *Filosofiia traditsionalizma (The Philosophy of Traditionalism).* Moscow: "Arktogeia-tsentr" 2002.

Dugin, Aleksandr. *Giperboreiskaia teoriia. Opyt ariosofskogo issledovaniia (The Hyperborean Theory. An Attempt at an Aryan Study).* Moscow: "Arktogeia," 1993.

Dugin, Aleksandr. *Misterii Evrazii (The Mysteries of Eurasia),* Moscow: "Arktogeia," 1996.

Dugin, Aleksandr. *Osnovy geopolitiki (The Foundations of Geopolitics).* Moscow: "Arktogeia," 1997.

Dugin, Aleksandr. *Russkaia veshch'. Ocherki natsional'noi filosofii. T. 1-2 (The Russian Thing: Sketches of a National Philosophy. Volumes 1-2).* "Arktogeia," 2001.

Dugin, Aleksandr. *Tampliery proletariata. Natsional-bol'shevizm i initsiatsiia (The Knights Templar of the Proletariate. National Bolshevism and the Rite of Initiation)*.Moscow: "Arktogeia," 1997.

Dugin, Aleksandr. *Tseli i zadachi nashei Revoliutsii (The Goals and Tasks of Our Revolution)*. Moscow: Fravarti, 1995.

Finseth, Ian Frederick. "Racist Publishing." Commonweal Institute (25 August 2006). http://www.commonwealinstitute.org/archive/racist-publishing. Accessed 6 October 2014.

Hofstadter, Richard. "The Paranoid Style in American Politics." In *The Paranoid Style in American Politics, and Other Essays.* New York: Alfred A. Knopf, 1965: 3–40.

Laruelle, Marlène. *Russian Eurasianism: An Ideology of Empire.* Translated by Mischa Gabowitsch. Baltimore, MD: The Johns Hopkins University Press, 2008.

Latukhina, Kira. "Prezident: Rossiia prodolzhit ukrepliat' svoi pozitsii v Arktike (The President: Russia Will Continue to Strengthen its Positions in the Arctic)." *Rossiiskaia gazeta* (28 August 2014). http://www.rg.ru/2014/08/29/arktika-site- anons.html. Accessed 1 September 2014.

MacDonald, Kevin. "What Makes Western Culture Unique?" In MacDonald, Kevin. *Cultural Insurrections: Essays on Western Civilization, Jewish Influence and Anti-Semitism.* Atlanta, GA: The Occidental Press, 2007: 271–99.

MacDonald, Kevin. *The Culture of Critique: An Evolutionary Analysis of Jewish Involvement in Twentieth-Century Intellectual and Political Movements.* Westport, CT: Praeger Publishers, 1998; 2nd edition, lst Books Library, 2002.

MacDonald, Kevin. "Parent-Child Play: An Evolutionary Perspective." In MacDonald, Kevin ed. *Parent-Child Play: Descriptions and Implications.* Albany, NY: State University of New York Press, 1993: 113–43.

MacDonald, Kevin. *A People That Shall Dwell Alone: Judaism as a Group Evolutionary Strategy.* Westport, CT: Praeger Publishers, 1994.

MacDonald, Kevin. *Separation and Its Discontents: Toward an Evolutionary Theory of Anti-Semitism.* Westport, CT: Praeger Publishers, 1998; 2nd edition, lst Books Library, 2003.

O'Neill, Robert M. *Free Speech in the College Community.* Bloomington, IN: Indiana University Press, 1997.

"Ot rektora MGU potrebovali uvolit' professor Aleksandra Dugina za prizyvy 'ubivat'' ukraintsev (Students demanded from the Provost of MGU have Professor Aleksandr Dugin fired for his calls to 'kill' Ukrainians.)" 16 July 2014. http://newsru.com/russia/16jun2014/dugin.html. Accessed 1 September 2014.

Remnick, David. "Letter From Moscow: Watching the Eclipse." *The New Yorker* (11 & 18 August 2914): 52–65.

Salter, Frank. "Is MacDonald a Scholar?" *Human Ethology Bulletin* 15:3 (September 2000): 16–22.

Schoenfeld, Eugen. Review of Kevin MacDonald's *A People That Shall Dwell Alone: Judaism as a Group Evolutionary Strategy.* In *Journal for the Scientific Study of Religion* 34:3 (September 1995): 408–10.

Stephens-Davidowitz, Seth. "The Data of Hate." *The New York Times.* 13 August 2014: SR4.

Shulevitz, Judy. "On Fighting Bad Ideas." http://www.slate.com/articles/news_and_politics/culturebox/2000/01/on_fighting_bad_ideas.html. Accessed 26 September 2014.

"Tainoe stanet iavnym. Dugin i Kurekhin. 1995 god. Efir pered vyborami v Gos. Dumu" (That Which is Secret Will Be Revealed. Dugin and Kurekhin. 1995. Broadcast prior to the Parliamentary Election.) https://www.youtube.com/watch?v=tqGjyMGhdqU. Accessed 26 September 2014.

Tuchman, Aryeh. "Cal. State University Professor Endorses, Fund-Raises for David Duke." Posted 1 July 2012 on "JHate: A Blog About Anti-Semitism." http://jhate.wordpress.com/2012/07/01/cal-state-university-professor-endorses-fund-raises-for-david-duke/. Accessed 12 August 2014.

Tucker, William H. *The Funding of Scientific Racism: Wickliffe Draper and the Pioneer Fund.* Urbana, IL: University of Illinois Press, 2002.

Umland, Andreas. "Dugin i MGU: pravoradikal'nyi ideolog kak professor vedushschego VUZa Rossii" (Dugin and Moscow State University: A Far-Right Ideologue as a Professor in Russia's Leading Institution of Higher Learning.") *Forum vostochnoevropeiskoi istorii I kul'tury* 1 (2013): 482–87. http://www1.ku-eichstaett.de/ZIMOS/forum/inhaltruss19.html. Accessed 12 August 2014.

Umland, Andreas. "Kulturhegemoniale Strategien der russischen extremen Rechten. Die Verbindung mit faschistischer Ideologie und metapolitischer Taktik im Neoeurasismus' des Aleksandr Dugin." *Österreichische Zeitschrift für Politikwissenschaft.* 33:4 (2004): 437–54.

"Vladimir Putin: Arktika—Vazhneishii region Rossii." RT (Russian Television) Broadcast, 29 August 2014. https://www.youtube.com/watch?v=ksg5x6kD_d8. Accessed 1 September 2014.

Walker, Shaun, Leonid Ragozin and Matthew Weaver. "Putin Likens Ukraine's Forces to Nazis and Threatens Standoff in the Arctic." *The Guardian* (29 August 2014). http://www. theguardian.com/world/2014/aug/29/putin-ukraine-forces-nazis-arctic. Accessed 1 September 2014.

Yurchak, Aleksei. "A Parasite From Outer Space: How Sergei Kurekhin Proved that Lenin Was a Mushroom." *Slavic Review* 70:2 (Summer 2011): 307–33.

II

Far-Right Politics and Internet Identities

Chapter Five

Identity, Tradition, Sovereignty

The Transnational Linkages of Radical Nationalist
Political Parties in the European Union

Glen M. E. Duerr

This chapter provides an examination of the formal transnational linkages between far-right, extreme political parties inside the European Union (EU), specifically investigating Identity, Tradition, Sovereignty (ITS), a pan-European (far) right-wing political party.[1] Although the political grouping only lasted for ten months, the prospect of a powerful transnational far-right party unsettled many people in Europe. Given that European elections often receive low turnout rates, it often happens that protest parties, including far-right, more extreme parties (characterized in this chapter as radical, nationalist political parties), are quite successful at the European level, and often obtain higher levels of support than in their normal domestic elections.

Cooperating across national borders is a function of working in an integrated Europe, and a driver of the entire European project. Many radical nationalist parties, however, are largely Euroskeptical, or Eurocritical, or they simply want their respective states to leave the organization altogether.[2] For this reason (among others), it is very difficult to operate across the boundaries of the EU and to have success as a political group at the supranational level. It is one thing to promote leaving the EU, as is the case with parties like the United Kingdom Independence Party (UKIP), it is another thing to work with like-minded parties within the structures of the EU.

ITS encountered some of these problems when the group was formed in January of 2007 in the European Parliament (EP). Members of the European Parliament (MEPs) from six member states joined forces to establish the group—an effort that requires significant transnational cooperation on the part of members. ITS subsequently disbanded, in November 2007, in part as a result of difficulties associated with working together on the European level. This chapter starts with an introduction to the background of ITS and an examination of how the party came together. The next section examines, in detail, the members of ITS and the inner workings of the party based, in part, on an interview with ITS Vice-Chairman, Philip Claeys, of Vlaams Belang in Belgium. This investigation then turns to the demise of ITS as a group in the EP noting points of contention between members of the party. Next, the discussion turns to other radical nationalist groupings that have the desire to become an official political party in Europe, but have not been able to create a large enough coalition. These include: the Alliance of European National Movements, the European National Front, and the European Alliance for Freedom. All of these groupings have been plagued by problems similar to ITS. Finally, this chapter also engages in a discussion of how radical nationalist parties are continuing their efforts to gain recognition and perhaps create another grouping the EP in future years. Given the ongoing nature of the Eurozone crisis that has persisted from 2008 through the time of writing (August 2014), this discussion will remain pertinent to the EU project because difficult economic times often contribute to the rise of radical nationalist parties, especially in Europe.

LITERATURE REVIEW

The right in Europe is described in a range of different ways including far-right, radical right, neo-fascist, or extreme. For the purposes of this analysis, however, the term radical nationalist parties will be used because there are many different terms that are often applied, but all of them imply a strongly nationalist sentiment as well as more radical political agendas. After all, there are numerous nationalist parties that seek independence that would not be considered right-wing, far-right, or extreme. These moderate nationalist parties typically belong to a European political group—the European Free Alliance—and coexist with other parties in the EP.[3] The term, "radical nationalist party" has a more succinct definition and refers not only to issues over national sovereignty, but also combines this concept with very harsh anti-immigration policies, and an overt desire to protect national sovereignty through advantaging the majority, titular ethnic group, and discriminating against others.

Many members of radical nationalist parties, in contrast, personally describe themselves as conservatives, right-wing parties, center-right parties, or patriots among other terms. The debate is a difficult one given the success of some parties, which have clearly attracted people in the mainstream of politics, but whose policies are rejected outright by all other parties in the system resulting in a "cordon sanitaire" of their involvement in national parliaments.[4] As a result, despite often-large shares of the vote, these political parties remain at the fringes of the electoral system and are not recognized by the other, more moderate parties in the system.

A basic premise of a political system is that political parties will compete for power and will often move toward the perceived center of the political spectrum as a means to win more votes and to gain power—the Downs Median voter,[5] which notes that parties will compete in a two-party system. The losing party in the system will find new ways to attract voters and will move to the political center to gain more support for the next election. However, political scientist Herbert Kitschelt argues that the Downs Median voter has limited applicability in systems with more than two parties. Kitschelt notes that parties on the political extremes actually have more of an incentive to stay on the extremes so as to maintain a presence in parliament.[6] European Studies scholar Hans-Georg Betz argues that there has been a recent increase in volatility in Western Europe politics since the 1980s, which has led to an increase in political disenfranchisement, which, in turn, has led to an increased number of protest parties—an increased number of radical nationalist political parties.[7] In an earlier publication, Betz (1993) defines the "radical, right-wing populist parties" in very definitive terms and lays out some of their main platforms and ideas:

> Radical right-wing populist parties are radical in their rejection of the established sociocultural and sociopolitical system and their advocacy of individual achievement, a free marketplace, and a drastic reduction of the role of the state. They are right-wing in their rejection of individual and social equality, in their opposition to the social integration of marginalized groups, and in their appeal to xenophobia, if not overt racism. They are populist in their instrumentalization of sentiments of anxiety and disenchantment and their appeal to the common man and his allegedly superior common sense.[8]

Betz (1998) later argues that since the end of the cold war, radical nationalist parties have gained salience in their respective systems; whereas, in the previous era—the end of World War Two to the end of the cold war—no such salience existed.[9] Radical nationalist political parties have become much more popular in recent years, and so it should be expected that eventually a political group would form in the EP.

Given that part of this chapter directly investigates radical nationalist parties in ITS—some of which come from Romania and Bulgaria—Bustikova and Kitschelt's (2009) work is particularly interesting as they argue that the nature of the former communist regime impacts contemporary politics. The authors found that two factors have encouraged the rise of the "radical right": a) highly polarized patrimonial regimes, and b) ethnic heterogeneity, where a titular nationalist is challenged by a small minority population.[10]

Both radical nationalist parties from Eastern Europe that contributed MEPs to ITS were from Romania and Bulgaria—two countries that scored highly on the factors leading to the rise of "radical right" parties.[11]

Sociologist Jens Rydgren's (2009) work is also useful for this project because his work focuses on who actually votes for radical nationalist parties. Rydgren argues that radical nationalists have thrived in Western Europe, but not merely on the basis of reaching out to people with high levels of social isolation—as is typically thought. Rather, the quantitative study finds that social isolation is a marginal factor when factoring in whether a person will vote for the radical right or not. In the article, Rydgren notes: "even humanitarian aid workers and members in human rights organizations are no less likely to vote for the radical right than people who are socially isolated."[12] Tim Bale et al (2010), in another informative contribution to this dialogue, describe the impact of radical nationalist parties on other parties in the system. The authors describe the effects of the growth of the radical nationalist parties on social democratic parties in Western Europe arguing that populist parties on the right appeal to, and often persuade, working class voters to switch allegiances.[13] Finally, political scientist Cas Mudde's (2013) recent work helps to place the impact of radical nationalist parties in proper context. Mudde argues that radical nationalist parties, despite their significant electoral successes, have limited influence on the politics in their respective countries. However, Mudde also notes that these parties have a number of factors in their favor such as the tabloidization of news, as well as the current economic crisis, which could further their progression.[14] Mudde concludes that while radical nationalist parties are merely a nuisance in the politics of Western Europe, these parties are now entrenched in a range of different countries, have learned from past mistakes, and now operate in a climate of the Eurozone crisis, which could lead to better electoral results.[15]

Very few scholars have investigated ITS in a specific and focused way. Two published academic works provide exceptions. Scholars Neil Fligstein, Alina Polyakova, and Wayne Sandholtz provide some information on ITS in their discussion of who is a European and what this means, and how this is affected by the growth of the EU.[16] The authors then examine, in one section of their paper, ITS and how European identity is characterized by a grouping of radical nationalist parties.[17] Political scientist, Nicholas Startin provides perhaps the most comprehensive examination of ITS. Startin notes the ITS came together, in part, over the need to survive as a unified bloc in the EP.[18] Another scholar, George Assenov Vassilev, has also completed extensive academic research into ITS. In a conference paper, the author makes some thought-provoking characterizations as he correctly describes the creation of ITS as "strange bedfellows" noting the agglomeration of secessionist and irredentist parties alongside parties that seek greater ethnic homogeneity.[19]

ARGUMENT, METHODOLOGY, AND THEORY

The common wisdom is that radical nationalist parties often do well in more challenging economic periods, which, in Europe, has been ongoing since the start of the "global" financial crisis in 2008. The popular narrative is that Adolf Hitler, for example, rose to power in Germany in the midst of the Great Depression. While some evidence is found at the national level, this evidence is limited because another Hitler did not arise out of other periods of deep recession in the 1970s or 1980s, for example.

The theory presented in this chapter is that radical nationalist parties will always play a role at the European level, simply given the fact that they will win seats because of Kitschelt's (1995) theory of party behavior in systems with three or more major political parties.[20] However, as argued by Startin (2010), given the nature of transnational cooperation, radical nationalist parties will have significant difficulty working together, which will make it very difficult to create a longstanding political group at the European level.[21] This chapter goes one step further and argues that the nature of nationalism— purporting one's national group above others—makes supranational coopera- tion very challenging because the goal of a radical nationalist party is protec- tion against all outside groups—including the people that they are supposed to cooperate with. This is not to say that it is impossible for another national- ist political bloc to form; rather, finding enough MEPs to pass the minimum threshold whilst maintaining a solid political program and congenial working relationships among members, is challenging.

This chapter also utilizes an in-person interview with Philip Claeys, the Vice-Chairman of ITS as a primary source of information, and is supple- mented by secondary sources in academia and journalism. Research was also conducted utilizing radical nationalist party websites, as well as the news record from the EP. Finally, field research was conducted before, during, and after the 22–25 May 2014 European elections in nine countries across the EU in order to assess the likelihood of another version of ITS rising in the future.[22]

IDENTITY, TRADITION, SOVEREIGNTY

ITS was created in early January 2007 as a grouping of twenty parliamentar- ians (twenty-three by May 2007) from seven EU states—France, Italy, Bel- gium, Austria, the United Kingdom, Romania, and Bulgaria.[23] The latter two countries were particularly controversial because Romania and Bulgaria en- tered the EU at the start of 2007, and the new MEPs from the Parti Romania Mare (Greater Romania Party) and the Ataka (National Union Attack from Bulgaria) allowed ITS to cross the twenty seat threshold needed to create a pan-European party—at that time, twenty members from at least six different countries.[24] ITS was welcomed as a bloc in the EP by former EP President, Josep Borrell of Spain, but former Socialist Group leader, Martin Schultz of Germany, argued that ITS did not fulfill the necessary criteria to join the EP because they did not share a political ideology.[25] However, Chairman of ITS, Bruno Gollnisch of France, responded that all members of ITS signed an agreement outlining their shared principles of which they agree—for this reason, Gollnisch argued that ITS should be allowed to create a transnational political bloc. President Borrell ultimately sided with Gollnisch and allowed the creation of ITS.[26] As a result of this decision, ITS gained membership in the EP and, as a result, received official funding from the EU (although, the political grouping was then shut out of official committee posts as a result of cordon sanitaire). ITS received €1 million (€50,000 for each member) as part of official recognition funded by the EU.[27]

ITS was created by a number of radical nationalist parties from across Europe including: Front National (FN) in France, Vlaams Belang (VB) in Belgium, Freiheitliche Partei Österreichs (FPÖ) in Austria, Greater Romania Party (GRP) in Romania, National Union Attack (NUA) in Bulgaria), Alternativa Sociale (AS), and Movimento Sociale-Fiamma Tricolore (MS-FT) in Italy, as well as one independent candidates from both the United Kingdom and Romania.

At its zenith, ITS consisted of twenty-three members including: seven members from FN, five members from the GRP, three members from VB, two members from two parties in Italy (including Alessandra Mussolini), one member from FPÖ, one member from NUA in Bulgaria, and one independent from both the UK and Romania.[28] The initial twenty members from at least six countries were then able to create ITS in the EP. (Since then, the threshold for entrance as a political grouping in the EP has been increased to twenty-five members from at least seven states.) ITS was created with a Chairman, Bruno Gollnisch from FN in France, and three Vice-Chairmen: Philip Claeys from VB in Belgium; Ashley Mote, an independent member from the UK; and Eugen Mihăescu from GRP in Romania.[29] In some ways, the creation of ITS with a president and three vice-presidents was a political compromise across different states, but, as noted earlier, cooperation between radical nationalist parties tends to be limited.

Initially, twenty MEPs came together to create ITS; but, as noted above, a total of twenty-three members were once part of the group. They included: Bruno Gollnisch, Jean-Marie Le Pen, Carl Lang, Marine Le Pen, Fernand La Rachinel, Jean-Claude Martinez, and Lydia Schenardi from FN in France; Andreas Molzer from FPÖ in Austria; Philip Claeys, Frank Vanhecke, and Koenraad Dillen from VB in Belgium; Alessandra Mussolini (AS) and Luca Romagnoli (MS-FT) from Italy; Daniela Buruiana, Eugen Mihaescu, Viorica Moisuc, Petra Popeanga, and Cristian Stanescu from the GRP in Romania;

Ashley Mote, an independent MEP from Southeast England in the UK—and a former member of the UK Independence Party (UKIP); and Dimitar Stoyanov, from NUA in Bulgaria.[30]

Mircea Cosea—an independent MEP from Romania joined the party in March 2007—the 21st member of ITS. Slavcho Binev and Desislav Chukolov, also from the same party in Bulgaria, joined ITS in May 2007 as the 22nd and 23rd members of the political grouping.[31] For a period of time in 2007, some observers noted that ITS was growing in size and could have become a larger political grouping within the EU.

However, in late 2007, the political unity within the party group started to unravel. When an Italian woman was killed (in Italy) by a Roma man of Romanian descent, Alessandra Mussolini (the granddaughter of Benito Mussolini) made comments about Romania that offended members of the GRP. In effect, Mussolini very negatively stereotyped Roma and Romanians, which was strongly condemned by most people and political parties in Europe. Ultimately, Mussolini's comments were not reconciled, which led to the withdrawal of the MEPs from GRP from the bloc—thus ending the political grouping because it no longer fulfilled the appropriate quota of twenty MEPs from six countries.[32]

POLICY PLATFORMS OF ITS

The present author, on 9 April 2010, visited the EP in Brussels, Belgium to conduct an interview with Philip Claeys, an MEP from VB in Belgium who also served as the Vice-Chairman of ITS during its time as a political group. By way of background, Philip Claeys first ran for a seat in the EP in 1999— in Belgium, parties provide a list of candidates for seats in parliament, and, depending on the percentage of votes received, parties will gain a commensurate number of seats. (In Belgium, the voting system is further complicated as seats are spread between Dutch, French, and German speaking voters.) In 1999, Vlaams Blok[33] won 15 percent of the vote giving the party two seats in the EP, which were held by Frank Vanhecke and Karel Dillen (the Chairman of Vlaams Blok). In 2003, when Dillen fell ill, Claeys replaced him in the EP. Claeys was then elected to the EP in 2004 when Vlaams Blok won 23 percent of the vote giving the party three seats in the EP. Once again Vanhecke took the first seat, Claeys the second, and Koenraad Dillen (the son of Karel Dillen) took the third. Finally, Claeys was re-elected in 2009 when VB won just under 16 percent of the vote, and winning two seats—once again, Vanhecke and Claeys took the seats.

During the interview a range of questions were asked on a broad range of topics. One question was posed to Mr. Claeys on the approach VB takes in

EP elections (which also happen to coincide with regional elections in Belgium). In response, he said:

> I approach them (the voters) with the typical themes of Vlaams Belang. . . . we campaigned on the Turkey issue; we are very much opposed to the possible accession of Turkey to the European Union. Then we campaigned for an EU that would be less bureaucratic, more democratic, and more accountable to voters, and, when we talk about member states, we see Flanders as a member state in the future. So these are the main themes: less bureaucracy, (less) mingling in our national affairs by Europe, no to Turkey, and no to the European immigration programme. So these were the big themes that we developed as part of our election campaign.

Most political parties have a set of defined (and evolving) policy platforms, but, given the nature of transnational politics in the EP, this can be more difficult. Therefore, the ITS grouping actually had common values rather than a unified set of political platforms. ITS MEP Andreas Molzer noted that ITS was put together with "minimal consensus" as a means of surviving together as a group.[34]

Given this "minimal consensus," it makes it difficult to define an explicit set of policies, but what can be stated is that most radical nationalist parties within ITS are nationalist and oppose immigration—and often migration within specific parts of the EU. Additionally, most parties also opposed the enlargement of the EU into Eastern Europe[35] as well as Turkey—as noted earlier by Mr. Claeys. Both Philip Claeys and Koen Dillen from VB wrote a book outlining their major objections to Turkey's accession bid.[36] According to research conducted by journalist, Alix Kroger, ITS stands for "the recognition of national interests," a "commitment to Christian values and the traditions of European civilization," and "opposition to unitary, bureaucratic European super state."[37] In reality, ITS has very stringent nationalist policies and some of the parties within the bloc have previously supported widespread deportations. Part of the irony of creating ITS is, for example, that the nationalism of FPÖ of Austria actually caused MEP Molzer to vote against the accession of Romania and Bulgaria into the EU.[38] This is another example of the irony of grouping nationalist parties together in a supranational grouping. ITS ignores the Christian admonitions to love the poor and destitute—even though many sub-Saharan African immigrants are very committed Christians. Moreover, many Christians across Europe and the world, would not approve of this association with ITS. The traditions of European civilization need to be specified more clearly, as does opposition to a unitary, bureaucratic European super state, because these arguments remain nebulous and ill defined.

PROBLEMS WITH FORMAL TRANSNATIONAL LINKAGES

ITS was not the first European party to encompass radical nationalist political parties. Jean-Marie Le Pen of FN, for example, led the Group of the European Right (GER) from 1984 to 1989 and then the Technical Group of the European Right (TGER) from 1989 to 1994.[39] The GER was made up of members from Italy's Italian Social Movement, from Germany's Die Republikaner, Greece's Greek National Political Union, and France's FN. (Briefly, a MEP from Northern Ireland's Ulster Unionist Party also sat with the GER.) GER ultimately disbanded over disagreements between the German and Italian MEPs over the status of South Tyrol—a German speaking community with a high degree of autonomy in northern Italy. In essence, transnational cooperation was very difficult for radical nationalists over the issue of opposing nationalisms.

The TGER was similarly made up of MEPs from France's FN, but was also joined by members from Germany's Republikaner party as well as from Belgium's Vlaams Blok party (now VB). The group collapsed after the 1994 elections when the Republikaner party failed to obtain the necessary 5 percent threshold to wins seats in parliament in Germany. This time, domestic politics in Germany disabled radical nationalist transnational cooperation.

Since 1994, the last time a radical nationalist group existed in the EP, the EU went through numerous changes including several rounds of enlargement. In 1995, Austria, Finland, and Sweden joined; in 2004, ten states from Central and Eastern Europe (Poland, Hungary, Czech Republic, Slovakia, Slovenia, Latvia, Lithuania, and Estonia) as well as two small states (Malta and Cyprus) from the Mediterranean; in 2007, Romania and Bulgaria; in July 2013, Croatia. These recent enlargements have changed the EU dramatically, and have also changed the nature of transnational cooperation—in essence the European project encompassing Western and Eastern Europe provides an institutional blockage against radical nationalist groups.

ITS dissolved in a manner reminiscent of the downfall of GER. Ultimately, ITS formally dissolved in November 2007 when Daniela Buriana and Cristian Stanescu from GRP both resigned from the party bloc, leaving only eighteen members of the political group.[40] The other three members of GRP all resigned earlier in the week, meaning that ITS could no longer sustain the necessary twenty members to maintain a group in the EP. Obviously, since the Romanian contingent in ITS was the second largest national grouping in ITS, the survival of the political group became infeasible.[41]

The withdrawal of the Romanian contingent from ITS came, as noted earlier, when Alessandra Mussolini of Italy made very inflammatory statements about Romanians after the murder of an Italian by a Romanian of Roma descent.[42] All five Romanian MEPs took exception to Mussolini's comments and left ITS to become independent members of the EP.

One of the major cleavages that contributed to the dissolution of ITS was due to the nature of the Schengen zone and EU level mobility rights for citizens from member states within the organization (and other states, like Switzerland that have also signed on). When a new country enters the EU, like Romania and Bulgaria did in 2007, every other country in the Schengen zone can impose up to a seven-year restriction on immigration into their country—this is known as the 2+3+2 formula. Countries can restrict immigration for two, five, or seven years. Since there is a significant economic asymmetry between most countries in Western Europe and countries in Eastern Europe (although some dynamic economies in countries like Slovenia and the Czech Republic are changing this distinction) a lot of migration flows from east to west, especially amongst young people born in Eastern Europe. Some Eastern Europeans go to work in blue-collar professions like construction or manufacturing, but many other well-educated Eastern Europeans go into information technology, law, engineering, and medicine. In some cases, a nationalist backlash develops in Western Europe, which, in the case of ITS, directly caused tension between MEPs. Opposing nationalism then increased tensions within the bloc, which then led to the easy dissolution of ITS over an argument between Italian and Romanian MEPs.

The brief history of ITS indicates the problematic nature of creating a radical nationalist political grouping and then having the various MEPs work with one another. In essence, national protection, opposition to immigration, and xenophobia do not lend themselves easily to transnational cooperation—in many respects these policies run counter to the European integration project. This is not to say that cooperation is impossible because the creation of ITS and several other nationalist party blocs has happened historically. Sharing similar political ideological beliefs is enough to create a political group; however, at the European level, discipline is required to allow MEPs to work together across national lines.

As Startin noted, "The very concept of political cooperation on a transnational basis is a troublesome one for RRPs (Radical Right Parties) and attempts to organize such cooperation have been mostly short-lived and unproductive."[43] One of the main reasons for this limited cooperation is the issue of immigration. Most parties associated with ITS have nationalist and anti-immigration platforms. This tends to cause tension with other states even if the goals are similar—reduce or eliminate immigration. Journalist, Matthew Tempest of the *Guardian* newspaper in the UK observed: "Ironically, given the hostility of the west European far right to expansion, immigration and Eastern Europe, it is Romania's entry that has made the caucus possible."[44] So, in order for ITS to function, the uneasy relationship was built between parties in Western Europe that typically oppose immigration from Eastern Europe, and nationalist parties from Eastern Europe itself.

Since the downturn of the global economy in late 2008 to the present in 2014, which affected economic output and unemployment in North America and Europe particularly hard, it is perhaps surprising that no other transnational political bloc (with a permanent position in the EP) has been formed to replace ITS. Even with the emergence of other radical nationalist political parties such as Golden Dawn in Greece, or, for example, FN's electoral performance in France gaining almost 18 percent of the vote in the 2012 Presidential election, there have been limits. At the 2014 European parliamentary election, however, one of the major stories was the success of FN in France, by not only winning the popular vote, but winning twenty-four of France's seventy-four EP seats. FPÖ of Austria won four seats, The Dutch Freedom Party (PVV) won four seats, Jobbik of Hungary won three seats, Golden Dawn of Greece won three seats, and VB of Belgium won one seat, so radical nationalist parties in some countries have seen a rise in support.

Only one new EP group was formed in the aftermath of the 2014 elections, the Europe of Freedom and Direct Democracy (EFDD) party. EFDD is a highly Euroskeptical political party, which is drawn largely from members of the UK Independence Party (UKIP) and comedian turned political activist, Beppe Grillo's Five Star Movement from Italy. The party was initially made up of 49 members from eight countries (the party now has 47 members from seven countries after the defection of one Latvian and one UKIP member), but is dominated by 23 UKIP members and 17 Five Star Movement members. Given the reliance on two parties, the status of the EFDD in the EP is tenuous because one more defection will dissolve the party. It is not defined here as a radical nationalist party (although some of the parties with the EP have radical, nationalist tendencies), but interestingly, the same conclusions apply to this more Euroskeptical party.

As already noted, one of the major points of contention has been the relationship between parties in Western Europe and parties in Eastern Europe. But, it seems strange that a statement made toward the GRP was, in part, a major catalyst for the dissolution of ITS, which still have not been resolved because a new political grouping could have been formed. Perhaps the biggest issue amongst members of ITS was due in part to the historic and geographic divide between Western and Eastern Europe. The statements made by an Italian toward Romanians was, in essence, the reason for the dissolution of ITS. In order for parties in Western Europe to continue appealing to their constituencies, the platforms of opposition to immigration is important; however, discouraging immigration from Eastern Europe was ultimately seen as offensive by members of the GRP. Thus, a paradox exists amongst the EP's radical nationalist members—the need for mutual support to create a party bloc, but the mutual antagonism that comes with limiting immigration into their respective states. Often members from VB or FN will welcome immigration from neighboring, Western European states, but discourage immigration from anywhere else in the world. In essence, opposing nationalisms makes cooperation extremely difficult.

The brief history of ITS exposes several different trends, indicative of the formation and dissolution of a grouping of radical nationalist parties at the transnational level. On the one hand, the formation of ITS shows that support for radical nationalist parties is significant enough across Europe for the institutionalization of this political position in the EP. On the other hand, however, the dissolution of ITS demonstrates that radical nationalist political parties are unable to resolve differences, or to maintain a unified presence in the EP.[45]

THREE NASCENT RADICAL NATIONALIST BLOCS

Since the collapse of ITS, three nascent political groupings for radical nationalist political parties have been formed—the Alliance of European National Movements (AENM), the European National Front (ENF), and the European Alliance for Freedom (EAF). These blocs are described as nascent because none have passed the necessary seat or country threshold required to enter the EP. In essence, radical nationalist parties are divided on their support for specific issues (such as immigration), as well as their ability to work with one another, which decreases their ability to form a political group in the EP.

The AENM was founded in 2009 and once consisted of several parties including: the British National Party (BNP) from the UK, FN from France, and Jobbik from Hungary.[46] The AENM was later joined by Front National from Belgium, NUA from Bulgaria, Fiamma Tricolore of Italy, Portugal's Partido Nacional Renovado, Spain's Movimento Social Republicano, and Ukraine's Svoboda (Ukraine is not presently a member of the EU).[47] However, several of these parties—most notably FN—have withdrawn from the group.

The AEMN website is still running and presents contemporary stories; although, as of the time of writing (August 2014), Bruno Gollnisch of FN was still listed as president on the English language site (FN has switched allegiance to the EAF discussed below) and Nick Griffin of the BNP was listed as the Vice President.[48] Officially, AEMN has only three members in the EP—all three from Jobbik—not enough to create a formal EP bloc. (Prior to the 2014 elections, AEMN also had two MEPs from the BNP in the UK.)

The second radical nationalist grouping is the ENF, which was founded in October 2004. Six parties are allied with ENF: Golden Dawn of Greece, National Democratic Party of Germany, New Force of Italy, National Revival of Poland, New Right of Romania, and Falange of Spain, but the bloc only has struggled to win any seats in the EP. (From 2009-2014, Roberto Fiore of the New Force in Italy was the only MEP.) So far, the group has had very little success and this does not look likely to change in the near future. Currently, ENF has four MEPs: three from Golden Dawn, and one from the National Democratic Party.

The EAF is the third grouping of radical nationalist parties, and was founded in 2010. EAF is made up of some prominent members of ITS since Franz Obermayer of FPÖ is the current president of the nascent group, and Marine Le Pen of FN and Philip Claeys of VB are the two Vice-presidents. According to the website, the political grouping also has members from the Netherlands, Italy, and Malta (as well as former members from Hungary, Lithuania, Germany, Sweden, and the UK).[49] After the 2014 European parliamentary elections, the party has thirty-three MEPs (twenty-four from FN, four from FPÖ, four from PVV, and one from VB) from four countries, which satisfies the criterion for the number of MEPs (at least twenty-five), but not from enough member states (now seven of twenty-eight).

As noted at the outset of this chapter, the hypothesis noted the ability for nationalist parties to elect members to the EP with little difficulty. Even fringe parties can win seats, especially in countries using a proportional representation system—this process is facilitated at the European level given very low levels of voter turnout.

From a logical standpoint, it would make sense that all nationalist parties would work together. However, given a level of animosity toward people in different states, and a desire to decrease migration and immigration, radical nationalist MEPs have been unable to form a viable bloc—and will struggle to do so in the future.

CONCLUSION

The brief history of ITS exposes a significant trend that hinders the emergence of a grouping of radical nationalist parties at the transnational level. On the one hand, the formation of ITS shows that support for nationalist parties is significant enough across Europe for the institutionalization of this political position in the EP. On the other hand, however, the dissolution of ITS shows that radical nationalist political parties are not able to resolve differences, nor keep a unified presence in the EP because of opposing nationalisms.

Although ITS has disbanded, it is important for policymakers within the EU to be wary of the development of another radical nationalist political bloc. Even though ITS failed, it is possible that another party will rise, especially if support for FN, VB, FPÖ, and others increases as a result of the recession—for some countries, a double dip recession—in Europe. Moreover, since EP elections usually only see low levels of turnout, it is possible that another bloc will rise and gain greater prominence within the EU, potentially threatening the larger integration project. However, even in the aftermath of the 2014 European parliamentary elections where some radical nationalist political parties were very successful, there has been no emergence of another, more radical political bloc, or with challenges from Euroskeptic states like the UK.

The existence of the AENM, the ENF, and the EAF is still a cause for some concern in the EP. Nonetheless, the same problems that confronted ITS are similarly faced by these three nascent groupings. All three groupings face significant challenges to creating a recognized bloc within the EP as only a handful of MEPs sit in ENF and EAF, and the AENM has not yet fulfilled the criteria to create a viable EP group. Furthermore, since radical nationalist parties are divided into three different groupings, it will be very difficult to gain official recognition in the EP—in essence, as hypothesized, the nature of radical nationalism makes transnational cooperation very difficult, if not impossible, because opposing nationalisms ultimately lead to conflict.

NOTES

1. Although ITS is widely known amongst people interested in the European Union, this grouping is not widely known. Two published academic works have specifically examined this political grouping in the EP: Neil Fligstein, Alina Polyakova, and Wayne Sandholtz, "European Integration, Nationalism and European Identity," *JCMS: Journal of Common Market Studies* 50, no. 1 (2012): 106–22; Nicholas Startin, "Where to for the Radical Right in the European Parliament? The Rise and Fall of Transnational Political Cooperation," *Perspectives on European Politics and Society*, 11, no. 4 (2010): 429–49.

2. The terms Eurocritical and Euroskeptical reflect a resentment of overt attempts by Europe to negate national sovereignty, but still implies support for free trade within the European Union.

3. Devashree Gupta, "Nationalism across Borders: Transnational Nationalist Advocacy in the European Union," *Comparative European Politics* 6, no.1 (2008): 61–80.

4. Cordon sanitaire effectively means that the party has been boycotted by all other parties—and sometimes the media. This means that they cannot work in a coalition government, or serve in cabinet positions.

5. Anthony Downs, "An Economic Theory of Political Action in a Democracy," *The Journal of Political Economy*, 65, no. 2 (1957): 135–50.

6. Herbert Kitschelt, *The Radical Right in Western Europe: A Comparative Analysis*. (Ann Arbor, MI: University of Michigan Press, 1995).

7. Hans-Georg Betz, *Radical Right-Wing Populism in Europe* (New York: St. Martin's Press, 1994), 2.

8. Hans-Georg Betz, "The New Politics of Resentment: Radical Right-Wing Populist Parties in Western Europe," *Comparative Politics* 25, No. 4 (1993): 413–27.

9. Hans-Georg Betz. "Introduction" in Betz, Hans-Georg and Stefan Immerfall, eds. *The New Politics of the Right: Neo-Populist Parties and Movements in Established Democracies* (Basingstoke, UK: MacMillan Press, 1998), 1.

10. Lenka Bustikova and Herbert Kitschelt, "The Radical Right in Post-Communist Europe: Comparative Perspectives on Legacies and Party Competition," *Communist and Post-Communist Studies* 42 (2009): 459–83.

11. Bustikova and Kitschelt, "The radical right in post-communist Europe," 473.

12. Jens Rydgren, "Social Isolation? Social Capital and Radical Right-wing voting in Western Europe," *Journal of Civil Society*, 5, no. 2 (2009): 129–50.

13. Tim Bale et al., "If You Can't Beat Them, Join Them? Explaining Social Democratic Responses to the Challenge from the Populist Radical Right in Western Europe," *Political Studies* 58 (2010): 410–26.

14. Cas Mudde, "Three decades of populist radical right parties in Western Europe: So what?" *European Journal of Political Research*, 52 (2013): 1–19.

15. Mudde, "Three Decades of populist radical right parties in Western Europe," 14–15.

16. Fligstein et al., "European Integration, Nationalism, and National Identity"

17. Fligstein et al., "European Integration, Nationalism, and National Identity," 19.

18. Startin, "Where to for the Radical Right in the European Parliament?" 440.

19. George Assenov Vassilev, "*Strange Bedfellows: Instrumental Opportunism in the Far-Right 'Identity, Tradition and Sovereignty' European Parliament Group*" (presentation, Annual Convention of the Midwest Political Science Association, Chicago, IL, April 3–6, 2008).

20. Herbert Kitschelt, *The Radical Right in Western Europe: A Comparative Analysis* (Ann Arbor, MI: University of Michigan Press, 1995).

21. Startin, "Where to for the Radical Right in the European Parliament?" 429.

22. The present author conducted field research on the European Parliament elections in Belgium, the Netherlands, Luxembourg, Germany, Austria, Slovakia, Hungary, the United Kingdom, and Spain, in May and June 2014.

23. Glen Duerr. "Domestic Ethnic Nationalism and Regional European Transnationalism: A Confluence of Impediments Opposing Turkey's EU Accession Bid" (presentation, Annual Convention of the International Studies Association, San Francisco, CA, 3–6 April, 2013), 24.

24. "Opening of the January Plenary Session - Welcome of Bulgarian and Romanian MEPs / Formation of a new political group," *European Parliament*, last modified, 4 December 2007, http://www.europarl.europa.eu/sides/getDoc.do?language=en&type=IM-PRESS&reference= 20070112IPR01903.

25. "Opening of the January Plenary Session - Welcome of Bulgarian and Romanian MEPs / Formation of a new political group."

26. "Opening of the January Plenary Session - Welcome of Bulgarian and Romanian MEPs / Formation of a new political group."

27. "Far-Right Wing Group Sidelined in European Parliament," *Deutsche Welle (dw.de)*, last modified, 2 February 2007, http://www.dw.de/far-right-wing-group-sidelined-in-european-parliament/a-2335201-1.

28. "Who's who in EU's new Far-Right Group," *BBCNews.com*, last modified, 12 January 2007, http://news.bbc.co.uk/2/hi/europe/6249513.stm.

29. "Ouverture de la Séance," *Parlement européen*, last modified, 4 December 2007, http://www.europarl.europa.eu/sides/getDoc.do?pubRef=-//EP//TEXT+IM-PRESS+20070112IPR01 903+0+DOC+XML+V0//FR.

30. Startin, "Where to for the Radical Right in the European Parliament?" 434.

31. Startin, "Where to for the Radical Right in the European Parliament?" 434.

32. Startin, "Where to for the Radical Right in the European Parliament?" 434.

33. Vlaams Blok is the precursor to Vlaams Belang. After being convicted by a Belgian court of inciting racism in 2004, Vlaams Blok was forced to disband. VB was then created as a new party, and largely maintains the same policy platforms.

34. Honor Mahoney, "Plans for European Far-Right Group Intensify," *EUObserver.com*, last modified, 8 January 2007, http://euobserver.com/political/23196.

35. Alix Kroger, "EU's Surprise Far-Right Coalition," BBCNews.com, last modified, 15 January 2007, http://news.bbc.co.uk/2/hi/europe/6254945.stm.

36. Philip Claeys, and Koen Dillen, *Turkey in the EU: A Bridge too far*, (Brussels: Egmont Publishing, 2008).

37. Kroger, "EU's Surprise Far-Right Coalition."

38. Ian Traynor, "Romania's First Gift to the European Union – A Caucus of Neo-Fascists and Holocaust Deniers," *Guardian*, last modified 7 January 2007, http://www.guardian.co.uk/politics/2007/jan/08/uk.eu/print.

39. "Who's who in EU's new Far-Right Group," *BBCNews.com*, last modified, 12 January 2007, http://news.bbc.co.uk/2/hi/europe/6249513.stm.

40. "End of the Identity, Tradition and Sovereignty Political Group as Romanian MEPs leave," *European Parliament*, last modified, 17 December 2007, http://www.europarl.europa.eu/sides/getDoc.do?language=en&type=IM-PRESS&reference=20071109BRI12778&secondRef=ITEM-003-en.

41. Vassilev, "Strange Bedfellows: Instrumental Opportunism in the Far-Right 'Identity, Tradition and Sovereignty' European Parliament Group," 4.

42. Honor Mahoney, "Far-Right European Parliament Group on Verge of Collapse," *EUObserver.com*, last modified, 8 November 2007, http://euobserver.com/political/25115.

43. Startin, "Where to for the Radical Right in the European Parliament?" 432.

44. Matthew Tempest, "British MEP Joins Far-Right Group," last modified, 11 January 2007, http://www.guardian.co.uk/world/2007/jan/11/eu.politics/print.

45. Duerr, "Domestic Ethnic Nationalism and Regional European Transnationalism," 24–25.

46. "BNP in Alliance with Nationalists," *BBCNews.com*, last modified, 12 November 2009, http://news.bbc.co.uk/2/hi/europe/8356284.stm.

47. "Alliance of European National Movements Expands to 9 Parties," BNP, last modified, no date given, http://www.bnp.org.uk/news/alliance-european-national-movements-expands-9-parties.

48. "Members," *AEMN.eu*, last modified, 14 June 2013, http://aemn.eu/members/.

49. "Board," European Alliance for Freedom (euralfree.org), last modified 14 June 2013, http://www.eurallfree.org/?q=node/66).

REFERENCES

"Alliance of European National Movements Expands to 9 Parties." *BNP*. Last modified unknown. http://www.bnp.org.uk/news/alliance-european-national-movements-expands-9-parties.

Bale, Tim et al., "If You Can't Beat Them, Join Them? Explaining Social Democratic Responses to the Challenge from the Populist Radical Right in Western Europe." *Political Studies* 58 (2010): 410–26.

Betz, Hans-Georg. "The New Politics of Resentment: Radical Right-Wing Populist Parties in Western Europe." *Comparative Politics* 25, No. 4 (1993): 413–27.

Betz, Hans-Georg. *Radical Right-Wing Populism in Europe*. New York: St. Martin's Press, 1994.

Betz, Hans-Georg. "Introduction." In *The New Politics of the Right: Neo-Populist Parties and Movements in Established Democracies*. Edited by Hans-Georg Betz and Stefan Immerfall. Basingstoke, UK: MacMillan Press, 1998.

"Board." *European Alliance for Freedom (euralfree.org)*. Last modified 14 June 2013. http://www.eurallfree.org/?q=node/66.

"BNP in alliance with nationalists." *BBCNews.com*. Last modified 12 November 2009. http://news.bbc.co.uk/2/hi/europe/8356284.stm.

Bustikova, Lenka, and Herbert Kitschelt. "The radical right in post-communist Europe: Comparative perspectives on legacies and party competition." *Communist and Post-Communist Studies* 42 (2009): 459–83.

Claeys, Philip, and Koen Dillen. *Turkey in the EU: A Bridge too far*. Brussels: Egmont Publishing, 2008.

Deutsche Welle. 2007. "Far-Right Wing Group Sidelined in European Parliament." Deutsche Welle (dw.de). Last modified 2 February 2007. http://www.dw.de/far-right-wing-group-sidelined-in-european-parliament/a-2335201-1.

Downs, Anthony. "An Economic Theory of Political Action in a Democracy." *The Journal of Political Economy*. 65, no. 2 (1957): 135–50.

Duerr, Glen. "Domestic Ethnic Nationalism and Regional European Transnationalism: A Confluence of Impediments Opposing Turkey's EU Accession Bid" (presentation, Annual Convention of the International Studies Association, San Francisco, CA, April 3-6, 2013).

European Parliament. 2007. "End of the Identity, Tradition and Sovereignty political group as Romanian MEPs leave." *European Parliament.* Last modified 17 December 2007. http://www.europarl.europa.eu/sides/getDoc.do?language=en&type=IM-PRESS&reference=2007 1109BRI12778&secondRef=ITEM-003-en.

Fligstein, Neil, Alina Polyakova, and Wayne Sandholtz. "European Integration, Nationalism and European Identity." *JCMS: Journal of Common Market Studies* 50, no. 1 (2012): 106-122.

Gupta, Devashree. "Nationalism across borders: transnational nationalist advocacy in the European Union." *Comparative European Politics* 6, no.1 (2008): 61–80.

Kitschelt, Herbert. *The Radical Right in Western Europe: A Comparative Analysis.* Ann Arbor, MI: University of Michigan Press, 1995.

Kroger, Alix. "EU's surprise far-right coalition." *BBCNews.com.* Last modified 15 January 2007. http://news.bbc.co.uk/2/hi/europe/6254945.stm.

Mahoney, Honor. "Plans for European far-right group intensify." *EUObserver.com.* Last modified 8 January 2007. http://euobserver.com/political/23196.

Mahoney, Honor. "Far-right European parliament group on verge of collapse." *EUObserver.com.* Last modified 8 November 2007. http://euobserver.com/political/25115.

"Members." *AEMN.eu.* Last modified June 14, 2013. http://aemn.eu/members/.

Mudde, Cas. "Three decades of populist radical right parties in Western Europe: So what?" *European Journal of Political Research*, 52 (2013): 1–19.

"Opening of the January plenary session - Welcome of Bulgarian and Romanian MEPs / Formation of a new political group." *European Parliament.* Last modified 4 December 2007. http://www.europarl.europa.eu/sides/getDoc.do?language=en&type=IM-PRESS&reference=20070112IPR01903.

"Ouverture de la séance." *Parlement européen.* Last modified 4 December 2007, http://www.europarl.europa.eu/sides/getDoc.do?pubRef=-//EP//TEXT+IM-PRESS+20070112IPR01903+0+DOC+XML+V0//FR.

Rydgren, Jens. "Social Isolation? Social Capital and Radical Right-wing Voting in Western Europe." *Journal of Civil Society* 5, no. 2 (2009): 129–50.

Startin, Nicholas. "Where to for the radical right in the European parliament? The rise and fall of transnational political cooperation." *Perspectives on European Politics and Society* 11, no. 4 (2010): 429–49.

Tempest, Matthew. "British MEP joins far-right group." *Guardian.co.uk.* Last modified 11 January 2007. http://www.guardian.co.uk/world/2007/jan/11/eu.politics/print.

Traynor, Ian. "Romania's first gift to the European Union - a caucus of neo-fascists and Holocaust deniers." *Guardian.* Last modified 7 January 2007. http://www.guardian.co.uk/politics/2007/jan/08/uk.eu/print.

Vassilev, George Assenov. "Strange Bedfellows: Instrumental Opportunism in the Far-Right 'Identity, Tradition and Sovereignty' European Parliament Group" (presentation, Annual Convention of the Midwest Political Science Association, Chicago, IL, April 3–6, 2008).

"Who's who in EU's new far-right group." *BBCNews.com.* Last modified 12 January 2007. http://news.bbc.co.uk/2/hi/europe/6249513.stm.

Chapter Six

Manipulating the Media

The German New Right's Virtual and Violent Identities

Helga Druxes

Global use of the Internet and new social media has undeniably changed political processes and the way individuals participate in them. Their low cost, technical sophistication, and ease of use provide a broad spectrum of political groups with tools to choreograph their public presence and appeal to potential supporters both nationally and transnationally.[1] Even though the Internet as a global medium is not a space beyond the reach of the law, efforts to legislate politically extreme content are usually aimed at protecting minors, and site shutdowns may be circumvented by moving to providers in countries with less restrictive hate speech laws. On steadily growing Web 2.0 platforms, users generate a massive amount of new content, which providers find hard to police, unless the community of users itself becomes involved in indexing problematic content. Moreover, young users fluidly migrate away from recently trendy platforms to new ones, for example, from MySpace to Facebook, or supplement their virtual profiles with Snapchat, a chat medium that, unlike its competitors, is not archived.

But just as easily as new social media can aid the spread of new forms of direct democracy, these media can also become tools for militant groups who wish to recruit new members and organize anti-democratic activities. The sheer volume of new video data that is being uploaded daily on social media platforms such as YouTube makes it difficult to proactively scan for illegal content. YouTube states for instance that each minute more than ten hours of new video material are uploaded.[2] The far right uses the Internet as a means of inserting itself into the public space opened up for "de-solidarization" by the economic crisis, the effects of globalization on the labor market, and anti-immigration politics. Within this space, the right claims a normalized, political agency. Increasingly, far right bloggers exhort followers to violent action across a transnational field of operations as a form of "legitimate" warfare against states they believe to be corrupt.

In some cases, neo-Nazi perpetrators even blur the boundaries between their online identity as video gamers and first-person-shooters. For example, in November 2011, a former member of "Free Net," a neo-Nazi blog, leaked more than 1,300 posts dating back to 2009 from a password-protected area of the site. In some of these messages, members of a radical group misleadingly called "Young National Democrats" invite others to participate in violence against the police and discuss strategies for taking over the National Democratic Party (NPD, the established national-socialist party) as its unofficial elite and most militant arm.[3] In July and August 2011, the British think tank Demos used Facebook advertisements to reach supporters of the far right in eleven countries and gathered over 10,000 questionnaire responses, which reveal "a spread of hardline nationalist sentiment among the young, mainly men."[4] A more recent symbolic event from 21 May 2013, is the public suicide of French neo-Nazi Dominique Venner at the altar of Notre Dame Cathedral, which, he blogged, was intended as a call to arms against "overpopulation" of France by Islamic immigrants and the recent legalization of gay marriage. In his Internet manifesto, he states: "[. . .] there need to be new gestures, spectacular and symbolic, to reawaken the memory of our origins. We are entering a time where words should be authenticated by actions."[5] With little delay, Marine Le Pen, the leader of the far-right Front National, quickly echoed by German far-right demagogue Götz Kubitschek, honored Venner for his career as a far-right historian and applauded his lone-wolf actionist tactics. Far-right identity politics à la Venner and other intellectuals of the international movement, *pace* Heidegger, are identitarian and nostalgic; they call for agonistic struggle: "In deciding oneself, in truly willing one's destiny, one becomes the victor over nothingness. There is no escape from this demand, because we have only this life where it is up to us to be fully ourselves or to be nothing."[6] However, such radical views do not appeal to all on the right spectrum. Even so, single extremist views can have a disproportionate spread on the net, as it is so easy to create and toggle rapidly between different sites, and duplicate a single opinion under a large number of aliases.

FAR-RIGHT VIEWS MOVE INTO THE MAINSTREAM

The new right has become adept at promoting a more acceptable form of casual racism via nationalist language couched in terms more acceptable to the mainstream. In Germany, this new trend became apparent in the aftermath of the Thilo Sarrazin controversy, which I discuss below. A percentage of the German public opposed Sarrazin's blatant eugenics, while others felt emboldened in their own free-floating racist nationalism, given that even a member of the Social Democratic Party (SPD) was uttering anti-Islamic and anti-immigrant views and gleaning lots of media attention. Since the SPD, traditionally a left liberal home for immigrant voters and the working class, did not dare expel him for these offensive polemics, such lack of opposition further seemed to legitimate his views. He is not an isolated case—formerly *bona fide* conservative German journalists like Udo Ulfkotte and Eva Herman, who now promote right populist esoteric views, also managed to mainstream these by using a daily right conservative web-based news show and a right-wing publisher, who also advertises in mainstream popular consumer magazines like *ADAC Motorwelt*.[7] In 2007, Herman was fired from her job as a channel one (ARD) TV-newscaster after she intervened in the German media debate about the low birth rate by praising Hitler's support payments for mothers and Nazi labor policies. Her book *Das Eva-Prinzip: Für eine neue Weiblichkeit* (The Eva-Principle: for a New Femininity, 2006) argued for a return to traditional gender roles and re-mythologized motherhood, attempting to interest middle-class German women once more in staying home and having babies. Ulfkotte, once a journalist for Germany's leading conservative newspaper, *Frankfurter Allgemeine Zeitung*, became a conspiracy theorist after the 9/11 attacks, publishing an incendiary tract, *The War In Our Cities - How Radical Islamists Undermine Germany* (2003). Like TV-personality Herrman, he lost his mainstream media job and established a publishing presence on the conservative populist fringe, warning against foreign radicals overwhelming Germany.

Here I want to emphasize the ubiquity of online activities on the far right—a single individual can toggle between multiple, simultaneous roles as online editor, local web host, and transnational conduit, and may have illegal real-life collaborations. For example, Thomas R. is known to have supplied the first safe house to the NSU after they went underground. Of course, youth online behavior does not necessarily translate into illegal public action, but far-right websites are adept at creating an attractive experiential life-world with opportunities for political participation via consumer products (far-right music purchases, or free CDs, regional concert advertisements, T-shirts, martial arts gear, and other lifestyle icons).[8] Most spectacularly, a group calling itself National Socialist Underground (NSU) was revealed in November 2011 to have committed at least nine murders of Turkish and Greek small business owners; they killed a policewoman and had attacked public sites with explosives. Members of this group, though small in number, moved around Germany unmonitored since at least before 1998, when their attempts at bomb making and weapons stockpiling came to the attention of law enforcement. At that time, they evaded arrest. The NSU made a DVD, which they mailed out to supporters. In it they boasted of their crimes and announced a sequel, "NSU II." As in the case of Anders Bering Breivik in Norway (July 2011), perpetrators of right-wing terrorism often conceive of their attacks as akin to making a film to advertise their actionism to potential emulators, or playing video games. Their hundreds of hours spent online harvesting email addresses on Facebook, playing *World of Warcraft*, and designing either a voluminous manifesto (Breivik) or a documentary collage of their crimes (NSU) created a simulacrum of effective offline political outreach, which then emboldened them to take further terrorist action.

Another use of the Internet involves forging connections across continents. The ongoing Munich trial of surviving NSU-member Beate Zschäpe uncovered collaborative transnational linkages between the American Ku Klux Klan and five police officials in the Baden-Württemberg region who, in 2001, were invited to join the "European White Knights of Ku Klux Klan." Two of these policemen, who were disciplined in 2005, continued on the force where they became colleagues of officer Michèle Kiesewetter, the one East German victim of the NSU, who was killed in 2007.[9] They were recruited by Achim S., the lead singer for the racist Swabian rock group *Celtic Moon*, who had traveled to Mississippi in fall 2000 to be inducted and named "Grand Dragon" of the new German branch of the U.S. Aryan hate group. Its goal was to "vouchsafe the future of the white European."[10] There are also East-West linkages between Uwe Mundlos, one of the two NSU killers and Thomas R., a neo-Nazi from the East German region of Sachsen-Anhalt who founded the far right group "Nationaler Widerstand Halle" (National Resistance of Halle), which in turn was interlinked with the German branch of the U.S. group "Blood & Honor," all of which illustrates the complex interconnections of the far right at the transnational, national, regional and individual levels.

In addition to these international and national linkages, virtual and local communities can be created. Both personal connections online and visits offline fostered the friendship between Thomas R. and Uwe Mundlos, which is alluded to in R.'s online link on his *National Observer* page to the neo-Nazi magazine *Der weisse Wolf* (White Wolf) as early as 2002, nine years before the full extent and geographic range of the NSU crimes became known to the general public.[11]

Radical right and right populist organizations in Germany infiltrate the mainstream by building up fraudulent virtual resumes via cheap and accessible Internet publicity, which in turn allow them to enter into publishing contracts with unsuspecting publishers, award each other prestigious prizes, make themselves into public figures, and generally mislead the public. I will give several examples of these strategies that have been succeeding all too well in the past few years and into the present. They create a virtual, low-cost presence able to reach and mobilize, even transnationally, large numbers of young sympathizers.

THE SARRAZIN CONTROVERSY SERVES UP A GOLDEN OPPORTUNITY

Interestingly, new radical right groups even copy left radical strategies to present themselves in public and pursue more violent tactics. First, I discuss the 2010 Sarrazin controversy. Thilo Sarrazin is a Social democrat politician and finance expert whose xenophobic views created an opportunity for far-right demagogues to glide to greater publicity in his wake. The fact that an avowed social democrat would vehemently oppose his own party on the issues of immigration and integration, seemed to some to create greater credence for his views. The right-wing group Institute for State Politics mimics government think tanks via its web presence and publishing ventures. Their messages of anti-immigrant hate are supported by pseudo-scientific Internet news sites such as *Sezession im Netz* or the anti-science *lifegen.de*, which foment moral panics by creating an apocalyptic tone about the future of Europe, so-called corruption of the "natural" environment through science, and produce a steady stream of global conspiracy theories. While the authors of these blogs, news sites and magazines may be few in number, their prolific, constantly updated output suggests far larger groups.

The 2010 controversy about Sarrazin's incendiary book *Deutschland schafft sich ab* (Germany aborts itself) shows that German conservative populists use the labor migrant as a trope for failed integration, fomenting hysteria in specific groups and age brackets (males between 20-29 and over 60 years old).[12] Although there is no truth to these racist and xenophobic claims, they did achieve some popular currency during the economic crisis that began in 2008, in the globalized society of a Germany unsure of its obligations both within the Euro zone and outside of "Fortress Europe."[13]

From the perspective of political parties in Europe with traditional lineages, today's right-wing extremism is ideologically diffuse and transgresses national boundaries. The real danger is the mainstreaming of radical-right views and their concentration from the periphery to the center of society.[14] The Internet is an integral part of the project of mainstreaming, as it is low-cost, ubiquitous, and readily available to large audiences. Currently, all the traditional German parties except for the Greens are shifting their rhetoric to the right in order to capture economically anxious and xenophobic voters.[15] We can see this move as a measure of the relative success and acceptance of right-wing ideas in the mainstream. The use of the new social media accelerates, transforms, and extends the reach of the right's message of rage and discontent, as it also targets multicultural Germans and rages against the very internationalization and global access from which the neo-Nazi movement itself profits (and absent which it would be nearly irrelevant, except in a national-historical context).

Recourse to "science" and "authorities" becomes another strategy of mainstreaming. Specifically, I analyze two examples from a gamut of choices favored by right extremists: the pseudo-academic study ("Der Fall Sarrazin") and the pseudo-scientific online forum (Lifegen.de). [16] Like the book by Sarrazin himself, these publications purport to be well-researched, and present spurious evidence for their claims. They quote "experts" in a format that simulates "balanced" debate, instrumentalizing *bona fide* publications and embedding these in a welter of pseudo-scientific propaganda that is suffused by an apocalyptic tone. Clever visual design choices and veiled rhetoric that carefully skirts the hate speech laws professionalize, modernize and mainstream their hate messages.

Why is this strategy more effective now than in the past? The accessibility and instant publicity of the net, chat rooms, diversified music styles, and a more modern dress code since 2004 have combined to create a distinctive "Erlebniswelt Rechtsextremismus" (right-wing extremist life-world) with more broad appeal. Moreover, fewer young people support traditional neo-Nazi parties like NPD or Liga Deutschland, organizing instead at the local level in an increasing number of local action groups, and sometimes even copying radical leftist strategies for clandestine action, music events, or self-presentation in the street. In light of such everyday pragmatic opportunism within a larger fluid and highly adaptable youth culture, it is no surprise that far-right self-presentation in print mimics accepted forms of political suasion: the tract, the news magazine, comment forums. However, the Internet handles and the repeated use of Germanic or medieval archaisms may signal the neo-Nazi credo of those who publish and market their texts via the net. For example, monikers like "Max Eichenhain," "gasgerd," "Ritter Jörg," using the Nazi flag's red-white and black color scheme on book covers, [17] or neo-Nazi numerology like 88 (the numerical value of the letter h, widely used code for Heil Hitler!), 14, a reference to Aryan Nation founder David Lane's indexed fourteen words, or 333 as a sign of the devil all signal far-right sympathies. For example, *Worst Case*, Georgescu and Vollborn's autobiographical account about job loss, unemployment, and their attempts to remake themselves as self-employed internet journalists, opens with a whole page of opaque sayings that include references to the number three. Ostensibly a narrative about a family's bootstrap rise from welfare and joblessness to self-employed success, it may easily be read as an allegory for neo-Nazi rebirth. Their repeated listing of "Glaube, Liebe, Hoffnung" (faith, love, hope) appeals both to Christian virtues and their perversion in traditional Nazi ideology. Oracular pronouncements like: "The one who is down and out will not be able to rise. We have the stuff to get back on top" or "Time moves forward in three steps, and we suffered in our bodies, souls and spirit given the circumstances" alternate with exhortations to: "stay alert. We trust only the written text, no longer the word." [18] The latter statement might be an

allusion to Hitler's *Mein Kampf* and to a predicted return to fascist supremacy in due time, which is also suggested by their final chapter title "Risen
from the ruins—the comeback." Vollborn and Georgescu employ a Hitlerian
vocabulary of crisis (will to survival, driven the world to ruin, shoals one
must navigate around) mixed with pseudo-scientific terminology like "the
scalpel of fate" and "to dissect luck from misfortune." According to Vollborn
and Georgescu, the state unfairly allocates resources to corporations and
other countries, while the middle-class family can hardly make ends meet.
Like leftists, they blame globalized capitalism for their economic woes, and
then they advocate suing to enforce the welfare rules as a strategy of profit-
ing from a corrupt system and hastening its demise. They feed on popular
anxiety about finances and changing visions of the family.

Sarrazin himself blends more recent neoliberal rhetoric about privatiza-
tion of state services and the citizen as entrepreneur of him- or herself with
the sixties' leftist belief that less state control of citizens is better. His polemic capitalizes on a general fear of globalization and losing out to migrants,
especially those from Arab countries and Turkey, which he derides as culturally regressive and lazy. He is obsessed with the declining German birth rate
and even sees this as a kind of obstinate feminist and atheist rebellion against
a biological mandate: "[. . .] the question remains of interest why a particular
nation would refuse to reproduce to a higher degree than another."[19] Terms
like inbreeding, conquest, hereditary gene pool of the population, derive
from a fascist eugenics and are entirely unscientific. He lists a jumble of
sources, some mainstream politicians and some nationalist extremists, some
mere anecdotes, flattering his readers to imagine themselves as instant experts. He is a regressive conservative, variously blaming foreign migrants,
highly educated German women, and the waning influence of Christian beliefs for joblessness, crime rates, and Germany's low birth rate. Sarrazin's
arguments are often illogical: on the one hand, he claims that true integration
would require a certain critical distance from the belief systems of the home
culture, but then chides educated women for their decision against motherhood, which in itself may arise from their feeling a sense of critical distance
toward Germany's lack of institutional support for working mothers.

Analogously, Vollborn and Georgescu want to undermine the government, yet urge their readership to extract the maximum in government subsidies, either by re-inventing themselves as entrepreneurs in the so-called "Ich-
AG" (a loan category that means entrepreneur of myself) to claim start-up
subsidies, re-negotiate mortgage payments, or demand more child support.
On their news site "Lifegen.de: Living Facts for Life Sciences" their anti-
government stance takes on a shriller tone, as they foment panic about bioterrorism, international policy failures and economic crisis.[20] Titles such as:
"Fukushima triggers global mental meltdown," "Nuclear power in Germany:
no usable plans for nuclear super meltdown," "Interview: a quantum code

determines our life after death," "U.S. porn industry targeted by disease researchers," describe foreign countries like Japan and the United States as sources of contamination. The authors state that 300,000 users accessed their site in 2009. The tangled web of deceptive avatars and cross-references that subtends their web activities documents the sheer technical malleability of virtual reality, but is used here—unlike in the VR gamer or chat community—to noxious propagandistic purpose.

Physicist Ulrich Berger traces the multiple pseudonyms of one of the Lifegen authors, Rolf Fröböse, untangling the web of cross-references and pseudo-endorsements by aliases, which form the core strategy of online right-wing authors.[21] At first glance, these tracts masquerade as real books. Furthermore, the line between crazed self-published tracts and substantive studies is blurred by the rise of on-demand publishing of academic treatises. It is doubtful that the average Internet user looking for alternatives sees through these practices. I see a parallel between the right-wing's use of Germanic mythology and the use of pseudo-science, insofar as both rubrics are interesting to people looking for explanatory systems and both presume specialized knowledge, yet actual expertise about these topics is limited to scientists and German culture experts. Schuppener argues that this is why "right extremists are able to act as carriers of elite knowledge."[22] The mainstreaming of rightist views is achieved by a maneuver embedding them in anti-globalization and anti-capitalist rhetoric tinged with cultural anxiety.

An example of this is a tract published by a younger generation rightwing privately funded "think tank," originating among the membership of Junge Freiheit, founded in 1985 from student guilds at Freiburg and Göttingen Universities. The tract promises to investigate the "causa Sarrazin."[23] The format of the publication mimics that of academic publications: it purports to be volume 15 in a series of scientific analyses by team of experts (who however are not listed by name), and it uses footnotes and a learned style. The tone is militaristic, casting Sarrazin in the role of a valiant provocateur, using polemics like live ammo ("Now he fired off the killer salvo: his book."[24] The authors laud Sarrazin for his basic convictions, as "conservative in the best sense," which they sum up as: social determinism, nationalism, hierarchy and defining one's own group against other groups ("erecting barriers") and the belief in hereditary genetic differences between population groups. In fact, this agenda is from the fascist playbook. The underlying militaristic tone of the tract is most likely drawn from the rhetoric of one of the main ideologues of this group, Götz Kubitschek, an army reservist whose strident endorsement of intellectual provocation as a basis for illegal action taking in the capacity of a "state of pre-civil war" is amply documented in a recent article.[25] The authors go on to cast Sarrazin as a valiant fighter for unpalatable social truths. Counter arguments are dismissed as reductionist, as examples of a p.c. scandal, and labeled "the [anti] Sarrazin campaign: chronicle of a politically correct failure."[26] Any serious criticism of his views is denigrated as "preparations for a successful public execution,"[27] which further emotionalizes the debate and allows a hagiographic rather than an analytical approach.

APPROPRIATING THE RADICAL LEFT PLAYBOOK

What is interesting about Kubitschek is that he borrows some leftist terminology from Enzensberger (who derived it from Nietzsche) and even got an endorsement from Bernd Rabehl, a former supporter of leftist revolutionary Rudi Dutschke:

> On the other side of the line—that is where the true revolutionary stands, in opposition to the world of the establishment, its licensed opposition included. That is where Rudi Dutschke, my youthful friend and companion, stood, and that is where I also see Götz Kubitschek. [. . .] The soldier-like and masculine demeanor that becomes apparent in K's public presentations, is both a part of his counter culture and a stylistic choice the better to provoke with; it does not contain any element of parody of the heroic chants of the past: Here we see someone at work who wants to be different! His very own combination of intelligence, the will to succeed, and responsibility are criteria for a future elite, which might be able to save society from collapse. It has to take shape in contradiction to the Zeitgeist and to everyday cowardice.[28]

A recent filmed interview with Kubitschek further emphasizes the right imitating protest strategies from the generation of 68 leftists: "Kubitschek carefully studies the strategies for agitation used by the 68ers—and he applies them [. . .] The right-wing intellectuals want to occupy the place of the left, with their spontaneous demonstrations, unannounced, fast [. . .]."[29]

The rightists behind Institut für Staatspolitik thus piece together an amalgam of leftist critique of the state apparatus and a self-quotation, a polemic that is short on evidence but long on reiteration of Sarrazin's racist and anti-multicultural shibboleths. They foment moral panic in public discourse by quoting patent untruths from their own publications, such as the right–wing magazine *Junge Freiheit* [Young Freedom], for which both Kubitschek and others in the group write.[30] Labeling Merkel's government "GDR-lite," they try to reactivate postwar fears of communist mind-control, and style Sarrazin into an oppressed dissident of the regime:

> Die Bundesrepublik Deutschland ist natürlich kein totalitärer Staat wie die DDR oder die Sowjetunion. Doch vielen Hütern der politischen Korrektheit ist totalitäres Denken nicht fremd. Ohne Zögern droht man dem, der die Diskursregeln verweigert, mit strafrechtlichen Konsequenzen, mit dem Verlust der beruflichen Existenz [. . .].

[Of course the Federal Republic is not a totalitarian state like the GDR or the Soviet Union. But many guardians of political correctness are no strangers to totalitarian thought. Without hesitation the one who refuses to play by the rules of polite discourse is threatened with legal consequences, with losing his professional livelihood.[31]]

More reputable news sources like the conservative *Frankfurter Allgemeine Zeitung* are also quoted, but it is easy to misattribute an outrageous quote listed right after the mention of the FAZ; however, as the copious endnotes reveal, many of the quotes hail from tabloids like *Bild* and *Welt,* or obscure conservative local newspapers. A recent filmed interview with Kubitschek further emphasizes the right copying protest strategies from the generation of 68 leftists: "Kubitschek carefully studies the strategies for agitation used by the 68ers—and he applies them [. . .] The right-wing intellectuals want to occupy the place of the left in society, with their spontaneous demonstrations, unannounced, agile [. . .]."[32] From actionistic words to deeds is not necessarily a big step for male neo-Nazis, as is currently emerging from the background of one of the NSU-murders. Captured text messages by neo-Nazi Thomas Starke (found guilty of supplying the NSU with explosives) dating back to the late 1990s, express outrage at diversity: "nothing but Turks, everywhere you look [in Dortmund], you can't believe the numbers." An East German supporter messages back: "That bad, is it? Then we know where to clean up next time." In the 1990s, the local right-wing music scene saw regular visits by Uwe Mundlos and Uwe Böhnhardt, the future NSU killers who traveled frequently to Dortmund to hang out with friends. On 4 April 2006, the NSU shot and killed Dortmund kiosk owner Mehmet Kubasik. "A possible motive may be their strategy of actionism as a means of communication," police profilers claimed. "The murder was to have served as a signal for right-wing extremists to commit more violence in Dortmund."[33] Social media skeptics who study the effect of these technologies on political identity building and activism have warned of a "tendency that web users get in contact only within ideologically homogeneous groups."[34] Thus, vigorous contestation of viewpoints may not ever happen. As Manuela Caiani and Linda Parenti state in *European and American Extreme Right Groups and the Internet,* "technologies could contribute to social ills, including violent conflict escalations, overwhelming flows of misinformation, and political polarization."[35]

FAR-RIGHT MEDIA STRATEGIES AND GOVERNMENT RESPONSE

The younger generation of new right writers who publish in *Junge Freiheit* and in *Sezession* further legitimate their standing by first co-founding, then awarding each other what sounds like a prestigious mainstream prize for journalism, the *Gerhard-Löwenthal Prize*. In 2008, Ellen Kositza, Kubitschek's wife, was the latest in a string of new right authors to receive it. Members of *Junge Freiheit* 'persuaded' the elderly widow of German-Jewish TV-journalist and camp survivor Gerhard Löwenthal into letting them republish her husband's memoir, and then co-endow the prize with the proceeds. In 2006, the committee awarded the prize to well-known geo-science journalist, Peter Scholl-Latour, who, as the video of the ceremony shows, is also very elderly and who, we can only hope, may not have any idea what group he is supporting by accepting the prize and coming to the 2008 event. The strategy of camouflaging themselves alongside famous icons of the press therefore appears to lift *IfS* and *JF* fascist propaganda to the level of objective political journalism.[36]

At present, the *Verfassungsschutz* (federal intelligence office) is beginning to become cognizant of these practices. Government and court intervention to stop right-wing swamping of the media sphere is long overdue. On 4 October 2011 a regional court in Mecklenburg-Vorpommern sued to shut down *AlterMedia*, a neo-Nazi news site with 4 million users, whose server is in the United States, but at the same time, a Berlin web hosting company *Strato*, a subsidiary of Telekom, refuses to shut down a neo-Nazi music site, *oposrecords*, with one million users and offensive hate speech, claiming that they are not responsible for content they host.[37] The site allows users to buy racial purity music and fan gear, even though marketing right-wing extremist content is illegal.

There is an institutional and governmental tradition of paying more critical attention to radicalism on the left than the right. The 2013 report on right-wing extremism emphasizes the dangers of far left and Islamist radicals, not objectively supported by their numbers or the frequency of such incidents. This report originates from a new anti-terrorist research center—the "Gemeinsame Abwehrzentrum Rechtsextremismus/ Rechtsterrorismus" (Joint Defense Center against Far-Right Extremism and Right-Wing Terrorism)— created in December 2011 after the NSU- murders came to light. The new center was attached to an anti-left radical terror unit, a legacy of the Baader-Meinhof gang's terrorist abductions of key political and corporate leaders, their police killings, bomb attacks, and armed robberies. Despite the shocking failure of intelligence about the NSU's murders, far-right crime is under-prosecuted even now. André S. is one of the four secondary defendants in the ongoing NSU-trial. He confessed that he bought a gun for Mundlos and Böhnhardt, almost certainly the Ceska used in the killings, but is not under arrest. More surveillance anxiety is projected, and more legal actions are pursued against leftist protesters—the last ten years of harsh legal rulings against anti-fascist protesters in the Dresden court system may serve as a case in point—than on homegrown local far-right terrorists and their supporters—in the NSU case, their support network is conservatively estimated to comprise around two hundred and fifty people.

CONCLUSION

In drawing conclusions from the evidence cited above we must note that not all right-wing populists are anti-Islamists; some, like Georgescu, who is a migrant himself, are anti-capitalist and anti-consumerist. But they do agree on the ideal of ethnic or national isolationism, that the welfare state suffers from resource scarcity and that therefore, it needs to restrict funding for the socially disadvantaged and limit immigration. Sociologist Wilhelm Heitmeyer's most recent study of xenophobia and other forms of group discrimination in eight European countries shows that, in fact, migrants in Germany constitute 10 percent of the population, but they are perceived by 50 percent of surveyed Germans as "too many."[38] Similarly, an approximate 7 percent of the population in Germany is Muslim, yet 46.1 percent of Germans surveyed feel that "there are too many Muslims in our country."[39] The study shows that despite the EU-wide regulation of migration, a perception persists that migrants should not have equal access to jobs and benefits, and that the native-born population should have precedence. Rightists like Sarrazin exploit such biases in order to revive fears about the changing demographic of Germany, without acknowledging that migrants adopt the receiving country's attitudes toward child bearing, and also attain higher levels of education over time. Sociologist Naika Foroutan documents, for instance, that third-generation Turkish-Germans are eight hundred times better educated than their immigrant forebears.[40] Indiscriminately labeling everyone of foreign heritage a migrant or every Turk a Muslim also confuses distinctions between those who are recent immigrants, those who are naturalized, those who are Muslim feminists, Christian, Alevite or Jewish Turks and so on. It is simply misguided, even delusional, to wish away a multicultural Germany, when it has existed de facto since at least the 1960s, if not much earlier, and was officially proclaimed a nation of immigration in the twenty-first century.

Fear of immigrants and the resultant cultural mixing may lead to homicidal rage against them and those who accept them. The danger of absorbing and publicizing one's own extremist views over the net as a form of self-empowerment became obvious in the 2011 mass killings of liberal youth in Norway. The killer, Anders Bering Breivik, disseminated a 1,500-page manifesto, much of which was cobbled together from other extremist sources on the net, convincing himself in the process that he was a warrior in the fight against Islamicization and multiculturalism. His virtual identity became more appealing than his everyday identity as an unsuccessful business owner. He was inspired to take action by the life world (*Erlebniswelt*) of the net, which suggests that speech acts create valid publicity, but in themselves are not enough to change society. As right-winger Kubitschek expresses it: "The one who has no power prepares himself for a long time and carefully, studies the reflexes of the media age and then forces public recognition via a coup. Because that is the measure of the provocateur's success: what does not make it into the media, does not exist in the world, did not happen as an event, did not catch fire."[41]

Extremist political agency is thus seen as dramatic and explosive, and necessarily outside democratic institutions, which are derided as corrupt or weak. While this conviction goes back to the radical leftists of the 1968 student movement, what is new today is the swamping of the media sphere with a proliferation of avatars and tracts masquerading as real people and bona fide sources. But this plastic medium is filled with strident discriminatory messages, which are echoed by cultural and economic anxieties from the mainstream. As the 2010 Heitmeyer study documents, a mutually binding social contract is eroding because higher-income elites no longer feel responsible for the socially weak.[42] This climate of "de-solidarization"[43] as Heitmeyer terms it, creates more room for right wing populists and their manipulation of the media sphere. Racists and xenophobes have adapted by veiling their language, claiming to wish preserve their own cultural heritage or specificity, while advocating the repatriation or exclusion of cultural others. By shifting away from race and into culture, and claiming that such cultural coherence and continuity existed in Europe's past, nostalgia for an imaginary "Judeo-Christian Occident" is created in opposition to an equally fantastical Islamic monolith.[44] In the present drama over the euro's viability, the climate in the German media is more conducive to national stereotyping, and will present a greater opportunity for the populist right to exploit the crisis for their own ends.

NOTES

1. Regina Wamper, Michael Sturm, Alexander Häusler, "Faschistischer Selbstbedienungsladen? Aneignungspraktiken der 'Autonomen Nationalisten' in historischer und diskursanalytischer Perspektive," in Jan Schedler and Alexander Häusler, eds. *Autonome Nationalisten: Neonazismus in Bewegung* (Wiesbaden: Verlag für Sozialwissenschaften, 2001), 284–85.

2. Thomas Günter, "Rechtliche Möglichkeiten gegen Rechtsextremismus im Internet," in Stephan Braun, Alexander Geisler, Martin Gerster, ed. *Strategien der extremen Rechten* (Wiesbaden: Verlag für Sozialwissenschaften, 2009), 642.

3. "Internes Forum geleaked," *Störungsmelder*, *Die Zeit* 6 November 2011, http://blog.zeit.de/stoerungsmelder/2011/11/06/internes-naziforum-geleaked---wir-sind-ja-nationalsozialisten_7401, accessed 7 November 2011.

4. Peter Walker and Matthew Taylor, "Far right on rise in Europe, says report," http://www.guardian.co.uk/world/2011/nov/06/far-right-rise-europe-report, accessed 7 November 2011.

5. See Dominique Venner, "La manif du 26 mai et Heidegger," http://www.dominiquevenner.fr/2013/05/la-m

anif-du-26-mai-et-heidegger/, accessed 22 May 2013. Translations mine. See Kim Wilsher, "Femen protester stages mock suicide at Notre Dame cathedral," *The Guardian*, 22 May 2013, http://www.guardian.co.uk/world/2013/may/22/femen-mock-suicide-notre-dame/print.

6. Venner, "La manif du 26 mai," 21 May 2013.

7. Personal communication from neo-Nazi expert and journalist Christoph Schultheis, Berlin, 16 October 2011.

8. Arne Zillmer, "White Rex - Nazimode aus Russland," 22 June 2013, http://blog.zeit.de/stoerungsmelder/2013/06/22/white-rex-nazimode-aus-russland_13291, accessed 25 June 2013.

9. Kirsten Haake, "Mehrere Polizisten waren Mitglied im Ku Klux Klan," http://www.zeit.de/ gesellschaft/zeitgeschehen/2012-10/polizisten-mitliedschaft-ku-klux-klan/komplettansicht, accessed 17 October 2012.

10. Wolf Schmidt, "Wie der KKK nach Schwaben kam," 10 August 2012, http://www.taz.de/Ku-Klux-Klan-Affaere/!99280/, accessed 11 August 2012.

11. Wolf Schmidt and Sebastian Erb, "Verbindungen vom NSU zum Ku Klux Klan: Viele Spuren führen zu Thomas R.," 15 August 2012, http://www.taz.de/Verbindungen-vom-NSU-zum-Ku-Klux-Klan/!99698/. Accessed 26 March 2014.

12. Sabine am Orde, "Auch die Unterschicht kauft Thilo: Psychologie der Sarrazin-Leser," *taz*, 1/10/11, http://www.taz.de/1/politik/deutschland/artikel/1/auch-die-unterschicht-kauft-thilo/, accessed 27 January 2011.

13. Institut für Staatspolitik, *Der Fall Sarrazin: Eine Analyse* (Albersroda: 2010). http://www.lifegen.de/index.php4, accessed 29 January 2011. This online "science" magazine is a daily forum of two right populists, Vlad Georgescu and Marita Vollborn, co-authors of a surprising number of Aryan purity hate tracts, in the guise of pseudo-scientific critiques of "contamination" in the German food industry. These authors have by now managed to simulate enough Internet credibility to infiltrate mainstream publishers and newspapers. Their proliferation strategies are indicative of various types of Internet presence (blogs, tweets, tracts, magazines, customer reviews on amazon.de, music, online youth sports fan clubs) on the extreme right, and are transparent enough to neo-Nazi followers.

14. For an account of the new boundary blurring between the radical right and right populists see Karin Priester, "Fließende Grenzen zwischen Rechtsextremismus und Rechtspopulismus in Europa?" *Das Parlament: Aus Politik und Zeitgeschichte*, (Bundeszentrale für politische Bildung: Frankfurt, November 1 2010), 33–39, http://www.bpb.de/publikationen/E8IL0Q,0,0,Extremismus.html, accessed 20 November 2010.

15. See Alexander Häusler, "Rechtspopulistisches Entwicklungsland?" *Lotta* 45 (Oberhausen: VFKB, 2011), 7–9. Sociologist Häusler gives many examples of the right populist rhetoric of the traditional parties, summing up: "Das rechtspopulistische Potential in Deutschland scheint trotz gegenteiliger Umfragen immer noch in das vorherrschende Parteiengefüge eingebunden zu sein." (9) (The right populist potential in Germany still seems contained within established party structures, surveys to the contrary.) However, he also concludes that "der Wunsch nach neuen rechten Formationen [ist] noch nicht aufgegeben worden." (the desire for new right formations has not been abandoned).

16. Regina Wamper, Michael Sturm, Alexander Häusler, "Faschistischer Selbstbedienungsladen? Aneignungspraktiken der 'Autonomen Nationalisten' in historischer und diskursanalytischer Perspektive," in Jan Schedler and Alexander Häusler, eds. *Autonome Nationalisten: Neonazismus in Bewegung* (Wiesbaden: Verlag für Sozialwissenschaften, 2001), 284–85.

17. Two recent examples are Thilo Sarrazin's racist diatribe *Deutschland schafft sich ab* (München: Deutsche Verlags-Anstalt, 2010), which alternates large blocks of white and black type against a red background, and Marita Vollborn and Vlad Georgescu's *Worst Case: Unser ganz erstaunliches Comeback nach Jobverlust und Sozialabstieg* (München: Hanser, 2009), which uses red and black type against a white background and presents a black bug on its back in the center. The bug is a "Zecke" (tick), an insult levied by neo-Nazis against leftists and punks, but also used as a label against the unemployed who are seen as parasites bleeding the welfare state dry. The combination of the color scheme and the image convey neo-Nazi signals, even if it is ambivalent whom the bug designates: the enemies, or the down-and-out authors themselves.

18. Georgescu and Vollborn, "Vorwort," x, xii, and x.

19. Sarrazin, *Deutschland schafft sich ab*, 344.

20. Georgescu was fired as an author from the web portal doc.de, because he published several opinion pieces about the German e coli outbreak in May/ June 2011 that claimed they were an act of foreign bioterrorism. See http://www.lifegen.de/newsip/shownews.php4? getnews=2011-06-24-5208&pc=s01, accessed 25 July 2011.

21. http://kritischgedacht.wordpress.com/2008/06/18/geheime-pr-des-zufalls/, accessed 25 July 2011.

22. Georg Schuppener, "Strategische Rückgriffe der extremen Rechten auf Mythen und Symbole," Stephan Braun, Alexander Geisler und Martin Gerster, eds. *Strategien der extremen Rechten* (Wiesbaden: VS Verlag der Sozialwissenschaften, 2009), 310–31; 326.

23. Institut für Staatspolitik, *Der Fall Sarrazin: Eine Analyse* (Rittergut Schnellroda, 2010).

24. Institut für Staatspolitik, 4.

25. Helmut Kellershohn, "Widerstand und Provokation: Strategische Optionen im Umkreis des Instituts für Staatspolitik," Stephan Braun, Alexander Geisler, Martin Gerster, eds. *Strategien der Extremen Rechten* (Wiesbaden: VS Verlag für Sozialwissenschaften, 2009), 259–89, 276–82.

26. *Der Fall Sarrazin*, 8.

27. Institut für Staatspolitik, 14.

28. Bernd Rabehl, http://www.jf-archiv.de/archiv06/200637090810.htm, accessed 30 July 2011.

29. Clemens Riha, "Auf dem Rittergut: Eine Begegnung mit Deutschlands Neuen Rechten," 3sat. de, 15.8.2011, http://www.3sat.de/mediathek/mediathek.php?obj=26378& mode=play, accessed 4 October 2011.

30. *JF* is used six times a news source, *Bild* is used twelve times, *Welt* is used twenty-one times. Conservative local papers like *Berliner Morgenpost*, *BZ*, and *Tagesspiegel*, are also liberally used.

31. Institut für Staatspolitik, 25.

32. Clemens Riha, "Auf dem Rittergut: Eine Begegnung mit Deutschlands Neuen Rechten," 3sat. de, 15 August 2011, http://www.3sat.de/mediathek/mediathek.php?obj=26378& mode=play, accessed 4 October 2011.

33. David Schraven, "Nazi-Netzwerk in Dortmund ist größer als vermutet," *Westdeutsche Allgemeine Zeitung*, 21 May 2013, http://www.derwesten.de/wirtschaft/nazi-netzwerk-in-dortmund-ist-groesser-als-vermutet-aimp-id7974205.html, accessed 21 May 2013.

34. See Manuela Caiani and Linda Parenti, *European and American Extreme Right Groups and the Internet* (Burlington, VT: Ashgate, 2013), 5.

35. Manuela Caiani and Linda Parenti, *European and American Extreme Right Groups and the Internet* (Burlington,VT: Ashgate, 2013), 5.

36. A related case is PAX Europa's 2011 awarding of the "Hiltrud Schröter Freiheitspreis" to Stefan Herre, the founder of *Politically Incorrect*, a grassroots anti-Islamic group. The deceased Hiltrud Schröter was an educator and Professor of Pedagogy at Frankfurt University, who (despite a lack of training in comparative theology) authored several critiques of Islamic theology, and whose name is being used to lend academic gravitas to the extremist anti-Islamic group *Bürgerbewegung PAX Europa* (Citizens' Movement Pax Europa), the founders of the prize. http://bpeinfo.wordpress.com/2011/06/11/stefan-herre-erster-preistrager-des-hiltrud-schroter-freiheitspreises-der-bpe/, accessed 7 November 2011.

37. Kathrin Haimerl, "Rechtsextreme Internethetzer im Netz der Justiz: Prozeß gegen Neonazi-Portal Altermedia," http://www.sueddeutsche.de/politik/prozess-gegen-neonazi-portal-altermedia-rechtsextreme-internet-hetzer-im-netz-der-justiz-1.1154773, accessed 4 October 2011. Adrian Bechtold, "Das lohnende Geschäft mit der Nazimusik," http://blog.zeit.de/stoerungsmelder/2011/10/01, accessed 1 October 2011.

38. Andreas Zick, Beate Küpper, Hinna Wolf, "Wie feindselig ist Europa? Ausmaße *Gruppenbezogener Menschenfeindlichkeit* in acht Ländern," Wilhelm Heitmeyer, ed. *Deutsche Zustände*, Folge 9 (Berlin: Suhrkamp, 2010), 47–48.

39. Zick, 50.

40. https://www2.hu-berlin.de/hcsp/de/1524/going-public/foroutan-sarrazins-thesen-auf-dem-prufstand-dossier-presseecho/, 24, accessed 29 July 2011.

138 *Druxes*

41. See Kellershohn, "Widerstand und Provokation," 280.
42. See Heitmeyer 2010, 127–34.
43. Heitmeyer 2012, 27.
44. In a debate about "Reden über Europa: Von der Zweck- zur Wertegemeinschaft?" in the Deutsches Theater on 23 October 2011 the moderator, Stephan-Andreas Casdorff, an editor of the Berlin newspaper *Tagesspiegel*, repeatedly alluded to an essential difference between a putative "Christlich-Jüdisches Abendland" as opposed to a Muslim Orient, but at least one panelist, the writer Navid Kermani, vehemently opposed this view. For an audio of the event, see http://www.allianz-kulturstiftung.de/dokumente_videos_de_und_en/11_lectures231011.mp3.

REFERENCES

Bürgerbewegung Pax Europa. "Stefan Herre erster Preisträger des Hiltrud Schröter Freiheitspreises." http://bpeinfo.wordpress.com/2011/06/11/stefan-herre-erster-preistrager-des-hiltrud-schroter-freiheitspreises-der-bpe/. Accessed 7 November 2011.
Braun, Stephan, A. Geisler and M. Gerster, eds. *Strategien der extremen Rechten*. Wiesbaden: Verlag für Sozialwissenschaften, 2009.
Claus, Robert, E. Lehnert, and Y. Müller, eds. *"Was ein rechter Mann ist . . .": Männlichkeiten im Rechtsextremismus*. Berlin: Dietz, 2010.
Foroutan, Naika. Sarrazins Thesen auf dem Prüfstand. https://www2.hu-berlin.de /hcsp/de/ 1524/going-public/foroutan-sarrazins-thesen-auf-dem-prufstand-dossier-presseecho/, 24. Accessed 29 July 2011.
Georgescu, Vlad and Marita Vollborn. *Worst Case: Unser ganz erstaunliches Comeback nach Jobverlust und Sozialabstieg*. München: Hanser, 2009.
Georgescu, Vlad. *Lifegen.de*. http://www.lifegen.de/index.php4. Accessed 29 January 2011.
Häusler, Alexander. "Rechtspopulistisches Entwicklungsland?" *Lotta* 45 [Herbst 2011] (Oberhausen: VFKB, 2011): 7–9.
Haimerl, Kathrin. "Rechstextreme Internethetzer im Netz der Justiz: Prozeß gegen Internet Portal Altermedia." http://www.sueddeutsche.de/politik/prozess-gegen-neonazi-portal-altermedia-rechtsextreme-internet-hetzer-im-netz-der-justiz-1.1154773. Accessed 4 October 2011.
Heitmeyer, Wilhelm. *Deutsche Zustände*. Folge 9. Berlin: Suhrkamp, 2010.
———. *Deutsche Zustände*. Folge 10. Berlin: Suhrkamp, 2012.
Institut für Staatspolitik. *Der Fall Sarrazin: Eine Analyse*. Albersroda, 2010.
Priester, Karin. "Fließende Grenzen zwischen Rechtsextremismus und Rechtspopulismus in Europa?" *Aus Politik und Zeitgeschichte: Extremismus*, (Bundeszentrale für politische Bildung: Frankfurt, 1 November 2010), 33–39, http://www.bpb.de/publikationen/E8IL0Q,0,0,Extremismus.html. Accessed 20 November 2010.
Rabehl, Bernd. "Götz Kubitschek: Der Revolutionär." http://www.jfarchiv.de/archiv06/200637090810.htm. Accessed 30 July 2011.
Riha, Clemens. "Auf dem Rittergut: Eine Begegnung mit Deutschlands Neuen Rechten." http://www.3sat.de/mediathek/mediathek.php?obj=26378&mode=play. Accessed 4 October 2011.
Sarrazin, Thilo. *Deutschland schafft sich ab*. München: Deutsche Verlags Anstalt, 2010.
Schedler, Jan and A. Häusler, eds. *Autonome Nationalisten: Neonazismus in Bewegung*. Wiesbaden: Verlag für Sozialmedien, 2011.
Störungsmelder, "Internes Forum geleaked." http://blog.zeit.de/stoerungsmelder/2011/11/06/internes-naziforum-geleaked---wir-sind-ja-nationalsozialisten_7401. Accessed 7 November 2011.
Venner, Dominique. "La manif du 26 mai." www.dominiquevenner.fr. Accessed 21 May 2013.
Walker, Peter, and Matthew Taylor. "Far Right on Rise in Europe, says report." http://www.guardian.co.uk/world/2011/nov/06/far-right-rise-europe-report. Accessed 7 November 2011.
Wefing, Heinrich. "Neustart: Die Politiker müssen das Netz beherrschen, sonst beherrscht das Netz die Politik." *Die Zeit* (Hamburg, 20 October 2011).

Willsher, Kim. "Femen protester stages mock suicide in Notre Dame cathedral." *The Guardian* 22 May 2013. http://www.guardian.co.uk/world/2013/may/22/femen-mock-suicide-notre-dame. Accessed 22 May 2013.

Chapter Seven

The Imitated Public Sphere

The Case of Hungary's Far Right

Domonkos Sik

"Being in crisis" is probably the most profound experience of the last few years that marks life not only in the United States, but also in Europe. The global consequences of the subprime mortgage crisis reached far beyond the economic sector; they generated transformations in the political sphere as well. In times of crisis, radical, extremist voices often gain strength and the principles of democracy are frequently attacked by populist arguments. This crisis, however, differs from previous ones, as modernization entered to a new era, the age of global information society.[1] In this constellation the whole context of democracy, populism, and radicalism changes as the fundamental structures of private and mass communication are transforming. The question is: how do these profound social changes affect the potential of radicalization? Are they creating an obstacle for populism, or are they instead weakening democracy by providing a tool for leading populist views?

In this chapter these questions are examined in the context of the post-socialist Hungary. First, the emergence of the far-right is introduced in the post-socialist constellation as a conjunction of several factors including the eroded democratic culture, the controversies of the multiparty system and the emergence of virtual public spheres. Secondly, the far-right virtual public sphere is analyzed from the perspective of Habermas's and Lash's critical theories of late modernity: the concept of an "imitated public sphere" is elaborated, which is based on ritualized communicative acts lacking any potential of mutually understanding the world. Finally those factors of political socialization are identified, which result in the susceptibility to such radical imitated public spheres including the lack of personal experiences of democratic interactions in the family, in the school or in the peer groups.[2]

CONTEXTUALIZING RADICALISM: THE CASE OF POST-SOCIALIST HUNGARY

After the collapse of state socialism in 1989, the consensus of the new political order was based on two pillars: the respect for democratic institutions and the transition from the dominance of state property into private property and a free market. These two elements expressed the general will of the people to rejoin Europe after the decades of belonging to the Soviet sphere of interest. Such a consensus united not only the political elite of the country, but also the majority of the population. The efforts of returning to the democratic world of Europe culminated in Hungary's becoming a member state of the European Union (EU) in 2004, which was approved by 84 percent of voters (with a voter turnout of 46 percent).

In the first fifteen years of the post-transition era the antidemocratic, extremist voices were marginal—if not completely unknown—in the public life of the nation. Radicalism existed only as a subculture, which, in the form of the Party of Hungarian Justice/ Truth and Life (MIÉP), gained minimal parliamentary mandates (only once in four parliamentary elections). However, the lack of open radicalism was not at all a consequence of acquiring a democratic political culture. During the fifty years of state socialism, civic culture was distorted to a great extent and the problematic heritage of authoritarianism and paternalism survived in the values, attitudes, and everyday practices of the majority.[3] This resulted on the one hand in the lack of trust in the state, disinterest in the public life, and an overall distortion of civic culture and political formation.[4] On the other hand, this heritage also led to the unchallenged emergence of prejudices against ethnic minorities, creating an intolerant, authoritarian civic culture.[5] This latent heritage of antidemocratic political culture is the first prerequisite for the emergence of radicalism in Hungary.

Despite their well-documented, continuous existence, these intolerant, antidemocratic tendencies remained latent until recent times. They broke into public life only gradually, as a consequence of internal and foreign political events and the formation of the adequate semantic frames. The first important factor, which prepared the ground for the emergence of radical ideas, was the polarization of party politics. Polarization began right after the transition, thanks to the traditional cleavages of the Hungarian political elite.[6] It created an extremely tense and aggressive public life in which parties positioned themselves not as rivals, but rather as enemies. Such a hostile atmosphere inevitably influenced the voters as well, resulting in a politically divided society.

While the mutual pragmatic and symbolic goal of EU membership effectively softened the division of the parties and the population during the first fifteen years of the third republic, after this was accomplished, a vacuum emerged. Suddenly there was not any shared value or goal able to generate common ground for the different memories of the troubled twentieth century and to bridge the gaps that separated the different political sides. Thus the two pillars of the foundation of the third republic, namely the respect for democracy and the free market, became less and less important. The democratic minimum gradually lost its normative force and party politics became reduced to a mere "techné of power." Essential debates about the past, the present, and the future, which might have served as the basis for redefining the Hungarian collective identity and potential social reforms, were never conducted. As the public sphere emptied, the majority of the population turned away from party politics, thinking of it as a basically suspicious terrain, which cannot really be changed by popular opinion, but in exchange does not really impact private life. The slow emptying of the public sphere and the consequent general disinterestedness was the second prerequisite for the emergence of the extreme right into mainstream politics.

If considered independently these factors, the latent antidemocratic heritage, the lack of a democratic minimum, and the disinterestedness of the majority did not increase the threat of expanding far-right ideas, but the combination of these elements created a tinderbox. As there was nothing left to stop the spreading of far-right ideas and sentiments, only the sparks were needed to inflame the public sphere. One of these sparks involved the scandal of Prime Minister Ferenc Gyurcsány: the leaking of a speech in which he admitted to misleading the public. The scandal resulted in the most violent protests and police reactions since the transition. This event became a symbolic turning point not only for the sympathizers of the far-right, but also for the wider public. Many concluded that the political elite as such are utterly corrupt, the social experiment of the transition has failed, and thus a radical change is needed, even at the cost of giving up the so-called democratic institutions.

The second spark was a shocking crime, committed by Roma people in Olaszliszka: a father was beaten to death in front of his family by angry relatives of a girl, who was presumed to have been hit by the car. This event has shaken the Hungarian public sphere especially after the far-right began exploiting it. The extreme right organizations tried to focus all the fears and frustrations on the Roma, while creating a panic, for which they would offer a "solution." The far-right systematically started to label different crimes as "gypsy crime" and used the Roma as a general scapegoat, having not only a tendency to commit crimes, but also to avoid work and misuse the system of social benefits.[7] The third spark was the spreading of the economic crisis in 2008, which resulted in high unemployment rates and a feeling of hopelessness in certain regions and social groups, especially amongst younger people living in rural areas.[8] Together these effects grounded a hysterical atmosphere including the elements of insecurity and political hopelessness.

Based on these shared experiences, gradually a political community was formed. However, as in case of any community, the radicals could not exist without a collective identity either, which provides the frames for a mutual understanding of the world. Collective identities are formed in public communicative processes, while relying on a certain "tradition."[9] Accordingly the emergence of the far-right should include a reference to this tradition and also to a space in which such communicative processes could occur. The origin of the far-right collective identity goes back to the interwar period, named the after its Governor, the Horthy-era. Interwar Hungary was born in the trauma of the Trianon treaty, resulting in the dissolution of the historical Kingdom of Hungary and the loss of 72 percent of its territory. The Horthy-system was founded on the political consensus of irredentism, which resulted in a centralized, authoritarian, nationalistic state. The different governments throughout the period were varying from central to far-right, which meant that while they all subordinated the democratic institutions to the goal of reclaiming lost territories, they differed in the extent of violating human rights. The blind revisionism resulting in antidemocratic practices culminated in the tragic participation of Hungarian authorities in the events of Holocaust and the elimination of almost the whole Jewish population in the countryside.[10]

During the historical period of state socialism, the ideological heritage of the Horthy-era, including nationalism, latent or explicit anti-Semitism, anticommunism, and authoritarianism, was persecuted: it could only survive as an underground, oppositional worldview. However, after 1989, the Hungarian right-wing parties slowly returned to the different threads of this heritage. The central right parties built a strong nationalist discourse, the main elements of which included the symbolic rehabilitation of the Horthy-era, the interpretation of the state socialist period as a gap in Hungarian sovereignty, and the labeling of the liberal-left wing parties as the inheritors of the Communist Party. The obvious conclusion of these narratives was the creation of an exclusive basis of legitimacy, which anoints the right-wing parties as the sole legitimate leaders of the country. While the central right parties instrumentalized interwar heritage in the daily political battles, the first radical Party (MIÉP), which seceded from the first central right Party (Forum of Hungarian Democrats, MDF), embraced it, with all its authoritarian, anti-Semitic features.[11] As a result, despite their common roots, the central and far-right distanced themselves from each other.

This distancing, however, never became a rupture: in opposition to the liberal-left parties an implicit mutual coalition prevailed, creating an overall ambivalent relationship. Within this relationship the central right parties played the dominant role. They relied on the far-right as a negative reference point: their consolidated character could be demonstrated through a comparison with more radical elements. In exchange, the central right forces did not participate in the complete isolation of the far-right, which the liberal-left parties repeatedly attempted to initiate. In this constellation the far-right party was doomed to permanent marginalization. Therefore, the fact that since 2009 the opposite is happening, and the new extreme right Party called Jobbik (meaning both Righter/ Better) became the third most popular Party, having 15 percent support amongst those having stable party preference, has come as a surprise to many analysts.

Several factors that have been referred to above may help to understand the sudden, unexpected popularity of the far-right, but considered independently they cannot explain the phenomena. The first group of explanatory factors originates in the social historical heritage: due to the lack of democratic political culture and high level of prejudices many people were susceptible to the antidemocratic narratives; they were simply unable to detect their dangerous aspect. The second group of factors originates in the dysfunction of mainstream parties and the distortions of the public sphere: due to the polarization of the political sphere, the lack of democratic minimum and the emptying of public debates, most of the voters turned away from party politics, leaving this type of political discourse and policy prey to extremist forces. The third group of factors is constituted by those events which enabled the elaboration of far-right interpretations of the world: the scandal of a left-wing Prime Minister, the police violence, the symbolic murder, and the economic crisis all created the conditions for generating panic and offering oversimplifying, populist solutions. The fourth group of factors originates in the right wing historical tradition, which provided the frames for building a political community: the ideological heritage of the interwar period provided the semantics for an interpretation of the past and present, while the shared roots with the central right parties prevented isolation.

In this constellation, one more element was lacking: the far-right political forces needed a communicative space, where they could organize their specific collective identity, independently from the dominant central parties. Attempts to create such public spheres were present since the formation of MIÉP. However, they were relying on the mediums of the printed press, radio, and television broadcast, which would have required more resources than the Party had to get their political message to the public. Thus these attempts could not reach a wider audience, resulting in the marginalization of the far-right forces.

This constellation has changed with the expansion of information society, especially with the Internet boom, which provided a surface, where radical ideology could have been spread countrywide with minimal cost.[12] The previously scattered communities and actions could have been connected and the radical sphere could start organizing itself on the cultural, economic, and political level.[13] The close relation between the expansion of a new medium and the radicalization is made evident by the age distribution of the supporters of Jobbik and the campaign strategy of the radical Party. Those younger generations are overrepresented amongst them, who are the main users of the new medium of information society, which was the main surface of the campaign of the Party as well.[14] In the following section this Internet-based public sphere is analyzed.

THE IMITATION OF A PUBLIC SPHERE

The public sphere plays a fundamental role in the political constitution of any community. This is where new norms and values may be born, elementary forms of freedom and recognition could be experienced, and autonomy can be practiced. In this sense, the public sphere has key importance for the community and the individual as well.[15] Because of its crucial role, however, not only the existence, but also the quality of the public sphere matters as well. In this sense the communicative practices constituting the public sphere require special attention. Communicative processes may be differentiated according to their rationality. Those debates can be called rational in which the participants can freely criticize any aspect (truth, rightness, honesty) of the speech acts and criticism is taken seriously. The opposite of this setting is the dogmatic or strategic use of language. In the first case criticisms are limited, or not responded to with further explanation and justification. In the second case criticisms are handled with manipulation or lies.[16]

This model of communication allows us to characterize the public spheres. In cases where the dominant form of interactions is free debate of equal partners, the public sphere actualizes the maximal rationality potential of communication. Therefore it fulfills its democratic function, provides a space for creating legitimate norms, and for experiencing freedom and mutual understanding. In those cases where the dominant form of interactions is dogmatic or strategic language usage, the public sphere is distorted. There the potential of communicative rationality cannot be actualized, legitimate institutions give their place to raw power relations, thus freedom or mutual understanding cannot be experienced.[17] In these cases the public sphere becomes a destructive force from a democratic point of view. Instead of fulfilling its function as a mediator between the everyday lifeworld and the administrative or economic systems, it becomes the tool of exploitation and alienation. Instead of criticizing the pathologies of late modern society, it becomes the obstacle of emancipation.

The above-mentioned influential critical theories of the public sphere were all elaborated before the rise of the information age; therefore they could not account for newly emerging challenges. According to critical analyses, the logic of information entirely reconfigures the classic or late modern frames of public sphere. While the public sphere is based on narrative semantic structures, which can be elaborated, reflected on, criticized, and defended, the functioning of information is much more limited. Information is a completely new form of social integration. It does not rely on a mutual understanding of the world. Instead it functions much more as stimulus. The stimuli of information stream continuously, thus coordinating action in real time. According to this logic, social integration depends on the connectedness of the actors to the same network of information. This model of mass communication eliminates the frames of not only traditional, but also modern human existence. It replaces the reflexive and communicative practices, with the unconscious, real time following of the streams of information. Therefore it fundamentally endangers all those levels, which rely on these practices: the reflexive-communicative construction of identity and the democratic control of public sphere. At the same time it threatens with a regression not only to traditional, but also to archaic, tribal forms of life.[18]

Accordingly, in the information age, there is an inherent tendency of distorting the emancipatory potential of the public sphere, which originates in the new medium of communication. The question remains: how this general tendency combines with the Internet-based public sphere of the far-right? In what follows the extreme right public sphere is analyzed on two levels. The most official level is the Facebook page of Jobbik, on which the supporters discuss current matters.[19] The most elaborated scene is the most popular extreme right news portal, the www.kuruc.info, where the radical discourse is produced. These two levels of the far-right public sphere have been monitored for three month in 2013 in order to reconstruct the most characteristic semantic and communicative patterns.

The weight of the Internet activity of the extreme right can be best demonstrated with the comparison of the sheer number of Facebook supporters: on 10 June 2014 Jobbik had more than 279,000 "Likes," the governing Party—having two third of the parliamentary mandates—has around 182,000 "Likes," while the second biggest left Party has around 124,000 "Likes." The fact that Jobbik has the greatest proportion of supporters being active online clearly indicates the importance of the Internet-based public sphere in the life of the radical side. The content of the Facebook page of Jobbik is obviously less extreme than the other analyzed scene. It functions much more as an entrance to the radical public sphere. It informs the supporters and those who are interested in the Party about the news, actions of the Party, cultural programs, and public and media events. Both the content and the presentation of this information are surprisingly moderate, compared to the far-right semantics appearing on other forums. The main goal is clearly not to frighten away the potential supporters with aggressive communication or controversial statements. Instead, the Facebook page imitates the façade of a usual, consolidated democratic party. In this sense its intention is to channel new supporters not to satisfy the needs of the core fans.

Accordingly, most of the topics appearing are not suspicious for someone unfamiliar with the stakes of political discourse. Most of the entries criticize the government or the EU from a nationalist point of view. Hot topics include the lack of defense of Hungarian interest, the limitation of foreigners' right to buy Hungarian soil, the corruption of the government and the defense of Hungarian minorities living abroad. Another big part of the entries is related to historical questions, commemorations, reevaluations of figures and events, with a special emphasis on Trianon and the interwar era. A third part of the entries directs the visitor deeper into the far-right public sphere. It includes advertisements of the Party media, of festivals and concerts belonging to the extreme right-skinhead subculture, and also camps and demonstrations. The fourth part of the entries, which occur in the smallest proportion, refer to those specific issues, which characterize the far-right discourses, such is the Roma question. As the last two types of contents are more controversial, they appear in the smallest proportion. In this way the central message is dosed in small amounts, while the façade of a consolidated Party is maintained.

Despite the careful communication of the Party, which aims to brand Jobbik as a responsible political force, the comments and interactions of the supporters highlight a completely different reality underneath the surface. On a semantic level the basic patterns of the far-right worldview directly appear. A strong "friend/enemy" distinction grounds the semantics,[20] dividing the political actors into the group of "true Hungarians" and the "enemies of Hungary." The enemies depending on their social status and the type of their activity are constituted of two subgroups. Those, who impair the honest Hungarians either with petty crime, violence or the abuse of the social security system, are identified with the unworthy, violent, ungrateful Roma. Those who undermine the prosperity of the Hungarians and Hungary on a general political level are identified with the cosmopolitan, liberal-left Jews. These two topoi frame the far-right discourses, serving as a basis of interpretation of the concrete fears and general anxiety of the supporters.

The category of the Roma is primarily used in those contexts, where fears of everyday life are the focus. The Roma are treated as the concrete enemy, who on the one hand endangers the material needs of the Hungarians by stealing or robbing them. On the other hand the Roma are the worthless rivals who get the scarce resources of the social security system, which rightfully belong to the honest Hungarians working for it. The category of the Jew is used to unveil the grand scheme of the global conspiracy against Hungarian interests. Any political actor who supports global trends on material level (e.g., by market liberalization) or cultural level (e.g., by giving place to global cultural products instead of local traditions) is characterized as a Jew. In this sense semantically the Roma and the Jew complement each other. Together they ground a linguistic universe, where the everyday fears and the general anxieties can be both interpreted in an essentializing manner. As the sources of the fears are attributed to ethnic categories, the enemy can be easily localized and frustrations can be targeted to concrete groups of people.

The discursive logic of friend and enemy is a dogmatic one: it does not allow debates, argumentations, criticism, and justification of validity claims, only alignment with the dominant distinctions. This characteristic is clearly present in the communicative processes of the Facebook page. The participants do not argue; rather they repeat phrases, which are treated as self-evident. In those few cases, where someone expresses an opinion, which does not accord with the canon, quickly many defenders appear, who instead of arguing, simply talk down the different opinion. In this sense the virtual communicative actions refer to a strict discursive field, with clear semantic contours and a dogmatic worldview. However this characteristic semantic field is not elaborated on the *Facebook* page itself. The main surface of these discussions is the kuruc.info portal, which is amongst the most read right wing political homepages: while the biggest central right sites like www.mno.hu have around 110,000 visitors a day, www.kuruc.info has around 96,000.[21] The portal is maintained from abroad, it hosts the far-right public sphere since 2006, despite several attempts to ban it.

It is divided into five thematic clusters: "anti-Hungarianism," "Gypsy crime," "gene cemetery," "politician crime," and "Jew crime." Probably these five pillars characterize best the semantic field of the far-right public sphere. At the center of the whole field there is an attempt to create hysteria and panic. The basis of the far-right worldview is the feeling of being threatened: as an individual and as a nation, from the inside and the outside, below and above. This strong emotional charge is fundamental in the sense that it proves the state of emergency, which state is the reason to give up any further need for justification. In state of emergency the reason gives its place to quick action, debate gives its place to dogmatic ideology and arguments give theirs to orders. Without this constant war atmosphere and the generalization of the extraordinary times, the far-right discourses could not exist. That is why it is crucial for them to maintain the emotional charge.

The five thematic clusters approach the topic of being threatened from a different angle. Under anti-Hungarianism those events and activities are discussed, which either offend the so-called Hungarian interests or criticize the activities of the far-right. Of course the intermeshing of these two different topics clearly serves strategic goals: within this semantic framing the criticisms of the far-right are treated as the attacks of the Hungarian interests as such. By mixing the friend/enemy distinction of the party with the friend/ enemy distinction of the nation, the former is justified by the latter and the interests of the far-right camp are reinterpreted as the interests of the nation. Combined with the emotional charge originating from the permanent state of emergency the equation of the national and party interests creates an antidemocratic, authoritarian atmosphere, where the directives of the party stand above criticism.

Under the label of politician crime, articles are collected which inform the public about corruption of the government. Such a section is surprisingly free from the far-right semantic frames: it usually does not blame the Roma or the Jews, but only reports the illegal activities of the former and present government. In this sense at first glance it is similar to those "watchdog" sites, which are devoted to the surveillance and civil control of the politicians. However in the far-right context the criticism of the politicians does not serve democratic purposes. Instead its aim is to introduce the utterly corrupt nature of the so-called "democratic" political elite. Instead of becoming an argument for bigger civil control and the development of democratic institutions, the news about the corruption of the politicians becomes an argument against democracy as such, which produced its corrupt elite. In this sense the suggested solution to the problems of democracy is the replacement of the democratic institutions with a political system founded on the moral supremacy of the self-appointed representatives of the nation.

This twisted implicit logic is even more paradoxical because, unsurprisingly, the www.kuruc.info itself does not do any investigative journalism. Instead it relies uncritically on the reports from magazines, which are in other contexts damned by the far-right as the trumpets of the anti-Hungarian conspiracy. This paradoxical relation to the democratic press expresses a deeper ambivalence in the far right's understanding of democracy. On the one hand the far-right semantics is contemptuous of the values of democracy: it explicitly despises the principles of tolerance and the rule of law. On the other hand however it exploits the protection provided by the same values: it argues against the banning of extreme right public voices in the name of free speech and it sues those who evaluate them as the inheritors of the Nazi mentality. The paradoxical relation to democracy on the semantic level creates a distorted civil culture, which is based on the expectation of political and social rights and the parallel exclusion of the unworthy social groups from the same universal rights.

The other three sections of the homepage, which constitute together the majority of the contents, are raw racist propaganda. They mix news and false-news and interpret them in a xenophobic manner by emphasizing the unworthiness, malevolence, ridiculousness or subordinated status of the Roma, the Jew or other ethnic or gender minorities. They lack the slightest attempt at objectivity, and in this sense their clear intention is to raise social tension and to maintain and channel fear and frustration. In a certain way these contents are the unique feature of the far-right semantics. The friend/enemy distinction of the true Hungarians and the others is not alien to the rhetoric of the central right parties either, while the criticism of the corruption originates in the civil society. However, open racism is tolerated only in the far-right community. The racist propaganda is quite homogeneous: in the edited articles, in the readers' letters, and the following forum discussions the same few stereotypes are repeated endlessly. In this sense they completely lack any communicative goals: they are not supposed to produce new information or to explain anything. As their essence is collective repetition, concerning their form and function they remind much more of tribal rituals or religious mantras.

According to Durkheim rituals played a central role in the tribal life of archaic society, as they provided the opportunity to reproduce collective consciousness and a common categorization of the world.[22] Habermas continues this line of though by suggesting that the originally non-linguistic rituals were gradually replaced by linguistic acts, which opened up a way of reflecting on the collective categories instead of simply reproduce them. In other words they allowed communicative rationalization.[23] From this point of view the virtual public sphere of the far-right expresses a regressive phenomenon. The ritual repetition of the same few racist stereotypes serves the purpose of reproducing a collective consciousness, which orients the understanding of the world and maintains a collective identity. Obviously such ritual practices exclude the potential of reflection, as they are in fact pseudo-communicative actions. Their function is not to understand the other or the world, but to create "collective effervescence" and through it a virtual community.

In sum, the far-right public sphere can be evaluated as an extremely limited public space. It lacks not only the rationality potential elaborated by Habermas, or the system critical potential mentioned by Arató-Cohen, but also lacks the existentialist potentials of experiencing individual freedom or recognition described by Arendt. Instead of all these potentials, the far-right public sphere seems to be based on negative sentiments. It is grounded by the feeling of being threatened on individual and collective level. This generalized fear is channeled into the public sphere creating a dogmatic semantics of friend/enemy, which groups are characterized by racist categories. Within these semantic frames the communication becomes limited as well. Its content and form both undermine the chance of reflection, which is normally an inherent potential of any communicative acts. Reflective speech acts are replaced with a pseudo-communicative practice resembling to archaic non-linguistic rituals. In this sense the far-right public sphere is an imitated public sphere: it does not fulfill the functions and potentials of the late modern public sphere, instead gives place to social regression.

Of course such patterns of far-right public sphere are not entirely new, as similar tendencies were present since the transition. However these tendencies were fragmented and could not constitute a coherent community until the appropriate medium of mass communication did not appear. With the emergence of the information society this constellation has drastically changed. A medium was born, which was perfectly compatible with the requirements of the far-right semantics and was capable of integrating the previously scattered far-right supporters. It provided a space, where the kind of limited, ritualistic communication could have been conducted, which organized the people with far-right mentality into a community sharing a common public sphere. In this sense the logic of information, which has been criticized by Lash for emptying the modern frames of reflection made a perfect match with the needs of the far-right community.

The information does not allow reflective evaluation of the contents, which is however a problem only for those political semantics, which rely on deliberation. From the perspective of the far-right, the information age had only positive consequences: with the help of the new medium those sporadic individuals, who are susceptible to the fundamentalist answers given to the challenges of late modernity could be easily accessed and integrated through a ritualized communication. Thus the emergence of information society gave a comparative advantage to the far-right parties. The medium of information raises several challenges for the parties relying on communicative rationality, which need to be adapted to. However the far-right parties, which neglect communicative rationality could instantly profit from its advantages, without a pressure of developing new forms of deliberation.

In this sense the far-right public sphere actualizes the worst fears of the information age. In it the medium and the content complement each other, mutually strengthening each other's devastating potentials. In the far-right public sphere the effectiveness of the web communication is combined with the intention of destroying the most important political results of the Enlightenment, while the alternative public spheres are in a comparative disadvantage. Thus the far-right parties threaten with social regression, the reemerging of archaic forms of life, based on ritualized reproduction of friend/enemy distinctions, neglecting the emancipatory achievements of the last two centuries. Of course, even if the danger grew recently, it is still far from becoming a dominant phenomenon. The majority is still not attracted by the far-right semantics. At this point, after analyzing the virtual public sphere of the far-right, the question concerning the preconditions of the attraction to the semantics appearing in it becomes the most important. In the last part of the chapter this question is analyzed.

SUSCEPTIBILITY TO RADICALISM: THE DISTORTIONS OF POLITICAL SOCIALIZATION

The information society provides the opportunity for the far-right public sphere to expand. However, beside the expansion of the extremist public sphere, the rise of information society also allows other semantics to emerge.

In this sense, radicalization is only one amongst the many potentials of the information society, such as the potential to develop new forms of democratic participation, deliberation, and civil society. The different reactions to the new potentials and challenges of the information society are the results of different paths of socialization and different experiences throughout the life course. In order to understand the functioning of the far-right public spheres, those socialization patterns needs to be identified, which create susceptibility to the radical semantics. As the far-right public sphere is founded on strong negative emotions, its constitution and potential transformations can be explained only from the perspective of those experiences, which evoke these feelings. Thus, as a last step, the results of a survey are introduced, which analyze the socialization processes of Hungarian students finishing high school.

Even if the analysis of young people does not substitute for an overall representative survey, there are several reasons why it fits to our goals. First of all, the eighteen–nineteen-year-old cohort is a generation which was born and educated after the transition, without any experiences from state socialist period. Furthermore, this generation is a native of the information society, which means that its members are the primary target group for the far-right virtual public sphere. Accordingly the analysis of the high school students provides an opportunity for a focused observation of those factors, which result in susceptibility to far-right semantics. In 2011 a representative survey has been conducted amongst Hungarian high school students.[24] More than four thousand school-leavers were asked about their family and school life, peer group relations, media consumption habits, opinions about the history, democracy, and radical values. In what follows the explanatory variables of the attraction to radical values are analyzed.

Radical values are measured by a principal component, created from a scale measuring ethnic prejudices[25] and attitude questions measuring authoritarianism.[26] The explanatory variables measured structural position (cultural, economic, and social capital), demographical variables (gender, family structure), the family memories about the twentieth century (Trianon, the Horthy-era, the Holocaust, state socialism), the family identity (being proud of nationality, knowledge, moral character), leisure time patterns (learning, individual amusement, family programs), family emotional life (alienated, caring), formal family communication patterns (dogmatic, strategic, rational), substantive family communication patterns (public issues, private issues), democratic experiences in school, media consumption habits (internet, TV), peer group relations (social network, communication patterns).

The following table summarizes the results of a linear regression, introducing those explanatory variables, which showed significant correspondence with the antidemocratic attitudes, plus the strength and the direction of the relation ($R^2 = 21$ percent).

THE EXPLANATORY VARIABLES OF ANTIDEMOCRATIC ATTITUDES

According to the results of the regression, we may conclude that antidemo-cratic attitudes are more frequent amongst males than females. This indicates the importance of gender socialization: males seem to have more experi-ences, which result in identification with prejudices and preferring of raw power over deliberation in social relations. Amongst the structural variables only cultural capital seems to have effect on the antidemocratic attitudes: the bigger is the parents' qualification, the smaller is the chance of susceptibility to radicalism. In the light of the lack of correspondence with other types of capital this sole relation may be interpreted as a key factor of political social-ization. It seems that susceptibility to antidemocratic values is primarily a cultural question, not a simple result of deprived structural position. The stakes of prejudices and authoritarian movements become visible only if the proper understanding of the nature of democracy is given. The lack of such implicit knowledge is one of the key factors of susceptibility to oversimplify-ing, populist semantics used by the far-right.

Besides demographic and structural factors, the quality of family life also plays a central role in the processes of political formation. In those families,

Table 7.1.   The explanatory variables of antidemocratic attitudes

name of explanatory variable	beta
gender	-,110
father's qualification	-,132
mother's qualification	-,096
aggressive emotional climate	,070
authoritarian father	,084
strategic family communication patterns	,094
talking about historical questions in family	-,069
Trianon as important historical event	,099
having a relative, who was a former member of the Communist Party	-,075
being proud to be Hungarian	,126
having nationalist symbols in the apartment	,087
religiousness	,060
amusement leisure time	,075
democratic experiences in school	-,121
talking about politics with friends	-,082

where the conflicts are settled in verbally or physically aggressive quarrels instead of discussion, or the father oppresses the family in an authoritarian manner, or the family communication is based on unscrupulous attempts to realize individual goals, instead of reaching mutual understanding, the chance of identification with antidemocratic values grows high. All these different attributes of family life refer to an elementary lack of interpersonal relationships based on intimacy and mutual recognition. Family life plays a crucial role in the democratic formation, as the family relationships are the first and foremost ground of practicing interactions as such. If these practices are characterized by alienated emotions, strict, unchangeable hierarchies, missing practices of peacefully handling conflicts, then the basic model of relating to the other and to oneself is equally damaged. Therefore a democratic model of organizing social life lacks any concrete grounds and becomes an unrealistic, empty ideal. Furthermore, without emotionally stable family background young people are more exposed to those emotional problems, which are transformed in the far-right public sphere into a generalized paranoid feeling of being threatened grounding the whole radical semantics. These are the reasons why young people growing up in families burdened with emotional and communicational pathologies tend to be more susceptible to values, which neglect or refuse democratic practices.

The historical consciousness is the next important factor in the preference or refusal of radical views. In those families where conversations about the experiences of the twentieth century occur frequently, the chance to choose antidemocratic values is smaller. In those families, where the Trianon treaty is a distinctive reference point in the interpretation of the past, the distancing from antidemocratic values is smaller. In those families having personal affiliations to the state socialist system the effect is the opposite. These correspondences reveal how memory affects political culture. On the one hand, as the twentieth century for Hungary was mostly about authoritarian political systems or dictatorships, talking about these issues in the family has the potential of raising awareness concerning any sort of radicalism. On the other hand, Trianon and involvement in state socialism are the two opposite reference points in collective memory. The former is the starting point of a narrative about the historical injustice, which the Hungarians have suffered, thus it is the foundation of any sort of nationalist worldview. The latter is the basis of a narrative which interprets state socialism as a special path of modernization instead of simply condemning it as a period of Soviet oppression. It is therefore the foundation of any sort of antinationalist worldview. Accordingly, the two family traditions determine the susceptibility to nationalism, which is the central element of far-right semantics.

The next group of variables expresses the identity factors in the process of acquiring antidemocratic values. In those families, where everyone is proud to be a Hungarian–and this is expressed in the placement of nationalistic symbols (e.g., a map of great-Hungary) in the apartment—there is a greater chance to identify with the radical semantics, building on these sentiments and symbols. The positive effect of religiousness requires a little more explanation. The Hungarian historical churches played an important political role in the Horhty-era, while being persecuted during the period of state socialism. This historical heritage made them the natural ally of the right-wing parties after the transition. Accordingly, the degree of religiousness is implicitly or explicitly a component of the nationalist identity, which explains why it opens a path to the antidemocratic political culture originating from it.

The positive effect of the leisure time spent with individual amusement can be understood best in comparison to the other two ideal types: the family and learning-centered free time. While these latter two types express a stable set of goals, the former expresses a lack of such clear orientation. In this sense the amusement leisure time, including playing with computers, watching TV and listening to music, expresses a loss of meaning, the missing of a prospect of a feasible life course. Without clear goals or means to realize goals the motivation to elaborate an identity and to aspire toward an ideal is impossible, which creates a vacuum and may easily cause frustration. This potential vacuum and frustration can be also exploited by the far-right semantics, which is exceptionally successful at channeling negative sentiments.

The last two variables indicate the extra-family factors of a socialization process resulting in susceptibility to radicalism. While family is the first and foremost terrain to practice interactions in general, the school is the first institution young people get into regular contact and peer groups are the first community of equals in one's life. Therefore both of them play a different, but equally crucial role. Being distinguished fields of practicing civic interactions, they are particularly important terrains of collecting experiences about institutions based on system logic and the potential of politically organizing a community. In case these experiences go wrong and they mirror an authoritarian institutional order or a community based on the principles of raw power instead of deliberation, then they could easily lead to a general disillusionment concerning the potential of democracy and result in antidemocratic orientation.

After surveying the explanatory factors affecting the antidemocratic attitudes we may conclude that the susceptibility to radicalism is basically a result of the parallel lack of key experiences. Those—especially male—young people, whose parents, because of their low cultural capital, do not understand or cannot explain the stakes of democratic principles; whose family life is based on unequal, arbitrary parent-child relations; whose family interactions are characterized by aggression instead of communication oriented to mutual understanding; who lack historical reflectivity and share a nationalist narrative of the past; whose family have a strong nationalistic or religious character; who miss any particular goal in life and float in their everyday life; and who do not have any democratic experience in the school or in their peer group community are particularly exposed to far-right semantics. Of course in themselves none of these factors result in antidemocratic attitudes, but their effect cumulates: the more factors are present the bigger is the chance to collect experiences, which orient toward radicalism.

CONCLUSION

In sum, we may conclude that the flourishing of the far-right in Hungary is based on many parallel tendencies. First of all, the authoritarian civic culture inherited from state socialism creates a general negligence in relation to the threats of antidemocratic semantics. Secondly, the negative experiences of the political life since the transition on the one hand increase this ignorance; on the other hand generate a strong anti-establishment atmosphere. Third, specific events created opportunity for the far-right to interpret complex problems in an oversimplifying, populist and racist manner. Fourth, the emergence of the information society created a medium fitting to the needs of the far-right public sphere. As these virtual forums fundamentally reshape the frames of reflection and communication, they are inhabited by the democratic political forces relying on deliberation slowly, which give a comparative advantage to the far-right using the virtual public sphere only for a pseudo-communication aimed at collective rituals, instead of communication oriented to mutual understanding. Finally, as such imitated public spheres provide extremely limited capacities, parallel distortions of process of political socialization are needed for the growing the far-right community.

As the analysis demonstrates, radicalization relies on factors, which are present on different levels of social processes. Factors like the social historical heritage, the daily political events, the transformations of modernity, and the political socialization processes together determine the potential of radicalization. On the one hand this conclusion has a reassuring consequence: the sudden radicalization of the majority in Hungary is improbable, as such a scenario would require drastic parallel changes on all these levels. On the one hand this conclusion has consequences for social policies oriented to lower the already dangerously high level of far-right influence: preventing further radicalization cannot be based only on anti-racist propaganda, it must influence all the above-mentioned levels. This means that the authoritarian political heritage needs to be combated, the political elite needs to eliminate the cold civil war atmosphere it created, symbolic events of anti-radicalism and collective democratic experiences are needed, the democratic virtual public sphere needs to be strengthened and most importantly the processes of political socialization need to be reformed.

NOTES

1. Manuel Castells, *The Rise of the Network Society, The Information Age: Economy, Society and Culture Vol. I.* (Cambridge, MA; Oxford, UK: Blackwell, 1996).

2. The notions of "far right," "extreme right," and "radical" are used as general terms referring to those political semantics and actors that explicitly refuse the basic principles and institutions of modern democracy. In addition, they have strong nationalist affiliation often complemented with xenophobic, racist or anti-Semitic sentiments, and populist political programs. All translations, unless otherwise indicated, are my own.

3. Tamás Keller, "The Position of Hungary on the Worldwide Map of Human Values." *Review of Sociology of the HAS 20*, no. 1, Domonkos Sik, "A Transformation of Action Coordination? A Critical Interpretation of the Hungarian Transition." *Review of Sociology of the HAS 20*, no. 2, Ildikó Szabó, *Political Socialization in Hungary* (Frankfurt/M., Bern, New York, Paris: Peter Lang, 1989).

4. Domonkos Sik, "Civic Socialization in Post-Transition Condition," *Politics, Culture and Socialization 2*, no. 3, Ildikó Szabó, *Nemzet és szocializáció. A politika szerepe az identitások alakulásában Magyarországon 1867–2006* (Budapest: L'Harmattan Kiadó, 2009).

5. György Csepeli, István Murányi and Gergő Prazsák, *Új tekintélyelvűség a mai Magyarországon* (Budapest: Aperion, 2010); Zoltán Fábián, *Tekintélyelvűség és előítéletek* (Budapest: Új Mandátum, 1999); Zsolt Enyedi and Ferenc Erős, eds., *Authoritarianism and Prejudice: Central European Perspectives* (Budapest: Osiris 1999); András Kovács, *The Stranger at Hand. Anti-Semitic Prejudices in Post-Communist Hungary* (Leiden and Boston: Brill, 2011).

6. András Körösényi, "Cleavages and Party System in Hungary," in *The 1994 Elections to the Hungarian National Assembly*, eds. Gábor Tóka and, Zsolt Enyedi (Stigma Verlag, 1999); Emilia Palonen, "Political Polarization and Populism in Contemporary Hungary," *Parliamentary Affairs 62*, no. 2.

7. Gergely Karácsony and Dániel Róna, "A Jobbik titka: A szélsőjobb magyarországi megerősödésének lehetséges okairól," *Politikatudományi Szemle 19*, no. 1.

8. István Grajczjár and András Tóth, "Válság, radikalizálódás és az újjászületés ígérete: a Jobbik útja a parlamentbe," in *Új képlet. A 2010-es választások Magyarországon*, eds. Zsolt Enyedi, Andrea Szabó and Róbert Tardos (Budapest: DKMKA, 2011).

9. Hans-Georg Gadamer, *Truth and Method*, translated by Joel Weinsheimer and D. G. Marshall (London: Continuum, 2004); Jürgen Habermas, *The Theory of Communicative Action vol.1: Reason and the Rationalization of Society*, translated by Thomas McCarthy, (Boston: Beacon Press, 1984).

10. Ignác Romsics, *Hungary in the 20th Century* (Budapest: Corvina—Osiris 1999).

11. László Karsai, "The Radical Right in Hungary," in *The Radical Right in Central and Eastern Europe Since 1989*, edited by Ramet Sabrina (Pennsylvania: The Pennsylvania State University Press, 1999); Áron Szele, "Extraordinary Situations-Extraordinary Means: The Regenerative Projects of the Hungarian Radical Right Yesterday and Today," *CEU Political Science Journal 7*, no. 2.

12. Even if the information society played a key role, it was not the only terrain of incubating a new extreme right identity. Gradually a new nationalist subculture emerged including its own music, leisure activity, symbols, and cultural practices capable of creating communities. See Margit Feischmidt, Rita Glózer, Zoltán Ilyés, Veronika Katalin Kasznár and Ildikó Zakariás, *Nemzet a mindennapokban – Az újnacionalizmus populáris kultúrája* (Budapest: L'Harmattan, 2014).

13. Balázs Barkóczi, "A hazai radikális jobboldal térhódítása az interneten," *Médiakutató 41*, no. 4.

14. Tamás Rudas, "A Jobbik törzsszavazóiról," in *Társadalmi riport 2010*, eds. Tamás Kolosi and István György Tóth (Budapest: Tárki, 2010); Lili Zentai "Utolsó, előre fuss! A Jobbik hajrája 2010-ben," in *Kritikus kampány. A 2010-es országgyűlési választási kampány elemzése*, eds. Gabriella Szabó, Zsuzsanna Mihályffy, Balázs Kiss (Budapest: L'Harmattan Kiadó, 2010).

15. Hannah Arendt, *The Human Condition* (Chicago: The University of Chicago Press, 1998).
16. Jürgen Habermas, *The Theory of Communicative Action vol.1: Reason and the Rationalization of Society*, translated by Thomas McCarthy (Boston: Beacon Press, 1984).
17. Andrew Arato and Jean L. Cohen, *Civil Society and Political Theory* (Cambridge: MIT Press, 1992); Jürgen Habermas, *Between Facts and Norms: Contributions to a Discourse Theory of Law and Democracy*, translated by William Rehg (Cambridge: Polity Press 1996).
18. Scott Lash, *Critique of Information* (London: Sage, 2002).
19. https://www.facebook.com/JobbikMagyarorszagertMozgalom.
20. Carl Schmitt, *The Concept of the Political*, translated by George D. Schwab (Chicago: University of Chicago Press, 2007).
21. The numbers originate from the database of www.webaudit.hu, downloaded on 10 June 2014.
22. Emile Durkheim, *The Elementary Forms of Religious Life*, translated by Karen E. Fields (New York: Free Press, 1995).
23. Jürgen Habermas, *The Theory of Communicative Action vol.2: Lifeworld and System: A Critique of Functionalist Reason*, translated by Thomas McCarthy (Boston: Beacon Press, 1984).
24. The survey was supported by the Hungarian Research Fund (project number: OTKA-K78579), for the detailed description of the research and further analyses about the preconditions of radical attitudes, see Domonkos Sik, *Demokratikus kultúra és modernizáció - Állampolgári szocializáció 20 évvel a rendszerváltás után* (Budapest: L'Harmattan, 2014).
25. The questions were: "Would it disturb you, if your classmate were an Arabian / a Roma/ a Chinese/ an African/ a German/ a Russian/ a Romanian/ a Serbian/ a Slovakian/ a Jew?"
26. The questions were: "How deeply do you agree with the following questions: Hungary needs a government, which does not simply talk, but smashes if needed/ Hungary needs to fight against the interior and external mischievous forces, in the name of national self-defense/ Finally one strong party would be needed, instead of the many arguing parties/ Military service should be obligatory?"

REFERENCES

Arato, Andrew and Cohen, Jean L. *Civil Society and Political Theory.* Cambridge: MIT Press, 1992.
Arendt, Hannah. *The Human Condition.* Chicago: The University of Chicago Press, 1998.
Barkóczi, Balázs. "A hazai radikális jobboldal térhódítása az interneten" (The Conquest of the Hungarian Far Right on the Internet). In *Médiakutató* 4 (2010): 51–61.
Castells, Manuel. *The Rise of the Network Society, The Information Age: Economy, Society and Culture*, Vol. I. Cambridge, MA; Oxford, UK: Blackwell, 1996.
Csepeli, György, István Murányi, and Gergő Prazsák. *Új tekintélyelvűség a mai Magyarországon.* (New Authoritarianism in Hungary). Budapest: Aperion, 2010.
Durkheim, Emile. *The Elementary Forms of Religious Life.* Translated by Karen E. Fields. New York: Free Press, 1995.
Enyedi, Zsolt and Ferenc Erős, eds. *Authoritarianism and Prejudice: Central European Perspectives.* Budapest: Osiris, 1999.
Fábián, Zoltán. *Tekintélyelvűség és előítéletek* (Authoritarianism and Prejudices). Budapest: Új Mandátum, 1999.
Gadamer, Hans-Georg. *Truth and Method.* Translated by Joel Weinsheimer and D. G. Marshall. London: Continuum, 2004.
Grajczjár, István and András Tóth. "Válság, radikalizálódás és az újjászületés ígérete: a Jobbik útja a parlamentbe" (Crisis, Radicalization and the Promise of Rebirth: the Way of Jobbik into the Parliament). In Enyedi Zsolt, Andrea Szabó, and Tardos Róbert, eds. *Új képlet. A 2010-es választások* Magyarországon. Budapest: DKMKA, 2011: 57–92.
Habermas, Jürgen. *The Theory of Communicative Action vol.1: Reason and the Rationalization of Society.* Translated by Thomas McCarthy. Boston: Beacon Press, 1984.

Habermas, Jürgen. *The Theory of Communicative Action vol.2: Lifeworld and System: A Critique of Functionalist Reason.* Translated by Thomas McCarthy. Boston: Beacon Press, 1987.

Habermas, Jürgen. *Between Facts and Norms: Contributions to a Discourse Theory of Law and Democracy.* Translated by William Rehg. Cambridge: Polity Press, 1996.

Keller, Tamás. "The Position of Hungary on the Worldwide Map of Human Values." In *Review of Sociology of the HAS* 1 (2010): 27–51.

Kovács, András. *The Stranger at Hand. Anti-Semitic Prejudices in Post-Communist Hungary.* Leiden and Boston: Brill, 2011.

Karácsony, Gergely and Dániel Róna. "A Jobbik titka: A szélsőjobb magyarországi megerősödésének lehetséges okairól" (The Secret of Jobbik: On the Potential Reasons of the Rise of the Hungarian Extreme Right). *Politikatudományi Szemle 1* (2010): 31–63.

Karsai, László. "The Radical Right in Hungary." In Sabrina P. Ramet, ed. *The Radical Right in Central and Eastern Europe Since 1989.* Pennsylvania: The Pennsylvania State University Press, 1999. 133–46.

Körösényi, András. "Cleavages and Party System in Hungary." In Tóka G and Enyedi Zseds. *The 1994 Elections to the Hungarian National Assembly.* Stigma Verlag, 1999.Lash, Scott. *Critique of Information.* London: Sage, 2002.

Palonen, Emilia. "Political Polarization and Populism in Contemporary Hungary." In *Parliamentary Affairs* 2 (2009): 318–34.

Romsics, Ignác. *Hungary in the 20th Century.* Budapest: Corvina-Osiris, 1999.

Rudas, Tamás. "A Jobbik törzsszavazóiról" (About the core voters of Jobbik). In Kolosi Tamás and Tóth István György, eds. *Társadalmi riport 2010*, Budapest: Tárki, 2010.

Schmitt, Carl. *The Concept of the Political.* Expanded Edition. Translated by George D.Schwab, Chicago: University of Chicago Press, 2007.

Sik, Domonkos. "A Transformation of Action Coordination? A Critical Interpretation of the Hungarian Transition." *Review of Sociology of the HAS* 2 (2010): 17–45.

Sik, Domonkos. "Civic Socialization in Post-Transition Condition." In *Politics, Culture and Socialization* 3 (2011): 257–71.

Sik, Domonkos. *Demokratikus kultúra és modernizáció - Állampolgári szocializáció 20 évvel a rendszerváltás után.* (Democratic Culture and Modernization—Civic Socialization 20 years after the Hungarian Transition). Budapest: L'Harmattan, 2014.

Szabó, Ildikó. *Political Socialization in Hungary.* Frankfurt/M., Bern, New York, Paris: Peter Lang, 1989.

Szabó, Ildikó. *Nemzet és szocializáció. A politika szerepe az identitások alakulásában Magyarországon 1867–2006.* (Nation and Socialization. The Role of Politics in Forming Identities in Hungary 1867–2006). Budapest: L'Harmattan Kiadó, 2009.

Szele, Áron. "Extraordinary Situations-Extraordinary Means: The Regenerative Projects of the Hungarian Radical Right Yesterday and Today." In *CEU Political Science Journal* 2 (2012): 123–44.

Zentai, Lili. "Utolsó, előre fuss! A Jobbik hajrája 2010-ben" ("Last, run to the first place! The charge of Jobbik in 2010"). In Szabó, Gabriella, Mihályffy, Zsuzsanna and Kiss Balázs, eds. *Kritikus kampány. A 2010-es országgyűlési választási kampányelemzése.* Budapest: L'Harmattan Kiadó, 2010.

Chapter Eight

Right-Wing Campaign Strategies in Sweden

Lara Mazurski

When the Sverigedemokraterna (translated as the "Sweden Democrats," hereafter SD) unveiled their campaign advertisement for the 2010 parliamentary election, they used a series of images positioning immigrants as scapegoats by creating a link between immigration and the domestic budgetary crisis. While the advertisement associates immigration and Islam with the economic failings of Swedish society, the SD also energized new forms of representation along with a new embodiment of Swedishness and conceptualizations of "the Other." On the surface, the controversial campaign ad identifies economic concerns and moral corruption with immigration, women, and Islam. Perhaps, as a result of this immediate and widespread association, the state's leading broadcaster, TV4, banned the advertisement for inciting hate speech before it even aired on Swedish television. The act of censorship thrust the ad center stage, with a subsequent flurry of international media coverage and the SD proclaiming unlawful persecution. Paradoxically, or, perhaps expectedly, censorship of the advertisement, and the ensuing public debate, dramatically increased awareness of the Party and its message.

By analyzing the SD campaign advertisement and the censorship surrounding it, I develop a critical understanding not only of representations of cultural, ethnic, or religious difference, but more specifically, of how the burqa is represented. At issue here is whether anti-immigrant discourses and popular notions of the Muslim woman, who is represented by the burqa as subjugated and victimized, have been condensed into a single body. Within the context of this ad, "otherness" is produced and reproduced through a complex combination of images, text, sound, and narration. Burqas are presented as parasitic and ubiquitous among immigrants; they symbolize an unknown threat. The recoding of the burqa's significance does not stop there. For example, the woman beneath the garment is not depicted as struggling to escape the patriarchy that has put her there. Instead, the ad advances the idea of the burqa as symbolic of that which Swedish society must fight to overcome: it is a symbol of a call for Swedish opposition to Islamic immigration.

In large part, the conversation that surrounded the SD in the 2010 election was concerned with questions of censorship and victimhood. Rather than engaging or opposing the act of censorship itself, in this chapter I look to the work of Judith Butler and her discussion of discursive censorship in *Excitable Speech: The Politics of the Performative* (1997). To do so, I analyze the representations and concepts deployed by this advertisement and illuminate the ways they are vulnerable to both reinterpretation and new citations. Butler's work on censorship matters here because it serves as a response to existing social concerns such as hate speech and censorship. Her work sheds light on how social and political acts like those performed or authorized by institutions are often reactionary in their political aims. Within the context of the censored SD ad, the act of censorship does not deliver its intended consequences, but rather diminishes public spaces for contestation. Indeed, censorship serves to counter its own effects and produces a new set of consequences that may even heighten the power of the speech that it sought to silence.

THE RIGHT WING IN THE POLITICAL CONTEXT OF CONTEMPORARY SWEDEN

Given the long-term entrenchment of politics and policies that have shaped the classic vision of the welfare state, Sweden has not provided receptive ground for right-wing populism. For decades the country has been considered "a viable alternative to Thatcherite neo-liberalism, while for many currents within Europe's dwindling group of ruling Socialist parties Sweden has come to represent the light beckoning at the end of a long tunnel of austerity and restructuring."[1] Jonas Pontusson's (1987) quote highlights Sweden's image as a safe haven for the Scandinavian project of Social Democracy juxtaposed against the impinging demands of neoliberalism. For more than seven decades, Sweden's liberal welfare state has been guarded by the Social Democratic Party (SAP) in conjunction with members of the left-wing bloc, composed of Social Democrats and Communists/ex-Communists, that stand in opposition to the right-wing bloc of Conservatives, Liberals, and the Center Party.[2] Since the postwar period, Sweden, like its Scandinavian counterparts, has experienced pronounced social, political, and demographic changes.[3] Immigration in particular has played a significant role in altering the model of "Swedishness," moving from an "ethnically homogenous population to one with mixed ethnic background."[4] With new population groups settling in, Sweden has worked to politically satisfy its inhabitants and introduce a new model that encompasses its burgeoning cultural diversity.[5]

In 1975 Sweden declared itself officially "multicultural," ushering in a model based on "equality," "freedom of choice," and "partnership."[6] The implementation of this "multicultural model" was a crucial moment in the recognition of the cultural diversity of immigrants and religious minorities in Sweden.

Yet with economic tensions mounting in the mid-1980s, followed by a number of challenges to its "immigration policy," Sweden would turn away from an official definition of "multiculturalism" in the 1990s.[7] Against the backdrop of entry into the European Union (1995), rising unemployment, and the emergence of neoliberal discourses on self-sufficiency, public sentiment began to change. Immigrants were no longer embraced as distinct minorities and the "multicultural model" was disavowed in favor of assimilationist policies.[8]

The move away from "multiculturalism" prepared the ground for a pan-European sentiment with populist right-wing parties emerging, such as the New Democracy, that brought with them illiberal and xenophobic rhetoric.[9] Targeting the vast numbers of asylum seekers and refugees who sought safety in Sweden during the Balkan conflict, the New Democracy initially drew a considerable amount of attention, but then disappeared a few years later. From the ashes of the far-right tradition, a number of neo-Nazi parties such as the Nordiska Rikspartiet (Nordic Realm Party) would emerge, and would be revitalized later in small splinter groups such as the Sweden Democrats.

Following the 2006 parliamentary election, the left-wing bloc, led by the SAP, experienced massive losses at the polls. In what would ensue, SAP party leadership was singled out for not focusing on the effects of the economic crisis, downplaying the consequences of unemployment, and for ignoring the needs of voters. This error in the left bloc's thinking served as a turning point; right-wing populists claimed that mainstream parties were out of touch with voters. It is in this climate that the Sweden Democrats would begin to emerge and bring their political viewpoints into the limelight.[10]

Formed in 1988, the SD self-identifies as a nationalist movement. In the late 1990s they renounced Nazism. In addition, they modified their provocative sentiments on abortion, on adoption from outside Europe, and on capital punishment.[11] Marked by a strong culturalist sentiment and an aversion to liberalism, the Party frequently wields accounts of "multicultural collapse" supported by xenophobic statements against ethnopluralism.[12] This sentiment is reflected in their manifesto from 2002: "The Sweden Democrats' primary political goal is to defend our national identity."[13] Not only does the SD position itself as a defender of the traditional Swedish nation state but it

also uses its status as a political outsider to drum up support from disenfranchised voters.

With its anti-immigrant sentiment, a high degree of disillusionment with
established political parties, concerns with unemployment, and the changing
face of Sweden, the SD mobilizes highly charged racial signifiers within
simplified debates. Such an agenda becomes visible in the strategic co-opting
of veiled Muslim women's bodies as "the other" in the controversial 2010
campaign ad, which would be subsequently censored. This is a useful entry
point for this critical discussion about the ways in which messages of cultural
inferiority and dysfunction are disseminated within the SD's campaign.

SVERIGEDEMOKRATERNA'S CAMPAIGN AD

Briefly, the Sweden Democrats 2010 election campaign ad depicts an aging
white pensioner in competition with a faceless mob of women in burqas. The
opposing sides are vying for the government's financial resources. The ad is
multifaceted, offering the viewer a number of narratives to interpret and
characterize the figure of the Islamic immigrant on cultural, religious, social,
and economic levels. Overall, the theme of this ad can be summarized as
"politics is about priorities" (reflecting the problems of stigmatization in
debates around Islamic integration and the wielding of "us" and "them"
categories).[14] The oppositional sentiment that characterizes the election ad
has been extremely controversial, leading to its banning, and by proxy it has
raised many concerns about how minority groups are represented in Sweden's media.[15]

The opening sequence of the advertisement begins with a quick glimpse
of the *Statsbudget* (state budget) on a numerical counter. The figure begins at
505,926,342,293 *krona*, Sweden's currency, but quickly decreases. A narrator's voice declares, "Politics is all about making priorities." Heavily edited
images follow that focus the viewer's eyes on a dimly lit room and two
bureaucrats, one male and the other female, who are sitting at desks and
processing handfuls of bank notes. Within this campaign video, narration and
imagery work hand-in-hand to reinforce the ad's visual binary structure.

The use of the female narrator's voice in the opening sequence, as an
anonymous and omniscient storyteller, helps reinforce the proposed objectivity and the truth-value of the message. In addition, the voiceover embeds a
gendered level into the ad. Throughout the clip, the narrator's voice functions
in conjunction with the actors through conceptual overlap: it is the voice of
authority reinforcing the SD's political message while also clarifying the
storyline and articulating the campaign's rhetoric. It is important to recognize
that from the start, the ad is framed as a factual account. The end result of this

visual and verbal persuasion is that ideological discourses of class struggle, gender, nationalism, and xenophobia begin to emerge as the truth.

As the ad continues, the two figures process *krona* from the stacks of cardboard boxes surrounding them. Images of the *Statsbudget* counter are interspersed with images of the bureaucrats, until a final tally of 100,000,000 is reached and dramatically flashes on the screen. The many references to bureaucracy and technology that appear in the opening sequence—the money-counting machines, emergency lights, and sirens—suggest a state of emergency. The triggers indicate that the viewer should be in a panic about the overburdened state budget.

Fast-paced editing increases the need for urgency. As the visual material accumulates and the ad proceeds, the narrator interjects: "Now you have a choice." After this point, which seemingly grants the voter agency and thereby empowers the viewer, a siren starts to sound and a flashing light illuminates the table where the bureaucrats are working. The voice continues, "What is your choice?"

The ad rhetorically declares a state of emergency with the viewer beginning to interpret the sirens and lights as the signals to take action. The moment of crisis is literally and metaphorically enacted. In the following seconds, two hand brakes appear from the ceiling directly in front of the bureaucrats, one inscribed with the word "*Pensioner*," ("Pensions" in English) and the other with "*Invandring*" ("Immigration"). The narrator declares, "Now you have a choice," and the sirens return, emphasizing the urgent need for the viewer to identify with the pensioner.

At this point, additional characters appear. The framing of the story begins to unravel and the visual significance of the narration emerges when the camera zooms in on an elderly white woman with a walker. A series of shots frames the walking woman, making it emphatically clear that she needs physical assistance. The walker draws the viewer's attention to the need for support while the woman "races" to pull the "Immigration" handbrake. The woman's frailty reminds the viewer that some support must come from the larger community. The pensioner's body represents the aging demographic of Sweden—and its need for increased health care—and serves as a signifier of the imagined Swedish nation state. As such, her body is used to both represent and interpolate the target audience for this political ideology.

Tobias Hübinette and Catrin Lundström (2011) explain that in "contemporary Sweden, the idea of being white without doubt constitutes the central core and the master signifier of Swedishness and thus of being Swedish, meaning that a Swede is a white person, and a non-white person is not a Swede."[16] This very element lies at the crux of the SD's ad, where the distinction between natives and foreigners is not only mobilized but also employed as a strategy. "Whiteness" serves as a signifier of native Swedes within the national imaginary of the SD, positioned against the "non-white-ness" of foreigners.[17]

The image of the pensioner, within the language of the SD's patriotism, does not immediately denote strength as usually presented within national discourses. Instead, the ad offers a more powerful reading that alludes to a "deserved" need for aging white pensioners. This woman is "anyone's"— and indeed *everyone's*—mother or grandmother, thus a representative of the "deserving" Swedish pensioner. Concepts such as "deserving" and "unde-serving" within this context echo the rhetoric of neoliberal globalization policies entailed in arguments about the political economy of the global labor market.[18] Since the 1970s such language has been used to distinguish be-tween those who are deemed "worthy" of social protection and "those who are not."[19] The moral redefinition of poverty within such rhetoric has been revitalized and mobilized to reinforce oppositional classifications of groups of people—those who require aid through no fault of their own versus those who are undeserving of help (i.e., the "unworthy poor").[20] It is these neolib-eral binaries that are employed by the SD within the logic of their political rhetoric, defining who is "deserving" of assistance and who are not.

BESIEGED BY BURQAS

In the following sequences, we as viewers witness the aging pensioner turn her head, and in her peripheral vision she sees a crowd of burqa-clad women besieging her. The image of the pensioner is now positioned against another cultural force, an invading army of covered women. In the series of quick shots that follow, the camera pans and focuses on the figures, five of whom are in black burqas and a sixth figure in a black niqab. Two are pushing baby carriages and appear from the darkness behind the pensioner. The camera then immediately offers a close-up of the grille covering one of the women's eyes. This close-up shot does a number of different things. It draws the viewers' attention to the burqa, it commands interest, and it pro-vokes a reaction from the viewers. The interaction among narration, image, and text works to highlight the agenda setting of the SD, toying with cues of "otherness" and images that highlight difference to prompt specific political reactions.

Valentino et al. (2002) have written about the ways such elements of visual framing work within political communication, specifically about vis-ible racial cues and how they work to heighten and elicit specific viewer attitudes about race in American political ads. For them, non-verbal but visual racial cues work in U.S. political ads, triggering racial responses in viewers (also known as racial priming). In the SD campaign ad a similar politics is at work in the framing of burqa-clad figures as "the other."

The ad's sequences create an image of religious Muslim women as imminent threats in a number of different ways. For example, burqa-clad figures are used to suggest a body that cannot be read—a body that is at first glance isolated yet physically present—serving as a challenge to the pensioner. The subtext is not nuanced or discreet: the bodies of the burqa-clad foreigners are positioned antagonistically in relation to the white Swedish body. This visual syntax suggests that a challenge is occurring within society and that pensioners have been betrayed and victimized by immigration and sacrificed to the needs of foreigners. The burqa-clad women are not presented as victims, nor are their children, but rather it is the Swedes who are suffering due to the demands of immigrants. The mob is used to marginalize the elderly Swedish woman—and the Swedes are empathetically presented as those who suffer. The narrator's voice returns and declares, "on the 19th of September you can choose the immigration brake above the pensions brake." The use of particular images and bodies inscribes specific subject positions upon viewers, leading them to believe that there are choices and priorities to be determined, based upon a particular indexing of these bodies.

In what follows, the mob appears to overtake the pensioner as hands reach for the respective handbrakes. As the ad fades out, the elderly women cannot grab the "Immigration" brake in time. Immigration triumphs. The image then freezes and the background transforms from black to white, as SD's logo appears. The narrator calls on the viewer to "vote [for the] Sweden Democrats." In this final scene the relationship among the visual imagery, embedded text, and the narrator's voice binds the narrative acts and establishes the stakes of the ballot through the aforementioned representations.

Problematically, the use of state finances and budgetary concerns as a framing device creates overtly simplistic representations in which pension and immigration funding are portrayed as mutually exclusive. This is an approach that takes economic conditions and represents them opportunistically, as a potential threat to established nationalist discourses. The idea that the budget cannot withstand more financial pressure attempts to persuade Swedish voters that the election is a contest between "us" and "them," a mutually exclusive choice.

The figures used to present national identity and the idea of "we the Swedish peoples," provide a double narrative. On the one hand, a crowd of burqa-clad women does not correspond to the reality of Swedish immigration. Instead these images reflect the xenophobic and Islamophobic discourses wielded by the SD within the election campaign. Their campaign not only deploys symbols of difference, such as burqas and niqabs, but more importantly uses them to aggravate the tensions and anxieties surrounding contemporary migration, particularly of Islamic refugees and asylum seekers. The double axes of these events highlights the inconsistencies that are used to drive the SD's controversial election campaign forward and also it offers a space where the gaps between reality and the imagination come to life.

To add more depth to this analysis it is important to consider the preliminary figures released by Statistics Sweden prior to the 2010 election. From a population of just over nine million inhabitants (9,340,000) in 2009, approximately 14 percent of Swedes were born abroad. The largest group was comprised of those born in Finland (173,000 persons), followed by those born in Iraq (117,000). Most pertinent to this discussion are the figures related to immigration prior to the 2010 election, when approximately 102,000 persons immigrated to Sweden during that calendar year. The largest segment of this group were emigrating Swedes, followed by Iraqis, and Somalis.[21] The motives for immigration differ from group to group, but many from the former Yugoslavia and Bosnia-Herzegovina, as well as from Iraq and Iran, represented in the numbers, were fleeing violent conflict.

Despite the logic associated with the numbers, the SD have intentionally targeted Islamic immigrants by using easily understood signifiers (burqas and niqabs). Divisively manipulating the empirical evidence, the SD has generally misrepresented Muslims or Islam as proof of the "failure of multiculturalism" by deploying certain kinds of bodies (burqas) as icons of failed immigrant integration to reflect the problems associated with social cohesion.[22]

The juxtaposition between the imagined native Swedes and foreigners serves as a symbolic enactment of the body politic as defined by the Party. The use of these bodies comments on the current social moment, suggesting that Swedish society is indeed a body (politic) in crisis. Returning to the aforementioned demographics, research shows that the fertility trends of Swedish-born and immigrant women have been similar for decades.[23] Statistics Sweden found that foreign-born women had a fertility rate of 2.21 children per woman whereas their Swedish counterparts reproduced at a rate of 1.82 children per woman.[24] It is important to note that fertility numbers related to foreign-born women also reflect integration patterns with lower birth levels at immigration which may increase and leveling out with time.

A contested conceptual territory appears, where nationhood is read through a nationalist lens provided by the SD. The commentary the Party offers on immigration—through the burqa-clad women—draws on a prior discourse already embedded in the burqa itself. And of course, the ad contributes to the perpetuation of these discourses. In the ad, the women in burqas are seen to be dangerous, both physically and mentally: we do not know who they are, what they want, or have any idea of their motives. The embattled juxtaposition of the elderly Swedish woman with the burqa-clad figures serves as a visual signifier of evil and good. The race enacted within the advertisement, the race to pull the immigration and/or pension lever, serves as an allegory and enacts specific kinds of boundaries the SD presumes to guard. As guardians of Swedish society the Party assumes the role of protecting an idealized nation state. The pensioner stands for deserved need, representing the need to protect Swedish society from perceived threats. Indeed, the burqa-clad women serve as bodies that threaten tradition and represent the ills of the contemporary nation state. For the SD it is this particular battle between the imagined past and the present that is enacted within the ad. In this respect, the advert is entirely in keeping with the Party's political platform, which is both anti-immigration and anti-Islam.

The framing of the burqa makes the ad significant: the controversial representation of the mob and the story that followed were core issues in the censoring of the ad. When Swedish television refused to broadcast the ad because it was deemed to contain race hatred, the ad quickly gained the attention of the international media, with the SD proclaiming that they were the victims of unlawful persecution. The next section will analyze the consequences of TV4's act of censorship. Here, the act of censorship emerges as a regulation of the social domain of speakable discourse, focusing on how censorship counters its own effect by diminishing public spaces for contestation. The significance of the term "speakable" within this context refers to how we think about what is thinkable, sayable, or legible in speech acts, highlighting the power of discourse.[25]

EXCITABLE SPEECH

By reading the campaign ad alongside Judith Butler's *Excitable Speech: The Politics of the Performative*, I will discuss the ways in which the regulation of speech via censorship displaces possibilities of actually *contesting* speech deemed "hateful" in the public sphere. Moreover, it is possible to theorize how speech and representation could be democratic sites of contestation that are never fixed or delineated in advance, and that are open to subversion or contestation. I am not suggesting that all discussions concerning forms of representation and textual narrative have been removed through censorship, but rather that such possibilities are always already governed by that which is commonly held as "truth" in the public sphere. Here, therefore, I will look at the SD's election advertisement and the subsequent censoring of the ad through Butler's work on censorship to examine how the act backfired and effectively silenced the group it sought to protect.

Although conventional discussions of censorship usually frame the act as something exercised by forms of government, the censorship enforced by TV4 to preempt any airing of the ad was intended to regulate content deemed offensive by the broadcaster.[26] For Butler, these measures "labor under a fear of contamination," in which the "attempt to purify the sphere of public discourse by institutionalizing the norms that establish what ought properly to be included there operates as a preemptive censor."[27] The immediate impact is, of course, that "such regulations introduce the censored speech into public discourse, thereby establishing it as a site of contestation, that is, as the scene of public utterance that it sought to preempt."[28] Indeed, Butler's insights prove applicable to the case of the SD ad. In re-circulating the *circumstances* of censorship, the media's "attempt to prevent Sweden Democrats (SD) from getting its message out have been counterproductive, handing the party the chance to portray itself as a victim of censorship" and heightening the speech as a site of contestation.[29] In terms of censoring the speech's dissemination, what became clear is that by mid-September 2010 (before the election), "after TV4 refused to air SD's campaign, the clip was viewed more than 600,000 times on YouTube."[30]

The claim of injury by language and representation takes us into unfamiliar territory, where we find ourselves ascribing agency to words and empowering them to injure us. In discourses concerning censorship, language is framed as having the ability to act upon us, against us, or on our behalf. In hate speech discourse, offensive speech is not only defined by the state but it is also literally enacted by the state. Here speech acts, as they have been defined by the state and solidified through hate speech laws have the ability to act or to "injure." Through this perspective, we as subjects are formed and constituted within the structure of language and are unable to break free of the conditions or decisions we might experience as a result of its power. Butler, by contrast, argues for the power of counter-narratives to emerge through the performative and through pluralistic public debate:

> The subject's production takes place not only through the regulation of that subject's speech, but through the regulation of the social domain of speakable discourse. The question is not what it is I will be able to say, but what will constitute the domain of the sayable within which I begin to speak at all. To become a subject means to be subjected to a set of implicit and explicit norms that govern the kind of speech that will be legible as the speech of a subject.[31]

Drawing from Butler's approach then, we can say that the problematizing representations and narratives found in the SD ad have the ability to interpolate us. Speech then serves as a totalizing object, that which precedes the text and exceeds the censor. As such, speech, from this perspective finds itself responsible for the production of offensive or hate material (speech).

In general, censorship is usually a state practice and has been a highly contested area. Critical accounts have attempted to focus upon the scope of such forms of speech—such as those deemed able to injure. In this case, arguments in support of censorship are often characterized as those that are a response to offensive speech: censorship is thus an act in response to that speech which is deemed problematic. But what the act of censorship does in this case is remove the possibility for those who are spoken for to respond to and contest the forms of representation that dominate the SD campaign ad. Therefore, any attempt to censor speech through such a programmatic reading makes the offensive speech inescapable. Butler explains that offensive speech, such as hate-speech, is a "category that cannot exist without the state's ratification . . . (that is) the state produces hate speech."[32] As such, reactionary or arbitrary acts of censorship are both counter-productive and harmful in their power to assign and delimit what is offensive and what is not.

When thinking in relation to the SD's campaign ad, the impact of the offensive speech—the message—is not delivered through the ad itself, but rather through the way in which the speech is conveyed. The deliberately delivered speech—contained in the ad through narrative accounts, texts, and forms of representation—does not originate in the ad itself. Rather, it is reiterated speech, language, meaning, and intent. The SD is not the originator of this message, as it has already been produced within historical discourse. The speaking subject is citational, which means the speaker uses such language as a demonstration of a community conveying a particular message. If speech is then understood as perlocutionary, meaning that speech leads to effects but is not itself the effect, then injurious speech is only problematic when it produces a set of effects. The subsequent effects of the language are crucial—what results from the utterances, in a performative sense. The performative force that results from these linguistic utterances, what the ad says or how it facilitates a set of effects for the viewer fosters its reiterability.

In light of this reading, the burqa is interesting in this particular ad and subsequent censorship because it is framed in a political discourse of stark either/or choices in both instances. In the ad, Swedes are compelled to choose between allocating resources either to burqas or walkers. When we censor the ad, we fear that representations of the burqa can and will contaminate public discourses. Censoring the ad positions TV4 as a protector of hate speech, to again speak on behalf of those represented in the ad. To support this claim, I look to how Butler expounds on the performative. She adds:

> If hate speech constitutes the kind of act that seeks to silence the one to whom it is addressed, but which might revive within the vocabulary of the silenced as its unexpected rejoinder, then the response to hate speech constitutes the "de-officialization" of the performative, its expropriation for non-ordinary means. Within the political sphere, performativity can work in precisely such counter-hegemonic ways. That moment in which a speech act without prior authorization nevertheless assumes authorization in the course of its performance may anticipate and instate altered contexts for its future reception.[33]

The burqa, as a link in a chain of citations in this ad, is censored because TV4 cannot imagine a counter-hegemonic speech emerging in public discourse to critique or repudiate the ad. As TV4's CEO Jan Scherman stated, "The film is contrary to the democracy clause in the Radio and Television Act and also against democracy clauses which the Sweden Democrats, among others, have adopted for the equality of all people regardless of whether it is the European Convention or the UN Charter."[34] He went on to explain that the ad "is also against the constitution act on freedom of speech that prohibits hate speech."[35] From a "need" to control our imaginings of burqas, and those who wear them, the regulation of the social domain of speakable discourse only further recirculates those toxic politicizations of the burqa. Because "we" cannot imagine a new critical emergence of insurrectionary discourses where the ad's unintelligible and unspeakable subjects *do* speak, the ad's depiction of the burqa rein scribes it as opaque and mute. The burqa, with all the attendant confusion of a social narrative in crisis, is drafted to fit and fill a momentary political need.

The act of restricting speech defined as injurious becomes, in turn, even more damaging. The minority group depicted in this ad has no form of recourse within the act of censorship and no way of engaging in a debate of the speakable. Intervening in such forms of discourse could have re-framed the debate within the context of the speech that was deemed injurious. To engage with these discourses in the public domain, those represented would have had the ability to counter, exceed, and confound the authoritative contexts from which they emerge).[36] By not allowing such forms of engagement to take place, the ability for such groups to engage in dialogue is compromised. The speech model that refers to race or religion is undermined and no longer works without producing additional problematic consequences. Racist discourse has been deployed in order to make false claims about the economic condition of the country, the relations between immigrant groups, and the prevalence of Islam within the country. The complex social and economic conditions that underlie such issues have been brushed aside in the service of a highly charged and politicized representation. Fortunately,

> the speech act, as a rite of institution, is one whose contexts are never fully determined in advance, and that the possibility for the speech act to take on a non-ordinary meaning, to function in contexts where it has not belonged, is precisely the political promise of the performative, one that positions the performative at the center of a politics of hegemony, one that offers a unanticipated political future for deconstructive thinking.[37]

By reading the burqa as a performative cultural objective, Sweden's public discourse has the capacity to gesture toward more of a politics of both hope and anxiety, a (Foucauldian) "politics of discomfort," where speech and representation are a democratic site of contestation, never fixed or delineated in advance. To seek a remedy in the public protection of speech, as TV4 has attempted to do, can only foreclose the field of intelligibility, and the ability of the burqa to speak back culturally.[38] On the other hand, to create the possibility for insurrectionary speech acts is to advocate a critical politics of discomfort in the hope of social change and progress.

CONCLUSION

This chapter analyzed a controversial campaign advertisement in the lead up to the 2010 Swedish general election. Sweden's nationalist party, the Sweden Democrats, created an inciting ad that both incorporates and participates in contemporary democratic debates about immigration, the scapegoating of migrants, the latest economic crisis, and foreign invaders clad in burqas. While the ad associates Islamic immigration with the failings of Swedish society, the SD also energized new forms of representation, a new embodiment of Swedishness, and updated representations of "the other." By analyzing the censored ad, I developed a critical understanding of ethnic, cultural, and religious representations as well as how speech regarding the burqa is managed in the contemporary political arena (the then 2010 election).

Taking my cue from Butler (1997), I have argued that censorship does not deliver its intended consequences, but rather diminishes public spaces for contestation. Censorship has the ability to counter its own effects, and in turn produce another set of consequences that heighten the power of the speech it intended to silence. In the SD election ad, a number of complex elements worked together to deliver a nuanced series of mutually reinforcing images and narratives. By refusing to air the ad on public television, the broadcaster acknowledged the politically regressive character of the video. Yet at the same time, the censorship of the ad served to underscore problematic representations of the burqa and immigrants. The act of censorship thrust the Party into the limelight with the SD proclaiming themselves victims of censorship. Coupled with the explosive power of the Internet and video hosting services such as YouTube, the ad quickly went "viral" and ensured that the party would lobby increased public support (locally and internationally). Mobilizing public sentiment with claims of injury, for the first time in Sweden's history the Sweden Democrats would enter parliament, as the sixth largest party with twenty seats and 5.7 percent of the vote. Despite TV4's preemptive censoring of SD's controversial campaign ad, the Party would have their victory with their message disseminated.

NOTES

1. Jonas Pontusson, "Radicalization and Retreat in Swedish Social Democracy." *The New Left Review* I, no. 165 (1987): 5–33. http://newleftreview.org/I/165/jonas-pontussen-radicalization-and-retreat-in-swedish-social-democracy.

2. Pontusson, "Radicalization," 6.

3. Harald Runblom, "Swedish Multiculturalism in a Comparative European Perspective." *Sociological Forum* 9, no.4 (1994): 623–40.

4. Runblom, "Swedish Multiculturalism," 624.

5. Runblom, "Swedish Multiculturalism," 624.

6. Christian Joppke and Ewa Morawska, eds., "Integrating Immigrants in Liberal Nation-States: Policies and Practices," *Toward Assimilation and Citizenship: Immigrants in Liberal Nation-States* (New York: Palgrave Macmillan, 2003), 13.

7. Yolande Jansen, *Secularism, Assimilation and the Crisis of Multiculturalism* (Amsterdam: Amsterdam University Press, 2013), 85.

8. Jansen, "Secularism," 85.

9. Anders Widfeldt, "Party Change as a Necessity – the Case of the Sweden Democrats," *Representation* 44, no. 3 (2008): 265.

10. Jens Rydgren, "Is Extreme Right-Wing Populism Contagious? Explaining the Emergence of a New Party Family." *European Journal of Political Research,* no. 44 (2005): 430.

11. Jens Rydgren, *From Tax Populism to Ethnic Nationalism: Radical Right-Wing Populism in Sweden.* (New York and Oxford: Berghahn Books, 2006), 108.

12. Rydgren, "Is Extreme Right-Wing Populism Contagious?" 109.

13. Quoted in Rygdren, "Is Extreme Right-Wing Populism Contagious? Explaining the Emergence of a New Party Family," 109.

14. Maarten Koomen et al. "Discursive Framing and the Reproduction of Integration in the Public Sphere: A Comparative Analysis of France, the United Kingdom, the Netherlands and Germany." *Ethnicities* 13, no. 2 (2013): 193.

15. Norman Fairclough, *Media Discourse* (London: Bloomsbury Academic, 1995): 17, 54.

16. Tobias Hübinette and Catrin Lundström, "White Melancholia: Mourning the Loss of "Good Old Sweden." *Eurozine* (2011), http://www.eurozine.com/pdf/2011-10-18-hubinette-en.pdf, accessed 14 August 2014.

17. Hübinette and Lundström, "White Melancholia."

18. Lisa Levenstein, "Deserving/Undeserving Poor." In *Poverty In The United States: An Encyclopedia of History, Politics and Policy,* ed. Gwendolyn Mink and Alice O'Connor (Santa Barbara: ABC-CLIO, 2004), 226–30.

19. Levenstein, "Deserving/Undeserving Poor," 226.

20. Michael Katz, *The Undeserving Poor: America's Enduring Confrontation with Poverty* (New York: Oxford University Press, 2013), 14.

21. Statistics Sweden. "Sweden's Population 31/12/2009, Preliminary Figures: Population Increases Amid Economic Crisis." (2009), http://goo.gl/TozMZN, accessed 14 August 2014.

22. Koomen et al., "Discursive Framing and the Reproduction of Integration in the Public Sphere: A Comparative Analysis of France, the United Kingdom, the Netherlands and Germany," 192.

23. Gunnar Andersson, "Childbearing after Migration: Fertility Patterns of Foreign-born Women in Sweden," *International Migration Review* 38.2 (2004): 747–74. See also Gunnar Andersson and Kirk Scott, "Labour-Market Status and First-Time Parenthood: The Experience of Immigrant Women in Sweden, 1981-97," *Population Studies* 59.1 (2005): 21–38.

24. David Landes, "Higher Birth Rates Among Sweden's Foreign-Born," *The Local: Sweden's News in English,* September 14, 2014, http://www.thelocal.se/20081103/15408.

25. Judith Butler, *Excitable Speech: A Politics of the Performative* (New York: Routledge, 1997), 128.

26. Butler, *Excitable Speech,* 77.

27. Butler, *Excitable Speech,* 129.

28. Butler, *Excitable Speech,* 130.

29. Casja Wikstrom, "TV4 Refuses to Air Sweden Democrat Ads," *The Local: Sweden's News in English,* 27 August 2010, http://www.thelocal.se/20100827/28622.

30. Wikstrom, "TV4."

31. Butler, *Excitable Speech,* 130.

32. Butler, *Excitable Speech,* 77.

33. Butler, *Excitable Speech,* 160.

34. Jan Scherman quoted in Casja Wikstrom, "TV4 Refuses to Air Sweden Democat Ads," *The Local: Sweden's News in English*, 27 August 2010, http://www.thelocal.se/20100827/ 28622, accessed 14 August 2014.
35. Scherman quoted in Wikstrom.
36. Butler, *Excitable Speech*, 159.
37. Butler, *Excitable Speech*, 161.
38. Butler, *Excitable Speech*, 161.

REFERENCES

Andersson, Gunnar, and Kirk Scott. "Labour-Market Status and First-Time Parenthood: The Experience of Immigrant Women in Sweden, 1981-97." *Population Studies* 59.1 (2005): 21–38.

Andersson, Gunnar. "Childbearing after Migration: Fertility Patterns of Foreign-born Women in Sweden." *International Migration Review* 38.2 (2004): 747–74.

Bordwell, David. *Narration in the Fiction Film*. London: Routledge, 1988.

Butler, Judith. *Excitable Speech: A Politics of the Performative*. New York: Routledge, 1997.

Coltrane, Scott, and Melina Messineo. "The Perpetuation of Subtle Prejudice: Race and Gender Imagery in 1990's Television Advertising." *Sex Roles* 42 (2000): 363–89.

Fairclough, Norman. *Media Discourse*. London: Bloomsbury Academic, 1995.

Helgesson, Stefan. "Modernism under Portuguese Rule." In *Literary History: Towards a Global Perspective*, edited by Anders Pettersson. Berlin: Walter de Gruyter, 2006. 118–56.

Hellstrom, Anders. "The Sweden Democrats Racism Scandal Will not be a Fatal Blow to the Party's Appeal to the Swedish Electorate." *The London School of Economics and Political Science EUROPP European Politics and Policy*. http://goo.gl/jwZUN3 .Accessed 12 December 2012.

Hübinette,Tobias and Catrin Lundström, "White Melancholia: Mourning the Loss of "Good Old Sweden."" *Eurozine* (2011): 1-6. http://www.eurozine.com/pdf/2011-10-18-hubinette-en.pdf.

Jansen, Yolande. *Secularism, Assimilation and the Crisis of Multiculturalism*. Amsterdam: Amsterdam University Press, 2013.

Joppke, Christian, and Ewa Morawska. "Integrating Immigrants in Liberal Nation-States: Policies and Practices." In *Toward Assimilation and Citizenship: Immigrants in Liberal Nation-States*, edited by Christian Joppke and Ewa Morawska. New York: Palgrave Macmillan, 2003. 1–37.

Katz, Michael. *The Undeserving Poor: America's Enduring Confrontation with Poverty*. New York: Oxford University Press, 2013.

Koomen, Maarten, Jean Tillie, Anja van Heelsum, and Sjef van Stiphout. "Discursive Framing and the Reproduction of Integration in the Public Sphere: A Comparative Analysis of France, the United Kingdom, the Netherlands and Germany." *Ethnicities* 13, no. 2 (2013): 191–208.

Landes, David. "Higher Birth Rates Among Sweden's Foreign-Born," *The Local: Sweden's News in English*, September 14, 2014. http://www.thelocal.se/20081103/15408.

Levenstein, Lisa. "Deserving/Undeserving Poor." In *Poverty In The United States: An Encyclopedia of History, Politics and Policy*, edited by Gwendolyn Mink and Alice O'Connor, 226–30. Santa Barbara: ABC-CLIO, 2004.

Pontusson, Jonas. "Radicalization and Retreat in Swedish Social Democracy." *The New Left Review* I, no. 165 (1987): 5–33.

Runblom, Harald. "Swedish Multiculturalism in a Comparative European Perspective." *Sociological Forum* 9, no.4 (1994): 623–40.

Rydgren, Jens. *From Tax Populism to Ethnic Nationalism: Radical Right-Wing Populism in Sweden*. New York and Oxford: Berghahn Books, 2006.

———. "Is Extreme Right-Wing Populism Contagious? Explaining the Emergence of a New Party Family." *European Journal of Political Research*, no. 44 (2005): 413–37.

Statistics Sweden. *"Sweden's Population 31/12/2009, Preliminary Figures: Population Increases amid Economic Crisis."* Stockholm, 21 December 2009. http://goo.gl/TozMZN. Accessed 14 August 2014.

"Sweden Democrats' Banned Commercial." YouTube video, 0:30. Posted by "bulletproof courier." 29 August 2010, http://youtu.be/AYavOiI-8uY.

Valentino, Nicholas A, Vincent L. Hutchings, and Ismail K. White. "Cues That Matter: How Political Ads Prime Racial Attitudes During Campaigns." *American Political Science Review* 96, no. 1 (2002): 75–90.

Widfeldt, Anders. "Party Change as a Necessity – the Case of the Sweden Democrats." *Representation* 44, no. 3 (2008): 265–76.

Wikstrom, Casja. "TV4 Refuses to Air Sweden Democrat Ads." *The Local: Sweden's News in English*, 27 August 2010. http://www.thelocal.se/20100827/28622 .

Chapter Nine

The "Identitarian Movement"

What Kind of Identity? Is it Really a Movement?

Fabian Virchow

On 20 October 2012, approximately seventy people occupied the roof of a mosque that was being built in the western French city of Poitiers. They brought along banners that said things like: "732 Génération Identitaire" and "Mosque Construction—Immigration—Referendum!"[1] The temporary occupation of the roof was the first publicity stunt of the group Génération Identitaire (GI), which formed as a youth group of "Le bloc Identitaire—Le mouvement social européen" (BI) (The Identitarian Block—The European Social Movement). The BI itself was officially established in April 2003 by former members of the group "Unité Radicale" (Radical Unity)—after BI had been banned because of one of their members had attempted to assassinate the French President. Since 2010, BI has been registered as a political party.

The place, time, and target of the stunt were not accidental. In the year 732 AD, during the battles of Tours and Poitiers, Charles Martell, the emperor of the Franks, had stopped the further incursion of Moors into the center of Europe. In a video message the mosque occupiers declared that their purpose was to spearhead the fight over national identity. According to GI just as in 732 AD, today the choice at stake is also, "live free or die."[2] Close to the time of the occupation, GI posted an Internet video that they labeled a "declaration of war." In it, young male and female interlocutors oppose policies of immigration and multiculturalism and complain about many slights that they, the indigenous populace, were facing.[3] This declaration was quickly translated into over ten languages and received 23,000 clicks in the French version alone. In several European countries, groups formed calling themselves "Identitarian" and also adopted the logo of the Greek letter lambda, shown in black font on a yellow circle. According to legend, this emblem had been carried on the shields of Spartan warriors. Looking closely at the German version of the "Identitäre Bewegung" (Identitarian Movement), we will investigate which identity markers its actors enlist and whether their designation as a movement is objectively correct. The study is anchored in rich background material on social movements, and studies on race theory in regard to the ethno-pluralism of the so-called New Right. Both print and digital publications of the German IB form the basis of our discourse analysis.

WHAT KIND OF IDENTITY?

A few years ago, Austrian cultural studies expert Peter Stachel Unbehagen noted "a more and more inflationary use of notions of 'identity' in social and cultural science,"[4] and reminded readers that it had become accepted "to speak of identity without specifying who or what was identical with whom."[5] Philip Gleason showed in his history of the use of the term identity in the U.S. American social sciences that Erik Erikson's psychological model provided a reading that understood individual identity as a largely stable nucleus of personality formed in one's childhood.[6] Identity concepts that derive from relational theory and symbolic interactionism, however, emphasize the process of constructing individual identity as well as its fluidity and processual nature, dependent on social interaction within specific contexts. In our contribution, identity is understood as the result of a psychosocial formation process that operates throughout our lives as we participate in social practices.

The representatives of IB also discuss their own understanding of identity. In the first issue of the German edition of their magazine "Identitäre Generation," one essay explicitly addresses the notion of identity in referring to a French theorist of the New Right, Alain de Benoist,[7] who claims that "the mere accident of being born French, Italian or German [. . .] alone does not define"[8] one's identity, but that belonging will only become relevant once an individual claims it to be personally meaningful. Identity is at first seen here as dynamic and capable of change; however, these characteristics vanish inexplicably once identity is transferred to the collective, to "peoples." These, claims the author, "have their own inner being and (ethnocultural) identity" that "markedly determine the awareness and actions of an individual" and confer on "all the diverse peoples of the world their own singular uniqueness."[9]

Confronted with the impossibility of being precise about what might constitute "Volk" with specific characteristics, representatives of IB counter with replies like "Every German (who is not a German citizen in name only) knows deep down who or what is German and who or what is not."[10] Such a statement betrays an inability to truly define "Germanness," and asserts that "Germanness" is derived from the "narrative of the nation": "the nation itself is the narrative, the master plan, that conjoins everything."[11]

Which narrative does IB offer via their written texts and visual products? Among its fundamental programmatic documents is the slim tract "The Identitarian Generation."[12] It unfolds an apocalyptic vision of the current situation in Europe. The present crisis, Willinger expounds, is more profound "als die Teilung Europas durch den eisernen Vorhang oder die Zerstörung unsres Kontinents durch die beiden Weltkriege"[13] (than the partition of Europe by the Iron Curtain, or the devastation of our continent by two World Wars). The crisis originates in "dem Geistigen" (the spiritual), because the continent has lost its "Lebenswillen" (will to live). This will to live is spelled out in bio-political terms: "Denn die größte Bedrohung Europas resultiert aus einer sich anbahnenden demographischen Katastrophe"[14] (The greatest threat to Europe results from a demographic catastrophe that is already underway). In this sense, IB opposes the plurality of choices about family life, against "selbstgewählte Kinderlosigkeit"[15] (personal choice to remain childless) and immigration to Europe, which they argue also create the danger of "Islamisierung" (Islamicization). Migrants who might practice their Muslim faith in many different ways, are here reduced to an undifferentiated whole and made out to be "dangerous Others."[16]

The generation of 1968 is being blamed for these developments in a simplistic and unilateral manner, as they promoted more liberalism and democracy in western societies.[17] In this point, the IB's mode of argumentation resembles the manifesto that Anders Bering Breivik published online.[18]

Among the largely Internet-based propaganda of the German-language IB, we can find myriad conflations of image and text to help us discern their worldview. First, the message of "eternal return" of specific cultural practices and lifestyles is implied in the image of a light-haired child running along a dirt path.[19] He wears felt clothing, leather shoes, and a little wooden sword, as well as a small leather bag tied around his waist. Behind the child the logo IB is visible. In the margins, above and below the image, is the statement "Die Geschichten unserer Vorfahren sind die Geschichten unserer Kinder" (The stories of our ancestors are our children's stories), referencing a key element of far right and biologically based *Weltanschauung*, according to which human society essentially does not change, but is ordered by constantly recurring laws, so that fundamental transformation is precluded. A close relationship to "nature" and therefore to "tradition" is evoked by an advertisement made by an IB-group in Stuttgart: in the foreground of the image we can see two little girls looking straight at the camera. Clothed in traditional Scandinavian outfits, they are located a little distance away from a farmer's shack, behind which open land and a lake stretch to the horizon.

Identity as a predetermined, stable quality of social collectives—one that articulates itself through specific cultural profiles, and through individuals who are shaped by them—embodies an important arena for the IB's visual representation. The IB group employs images and targeted words to describe what, according to them, might be a desirable "identity": it has to be non-Muslim and non-migrant.

The IB-group from Bremen depicts hetero-normative families in several image choices. One image shows a couple in profile, kissing. She clutches a baby to her breast; the man protectively clasps the woman's hand. In the center of the image between the two adults we see IB's logo. A different motif, generated by IB Bremen, refers to a popular cartoon series by deploying the sentence "Liebe . . . ist mehr als ein Wort" (love . . . is more than just a word) where it occupies the upper third of the image in order to attract the viewer's attention. Below the text we see several silhouettes: first, a hetero-sexual couple kissing, then a couple consisting of a pregnant wife and a hetero-normative small family, including a husband and two children. The final element is an old couple sitting close to each other on a bench—a motif that evokes clichéd scenes of long-time couples spending their sunset years together. The message of the visual elements combined with the titles suggests that a heterosexual relationship would work throughout one's life, so long as reproductivity is at its core.

The rising sun is another visual trope implying new hope for the future, and it can be found in many interpretive schemata of the IB movement as a whole. For example, IB Germany disseminates a combination of image and text in which we can see the rays of the rising sun warming a rough sea and a rocky shore—this shore motif was selected to visually reference the economic crisis in Cyprus going on at that time. Viewers could distinguish the IB logo partially visible in the lower left corner, and in the upper left corner, the text "Wir lieben" (we love) was placed. Two alternatives for completion of the statement were offered: for one, the word "Europe" in the lower right corner, with the letter O shaped like the IB-logo. The other option was put at the lower margin of the image: " . . . nicht den Euro! Für ein Europa der Vaterländer und der Regionen!" (. . . not the Euro! For a Europe of homelands and regions!).

The "identity" offered by IB sets itself off against classical racist theories that stress the superiority of one race over others, instead emphasizing the "right to diversity." However, this right is identified with a duty to diversify according to the parameters of the claimed "ethno-cultural identity," so that a co-existence of a folk collective delimited by apartheid is being promoted.

In point of fact, it is impossible to try and hermetically define ethnic belonging and a collective identity that might derive from it.[20] If ethno-culturalist concepts deploy "culture" as a marker of difference and postulate a separation line between what is one's "own" and what is "foreign," then this is a purely voluntaristic assumption.

In the opinion of the IB—and of the Extreme Right in general—the struggle for "identity" expresses a "question of life and death,"[21] as stated by Lichtmesz in reference to the extreme right intellectual Hans-Dietrich Sander. Since, as they view it, identity creates meaning—and the one able to create such meaning would also possess the ability to dominate—the question of 'identity' then needs to be seen as a question of power.

IS IT REALLY A MOVEMENT?

Following Joachim Raschke, a social movement is "ein mobilisierender kollektiver Akteur, der mit einer gewissen Kontinuität auf der Grundlage hoher symbolischer Integration und geringer Rollenspezifikation mittels variabler Organisations- und Aktionsformen das Ziel verfolgt, grundlegenden sozialen Wandel herbeizuführen, zu verhindern oder rückgängig zu machen"[22] (a collective actor [is one] who mobilizes others on the basis of high symbolic integration and slight role specification, who deploys varied forms of organization and action-taking, and who pursues the goal of bringing about either profound social change, preventing it from happening, or undoing it). Even if some of these criteria may seem a bit vague, taken together they allow us to distinguish social movements from single protest events, and movements from social parties and interest groups. There can be little doubt that IB wants to bring about fundamental social change. As in other societies of the global north, and despite the ongoing resistance of conservative forces and parties who vigorously debate these changes, people in Germany and Austria have to come to realize that immigration is here to stay, and that it lastingly transforms the receiving countries.[23] Similarly, the hetero-normative paradigm has lost much of its appeal. Despite these incontrovertible facts, IB would like to undo such gains in ethnic, sexual and religious diversity. In this regard, their project is more ambitious than merely correcting the drift within individual political areas.

The forms of action-taking IB chooses are first and foremost unconventional forms of political participation. In the German-language context, we need to mention the following actions as exemplary. In October 2012, IB organized a flash-mob at the opening of an intercultural festival in Frankfurt. They played hard rock, true to their motto "Multikulti wegbassen" (blast away multiculturalism). Two months later, in Vienna they performed a similar event at a dance workshop that promoted intercultural tolerance. In February 2013, supporters of IB in Vienna participated in a church occupation, an action intended to highlight the plight of asylum seekers. There, IB came forward with a fictive asylum seeker called "Sepp [Josef] U." to suggest that it was really native Austrians who needed special protection. In March 2013, a group of seventeen IB supporters in Hamburg clashed with a counter protest during their own march against the building of a mosque. Their failed action was given the title "17 against 700" and marketed virtually, drawing a comparison to the three hundred Spartan warriors who, according to legend, had bravely opposed the superior force of the Persian army.

Even if the IB group's total number of actions is small and can be mostly found on the Internet, their forms of action correspond to those of other social movements. Both in print and on the Internet, their publications show the rudiments of a shared self-conception regarding the outlining of problems and desirable alternatives, which is a critical feature for every social movement's collective identity and its transactional ability. Nonetheless, the fact that IB mostly expresses their agenda online, which is especially true for Germany and less so for Austria, and that concerted political events are still rare, indicates a structural problem. Only concerted political action-taking at a concrete event with its emotional and cognitive experiences can establish trust and stable social connections among these activists, and are necessary for the lasting existence of a social movement.

Given that the IB group conceives of itself as "active promoters of the deed," the relative absence of political actions in the public arena is astonishing. The group inflates the importance of deeds to counter the supposed decadence of western societies, which is symbolically represented in the 1968 movement. Then again, IB hopes for greater media presence if its members perform provocative public stunts. A leading IB-activist in Austria is impressed, for instance, by actions of the French Identitarians. They had placed stickers over city and street signs with slogans like "Straße der Burka" (street of burqas) or "Istanbul?" to attract attention to negative effects of immigration and Islam. Once plans for the building of a mosque would become public knowledge, this group would startle locals with an Islamic muezzin's wake-up calls via speakers, and then leaflet.[24] A reason for their orientation toward actionism can be seen in the rhetoric of the fateful hour, which suggests that only immediate forceful deed might prevent disaster from striking. Back at the dawn of the twentieth century, we witnessed a similar negative view about the passage of time that was held in common by many diverse right extremist movements.

A visual appeal to action, decisiveness, and fighting spirit can also be found in other advertisements, which not only supply text to illustrate the "will to create change" but the image of a black superhero character, who kneels on one leg, with the other one bent, and has punched the ground with his fist so that big cracks appear: therefore, he has shaken it to the core. In a different image, distributed by the IB group in Stuttgart, we can see a fair-skinned youth who holds a homemade firebomb that is already lit. As is the case with other far-right groups who use this as a legitimation strategy, IB uses many references to "crime by foreigners." A frequently profiled case is the death of a young man in the town of Weye near Bremen, who was killed in an altercation with other youths. Some of these youths were from immigrant families, which easily enables the far right to use the case for publicity and to devote visual representations to the victim. Not only do they post photos combined with apparently spontaneous politicized claims, such as "Wir sind Daniel. Wir sind DEUTSCH" (We are all Daniel. We are GERMAN) together with the IB logo, they also post photos of so-called commemorative marches from remote areas of Germany and images of Christian mourning rituals.

The pathos in the style of many of IB publications matches their call to action. Short statements make assertions, but these are rarely founded upon empirical or theoretical evidence. Young people are targeted with this kind of rhetoric, so that they might feel part of an active, belligerent movement.

Their self-presentation as a "new force" in the political arena deliberately reactivates myths that the IB feels to be of paramount importance, because they supposedly express a truth or status value. Myths, they state, "geben dem Dasein in der Welt einen Halt und einen Sinn" (give support and meaning to our existence in the world) and are imbued with "mobilisierende Macht" (the power to mobilize).[25] The Enlightenment is demonized as "Todfeind des Mythos"[26] (archenemy of myth), and blamed for destroying "jedes organische Gemeinschaftsgefühl"[27] (any kind of organic communitarian feeling).

In the thought process of the far right, myths harken back to a Golden Age located in the past, yet also express which values and attitudes are needed to overcome the current "decadent social order." The IB's key mythical touchstone is the Spartans. The battle of Thermopylae in particular represents an opportunity to remind people of "die Notwendigkeit heroischer Mythen und die Bereitschaft zum Handeln in Zeiten der Not zu erinnern. Der Wille zur Tat fand hier einen weltgeschichtlichen Ausdruck und manifestiert einen Grundpfeiler abendländischer Identität"[28] (the necessity of hero myths and the readiness for action in times of need. The will to act expressed itself at this moment and manifests a pillar of Western identity). From its perspective, the IB states that myths of Greek antiquity have organizing and mobilizing power, coming back to life in the Poitiers mosque occupation: "Wer solche Aktionen sieht, der will dabei sein, will zu dieser kühnen Mannschaft gehören, die vom Hass umbrandet, mit frechem, freien Lachen einer ganzen Welt ihr 'Ego non' entgegenstellt"[29] (Anyone who witnesses such an action will want to be part of it, will want to belong to this daring band of men, who oppose waves of hatred with their own impertinent, free laughter and who call out "not I" against the whole world).

Even the symbol of the Identitarian movement, the Greek letter lambda enclosed by a circle, is connected by them to the Spartan warriors of the fifth century BC, who supposedly bore it on their shields. The IB admit that the strategic value of the Spartan mission led by King Leonidas at Thermopylae is actually quite dubious, despite that, the battle is eulogized as "sagenhafte Ruhmestat" (glorious deed of mythical proportions) and as "Kern der Historienbildung um den legendären Stadtstaat, dessen Mythos bis heute die Menschen fasziniert und in Tagen ethnisch-kulurellen Verfalls"[30] (as focal point around which history was made and its legendary city state, whose myth fascinates people until now and in our own era of ethic and cultural decay) can supply a point of connection. The IB demands our reorientation toward "heroische Werte sowie den Willen zur Tat in Zeiten äußerster Bedrängnis" (heroic values and the will to take action in troubled times), including being prepared to sacrifice one's own life, and is finally glorified as "höchste Bewährung der Mannheit"[31] (greatest test of masculinity).

Similar to other contexts for far-right self-promotion, the IB also repeatedly uses the term "youth" in a positive manner. They believe youth to embody virility, the will to act, and an impulse to perform great deeds: "Wir als Angehörige der Jugend Europas haben noch nicht die Möglichkeit zu handeln—reißen wir uns heraus aus der allgemeinen Lethargie und dem vorherrschenden Pessimismus—nehmen wir unser Schicksal in die Hand!"[32] (As members of Europe's youth, we do not yet have the opportunity to act— let's tear ourselves away from the dominant mood of lethargy—let's seize our fate!). The prominent use of the term "young generation" suggests that one political spokesperson might actually represent a whole cohort and bundle together their experiences and emotions, in light of the economic crisis in so many European countries. Part of their strategy of appealing to young people, is to use familiar elements of pop culture, such as the character Cartman from the series South Park, to whom they impute the motto "Respect my identity," or references to the graphic novel series 300, written by Frank Miller in 1998, which was made into a film by Zack Snyder in 2007. The Persians are depicted as decadent and degenerate, as a never-ending tide of invaders. Against them are the Spartan Hoplites, drawn as pure, muscular, invincible and implacable warriors, and therefore quite contrary to the Persian army.

The IB's self-awareness as a "generation" also furthers the distinction from the generation of 1968, which is blamed for the crisis in Europe today—defined by tides of immigration, and religious and sexual pluralism. It is remarkable that even right after German unification, the far right tried to adopt the moniker "89ers" in order to undo the liberalism and democracy they retroactively ascribe to the work of the 68ers, and to assign new importance to one's own identification with the German nation.

Since the beginning of 2014, there have been several initiatives of IB to shape co-operations and networking on a more permanent level. At a reunion in Fulda, around eighty people debated the current situation and future outlook of IB and, in April 2014, elected Nils Altmieks as their leader. In addition, a few groups of IB were tasked with organizing and coordinating in specific regions. Those present voted to establish "Kompetenzteams" (teams for competence) that would be given specific charges. In one far-right magazine, an author comments on these decisions as "Schritt weiter in Richtung organisierter Strukturen und professionellen Handelns" (step forward in the direction of organized structures and professionalism).[33]

A further tool for networking among the groups and activists is an "Identitarian Fanzine" which first appeared in March 2013, but did not appear regularly. In Austria, a publication appears now and then with programmatic contributions. On an Internet homepage, text contributions and videos are posted.[34] A linked online shop sells t-shirts with, for example, logos like Lampedusa Coastguard, Nietz-Che, Schmiss (a dueling scar) happens, or bye bye, equality.[35]

Every social movement also needs "free spaces" that offer tangible protection against opponents, and which serve to reassure the group and allow for communication about ideological beliefs, strategic planning and tactical co-ordination. These can be guaranteed within a broad range of contexts, from families to political meetings.[36] IB Germany recently created two new meeting points: in July 2013, a new "Zentrum für Jugend, Identität und Kultur" (Center for Youth, Identity and Culture) opened in Dresden, and in Hesse, in a small town near Frankfurt, the "Projektwerkstatt Karben" (Karben project lab) opened its doors. Both offer meeting spaces for the IB. "Arktos," a joint British- Swedish publisher, organized several international reunions to discuss "Identiarian ideas," which Austrian and German representatives attended. This venture needs to be seen as a way of providing free spaces in order to facilitate consensus about fundamentals, strategies and tactical decisions.

CONCLUSION

The IB's own motto "0% Rassismus—100% Identität" (Zero Racism—100 percent Identity) appears true only at a quick cursory glance. In real terms, the IB stands for a form of differentialist or culturalist racism,[37] which distinguishes itself from classic racism defined by superiority, but substantively still constructs various collectives, or, "Völker" (national tribes), defined by specific characteristics that cannot be verified. As far as political theories and action guidelines, such equivocations do not make that much of a difference. Blaming multiculturalism and cultural mixing, they create nuanced stories about white victimhood and demands for repatriation of non-Whites out of Europe. Elsewhere, IB attacks liberalism, the principle of human rights and equality in favor of a return to a hierarchical social model governed by traditional gender roles, rendering values like discipline, courage, and loyalty newly desirable.

In a relatively short time, the Identitarian Movement succeeded in attracting notice with just a few spectacular public demonstrations. In Germany, they can be typified as a proto-movement. Several factors common to social movements can be seen, while others are absent. It is possible that the German IB will develop into an organization with solidified structures, assigned roles, and tasks. As a network of actors, they are being watched by rival political projects of the Far Right.

While those groups notice with respect that the IB adds a new political style to the mix, and that they managed to create a successful political brand by combining colors, concept and historical themes, they also criticize IB for its lack of public spokespersons who might become identified as the face of the movement, or their focus. For example, they write that one reads "man bei den Identitären viel vom Zorn und vom kommenden Aufstand [lese], sieht aber keinen Kopf, der—angetrieben von diesem Zorn—alles auf eine Karte setzte" (a lot about anger and the coming uprising, but see no leader who, motivated by this anger, would stake everything on a single card).[38] Finally, the IB is also criticized for not being confrontational enough[39] in its political self-positioning and in taking a stand.

The "Junge Nationaldemokraten" (Young National Democrats) (JN), the youth organization of the essentially fascistic "Nationaldemokratischen Partei Deutschlands" (German National Democratic Party) (NPD), sees the main virtue of IB in its placement of a topic on the public agenda that they also care about. They hope to connect to it, because "eröffnen sich dadurch neue Chancen, um Begrifflichkeiten zu nutzen und unter Umständen zu prägen, die weder verbrannt noch negativ besetzt sind" (new chances open up for using terms or coining new concepts which are not exhausted, or may carry negative connotations).[40] This is why the JN created a new campaign under the motto "Werde, der du bist" (Become the one you are) and uses as its symbol a white palm reaching out to the viewer. The goal of the campaign is:

> unsere europäische ethno-kulturelle Identität gegen Islamisierung und die komplette Verblödung durch US-amerikanischen Konsumimperialismus zu verteidigen. Unser Bollwerk gegen ungezügelte Masseneinwanderung und den geistigen Verfall aller Traditionen ist das bewußte Bekenntnis zur eigenen Identität.[41]
> [to defend our European ethno-cultural identity against Islamicization and the complete dumbing down by US-American consumer imperialism. Our fortress against uncontrolled mass immigration and the spiritual decay of tradition is the affirmation of our own identity.]

A striking parallel between the positions of IB and JN becomes evident; whether it is actually the JN or the IB who more successfully advertise with these beliefs and obtain primary control over the term "identity" remains to be seen. After all, in the JN there are members who demand joint action between the two groups,[42] in the hope that cadres who are ideologically sound and dynamic will emerge in the course of campaigns, in the end throwing in their support with the JN's political agenda.[43]

NOTES

1. Translation from the German by Helga Druxes.
2. Unknown author, "Mosque at Poitiers Occupied Génération Identitaire demand vote on mass immigration and mosques," http://www.youtube.com/watch?v=spTr0L2G9yM, accessed 28 July 2014. This version received around 10,800 clicks.
3. Génération Identitaire, "Déclaration de guerre," http://www.youtube.com/watch?v=5Vnss7y9TNA, accessed 28 July 2014.
4. Peter Stachel, "Identität," *Archiv für Kulturgeschichte* 87, 2 (2005): 396 and 397.
5. Stachel, "Identität," 397–98.
6. Philip Gleason, "Identifying Identity: A Semantic History." *The Journal of American History* 69, no. 4 (1983): 910–31; Margaret Wetherell, "The Field of Identity Studies," in *The SAGE Handbook of Identities*, eds. Margaret Wetherell and Chandra Talpade Mohanty, 3–26 (Los Angeles: Sage, 2010).
7. Hanspeter Siegfried, "Kulturrevolution von rechts?" Widerspruch 11, no. 21 (1991): 76–94.
8. Mm, "Identität. Der Begriff einer Wende." *Identitäre Generation*, 2013, 18.
9. mm, "Identität," 18.
10. Martin Lichtmesz, "Verteidigung des Eigenen." *Burschenschaftliche Blätter* 127, no. 4.
11. Lichtmesz, "Verteidigung," 152.
12. Markus Willinger, *Die Identitäre Generation* (London: Arktos Media, 2013).
13. Willinger, *Die Identitäre Generation*, 7.
14. am. "Europa in der Krise," *Identitäre Generation*, 2013, 4.
15. am. "Europa," 4.
16. Douglas Pratt, "Islamophobia: Ignorance, Imagination, Identity and Interaction." *Islam and Christian-Muslim Relations* 22, no. 4 (2011): 379–89.
17. Gerrit Dworok and Christoph Weissmann, eds, 1968 und die 68er. Ereignisse, Wirkungen und Kontroversen in der Bundesrepublik (Wien/Köln/Weimar: Böhlau, 2013).
18. Stephen J. Walton, "Anti-Feminism and Misogyny in Breivik's 'Manifesto.'" *NORA—Nordic Journal of Feminist and Gender Research* 20, no. 1 (2012): 4–11.
19. In fact, IB defines their view of the shape of history as cyclical. See mm. "Mensch und Welt" *Identitäre Generation*, 2013, 24.
20. C. W. Stephan and W. G. Stephan, "The Measurement of Racial and Ethnic Identity." *International Journal of Intercultural Relations* 24, no. 5 (2000): 541–52; Siniša Malešević, "The Chimera of National Identity." *Nations and Nationalism* 17, no. 2 (2011): 272–90.
21. Martin Lichtmesz, "Die dreifache Wurzel der Identität." *Sezession,* May 2013, 24.
22. Joachim Raschke, *Soziale Bewegungen. Ein historisch-systematischer Grundriß* (Frankfurt/New York: Campus, 1985), 77
23. Simon Green, "Immigration, Asylum and Citizenship in Germany: The Impact of Unification and the Berlin Republic." *West European Politics* 24, no. 4 (2001): 82–104; Merih Anil, "No More Foreigners? The Remaking of German Naturalization and Citizenship Law, 1990-2000." *Dialectical Anthropology* 29, no. 3–4 (2005): 453–70; Hartwig Pautz, "The Politics of Identity in Germany: the *Leitkultur* Debate." *Race & Class* 46, no. 4 (2005): 39–52; Roger Karapin, "Protest and Reform in Asylum Policy." *German Politics and Society* 28, no. 1 (2010): 1–45; Joyce Marie Mushaben, "From Ausländer to Inländer. The Changing Faces of Citizenship in Post-Wall Germany." *German Politics and Society* 28, no. 1 (2010): 141–64.
24. Patrick Lenart, "Identitäre Aktionsformen." *Sezession,* May 2013, 29–30.

25. jf, "Die Neugeburt des Mythos." *Identitäre Generation*, 2013, 6.
26. jf, "Neugeburt," 6.
27. jf, "Neugeburt," 9.
28. Sebastian Pella, "Identitäre Bewegung: Historische Wurzeln im antiken Sparta." *Neue Ordnung*, 2013, 19.
29. jf, "Neugeburt," 11.
30. Pella, "Identitäre," 21.
31. Pella, "Identitäre," 21.
32. am. "Europa," 5.
33. Ulli Vader, "'Liebe zu Deutschland,'" *Zuerst!*, June 2014, 36.
34. http://www.identitaere-generation.info/, accessed 28 July 2014.
35. https://www.phalanx-europa.com/de/, accessed 28 July 2014. A "Schmiss" is a scar in the face of male members of student fraternities who duel as proof of their manhood and courage with epees.
36. Francesca Polletta, "'Free Spaces' in Collective Action," *Theory and Society* 28, 1 (1999): 1-38. Robert Futrell and Peter Simi, "Free Spaces, Collective Identity, and the Persistence of U.S. White Power Activism," *Social Problems* 51, 1 (2004): 16–42.
37. Pierre-André Taguieff, *Die Macht des Vorurteils. Der Rassismus und sein Double* (Hamburg: Hamburger Edition, 2000), 22 ff.
38. Götz Kubitschek, "Schauen, suchen, denken." *Sezession,* May 2013, 8.
39. Dorian Rehwaldt, "'Doppelt bestrafte Generation.'" *Zuerst!* , December 2012, 60; Michael Schäfer, "Identitäre Bewegung—Pro und Contra." *Der Aktivist* , 2012, 11/12.
40. Andy Knape, "Wir starten durch—kommt Ihr mit uns?" *Der Aktivist* 2012, 30.
41. Michael Schäfer, "Werde, wer DU bist!" *Deutsche Stimme*, February 2013, 16.
42. Malte Hansen, "Kampf um die Identität—Teil II." *Deutsche Stimme* , April 2013, 16.
43. Schäfer, "Identitäre," 12; Malte Hansen, "Kampf um die Identität—Teil I." *Deutsche Stimme* , March 2013, 16.

REFERENCES

Alexander, Bryant Keith. "Racializing Identity: Performance, Pedagogy, and Regret." *Cultural Studies M Critical Methodologies* 4, no. 1 (2004): 12–24.

am. "Europa in der Krise." *Identitäre Generation*, 2013, 4–5.

Anil, Merih. "No More Foreigners? The Remaking of German Naturalization and Citizenship Law, 1990-2000." *Dialectical Anthropology* 29, no. 3-4 (2005): 453–70.

Benoist, Alain de. "Metapolitik der Identität." *Sezession,* May 2013, 20–22.

Dobratz, Betty A. "The Role of Religion in the Collective Identity of the White Racialist Movement." *Journal for the Scientific Study of Religion* 40, no. 2 (2001): 287–302.

Dworok, Gerrit and C. Weissmann, eds. *1968 und die 68er. Ereignisse, Wirkungen und Kontroversen in der Bundesrepublik.* Wien/Köln/Weimar: Böhlau, 2013.

Futrell, Robert and Pete Simi. "Free Spaces, Collective Identity, and the Persistence of U.S. White Power Activism." *Social Problems* 51, no. 1 (2004): 16–42.

Gallaher, Carolyn. "Identity Politics and the Religious Right: Hiding Hate in the Landscape." *Antipode* 29, no. 3 (1997): 256-277.

Génération Identitaire, "Déclaration de Guerre." http://www.youtube.com/watch?v=5Vnss7y9TNA. Accessed 28 July 2014.

Gleason, Philip. "Identifying Identity: A Semantic History." *The Journal of American History* 69, no. 4 (1983): 910–31.

Green, Simon. "Immigration, Asylum and Citizenship in Germany: The Impact of Unification and the Berlin Republic." *West European Politics* 24, no. 4 (2001): 82–104.

Hansen, Malte. "Kampf um die Identität—Teil I." *Deutsche Stimme* , March 2013, 16.

Hansen, Malte. "Kampf um die Identität—Teil II." *Deutsche Stimme* , April 2013, 16.

Hill, J. D., and T. M. Wilson. "Identity Politics and the Politics of Identities." *Identities: Global Studies in Culture and Power* 10, no. 1 (2003): 1–8.

Hoffgaard, Henning. *Junge Freiheit,* 01 March 2013, 7.

Holland, D., G. Fox, and V. Daro. "Social Movements and Collective Identity: A Decentered, Dialogic View." *Anthropological Quarterly* 81, no. 1 (2008): 95–126.

jf, "Die Neugeburt des Mythos." *Identitäre Generation*, 2013, 6–12.

Josey, Christopher S. "Hate Speech and Identity: An Analysis of neo-Racism and the Indexing of Identity." *Discourse & Society* 21, no. 1 (2010): 27–39.

Karapin, Roger. "Protest and Reform in Asylum Policy." *German Politics and Society* 28, no. 1(2010): 1–45.

Klandersmans. B., J. M. Sabucedo, M. Rodriguez, and M. de Weerd. "Identity Processes in Collective Action Participation: Farmers' Identity and Farmers' Protest in the Netherlands and Spain." *Political Psychology* 23, no. 2 (2002): 235–51.

Knape, Andy. "Wir starten durch—kommt Ihr mit uns?" *Der Aktivist* 2012, 30–31.

Kubitschek, Götz. "Schauen, suchen, denken." *Sezession,* May 2013, 6–9.

Lenart, Patrick. "Identitäre Aktionsformen." *Sezession,* May 2013, 28–31.

Lichtmesz, Martin. "Verteidigung des Eigenen." *Burschenschaftliche Blätter* 127, no. 4 (2012): 151–52.

Lichtmesz, Martin. "Die dreifache Wurzel der Identität." *Sezession,* May 2013, 24–27.

Malešević, Siniša. "The Chimera of National Identity." *Nations and Nationalism* 17, no. 2 (2011): 272–90.

mm. "Identität. Der Begriff einer Wende." *Identitäre Generation*, 2013, 17–20.

mm. "Mensch und Welt" *Identitäre Generation*, 2013, 22–24.

Morozov, V. and B. Rumelili. "The External Constitution of European Identity: Russia and Turkey as Europe-Makers." *Cooperation and Conflict* 47, no. 1 (2012): 28–48.

Müller, Ulrike Anne. "Far Away So Close: Race, Whiteness, and German Identity." *Identities:Global Studies in Culture and Power* 18, no. 6 (2011): 620–45.

Mushaben, Joyce Marie. "From Ausländer to Inländer. The Changing Faces of Citizenship in Post-Wall Germany." *German Politics and Society* 28, no. 1 (2010): 141–64.

Owens, T. J., D. T. Robinson, and L. Smith-Lovin. "Three Faces of Identity." *Annual Review of Sociology* 36 (2010): 477–99.

Pautz, Hartwig. "The Politics of Identity in Germany: the *Leitkultur* Debate." *Race & Class* 46, no. 4 (2005): 39–52.

Pella, Sebastian. "Identitäre Bewegung: Historische Wurzeln im antiken Sparta." *Neue Ordnung*, 2013, 19–21.

Polletta, Francesca. "'Free Spaces" in Collective Action." *Theory and Society* 28, no. 1 (1999): 1–38.

Polletta, F., and J. M. Jasper. "Collective Identity and Social Movements." *Annual Review of Sociology* 27 (2001): 283–305.

Pratt, Douglas. "Islamophobia: Ignorance, Imagination, Identity and Interaction." *Islam and Christian-Muslim Relations* 22, no. 4 (2011): 379–89.

Raschke, Joachim. *Soziale Bewegungen. Ein historisch-systematischer Grundriß.* Frankfurt/ New York: Campus, 1985.

Rehwaldt, Dorian. "'Doppelt bestrafte Generation.'" *Zuerst!* , December 2012, 59–60.

Schäfer, Michael. "Identitäre Bewegung—Pro und Contra." *Der Aktivist* , 2012, 10–12.

Schäfer, Michael. "Werde, wer DU bist!" *Deutsche Stimme*, February 2013, 16.

Siegfried, Hanspeter. "Kulturrevolution von rechts?" *Widerspruch* 11, no. 21 (1991): 76–94.

Spektorowki, Alberto. "The New Right: Ethno-Regionalism, Ethno-Pluralism and the Emergence of a neo-Fascist 'Third Way.'" *Journal of Political Ideologies* 8, no. 1 (2003): 111–30.

Stachel, Peter. "Identität." *Archiv für Kulturgeschichte* 87, no. 2 (2005): 395–425.

Stephan, C. W., and W. G. Stephan. "The Measurement of Racial and Ethnic Identity." *International Journal of Intercultural Relations* 24, no. 5 (2000): 541–52.

Taguieff, Pierre-André. *Die Macht des Vorurteils. Der Rassismus und sein Double.* Hamburg: Hamburger Edition, 2000.

Vader, Ulli. " 'Liebe zu Deutschland.'" *Zuerst!,* June 2014, 36–37.

Walton, Stephen J. "Anti-Feminism and Misogyny in Breivik's 'Manifesto.'" *NORA—Nordic Journal of Feminist and Gender Research* 20, no. 1 (2012): 4–11.

Weßels, Bernhard. "Discontent and European Identity: Three Types of Euroscepticism." *Acta Politica* 42, no. 2 (2007): 287–306.

Wetherell, Margaret. "The Field of Identity Studies." In *The SAGE Handbook of Identities*. Edited by Margaret Wetherell and Chandra Talpade Mohanty, 3–26. Los Angeles: Sage, 2010.

Willinger, Markus. *Die Identitäre Generation*. London: Arktos Media, 2013.

III

Homophobia, Race, and Radicalism

Chapter Ten

Singing for Race and Nation

Fascism and Racism in Greek Youth Music

Alexandra Koronaiou, Evangelos Lagos,
and Alexandros Sakellariou

The economic and social collapse that Greece has been experiencing since 2010 has indelibly marked both the society and the political system.[1] The crisis, as well as the complete failure to tackle it effectively either on the national or European level, brought to the surface, magnified, and accelerated extensive and profound socio-political processes that were developing during the last two decades. These crystallized in the two successive national elections in 2012 May and June and provoked an extensive restructuring of the Greek political system.

These elections took place in a climate of sharp political conflict caused by successive waves of austerity and recession that had already provoked the spike in unemployment and exacerbated the conditions of extreme poverty which created a severe humanitarian crisis for large parts of the population. The collapse of the already anaemic social policy and services had resulted in a dramatic impact on people's everyday lives: there was a marked increase in the number of people who could not afford even the day's meals, more than 1.3 million unemployed, 64 percent youth unemployment, 3.9 million below the poverty line, 70 percent of households cutting back on food expenses, more than 3,000 suicides in three years, a dramatic explosion of homelessness rates and of those without access to basic social services, health, and social security rights. These conditions triggered a series of sociopolitical developments that strongly challenged the balance of power within the Greek political system, which had been dominant for the last four decades.

One of the most salient developments is the remarkable electoral success and entry into the Greek Parliament of a formerly marginal political formation of the extremist neo-Nazi right. In 2012, Laikos Syndesmos Chryssi Avgi (Popular League Golden Dawn) succeeded in attracting 7 percent of the vote (from 0.29 percent in 2009) and in winning eighteen seats in the Greek Parliament, thus enabling it to generate an extreme xenophobic-racist and authoritarian discourse focused on anti-migrant scapegoating and on the violent and absolute rejection of the Third Greek Democracy's political system that had been established in 1974 after the collapse of the seven-year military dictatorship.[2]

Golden Dawn's impressive electoral leap as well as its constantly rising influence, according to the subsequent opinion polls, particularly among young people, has attracted the media's and the public's great interest and concern for the unexpected electoral success of a neo-Nazi organization, known for its extremist discourse and practice.[3]

This chapter examines one specific aspect of Golden Dawn's strategy to reach and recruit young Greeks and to shape and propagate a neo-Nazi political identity: namely the Party's establishment of a White Power music scene within youth music and culture. For this purpose, we focus on the analysis of Greek White Power songs in order to investigate their ideological content as well as to highlight their relation to Golden Dawn's ideology and effort to develop and disseminate its neo-Nazi identity among Greek youth.

In this context, we draw on the international debate about fascist/neo-Nazi ideology and politics, in particular the work of Roger Griffin and his definition of "generic fascism." Griffin's work has been of great importance as it has refreshed the theoretical interest in fascism and offered an elaborate conceptual framework for the analysis of fascist ideology. According to Griffin's ideal-typical approach, the core of fascist ideology consists of a "vision of the nation being capable of imminent phoenix-like rebirth from the prevailing crisis and decadence in a revolutionary new political and cultural order embracing all the 'true' members of the national community."[4] In this framework, the notion of "palingenetic ultra-nationalism" is central in summarizing the combination of revolutionary, exclusionist, mythologized, authoritarian, and racist qualities of a nationalist discourse obsessed with "degeneration and regeneration as socio-historical realities"[5] that Griffin highlighted as the fundamental fascist socio-political discourse.

We trace such discursive threads within Greek White Power songs and build upon international research on extreme right and neo-Nazi identities and cultures as well as on the preliminary findings of our ongoing research in the MYPLACE[6] research project regarding Golden Dawn and its appeal to Greek youth. Our aim is to offer an overview and an understanding of Greek neo-Nazi musical identity within Greek youth culture, thus contributing to the understanding of contemporary youth political identities.

At the time of writing, Golden Dawn had once again monopolized public interest following the Greek government's decision to react against two consecutive violent attacks that the Party's storm troopers had perpetrated. In the first case, members of the Communist Party's Youth (KNE) had been attacked by Golden Dawn members and supporters during a postering action. In the second case, a small group of young antifascists had been attacked by numerous Golden Dawn storm troopers, resulting in the cold-blooded murder of a thirty-four-year-old antifascist rapper. The (inter)national shock that the second of these attacks caused and the ensuing outrage and protests lead the police and the judicial system to react against the Party and its leadership by initiating a full judicial investigation and by pressing charges. The public prosecutor's request for investigation includes a large number of criminal cases, e.g., attacks against immigrants that were still not related immediately to Golden Dawn, although they had already gone to the police. The outcome of the investigation's first phase was the arrest of six Golden Dawn leading MPs together with many Party members and the pre-trial detention of three others, including the Party's leader and deputy leader as well as of other members and local branch Party officials. At the same time, the media rediscovered the violent Nazi character of Golden Dawn and reported on its hate practices while emphasizing the Party's connection with young people and youth culture. The outcome of the second phase of the investigation was the imprisonment of three more MPs, while the rest of them are free either under various restrictions, e.g., not to leave the country, not to participate in the Party's public assemblies, etc. or on bail. Furthermore, during the investigation two of the Party's MPs stated that they did not know about the Party's criminal activities and since then they declared that they are not affiliated with Golden Dawn and are considered as independent MPs in the Parliament.

THE RISE OF NEO-NAZISM IN GREECE: GOLDEN DAWN AND YOUNG PEOPLE

Golden Dawn's settling into the Greek political system had provoked a massive wave of accounts and debates about the causes, the meaning and the dynamic of the Party's electoral success. The "Golden Dawn debate" became even more heated when vote analyses revealed the Party's effectiveness in attracting a high proportion of the youth vote, in fact, the second highest among all parties. The youth and young adult vote for Golden Dawn ranged from 10 to 14 percent in the May/June exit polls for the eighteen to twenty-four age group and from 13–16 percent for the twenty-five to thirty-four age group, setting off many questions and great anxiety not only about the political meaning of the youth vote, but also about the dynamic it unveiled. Anxiety escalated when Golden Dawn's penetration throughout Greek youth became evident also in the educational system, particularly in secondary schools. Groups of school students appeared to openly express their support for Golden Dawn, they displayed the Party's symbols (including swastikas and the Nazi salute), intimidated and attacked political opponents, teachers and classmates of non-Greek origin, and recruited fellow students. The situation quickly escalated into fierce antagonism and conflict between groups supporting Golden Dawn and anti-fascist groups that were formed in reaction to the Party's aggressive presence in schools.

Golden Dawn's official discourse hails such developments, proclaiming that in future elections an "intergenerational battle" will take place with the majority of the Greek youth taking the side of Golden Dawn.[7] As they declared when an "Observatory for the Prevention of School Violence and Intimidation" was announced, any attempts to contain Golden Dawn's influence on youth "will ultimately fail, because we have won the youth from you [i.e. the mainstream parties] once and for all."[8] In their official websites they present young people's support of Golden Dawn as a result of youth's rejection of the corrupt and treacherous political system of parliamentary democracy and of the lies from liberal and socialist parties. On the contrary, Golden Dawn tells young people the truth and it articulates their heroic will for a radical change that will restore the nation and the people from the dramatic conditions they have been cast into.[9]

In this context, youth is, for Golden Dawn, a vital force with respect to radical change and to establishing a "New Nation" and a new political regime run by the "worthy" ones in order to vindicate the interests of the nation. Golden Dawn calls systematically upon a nationally awakened new generation that shall oppose and fight party democracy and its liberal and socialist variants.[10] This would be a generation of nationalists that shall crush Greece's enemies and will salvage Greek civilization from the capitalists' and the invading "barbarian immigrants" with the left's support.[11] Their discourse promotes a heroic attitude of "us against all others," thus presenting the Party as the only political agent that fights for the true interests and aspirations of the people, the youth and the nation.[12]

Despite the Party's denial that it recruits young people in schools, Golden Dawn's political activities attract young people of all age groups, while lately the Party has been organizing "history courses" for the nationalist education of young people, even at primary level. Golden Dawn's public activities reveal that young people are involved in much of its social activism, particularly in food and blood donations "for Greeks only" and in public events and commemorations. Moreover, the rise in racist violent attacks by young people against immigrants has raised concerns that actually Golden Dawn encourages such attacks as a kind of "initiation rite" to the Party's political practice, an accusation that Golden Dawn officially rejects, but which can be read in the recent public prosecutor's request that led to the arrest and pre-trial detention of the Party's leader and of prominent members and MPs.

The ideologically and politically charged debate on Golden Dawn's infiltration of a segment of Greek youth initially emphasized the role of the crisis, austerity, and especially of youth unemployment that in May 2013 exceeded 64 percent for those under twenty-five.[13] It interpreted the Golden Dawn youth vote as a consequence of young people's feelings of rage and despair due to the economic and social collapse of the country. According to such arguments, the impulsive nature of youth transformed rage and despair into electoral support for an extremist organization, thus expressing young people's will to punish the political system, which they held responsible for the destruction of their future.

However, this approach failed to account for the specific ideological and political choice that Golden Dawn young voters were making by supporting the Party. In other words, it had been unable to explain why these young people chose to vote for a neo-Nazi organization and not for any other parties that were also opposed to those whom the young people were blaming for the country's plight. To answer such questions, we need to take into account the ideological and political significance of young people's support for an ultra-nationalist, authoritarian, and racist organization that denounces democracy altogether and promises instead the nation's rebirth and the people's salvation through a national-socialist revolution that would establish an oligarchic and militaristic regime.

Our research for the MYPLACE project confirms the need for such an approach. It reveals a remarkable ideological and political connection between young voters and the Party's ideology and politics. Many of Golden Dawn young voters appear to be extremely dismissive of parliamentary democracy (or of any kind of democracy), political parties, and politicians. They express hostility toward liberal and left-wing ideology and politics: they are proudly nationalist, overtly or implicitly racist and xenophobic; in addition, they favor authoritarian and militaristic solutions, and support the political use of violence, while they avoid expressing criticism for the Party's choices and activity and dismiss all accusations of Nazism as systemic media fictions that aim to discredit the Party.

Remarkably, these characteristics coincide with important ideological and political developments and trends among Greek youth, namely, the alarming strengthening of nationalism, authoritarianism, and xenophobia that social surveys repeatedly have been tracking since the end of the 1990s.[14] Such trends among Greek youth were mirroring similar developments in the general population signifying the development of a wider political process that had resulted in 2007, for the first time since 1977, in the parliamentary representation of an extreme right political party. LAOS had already become a presence five years before Golden Dawn's impressive invasion of the Greek political system. In the 2012 elections LAOS suffered a spectacular collapse and its voters massively supported Golden Dawn as well as other predominantly right-wing parties.[15]

The question of Golden Dawn's political success in Greece, then, needs to be analyzed and understood in relation to wider ideological and political developments and trends that cannot be attributed solely to the current crisis. In this sense, Golden Dawn's political and electoral success is not just an accident caused by rage and protest against the destructive consequences of the crisis, austerity, and recession. Instead, it should be understood as the result of profound socio-political processes that had already been present and developing in Greek society for the last two decades, magnified and sharpened by the country's collapse and the deconstruction of the dominant balance of power in the Greek political system which was caused by the onset of the crisis.

Thus, the investigation of young peoples' support for Golden Dawn needs to take into account the ideological bonds that the Party has developed with a segment of Greek youth. These bonds constitute a central part of Golden Dawn's ideological strategy (even from the time of its early formation in mid 1980s as a political organization comprised mainly of young militant national-socialists)[16] concentrating on the shaping of a neo-Nazi cultural and political identity among Greek youth. In this context, Golden Dawn's influence on Greek youth culture is of crucial importance for the understanding of contemporary youth political identities and political engagement.

YOUNG PEOPLE, MUSIC, AND RIGHT-WING EXTREMISM

Music is a key issue for the study of youth subcultures and its role has been investigated since the 1960s. T he mixing of music and politics has come to exert an enormous influence on popular culture [17] and the combination of music and politics that takes place in social movements is an important, if often overlooked, source of cultural transformation.[18] Music and songs influence people's ideas, memories, and lives; it participates in the construction of meaning and can constitute a central aspect of collective identity formation.[19] National anthems are among the most typical examples of music's socio-political uses.[20] Thus, the imagined community of the nation is reproduced through nationalist music[21] that plays a specific role in erasing the voices of the nation's internal " others" and of foreigners,[22] especially when nationalist groups and parties are in power.

Music and songs are also crucial for social movements. Songs provide channels of communication for activists within movements, but also between different movements and between movement generations,[23] because music enters easily into collective memory. Likewise, music plays an important role in right-wing or neo-Nazi groups and social movements. As other researchers have shown,[24] extreme-right (White Power) music facilitates the formation and framing of young people's political identity and ideology. For nationalist movements, as well as for all social movements in general, identity construction is central in their politics.[25] Nationalist identity, in particular, involves a re-interpreted historical past that is often considered as important a terrain of practice as the present, or even more important than the present.[26] Corte and Edwards[27] summarize their research, arguing that White Power music plays an important role in supporting racist movements by recruiting adherents, by cultivating in young people a sense of collective identity, and by providing financial resources. However, we should always remember that all these extreme groups and White Power music bands have an historical paradigm: Nazi Germany. Joseph Goebbels himself asserted that music is a very crucial factor for the Hitler's Youth, since music's task was to uplift the emotions: "it goes without saying that the phalanges of our youth are singing while marching in the streets."[28] Following that, Friedrich W. Herzog the editor of the journal *Die Musik* wrote in 1934 that: "we want a music that will be full of the expressive power of the national-socialist idea."[29] We need to keep in mind the historical roots of nationalist music and the role music played in the formation of nations. Furthermore, we have to remember that such groups play a social role which is not only related to music, but also to social participation, the sense of belonging, ideology, and of course the imagined community of the nation.

Hence, the study of the White Power scene is important for the analysis and understanding of the cultural dimension of extremist right-wing movements, since its use reveals a particular political intentionality to prevail over cultural forms external to it that are then reconfigured to serve socio-political needs, namely to strengthen participation, the sense of belonging, and of course the neo-Nazi re-interpretation of the imagined community of the nation. In this context, studying the White Power music scene is important for the understanding of extreme-right and neo-Nazi propaganda strategies, because of the scene's penetration in youth culture, as well as because of the development of a sense of a community of activists that connects and coordinates individuals and groups on an international scale.[30] Recordings, magazines and fanzines, live concerts, the Internet, and social media have proved to be particularly useful in reproducing and propagating neo-Nazi ideas and identities using youth culture and music as its vehicle as well as in forming and configuring the activist character of neo-Nazi politics.[31]

THE GREEK WHITE POWER SCENE:
SINGING FOR NATIONAL GLORY, BLOOD, AND HATE

Music has a peculiar status in neo-Nazi culture. It is perceived and understood within a militant-activist framework that privileges political propaganda and networking, that is, expressive, communicative or participatory uses
of music over aesthetic or recreational ones. Its role is important but also
ancillary. It has no intrinsic value and becomes meaningful only as a means
of recruiting young people and propagating fascist and racist ideology, that
is, within the framework of propaganda.

   Golden Dawn is no exception to this characterization. In fact the development of the Greek White Power music scene has been its own achievement.
Youth music, the Internet, and social media, as well as football fan culture
were targeted as Golden Dawn's main fields of interest in its effort to recruit
young people.[32] For this purpose, and building upon the marginal in Greece
skinhead culture, Golden Dawn adopted a strategy from the British far right/
neo-Nazi parties and organizations of the late 1970s and 1980s that aimed at
reaching young people through youth music subcultures. The formation in
late 1990s of the Party's youth division ("Youth Front") and the issuing of its
magazine *Antepithessi* ("Counterattack") were Golden Dawn's first moves in
reaching a wider youth audience that had become more susceptible to the
nationalist discourses that dominated the Greek public sphere in the 1990s.
This had been a crucial period for Golden Dawn's development, a period
during which nationalist and xenophobic discourses were established in the
Greek public sphere following the first massive outbreak of immigration to
Greece (after the collapse of the Albanian political system and economy) and
FYROM's[33] claiming the term "Macedonia" as its official name in the early
1990s. As the Party's main ideological instructor explained in 1999, ". . .
Youth Front was formed as an attempt to exploit ideologically and politically
the already very positive climate that existed in a large part of youth. From
the first moment we felt that penetration into these circles would become
much easier if we used those sectors in which youth is massively present,
such as music and football stadiums."[34]

   The Party's connection to the international White Power music movement
through the B&H network was pivotal to this strategy. After its establishment
in 1999 by "a group of nationalists and national-socialists (mainly members
of Golden Dawn) . . . ,"[35] the Greek branch of B&H, Blood and Honour
Hellas (B&HH) became the most important focal point for the Greek White
Power music scene. Following Ian Stuart Donaldson's remark that "a pamphlet is read only once, but a song is learnt by heart and repeated a thousand
times"[36] Golden Dawn succeeded, through B&HH, in establishing a White
Power music scene that houses and supports bands, record companies, and
live concerts, publishes magazines and fanzines, sells CDs and ancillaries (t-

shirts, hats, badges, etc.), connects with their international counterparts, uses the Internet extensively, and produces music that ". . . is not simply a means of entertainment. It is a means of spreading our ideas and values [. . .]. Our music is an ideology that can be listened to."[37]

On the official blog of the Party's youth division (Youth Front) there are many articles and news items about the white power scene in Greece and abroad. In one of them, entitled "Our Music,"[38] they describe music as something different from a mere means of entertainment, which it usually is for the majority. For Golden Dawn, music is rather a medium of propagation of their ideas and values, a way to express different forms of their nationalist worldviews and way of life. They insist that their music has a clearly anti-commercial outlook due to its status as part of a subculture, which is mostly important, as they note, for the young people, who today, more than ever, need Golden Dawn's ideas and values.[39] Such instrumental approaches to music that perceive it as an ideological weapon in the effort to strengthen and propagate neo-Nazi culture and politics are typical of the B&H attitude toward music and they are strongly highlighted in the texts produced by the White Power music scene in general.[40] This is why "antepithessi" reproduces the view of the Italian White Power band Hate for Breakfast, at its note on the band's dissolution so as, according to the band's members, to be able to completely devote themselves to the national-socialist struggle: "Fuck music and concerts. Long live Fascism. For a superior spirit!"[41]

The first decade of the twenty-first century was very successful for B& HH and the Greek White Power scene. The general trend toward a strengthening of nationalist and xenophobic discourses in Greek society and in the political system aligns as well with Golden Dawn's growing visibility and influence. Consistent with this trend, the Greek White Power scene demonstrated considerable growth. Bands, musical styles, live concerts, and recordings multiplied while the Internet and social media opened the scene to a wider youth audience.[42] During this decade Greek White Power stopped being confined to Oi/RAC (Rock Against Communism) and skinhead culture. Although these remained at the heart of the scene, hardcore, thrash metal, black metal, and even hip hop music were also added. Besides, Golden Dawn itself strongly benefited from the Greek White Power development, as the latter operated under the Party's absolute control through the B&HH. It is worth noting that four prominent Golden Dawn members, two of whom were elected MPs in the June 2012 elections, are members of White Power bands that have been systematically promoted by B&HH.[43] Thus, the ideological identification between the official Golden Dawn dogma and the songwriting production of White Power bands, as well as their participation in Golden Dawn events, particularly the annual Greek Youth Festival should cause no surprise.

SINGING NAZISM[44]

Golden Dawn's control over the White Power scene in Greece is reflected in the very names of the bands, in the lyrics of the songs, and in the symbols that are used by bands and audience alike. The direct or indirect appearance of Golden Dawn slogans or of the Party's name in song titles and lyrics is quite common.[45]

Just as often there are direct or indirect references to historical Nazism. Here the Greek fans of Adolf Hitler express their faith in National Socialism as well as their hope for its revival and ultimate victory. They also strive to purify and restore the Greek Nazi collaborators during the German occupation of the country in WWII (1941–1944). Thus, Pogrom, the band of a Golden Dawn MP, sing: "we love the national coat of arms, head shaved, nationalism, army and arms raised."[46] The band Maiandros (meander)[47] believe that "national-socialism is the medicine"[48] for what they see as the contemporary social decline and pathology, while the White Pride Rockers look forward to fascism's rebirth and they warn: "In Dresden's ruins the Phoenix is born and white Europe rises again/ [. . .] we will return and this time we will be stronger and the earth will tremble."[49]

More openly, Hellenic Stompers, the White Power band of another party member, glorify the Greek Nazi collaborators during the German occupation period and close the song shouting, "Sieg Heil" ("Hail Victory"), the famous Nazi salute and slogan that prominent members of Golden Dawn as well as its leader use quite frequently (in its Greek translation as "Zito i Niki") when they conclude their texts and speeches[50]: "It came at last this moment that the blooded earth will be purified/ [. . .] Hellenic SS greet the sun/ [. . .] war and horror prevail."[51]

In the same spirit, but with evident anxiety for the acquittal of Nazi collaborators from their historical condemnation as traitors, No Surrender (an emblematic Golden Dawn and B&HH band) sing about their grandfather who was an SS trooper: "In my house you can see a photo of my grandfather/ totenkopf, boots and black uniform/ proud he was, proud I am too, one nation and people, one leader."[52] Subsequent verses reveal that the grandfather had joined the Greek Nazi collaborationist troops (often called the "Greek SS") killing communist guerrillas in order to protect the Greek Macedonia from communist control. Fighting against the Greek resistance he was fighting to liberate Greece from communism.

This song accurately summarizes Golden Dawn's historical revisionism regarding the role of Greek Nazi collaborators. Here they are heroically presented as fighting against communism in order to protect Greek Macedonia from communist control, while the Greek resistance (ELAS guerrillas, i.e., the Greek Communist Party and its partisans) is identified with the black marketeers who controlled the market and is characterized as treasonous.

This is a common Golden Dawn historical distortion that seeks to challenge the relationship of black marketeers with Nazi collaborators in order to remove the stigma of the traitor from itself and to present them as patriots and nationalists who in fact opposed communism. Moreover, its goal is to challenge the Communist Party's actual national struggle and final victory against the Nazi occupation and to undermine the wide social recognition of its fight against Golden Dawn's ideological and political fathers.

Neo-Nazi historical revisionism has great importance for Golden Dawn as a political party, since it is only through such heroicization of Greek Nazi collaborators and the corresponding devaluation and dismissal of the anti-Nazi fight during the WWII Greece (that turns the Nazi collaborators into the "real National Resistance") that Greek neo-Nazis can claim the title of "patriot" and of the nation's defenders. This is precisely the reason why Golden Dawn organizes and participates in commemorative public events for the Nazi collaborators in which the latter are represented as nationalist martyrs who were murdered by the communists because of their determination to protect the country from communist control. In its effort to diffuse this brand of revisionism, Golden Dawn has extensively applied the term "National Resistance," aspiring to reach wider electoral audiences. Thus, they invite Greek citizens to join and vote for the Party that is presented as the "only National Resistance"[53] against traitors, immigrants, Zionism, capitalist speculators and Marxist internationalists.

As expected, Greek neo-Nazi revisionism could not exclude the Holocaust. Nevertheless, a differentiation between Greek White Power bands and Golden Dawn's official position on the Holocaust must be noted. Whereas Golden Dawn's MPs identify themselves publicly as "Holocaust deniers," activating the neo-Nazi set of arguments, typical for this purpose, Pogrom, the White Power band of a Golden Dawn MP celebrates and praises Auschwitz and the extinction of Jews: "Juden Raus!/ Fuck Wiesenthal, Fuck Anne Frank, Fuck the whole race of Abraham/ David's star makes me sick, Ah, how I love Auschwitz."[54]

In any case, the differentiation between White Power bands and Golden Dawn's official discourse regarding the enthusiastic endorsement or denial of the Holocaust seems to be superficial. The photographs and the accompanying comments that a Golden Dawn parliamentary candidate publicized on the Internet upon his return from a visit to Dachau[55] indicate that the whole-hearted endorsement of the Holocaust is shared by Golden Dawn core members despite the public rhetorical tactics that the Party has adopted, especially since their electoral success.

Jews represent a fundamental enemy for White Power bands as well as for Golden Dawn. As A. Shekhovtsov observes, in White Power song writing, Jews personify the qualities of both the demonized "Other" and of the "System" representing, thus, the two faces that the "forces of evil" assume in neo-Nazi culture and politics.[56] They represent the "villainous foreigner" that defiles the white race with their inferior and negative cultural and racial characteristics, but they are also seen as the almighty owners of the dominant economic and political system who seek to destroy the white nations and to enslave all peoples in its interests. In this context Jews are blamed for the decline of Greek society that has been caused through capitalist greed, multiculturalism, globalization, and the treasonous governments that the Jews control economically through capital and politically through Zionist politics. The White Power "Zionist Occupation Government" theme that perceives governments as controlled by global forces under Zionist command is reproduced by the Greek White Power bands and coincides with Golden Dawn's interpretation of the migration issue in the context of globalization. Both the Party and the bands perceive immigration as a form of invasion that aims to corrupt Aryan races and cultures and to exterminate white peoples through the multicultural society that capitalism and Zionism impose.[57] "The foreigners at last show their real faces/ they respect nothing/ and our Jewish governors built mosques for them,"[58] Maiandros sings, while Pogrom despises and threatens immigrants in Greece: "I see them in squares, I see them at work/ I see them in the sea too, they dirty the waters/ If they stay in Greece, they will pay dearly."[59]

Immigrants are treated as "invaders" and "garbage" that murder Greeks, pollute the country, and alter its culture . Along with Turks, Muslims, nonwhites, as well as anarchists, leftists, and democrats, they are the main "villainous others," whereas politicians, the state, and the capitalists represent the "system." Both groups of enemies are despised by White Power bands and they are treated with condemnation and violence. Thus, the band Hellgrinder urges: "Slay a politician, slay an Albanian, an anarchist son of a bitch/ slay a Turk, slay a Muslim scum, slay a nigger."[60]

The common element between these two groups of enemies is that they both destroy the Greek nation and race. But White Power bands hate particularly politicians, anarchists, and democrats for yet another reason: they are the nation's traitors, since they are of Greek origin but they turn against national interest, as this is understood by this extreme-right culture. Accordingly, White Front Thessaloniki sing about the "coward anarchists, pillars of the state"[61] who choose to betray the nation aligning with the state, the law, and the police. The band Mahen urges: "Slay a politician, a democrat/ their regime is a sham."[62] The hatred that White Power bands express for politicians, anarchists, leftists, and democrats as well as for capitalists— in fact for everyone other than neo-Nazi movements and parties—derives from their anti-systemic rhetoric that groups all political opponents in one single category, that of the nation's traitors. This attitude echoes Golden Dawn's adoption of Adolf Hitler's propaganda strategy to equate and classify as a single group all political opponents in order to present the people with a single enemy—a gesture that simplifies political struggle and unifies members and supporters against one single adversary. Golden Dawn put this strategy into practice by adopting the slogan "Against All," which also includes other conservative and far-right parties and organizations that differentiate themselves from Golden Dawn.[63] That is why Maiandros warns: "But phoney patriots too will get the shot."[64]

Such a culture of hate and violence is a source of pride and determination for the members and the supporters of White Power music scene, while Golden Dawn incorporates it within its concept of a new National Resistance that confronts the nation's enemies and traitors and will free the nation and the people.[65] This kind of music also offers a heroic sense of struggle for ideals and values and a sense of community with a purpose. In this spirit White Front of Thessaloniki sing: "Consciously have chosen the denial of law/ Brave at heart, brave to the soul against decay and decadence/ [. . .] We live hard because we have ideas. Against all!"[66]

Heroism and the sense of a "fighting us," that is, of a community of fighters against evil forces that threaten the nation, is again another central theme in Golden Dawn discourse. It is repeated in most ideological texts and it is highlighted and celebrated in party speeches and events.[67] The theme is also materialized in the Party's (para)military appearance and in its mode of collective action and it is reflected in the militaristic images that White Power songs paint for party activists, their fights and forthcoming victory.

Their struggle is directed against the national decay and decadence caused by the traitors' actions. Greed, corruption, immorality, devaluation of national ideals and symbols, and subjection to the interests of the nation's external enemies are the main characteristics of the national decline that Greek White Power bands are fighting against. Maiandros describe a grim picture of Greece's decline: "Our society below zero, moral values have all gone/ [. . .] Garbage and foreigners, national decline/ Jewish government, absolute languish."[68]

The theme of treason is widely used in White Power song writing as well as in Golden Dawn discourse. It serves the appropriation of the concept of nation by the National Socialists. It encapsulates the ultra-nationalist interpretation of the country's problems, stigmatizes political opponents, and justifies the neo-Nazi obsession with extreme violence and the physical extinction of their opponents. It is also closely connected to the themes of decline and national danger, of revenge, and of national rebirth after the final victory of the national-socialist revolution that will violently avenge and exterminate the traitors. Golden Dawn's Youth also pride themselves on instilling fear in traitors, while even pop songs that Golden Dawn local branch members compose include such warnings: "From the phalanx's path they flee all the nation's enemies/ From traitors the city empties/ When Golden Dawn passes, when Golden Dawn passes"[69] or "And when we will be lined up like soldiers/ Woe and alas, traitors we will find you."[70]

Revolution is yet another common theme both in White Power songs and Golden Dawn ideology and politics. The prospect of a future revolution supports their anti-systemic rhetoric and again justifies violence: "In revolution we loose our minds/ For all our enemies we will become a threat/ [. . .] Verbal bullets and real ones comrades. "[71]

The victory of the national-socialist revolution will lead to the nation's rebirth through the ashes of decadent Greece. White Power songs promise freedom, glory, and power for the Greek nation after the victorious revolution. National pride will be restored and the nation's glorious past will be revived, while Greece will be recognized and honoured by Aryan Europe: "Nationalists dressed in black will parade and the Greeks, free, the victory will celebrate/ [. . .] Great will our country and Europe be/ Our Aryan brothers will be first to hail us."[72]

The conception of the nation's rebirth through the ashes of decadent Greece that will be destroyed by the nationalist/national-socialist revolution in order for a "New Nation" and a "New Greek People" to be created is central to Golden Dawn's ideology. The official party anthem centres on the revival of the nation's mythologized past and on the demand for a New Nation: " Followers of Great Ancestors, sons of Glorious Fighters/ We are the New Spartans with our Brave Heart/ [. . .] We Want a New Hellas [Greece]/ That Will Cover All Earth."[73]

In Golden Dawn's ideological texts this conception is elaborated and analyzed to produce a vision of the nation's phoenix-like resurrection that will relieve it from internal and external enemies, restoring its past glory. This kind of "palingenetic ultra-nationalism"[74] requires a revolutionary process of national purification and rebirth, one that results in a "universal rupture of an era and a people with everything that preceded in its historic course" and in the "transformation of the Folk Community's thinking" in order to reconstruct it and to build the "National People's State."[75] It is a revolution that "does not seek to salvage anything from the established economic and social interests that drive Nations, Peoples and Civilization to decline" and is seen as "the only absolute and real revolution because it seeks to give birth to new moral, spiritual, social and mental values."[76] These values will mark the "re-Hellenization" of the state and the people through "the final eradication of those Semitic elements which have been cultivated for many decades in our People" such as "individualism, selfishness, political opportunism, the rampant pursuit of profit, indifference for the future of the Race and of the Homeland" and by putting "first the splendor of Faith in the Greek Blood, the operative force of the achievements of the Greek Nation."[77] This vision of revolutionary national rebirth is complemented by that of the Greek nation's supremacy that constitutes the ultimate promise of both Golden Dawn and White Power bands for a "New Hellas" and that will eradiate as a "New Alexandria" (Maiandros) and "will cover all Earth."

CONCLUSION

The Greek White Power bands sing about nation, race, blood, decline, treason, hatred, revolution, and the violent revival of the mythologized Greek past. They create a cultural universe in which hatred and the worship of violence dominate and they are directed against all those who do not comply with Aryan requirements or do not align with the imperatives of racial ultra-nationalism. The music uses anti-systemic rhetoric and openly declares its devotion to National Socialism while at the same time it revises and inverts, in order to appropriate them, core public conceptions of the country's historical past such as the National Resistance against the WWII Nazi occupation of Greece as well as Greek antiquity. Finally, it promises revenge and the violent punishment of those who are held responsible for the country's decline heralding a free and glorious future built upon the ruins of the decadent present.

As it operates under the ideological and political control of Golden Dawn, the White Power scene reproduces the latter's central ideological themes, thus functioning as a fundamental ideological tool for the propagation of neo-Nazi ideas and practices through youth culture and music. The White Power scene cultivates a sense of a fighting community of activists that struggle against stronger enemies for the county's salvation and the restoration of Aryan supremacy. It uses international networking and the promotion of cultural products through traditional media and the Internet in order to reach and indoctrinate young people. It exploits the strong presence of nationalist and xenophobic discourses in the Greek public sphere for the last two decades attempting to appropriate and channel youth's reaction to the present socio-political collapse of the country.

The Greek White Power scene has helped Golden Dawn capitalize on widespread nationalist and xenophobic public discourses and feelings in order to construct a cultural-political identity that identifies patriotism with nationalism and the latter with National Socialism. It is a "heroic" identity that attacks all other identities demanding their subjection or their extinction. Racial nationalism as well as intolerance and hatred toward all other identities are the fundamental elements upon which a "New Greece," a "Great Greece," will be built after the victory of the national-socialist revolution that will cleanse the nation from all incompatible to neo-Nazi identities.

In conclusion, it can be argued that the White Power scene in Greece popularizes Golden Dawn ideology among young people opening a cultural space for the diffusion of the characteristic to fascism ideology of "palingenetic ultra-nationalism" and the corresponding to it neo-Nazi identities and politics. It does this by infusing National Socialism, racism, and authoritarianism in youth cultural forms and practices building on both the widespread nationalist and xenophobic discourses that already for a long time characterized the Greek public sphere and politics and young people's rage about the country's present plight. In these ways, it contributes to the establishment and growth of a popular neo-Nazi ideological current in contemporary Greek society.

NOTES

1. We would like to thank our colleagues, Stelios Kymionis, and Aris Deliveris for their ideas and fruitful comments during the preparation of this chapter.

2. While we were working on this chapter Golden Dawn managed to raise its political influence in the European elections of 25 May 2014 gaining the third place with 9.39 percent of the votes and electing three members in the European Parliament.

3. Maria Margaronis, "Fear and Loathing in Athens: The Rise of Golden Dawn and the Far Right," *The Guardian*, 26 October 2012, http://www.theguardian.com/world/2012/oct/26/golden-dawn-greece-far-right; and Augustine Zenakos, accessed 1 September 2013; "Golden Dawn, 1980-2012. The Neo-Nazis' Road to Parliament," *Reports from the Edge of Borderline Democracy*, 25 October 2012, http://borderlinereports.net/2012/10/25/report-golden-dawn-1980-2012-the-neonazis-road-to-parliament/, accessed 1 September 2013.

4. Roger Griffin, "The Palingenetic Core of Generic Fascist Ideology," in *Che Cos'è il Fascismo? Interpretazioni e Prospettive di Ricerche*, ed. Alessandro Campi (Roma: Ideazione Editrice, 2003), 97–122.

5. Griffin, "The Palingenetic Core of Generic Fascist Ideology," 102.

6. MYPLACE, Memory, Youth, Political Legacy and Civic Engagement, Grant No: FP7-266831 http://www.fp7-myplace.eu/index.php.

7. "Σαρώνει η Χρυσή Αυγή στη Νεολαία" (Golden Dawn sweeps among youth), 27 November 2012, accessed 27 August 2014. All translations, unless otherwise indicated, are our own. http://www.xryshaygh.com/index.php/enimerosi/view/sarwnei-h-chrush-augh-sth-neolaia#.UhRkMGew69s.

8. Antiochos, "Παρατηρητήριο για την Ανάσχεση της Χρυσής Αυγής στα Σχολεία φτιάχνει το Υπουργείο Παιδείας" (Observatory for the Containment of Golden Dawn Set up by the Ministry of Education), 25 November 2012, http://www.xryshaygh.com/index.php/enimerosi/view/parathrhthrio-gia-thn-anaschesh-ths-chrushs-aughs-sta-scholeia-ftiachnei-to#. UhRljGew69s, accessed 27 August 2014.

9. Spyridoula, "Γιατί η Νεολαία Προτιμά τη Χρυσή Αυγή" (Why youth prefer Golden Dawn?), 17 December 2012, http://www.xryshaygh.com/index.php/enimerosi/view/giati-h-neolaia-protima-thn-chrush-augh2#.UhRs4Wew69s,last, accessed 27 August 2014.

10. Evangelos Karakostas, "Εθνικιστική Επανάσταση" (Nationalist Revolution), 20 October 2012, http://www.xryshaygh.com/index.php/enimerosi/view/ethnikistikhepanastash#. UhSE4Gew69s, accessed 27 August 2014.

11. Floga tou Tainarou, "Αντιρατσισμός: Το Νέο Προσωπείο του Ανθελληνισμού" (Anti-racism: The new mask of anti-Hellenism), 5 June 2013, http://www.xryshaygh.com/index.php/enimerosi/view/antiratsismos-to-neo-proswpeio-tou-anthellhnismou#.UhSB7mew69s,   accessed 27 August 2014.

12. Evangelos Karakostas, "Η Πίστη μας, το Κίνημα, η Νίκη!" (Our Faith, the Movement, the Victory!), 6 August 2013, http://www.xryshaygh.com/index.php/enimerosi/view/h-pisth-mas-to-kinhma-h-nikh#.UhRx7Wew69s, accessed 27 August 2014.

13. "ΕΛΣΤΑΤ: Στο 27.6 percent το Μάιο η Ανεργία—στο 64.9 percent στους Νέους" (ELSTAT: Unemployment at 27.6 percent on May—64.9 percent in youth)," 8 August 2013, http://www.skai.gr/news/finance/article/239394/elstat-dramatiki-epideinosi-tis-anergias-sto-276-to-maio-f/, accessed 27 August 2014.

14. General Secretariat for Youth, VPRC Institute, *Οι Νέοι της Εποχής μας* (*The Young People of Our Times*), Athens: Papazissis, 2000; General Secretariat for Youth, *Youth in Greece Today*, General Secretariat for Youth (May 2005); and Chara Stratoudaki, "Εθνος και Δημοκρατία, Όψεις της Εθνικής Ταυτότητας των Εφήβων" (Nation and Democracy, Aspects of adolescents' National Identity), *Journal of Social Research* 116 A (2006): 23–50.

15. The Popular Orthodox Rally (LAOS) emerged from within the conservative party of New Democracy formulating an authoritarian, nationalist, and xenophobic discourse and got 3.80 percent and 5.63 percent in the 2007 and 2009 national elections respectively. LAOS collapsed electorally and politically during the summer 2012 national elections, following its integration to the "austerity bloc" as well as its participation to the preceding coalition government that implemented harsh austerity measures.

16. Dimitris Psarras, *Η Μαύρη Βίβλος της Χρυσής Αυγής* (*The Black Bible of Golden Dawn*) (Athens: Polis, 2012), 53–56.

17. Ron Eyerman and Andrew Jamison, *Music and Social Movements. Mobilizing Traditions in the Twentieth Century* (Cambridge: Cambridge University Press, 1998), 1.

18. Eyerman and Jamison, *Music and Social Movements*, 4.

19. Eyerman and Jamison, *Music and Social Movements*, 161.

20. Philip Bohlman, *The Music of European Nationalism. Cultural Identity and Modern History* (Santa Barbara-ABC CLIO, 2004).

21. Benedict Anderson, *Imagined Communities* (London: Verso, 1991).

22. Bohlman, *The Music of European Nationalism*, 20.

23. Eyerman and Jamison, *Music and Social Movements*, 161.

24. Hilary Pilkington et al., *Russia's Skinheads. Exploring and Rethinking Sub-Cultural Lives* (Abington: Routledge, 2010); Chiara Pierobon, "The Role of the Music in the German Extremist Right Wing Movements" (Paper presented at the 9th Conference of the European Sociological Association, Lisbon 2-5 September, 2009); Ugo Corte and Bob Edwards, "White Power Music and the Mobilization of Racist Social Movements," *Music and Arts in Action* 1 (2008).

25. Jane Jenson, "What's in a Name? Nationalist Movements and Public Discourse," in *Social Movements and Culture*, edited by H. Johnston and B. Klandermans (Minneapolis: University of Minnesota Press, 1995), 107.

26. Jensen, "What's in a name?," 107.

27. Corte and Edwards, "White Power Music and the Mobilization of Racist Social Movements," 17–18.

28. Lionel Richard, *Ναζισμός και Κουλτούρα* (*Nazism and Culture*) (Athens: Astarti, 1999), 202.

29. Richard, *Ναζισμός και Κουλτούρα* (*Nazism and Culture*), 203.

30. Timothy S. Brown, "Subcultures, Pop Music and Politics: Skinhead and 'Nazi Rock' in England and Germany," *Journal of Social History* 38 (2004); Corte and Edwards, "White Power Music and the Mobilization of Racist Social Movements"; Robert Futrell, Pete Simi, and Simon Gottschalk, "Understanding Music in Movements: The White Power Music Scene," *The Sociological Quarterly* 47 (2006).

31. For example, see *The Sounds of Hate, The White Power Music Scene in the United States 2012*, ADL, 2012 http://www.adl.org/assets/pdf/combating-hate/Sounds-of-Hate-White-Power-Music-Scene-2012.pdf ; U. Corte and B. Edwards (2008), http://www.diva-portal.org/smash/get/diva2:355075/FULLTEXT01.pdf.

32. Psarras, *Η Μαύρη Βίβλος της Χρυσής Αυγής* (*The Black Bible of Golden Dawn*), 308.

33. The Former Yugoslav Republic of Macedonia.

34. Giorgos Mastoras, "Η Πορεία μας" (Our Course), Antepithessi, 3 (1999), quoted in Psaras 2012, 309.

35. Giorgos Mastoras, *Η Ιστορία της White Power Μουσικής* (*The History of White Power Music*) (Athens: Lonchi/Antepithessi, 2003), 161.

36. Quoted in Mastoras 2003 and Shekhovtsov 2012, 291.

37. "Η Μουσική μας" (Our Music), 17 April 2010, http:// antepithesi.wordpress.com, accessed 7 August 2013.

38. "Η Μουσική μας" (Our Music).

39. "Η Μουσική μας" (Our Music).

40. "Η Μουσική είναι η Ταυτότητά μας" (Our Music is our Identity), http:// www.terrapatria.gr/, accessed 11 August 2013.

41. "Διαλύθηκαν οι Hate for Breakfast" (Hate for Breakfast dissolved), 24 November 2009, http://antepithesh.wordpress.com/2009/11/24/, accessed 11 August 2013; and "Τίτλοι Τέλους για μια Σπουδαία Μπάντα" (End titles for a great band), 4 January 2010, http://antepithesh. wordpress.com/2010/01/04/, accessed 11 August 2013.

42. Charis Symvoulides, *Oi! Η Μουσική των Skinheads (Oi!—Skinheads Music)* (Ioannina: Isnafi, 2008); Sofia Tipaldou, "Rock for the Motherland: White Power Music Scene in Greece," in *White Power Music: Scenes of Extreme—Right Cultural Resistance*, edited by Anton Shekhotsov and Paul Jackson (Searchlight Magazine: University of Northampton, 2012); Eleni Isis Mouza, "Η Μουσική Σκηνή της White Power Rock και το White Power Movement. Μια Έρευνα σε Ιταλικά και Ελληνικά Διαδικτυακά Forum" (The White Power Music Scene Rock and the White Power Movement. A Survey in Italian and Greek Internet Forum) (MA Thesis, National Kapodistrian University of Athens, 2011).

43. These White Power bands are: Iron Youth, Hellenic Stompers, Pogrom, and Naer Mataron.

44. All quoted lyrics in this chapter are the authors' translations of the Greek language originals, which are available on the Internet. They can all be found in the respective sources listed in the "Discography" section. The authors use the forward slashes (/) to indicate not necessarily separate lines, but often the rhymes in the original.

45. "We love songs about Greece and honour/ lyrics about blood and fatherland" (Pogrom, echoing both, Golden Dawn's slogan "Blood-Honour-Golden Dawn" and the B&H's title); "Anarchists and Bolsheviks, this land does not belong to you" and "Against All" (White Front Thessaloniki , both Golden Dawn slogans); "Our day that is coming soon will appear/ to rise at last the golden dawn" and "Blood-Honour-Golden Dawn" (Maiandros) .

46. Pogrom, *Ροκ για την Πατρίδα* (*Rock for the Fatherland*), CD Rock for the Fatherland, Gammadion Productions, 2006, http http://www.youtube.com/watch?v=OtbkqsII9AQ, accessed 27 August 2014.

47. The Meander is the official Golden Dawn party symbol.

48. Maiandros, *Χρυσή Αυγή* (*Golden Dawn*), 2010, http http://www.youtube.com/watch?v= 3nKy12JrLzE, accessed 27 August 2014.

49. White Pride Rockers. *Θα Τρέμει η Γη* (*The earth will tremble*), http://www.youtube. com/watch?v=wbFTHJD5gJU, accessed 27 August 2014.

50. Giorgos Mastoras, "Η Χρυσή Αυγή και το Σάπιο Καθεστώς" (Golden Dawn and the Rotten Regime), 14 August 2013, http://www.xryshaygh.com/index.php/enimerosi/view/h-chrush-augh-kai-to-sapio-kathestws#.UhOQ8dJM98E, accessed 27 August 2014; and "Το Χρυσό Κλουβί του Καπιταλισμού" (The Golden Cage of Capitalism), 10 July 2013, http:// www.xryshaygh.com/index.php/enimerosi/view/to-chruso-kloubi-tou-kapitalismou, accessed 27 August 2014.

51. Hellenic Stompers. *Ελληνικά SS* (*Hellenic SS*), CD Dimios, Gammadion, 2007.http:// www.youtube.com/watch?v=8LghjxwDvnk. Accessed 27 August 2014.

52. No Surrender. *Ο Παππούς μου ήταν στα SS* (*My grandfather was in SS*) http:// www.youtube.com/watch?v=MqjGVrZc270, accessed 27 August 2014.

53. "Έλα στη Χρυσή Αυγή, Εθνική Αντίσταση" (Join Golden Dawn, Join the National Resistance), http://www.youtube.com/watch?v=tggt-NixAd8, accessed 27 August 2014; and "Έλα στην Εθνική Αντίσταση, Ψήφισε Χρυσή Αυγή" (Join the National Resistance, Vote for Golden Dawn), http://xryshaygh.blogspot.gr/2012/05/blog-post_1674.html, accessed 1 September 2013.

54. Pogrom, *Άουσβιτς (Auschwitz)*. https://www.youtube.com/watch?v=BbZQuWSnKrU, accessed 27 August 2014.

55. "Υποψήφιος Βουλευτής της Χρυσής Αυγής Χαμογελά στο Κολαστήριο του Νταχάου " (A Golden Dawn MP candidate visiting Dachau smiling), http://news-piper.blogspot.gr/2012/05/blog-post_8286.html, accessed 27 August 2014.

56. Anton Shekhovstov, "European Far-Right Music and its Enemies," in *Analyzing Fascist Discourse: European Fascism in Talk and Text*, edited by Ruth Wodak and John E. Richardson (London: Routledge, 2012), 289.

57. Apostolos Karaiskos, "Σιωνισμός και Παγκοσμιοποίηση " (Zionism and Globalization), 25 September 2012, http://www.xryshaygh.com/index.php/enimerosi/view/siwnismos-kai-pagkosmiopoihsh, accessed 27 August 2014; and "France24 και Αφρικανοί Λαθροεισβολείς σε Οχετό Λάσπης κατά της Χρυσής Αυγής" (France24 and African Clandestine Intruders Throw Sludge Against Golden Dawn), 16 July 2013, http://www.xryshaygh.com/index.php/enimerosi/view/france24-kai-afrikanoi-lathroeisboleis-se-ocheto-lasphs-kata-ths-chrushs-au#.UjbMzX8SO9h, accessed 27 August 2014.

58. Maiandros, *Χρυσή Αυγή* (*Golden Dawn*), 2010, http://www.youtube.com/watch?v=3nKy12JrLzE, accessed 27 August 2014.

59. Pogrom, *Μίλα Ελληνικά ή Ψόφα* (*Speak Greek or Die*), https://www.youtube.com/watch?v=nGIbWaIEsGY#t=46, accessed 27 August 2014.

60. Hellgrinder, *Σφάξε έναν Αλβανό* (*Slay an Albanian*), http://www.youtube.com/watch?v=zRc_mrXmS5s, accessed 27 August 2014.

61. White Front Thessaloniki, *Εναντίον όλων* (*Against All*), CD Rock for the Fatherland, Gammadion Productions, 2006, http://www.youtube.com/watch?v=tXM-dv6Z21A, accessed 27 August 2014.

62. Mahen, *Σφάξε έναν Πολιτικό* (*Slay a Politician*), CD Heroes, Self-Released, 1998, http://www.youtube.com/watch?v=FW68zFS7hgc&list=PL1F1ACA2736F73DA1, accessed 27 August 2014.

63. Psaras, *Η Μαύρη Βίβλος της Χρυσής Αυγής* (*The Black Bible of Golden Dawn*), 136-38.

64. Maiandros, *Χρυσή Αυγή* (*Golden Dawn*), 2010, http://www.youtube.com/watch?v=3nKy12JrLzE, accessed 27 August 2014.

65. "Πολιτικό Απελευθερωτικό Κίνημα η Χρυσή Αυγή" (Golden Dawn, Political Liberation Movement), 4 June 2013, http://www.xryshaygh.com/index.php/enimerosi/view/politiko-apeleutherwtiko-kinhma-h-chrush-augh#.Uhif3NK-18E, accessed 27 August 2014; and "Ιδεολογική και Πολιτιστική Αντεπίθεση" (Ideological and Cultural Counterattack), 27 March 2013, http://www.xryshaygh.com/index.php/enimerosi/view/ideologikh-kai-politistikh-antepithesh#.UhihTtK-18E, accessed 27 August 2014.

66. White Front Thessaloniki, *Εναντίον όλων* (*Against All*), CD Rock for the Fatherland,>Gammadion Productions, 2006, https://www.youtube.com/watch?v=tXM-dv6Z21A, accessed 27 August 2014.

67. Kostas Alexandrakis, "Η Παρακμή των Νεοελλήνων και ο Ηρωικός Τρόπος Ζωής" (The Modern Greeks' Decline and the Heroic Way of Life), 21 August 2013, http://www.xryshaygh.com/index.php/enimerosi/view/h-parakmh-twn-neoellhnwn-kai-o-hrwikos-tropos-zwhs#.Uhi_SNK-18F, accessed 27 August 2014.

68. Maiandros, *Χρυσή Αυγή* (*Golden Dawn*), 2010, http://www.youtube.com/watch?v=3nKy12JrLzE, accessed 27 August 2014.

69. Youth Front Hymn, *Χρυσαυγίτες στο δρόμο περνάνε* (*Golden Dawn members pass on the street*), http://www.youtube.com/watch?v=eegypZ0gZe8, accessed 27 August 2014.

70. Maria Athanassopoulou, *Χρυσή Αυγή* (*Golden Dawn*) , 2012, http://www.youtube.com/watch?v=vXU_HDFsI-0, accessed 27 August 2014.

71. Maiandros, *Χρυσή Αυγή* (*Golden Dawn*), 2010, http://www.youtube.com/watch?v=3nKy12JrLzE, accessed 27 August 2014.

72. Maiandros, *Χρυσή Αυγή* (*Golden Dawn*), 2010, http://www.youtube.com/watch?v=3nKy12JrLzE, accessed 27 August 2014.

73. Ύμνος της Χρυσής Αυγής (*Hymn of Golden Dawn*), http://www.youtube.com/watch?v=I3_g8oSm3MY, accessed 27 August 2014.

74. Griffin, "The Palingenetic Core of Generic Fascist Ideology."

75. "Ταυτότητα" (Identity), http://www.xryshaygh.com/index.php/kinima, accessed 27 August 2014.

76. "Ταυτότητα" (Identity).
77. Evangelos Karakostas, "Εθνικιστική Επανάσταση" (Nationalist Revolution), 20 November 2012, http://www.xryshaygh.com/index.php/enimerosi/view/ethnikistikh-epanastash#. UhixNNK-18E, accessed 27 August 2014.

REFERENCES

Anderson, Benedict. Imagined Communities. London: Verso, 1991.
Bohlman, Philip. The Music of European Nationalism. Cultural Identity and Modern History. Santa Barbara: ABC-CLIO, 2004.
Brown, Timothy S. "Subcultures, Pop Music and Politics: Skinhead and 'Nazi Rock' in England and Germany." In Journal of Social History 38, 1 (2004): 157–78.
Corte, Ugo and Bob Edwards. "White Power Music and the Mobilization of Racist Social-Movements." In Music and Arts in Action 1,1(2008): 4–20.
Eyerman, Ron and Andrew Jamison. Music and Social Movements. Mobilizing Traditions in the Twentieth Century. Cambridge: Cambridge University Press, 1998.
Futrell, Robert, PeteSimi, and Simon Gottschalk. "Understanding Music in Movements: The White Power Music Scene." In The Sociological Quarterly. 47 (2006): 275–304.
Griffin, Roger. "The Palingenetic Core of Generic Fascist Ideology." In *Che Cos'è il Fascismo? Interpretazioni e Prospettive di Ricerche*. Edited by Alessandro Campi, 97-122. Roma: Ideazione Editrice, 2003.
Griffin, Roger. *Fascism* . Oxford: Oxford University Press, 1995.
Jenson, Jane. "What's in a Name? Nationalist Movements and Public Discourse." In Social Movements and Culture . Edited by Hank Johnston and Bert Klandermans. Minneapolis: University of Minnesota Press, 1995. 107–26.
Kaplan, Jeffrey, ed., Encyclopedia of White Power: A Sourcebook on the Radical Racist Right. Maryland: Altamira Press, 2000.
Loow, Helene. "White Power Rock n Roll: A Growing Industry." In Nation and Race: The Developing Euro-American Racist Subculture. Edited by Jeffrey Kaplan and Tore Bjorko. Boston: Northeastern University Press, 1998. 126–47.
Lowles, Nick and Steve Silver, eds. White Noise. Inside the International Nazi Skinhead Scene. London: Searchlight, 1998.
Margaronis, Maria. "Fear and Loathing in Athens: The Rise of Golden Dawn and the Far Right." *The Guardian*, 26 October 2012. http://www.theguardian.com/world/2012/oct/26/golden-dawn-greece-far-right . Accessed 1 September 2013.
Mastoras, Giorgos. *Η Ιστορία της White Power Μουσικής* (*The History of White Power Music*). Athens: Lonchi/Antepithessi, 2003.
Mouza, Heleni Isis, *Η Μουσική Σκηνή της White Power Rock και το White Power Movement. Μια Έρευνα σε Ιταλικά και Ελληνικά Διαδικτυακά Forum* (*The White Power Rock Music Scene and the white Power Movement. A Survey in Italian and Greek Internet Forum*). MA Thesis, National Kapodistrian University of Athens, 2011.
Pierobon, Chiara. "The Role of the Music in the German extremist right-wing movements." Paper presented at the 9 th Conference of the European Sociological Association, Lisbon, 2-5 September, 2009.
Pilkington, Hilary et al., Russia's Skinheads. Exploring and Rethinking Subcultural Lives. Abington: Routledge 2010.
Psaras, Dimitris. *Η Μαύρη Βίβλος της Χρυσής Αυγής* (*The Black Bible of Golden Dawn*). Athens: Polis, 2012.
Richard, Lionel. *Ναζισμός και Κουλτούρα* (Nazism and Culture) . Translated by Loiska Avagianou. Athens: Astarti, 1999.
Shekhovtsov, Anton. "European Far-Right Music and Its Enemies." In Analyzing Fascist Discourse: European Fascism in Talk and Text. Edited by Ruth Wodak, John E. Richardson. London: Routledge, 2012. 277–96.
Simi, Pete and Robert Futrell. "Cyberculture and the Endurance of White Power Activism." In Journal of Political and Military Sociology, 34, 1 (2006): 115–42.

Simi, Pete and Robert Futrell. *American Swastika. Inside the White Power Movement's Hidden Spaces of Hate*. Lanham, MD: Rowman & Littlefield, 2010.

Stratoudaki, Chara. "Έθνος και Δημοκρατία, Όψεις της Εθνικής Τυατότητας των Εφήβων" (Nation and Democracy, Aspects of adolescents' National Identity). In *Journal of Social Research* 116 A (2006): 23–50.

Symvoulides, Charis. *Oi— Η Μουσική των Skinheads (Oi!—Skinheads' Music)*, Ioannina: Isnafi, 2008.

Tipaldou, Sofia. "Rock for the Motherland: White Power Music Scene in Greece." In *White Power Music: Scenes of Extreme-Right Cultural Resistance*. Edited by Anton Shekhotsov and Paul Jackson. Searchlight Magazine: University of Northampton, 2012.

Zenakos, Augustine. "Golden Dawn, 1980–2012. The neo-Nazis' Road to Parliament." *Reports from the Edge of Borderline Democracy,* 25 October 2012. http://borderlinereports.net/2012/10/25/report-golden-dawn-1980-2012-the-neonazis-road-to-parliament/. Accessed 1 September 2013.

DISCOGRAPHY

Athanassopoulou, Maria. *Χρυσή Αυγή (Golden Dawn)*, 2012. http://www.youtube.com/watch?v=vXU_HDFsI-0 . Accessed 27 August 2014.

Hellgrinder. *Σφάξε έναν Αλβανό (Slay an Albanian)*. http://www.youtube.com/watch?v=zRc_mrXmS5s. Accessed 27 August 2014.

Hellenic Stompers. *Ελληνικά SS (Hellenic SS)*, CD Dimios, Gammadion, 2007. http://www.youtube.com/watch?v=8LghjxwDvnk. Accessed 27 August 2014.

Iron Youth. *When that Day Comes*, CD Respect/Defend/Create, 2001. http://www.youtube.com/watch?v=9Mu5fxaGv6I . Accessed 27 August 2014.

Mahen. *Σφάξε έναν Πολιτικό (Slay a Politician)*, CD Heroes, Self-Released, 1998. https://www.youtube.com/watch?v=FW68zFS7hgc&list=PL1F1ACA2736F73DA1 . Accessed 27 August 2014.

Maiandros. *Χρυσή Αυγή (Golden Dawn)*, 2010. http://www.youtube.com/watch?v=3nKy12JrLzE. Accessed 27 August 2014.

No Surrender. *Ο Παπούς μου ήταν στα SS (My grandfather was in SS)*. https://www.youtube.com/watch?v=MqjGVrZc270 . Accessed 27 August 2014.

Pogrom. *Ροκ για την Πατρίδα (Rock for the Fatherland)*, CD Rock for the Fatherland, Gammadion Productions, 2006. http://www.youtube.com/watch?v=OtbkqsII9AQ Accessed 27 August 2014.

Pogrom. *Άουσβιτς (Auschwitz)*. https://www.youtube.com/watch?v=BbZQuWSnKrU. Accessed 27 August 2014.

White Front Thessaloniki. *Εναντίον όλων (Against All)*, CD Rock for the Fatherland, Gammadion Productions, 2006. https://www.youtube.com/watch?v=tXM-dv6Z21A. Accessed 27 August 2014.

White Pride Rockers. *Θα Τρέμει η Γη (The earth will tremble)*. http://www.youtube.com/watch?v=wbFTHJD5gJU. Accessed 27 August 2014.

Ύμνος της Χρυσής Αυγής (Hymn of Golden Dawn). http://www.youtube.com/watch?v=I3_g8oSm3MY. Accessed 27 August 2014.

Youth Front Hymn. *Χρυσαυγίτες στο δρόμο περνάνε (Golden Dawn members pass on the street)*. http://www.youtube.com/watch?v=eegypZ0gZe8. Accessed 27 August 2014.

Chapter Eleven

"The Order of the Vanquished Dragon"

The Performance of Archaistic Homophobia by the Union of Orthodox Banner Bearers in Putin's Russia

Alexandar Mihailovic

As many prominent Russian Orthodox commentators have remarked with chagrin (most notably the cleric Fr. Vsevolod Chaplin), the Internet footprint of the Union of Orthodox Banner Bearers is considerably larger than its membership, or role in serious discussions about the directions of the Church.[1] The group's protests are carefully structured enactments of épatage. We are made to understand that the eclectic "uniform" of the Union of Orthodox Banner Bearers (black t-shirts emblazoned with fanciful pastiches of Orthodox crosses with elements of Celtic runes, skulls and Iron Crosses) is itself an indication that all protest is first and foremost about provocation. Through its website, video blogs and vKontakte page, the Union of Orthodox Banner Bearers has served as something of a midwife in facilitating the new media birth of exhibitionistic performances of xenophobic absolutism in contemporary Russian political life. Groups such as the Union of Orthodox Banner Bearers employ categories of sexuality as a stratagem for redefining the concept of "foreignness."

A curious feature of militantly homophobic religious groups in Russia is the fact of their eclectic theatricality: much of their heraldry and costumes is derivative of Tolkien's *The Hobbit* and *The Lord of the Rings* trilogy, and draws on details from pop-historical accounts about the court of Vlad the Impaler, Ivan the Terrible's elite security force of the *Oprichnina,* and the Order of the Teutonic Knights. The self-conscious archaizing tendency among such groups is particularly evident in their performance of collective prophylaxes against the "foreign threat" of homosexuality. The reflexive Germanophilia of many Skinhead and neo-Nazi groups has been a significant obstacle to their wider appeal, among a population that has largely remained mindful of the tragic legacy of the Second World War.

I will argue that the archaizing tendency has a distinct logic, in attempting to bring about a firmer ideological coalition between neo-Nazi movements and the Russian Orthodox Church through the stratagems of ritualized public performances that seek to hybridize different symbolic codes among the Russian far right. In their high-profile campaign against homosexuality, the Union of Orthodox Banner Bearers seeks to appeal to the anxieties of Skinhead groups about the weakening of group solidarity among Russian men by speaking a xenophobic language that identifies the threat of collective emasculation as originating not only in ethnic minorities, but also (and perhaps more dangerously) among European and American supporters of the LGBTQ movement and their Russian quislings. The Union of Orthodox Banner Bearers finesses a striking reversal of ideological values, presenting the enemy as the same Europe that the Skinheads regard as the nominal carrier of the Aryan legacy. The relations between the young and the older participants that we see in the Union's protest actions (which are widely available on their website and YouTube) seem to underscore the virtue of obedience, that youth should emulate the lessons of posterity and esteemed traditions as a safeguard against their susceptibility to the "foreign" influences of polymorphous sexuality and the culture of the West. In a country where Skinhead groups conspicuously lack older mentors yet fetishize the concept of authority while also having a largely hostile attitude to the Russian Orthodox Church,[2] the Union of Orthodox Banner Bearers positions itself as a brotherhood of hirsute elders who are able to instruct rightist youths in the appropriately intimate, yet non-sexual relations among males, and to serve as a bridge for them to engage with institutions of state power.

On the most basic level, the Union of Orthodox Banner Bearers' penchant for theatricality and parades is meant to serve as a counterweight to LGBT Pride parades planned for St. Petersburg and Moscow. Their political differences notwithstanding, the Union of Orthodox Banner Bearers and anti-Putin performance art groups such as Voina ("War") both act up for the cameras in ways that suggest an understanding of political performance as a digitally recorded act. The Union of Orthodox Banner Bearers has consistently demonstrated an interest in the notion of nationalist and conservative protest as a religious procession that obtains power only when it is captured in a series of images. Their protest is a form of performance art, in search of its own videography.

NEW STRATEGIES FOR MEDIEVAL CONFLICTS: MODERNITY ON DIGITAL TRIAL

Certainly the conditions would seem ripe for the Union of Orthodox Banner Bearers' use of homophobia as a catalyst for ideological hybridization. According to the recent, and much discussed, survey conducted by the Levada Center in Moscow, attitudes in Russia toward same-sex love remain strongly negative, and in some matters have become increasingly so. The number of homophobic protests in Russia has significantly increased since 2005, when LGBT groups first submitted requests to hold Gay Pride parades in Moscow and St. Petersburg, and has further intensified from the time of the ratification on 7 March 2012 in the Russian Duma of an ambiguously worded law against "homosexual propaganda." The law (which was initially adopted by St. Petersburg, Ryazan', Arkhangelsk, and Nizhnii Novgorod) criminalizes speech about acts that have been decriminalized in Russia since 1993. The Levada Center reports that at the beginning of 2013, 87 percent of the entire respondent pool was opposed to gay pride parades in the major cities, whereas in 2010 the figure was 82 percent and, in 2005, 74 percent. The conductors of the survey note that even the more politically liberal demographic of respondents between the ages of twenty-five and forty tended to have homophobic views that outweighed their otherwise socially tolerant attitudes.[3] Judging by the numerous videos posted on Youtube and vKontakte of protest marches against demonstrations for LGBT rights, the majority of the anti-gay demonstrators in fact fall within that younger demographic.

One Internet protest, which appeared on the site of an apparently affiliated organization called "The Order of the Vanquished Dragon, in the Name of Saint George the Conqueror," has generated a considerable and varied response in blogs and discussion forums. An examination of the website of "The Order of the Vanquished Dragon" initially seems to offer clear-cut answers about the group's mission and identity, but little about its activities and even less about its composition. Every page of the group's website is capped by a heraldic logo, with the phrase "The Order of the Dragon 'Dracula'" written in large type, and the prolix name of the group "The Order of the Vanquished Dragon, in the Name of Saint George the Conqueror" written in a smaller and more modern font underneath it. What is the relation between these two entities? Is "The Order of the Dragon 'Dracula'" the umbrella organization of "The Order of the Vanquished Dragon, in the Name of Saint George the Conqueror," or do the two names in fact refer to the same entity, which has various names that reflect the different stages of its historical struggle, and politically evangelizing mission?

Although this is a question which we will answer in due course, for the time being it should suffice to say that the custodians of the site seem to be playing with the viewer's appreciation of a powerful continuum that appears under different names, both as a reflection of its impressive pedigree and need to conceal itself under a shifting nomenclature. We are confronted with the implication that the need for such code names has passed, because of the perilous hour that has struck: the battle lines are now drawn, and the cold war between irreconcilable value systems has already shifted into a highly visible and volatile conflict. For a Russian consumer, the analogies of this formerly 'secret' history of cultural conflict to post-Soviet pop cultural products such as Timur Bekmembetov's *Night Watch* films—with their CGI-inflected narrative about a "cold peace" between centuries-old forces of light and darkness, shattered in present-day Moscow—is striking, and perhaps intentional. The home page of the site foregrounds an essay with the provocative title: "Vlad Dracula and the Proliferation of Kikes (*Vlad Drakula i zhidovstvuiushchie*)," a rambling pseudo-historical narrative that asserts and follows a coalition between Renaissance humanism with a rising Jewish influence in central Europe. In the view of the essay's author Aleksandr Getmanov (whose name is very likely a pseudonym, referencing the title of a Cossack leader [Russian *getman*; Ukrainian *hetman*]),[4] the early days of block printing in Saxony represents the fatal point of intersection between an immorally desacralized culture of the West and the machinations of Jewry. The content of this text makes the viewer aware of the formatting of the screen, which is suggestive of an unfurled scroll manuscript, or (by association with certain manuscript traditions from the Russian medieval context), a document written on a birch bark. This page serves as a kind of template for hermeneutically processing pages of interpellated visual and textual information elsewhere on the site for "The Order of the Dragon 'Dracula.'" As demonstrated by any act of reading the text "Vlad Dracula and the Proliferation of Kikes" against its tableaux of images—which follow a sequence of photographic and cartographic panoramas and representations of war and civilian massacres, culminating in the distinctly non-violent portraits of early forms of printing—scrolling down becomes a form of *askesis* for the viewer, from bad to worse to somewhat better.

The entire page serves as further evidence for the scholar Tatiana Chumakova's contention that the fascination in contemporary Russian political and pop culture with the idea of medieval culture represents, above all, a rejection of the ideal of reason. In this revisionist idealization of a certain (faux) Medievalism, with the Soviet period and Western culture as a whole emerging as variants of the French Enlightenment that some postmodernist thinkers (taking a cue from Foucault and members of the *tel quel* group) portray as hypocritical, soulless and at the very least covertly totalitarian.[5] The archaizing tendencies of the home page of "The Order of the Dragon 'Dracula'" evokes pre-modern ways of reading, by using the screen not so much as a surface on which a text is projected, but as prosthesis for the processing all visual information. As Alexander Galloway writes in his recent study about the confluence between old and new forms of entertainment and informatics within social media, the interface of the computer or phone screen is "less a surface [than] a doorway or window"; it is not "something that appears before you but rather is a gateway that opens up and allows passage to some place beyond."[6] By using the screen more as a guide for iconographic parsing than as a domain for textual archiving, the home page of "The Order of the Dragon 'Dracula'" is meant to introduce its audience to the pre-modern experience of an illuminated manuscript.

SPIRITUAL PROPHYLAXIS AND THE FOREIGN THREAT OF HOMOSEXUALITY

For the media-savvy Russian viewer (whose average demographic would be a person in their twenties or thirties) the discursive, incomplete and highly eccentric home page of "Order of the Vanquished Dragon" serves as a prompt and goad to search elsewhere on the site, for more information about the goals and activities of the organization. A cursory walk through the site adds the name of another organization: the Union of Orthodox Banner Bearers. An entire page is devoted to full online versions of its journal *Sacred Banner* (*Sviashchennaia khorugv'*). Little information about this organization—whose activities, judging from the contents of the journal, seem to be real—is made available on the site for "Order of the Vanquished Dragon." The highly involuted structure of the site (which is highly evocative of what the medievalist Dmitri Likhachev notes as the stylistic hallmarks of old Russian literature: the love of redundancy, sententiousness and incantatory list-making)[7] eventually brings the viewer to the bewildering conclusion that neither the "Order of the Vanquished Dragon" and the "The Order of the Dragon 'Dracula'" is an actual organization: they are merely different avatars for the Union of Orthodox Banner Bearers. With no call for membership on the website—or even list of the officers of the group—the viewer comes to the realization that the latter two groups are entirely fictional.

The site is distinctive for evoking a gaming format, but with the peculiar variation that it is not individuals who take on multiple identities, but organizations and collectives. Here the Union of Orthodox Banner Bearers seems to be addressing an audience of Russian gamers. Writing about the emerging configuration of the Russian gaming community in 2010 and 2011, Catherine Goodfellow notes that the construction of identities among Russian gamers reflects a highly idiosyncratic willingness to scuttle the unitary self, as expressed through the serial experiencing of corporate as well as individual identities: "[y]oung Russian gamers [. . .] have the opportunity to enter Russian, American, Pacific Asian and European virtual worlds and in so doing, try on different aspects of cultural identity and simultaneously reflect on their own Russian national identity."[8] In their design of the site for "Order of the Vanquished Dragon," the Union of Orthodox Banner Bearers place particular emphasis on the merging of the individual gamer with the group. The instructional point of this treatment of the group as an agent or player would seem to be that a person can never be a viable moral or even ontological category, whereas an organization is. The viewer is made to embark on a quest for information, which (in keeping with the configuration of gaming platforms) is never completely satisfied. For all of the considerable evidence pointing to the Matrioshka-like nestling of "Order of the Vanquished Dragon" within "The Order of the Dragon 'Dracula,'" and the latter's status as a subset of the Union of Orthodox Crusaders, the link for the official site of the last of these organizations (http://www.pycckie.org/) is nowhere listed on the site for "The Order of the Dragon 'Dracula.'"

Such coyness about origins, affiliations, and actual professions of faith serves to encourage a view of the activities of the Union of Orthodox Banner Bearers as being sprawling, open-ended and possibly inclusive. With its congeries of anti-Semitism, homophobia, anti-bolshevism, anti-modernity, and monarchism leavened with an accommodating attitude toward Russian President Vladimir Putin's policies, the Union of Orthodox Banner Bearers positions itself as a kind of unruly—yet nonetheless welcoming—round table for different elements of the Russian conservative mainstream, reproducing what Valeriia Novodvorskaya (the former head of the Democratic Union) has called Putin's "comedies of national reconciliation."[9] Highly characteristic of what might be termed a Russian form of rightist eclecticism, the Union manifests a highly charitable attitude toward the Stalin period and its political legacy, offering criticisms of it that are wrapped in mild reproofs that are distinctly absent from its blistering condemnation of Lenin. It is amidst this tyranny of small differences that the Union of Orthodox Banner Bearers casts the fear of homosexuality as a core value among the silent majority of Russians.

Certainly what we see and experience on the page from "The Order of the Dragon 'Dracula'," titled "The Spiritual Oprichnina, or DEATH TO FAGGOTS!" serves as a vivid reminder of the Internet as a hybridized medium that owes its structure variously to cinema, the personal diary, and the historical chronicle.[10] The homophobic web page of "The Order of the Dragon 'Dracula'" is formatted in ways that are expressive of traditional visual and literary diegetic conventions. In their assertion of the primacy of the act itself over the medium of its representation—by defining the page of their site as a portal for joining an event rather than a site that *becomes* a happening— Union of Orthodox Banner Bearers underscores a distinction between homosexual feelings and acts. As we shall see, this distinction plays a key role in understanding (and excusing) the seemingly self-aware homoeroticism of the page "The Spiritual Oprichnina." These men see themselves as both the elite security force of Ivan the Terrible and (in keeping with the ahistorical, quasi-Medievalist mash-up that distinguishes the site as a whole) monks, with the young participants serving as novitiates under the stern guidance of older men. What we see on this particular page is a conception of exorcism as a rite that is too disturbing and profane to be enacted before a directly witnessing larger public, or laity. But the Internet is a useful setting for the act of purification not simply because it removes us from direct contamination of occupying the same physical space. Here, the Internet serves as a prophylactic filter, or buffer, for a second, and perhaps more important reason: it can do righteous battle by transmuting its nemesis into something less harmful, through a reformatting of it into a digital setting. As Pierre Lévy wrote in one of his early, and especially utopian, discussions about cyberspace, "[d]igitization enables us to create, modify, and even interact with messages, atom of information by atom of information, bit by bit [thereby enabling us to] retain the timbre of a voice or instrument, while using it to play a different melody."[11] Digitization becomes, in other words, a form of useful and necessary violation of older patterns of being.

On the web page "The Spiritual Oprichnina," this idea of reformatting as the actual, or real moment of exorcism takes on the most vivid expression in the "killing" of the spirit of homosexuality, depicted in a series of photographs that demonstrates the group's repeated attempts to cast out demons from a Russian edition of the magazine *Queer.*[12] Yet the scroll of still images that follows suggests that this act of exorcism is powerfully erotic in its own right. As a first step in this rite, pages were torn out from the magazine, and photographs showing "naked, buff men" (*golye nakachennye muzhiki*) were nailed to a fence. The young man Mikhail who had tried to exorcise the magazine by shooting at it with a homemade arrow (fashioned from an aspen branch) had failed. Enough of these desultory attempts! The elder Leonid Donatych Simonovich-Nikshich (the ordained Russian-Serbian priest who is the leader of the group) mutters to another young man, "Yura, bring the spear!" As even Yura fails, Leonid impatiently grabs a knife, and stabs at another image in the magazine of a cross-dressing man. The photograph at first "emits such a howl and squeal!!!," then finally groans and falls silent. The instant of the demon's actual silencing is denoted by a color negative image. In a peculiar coda to the histrionics of the exorcism (which also include the demon emitting a "horrific roar" (*strashnyi rev*) at being poked with the spear), the narrative concludes with the statement that it was thus that the "everyday symbolic act of the NEW RUSSIAN SPIRITUAL OPRICHNINA took place." We are made to understand that the entire process was a record of an actual exorcism that serves as a paradigm for the viewer to understand and vanquish his own homoeroticism, and that we need to read the entire page in the same manner that we read the homepage: the act of scrolling down represents a descent into a Hell, a harrowing experience that is incrementally leavened with the promise of a provisional redemption.

TOWARD A PHILOSOPHY OF THE SHARED EVENT: ARCHAIZED HOMOPHOBIA AS DESEXUALIZED INTIMACY

Since the sentencing in August 2012 of the punk art collective Pussy Riot for its protest performance in Moscow's Church of Christ the Savior, certain ideological formulas and terms from Russian Skinhead and neo-Nazi movements have become more clearly mainstreamed into the political language of the state-controlled media in Russia. The archaizing tendency among groups such as the Union for Orthodox Banner Bearers is particularly evident in their performance of collective prophylaxes against the "foreign threat" of homosexuality. Several of these groups have staged what can be plausibly understood as their own versions of performance art, in which the public square of the Internet is seen as being the most rhetorically venue for attacking the values and—most significantly—the publications of the LBGT community. A great deal of the page "The Spiritual Oprichnina" emphasizes that homosexuality is false (and therefore evil) by virtue of already being a media representation. A young man shooting an arrow, at the behest of an older man, into the photograph of the backside of a transgender person from the magazine *Queer* is not, as we might think, an instance of homosociality tipping over into open eroticism; rather, it is a calculated meta-iconographical moment that references St. Sebastian and the notion of homosexuality as a sickness of a modernity defined by the explosion of mass print reproduction.[13] And how else can we explain the fact that the relations among the men in "The Spiritual Oprichnina, or DEATH TO FAGGOTS!" clearly references the homosexual orgy from the novel *Day of the Oprichnik*, written by an author whose work has been publicly burned by the Union of Orthodox Banner Bearers themselves? On the Union's website, the call of the elder Leonid for a novitiate to spike the back of a gay man echoes the shout of "[d]on't be scared, greenhorns!" that the mentor Batya (whose name is an honorific title, meaning "esteemed father") makes in Vladimir Sorokin's novel, to his own group of young apprentices as he and they intimately join together in an "oprichnik *caterpillar*."[14] As in Sorokin's novel, the novitiates study under harsh but fair teachers, with the difference that the elderly *oprichniki* on the Union's web page are proudly asexual, and are thus able to break the spirit of sodomy. Only the elderly leader is able to resist—and therefore exorcise—homoerotism. Younger men, however, might be tempted by the force that they are expelling. Indeed, all of the videos of the group posted on the Internet have only the leader Leonid Simonovich-Nikshich and the artist Igor Miroshnichenko (the second oldest member of the group) carry out the shredding and burning of images of Madonna, Elton John, and Pussy Riot. In ways that are surprisingly open, the Union of Orthodox Banner Bearers acknowledges not just the homosociality, but also the homoeroticism within their own group. From the perspective of performance as a ritualized practice, the Union dissolves the binary of heterosexual/homosexual, by freely acknowledging the vividly sexualized aspect of their group work. The web page "The Spiritual Oprichnina" bristles with what Eve Kosofsky Sedgwick terms the "less stable and identity-bound understandings of sexual choice," whose multiple points of overlap and intersection create highly distinctive "performative effects [within] a self-contradictory discursive field."[15] In effect, the Union of Orthodox Banner Bearers recognizes erotic polymorphousness as the natural state of things, seeing in *all* forms of sexuality nothing more than a congeries of destructive forces that need to be purged of their content of disobedience and submerged pride. In one interview posted on the main website for the organization, Simonovich-Nikshich even compares Madonna to himself, by referring to her as a priest ("Madonna kak sviashchennik"), as if to underscore the role of the performative charisma of the spiritual teacher, as the only figure who can come into contact with natural instincts without themselves being overwhelmed by them.[16]

The fact that the Union of Orthodox Banner Bearers ultimately insists on the *symbolic* nature of the represented rite suggests that the page serves as a medium for rendering the quotidian into the sacred. The Russian verb for scrolling down on a screen (*prokruchivat' / prokrutit'*) can, in other contexts, also be used to refer to an apparatus playing an audio or video recording, such as a disk or tape. Here, both senses of the Russian "scrolling" are suggested, with the page becoming both an instance of transposition into another medium and a site for the conjoining of disparate individuals that Mikhail Bakhtin, in a homonymic pun, calls the event (*sobytie*) of "co-being" (*so-bytie*). The 1986 publication of Bakhtin's early (and unfinished) manuscript "Toward a Philosophy of the Act" prompted Russian nationalist philosophers such as Yuri Davydov (already emboldened by the beginnings of *glasnost'* under Gorbachev) to articulate a notion of personal responsibility not as a Kantian imperative, but rather as an unfolding of call-and-response within a national community. Particularly interesting to Davydov and other nativist commentators (most notably Bakhtin's former student Vadim Kozhinov) was the critic's insistence that "the unitary yet complex event" consists not of its participants "co-experiencing" with particular others, but rather of each occupying a position outside of themselves (*vnenakhodimost'*) that is expressed in the totality of their relations with all others.[17]

Bakhtin's conception of the "happening" as a totality of interlocking realms of experience that blurs the significance of particular acts of intimacy is remarkably productive in explicating the totality of multiple frames of reference on a site such as "The Order of the Dragon 'Dracula,'" with its plethora of names for one organization, and assertion that homoeroticism can be neutralized by being reconfigured into a different representational context. In its understanding of Internet images as largely defanged representations of sin, the Union also selectively references the Orthodox conception of the icon as the only esthetic realm that is truly participative for the viewer. With its warped proportions and reverse perspective, the icon endeavors to bring the viewer into contact with the "prototypes" of the Divine figures it portrays, yet can only do so fully when it is located within a consecrated space. [18] According to the new media dispensationalism of the Union of Orthodox Banner Bearers, the proliferation of images in digitized form within a user community provides the opportunity for objectifying—and therefore nullifying—them. To paraphrase Susan Sontag, the medium of the Internet becomes the solvent for immorality.

CONCLUSION

The notion of performance as a rite—as an act that is equally capable of purifying or polluting—brings greater clarity to the clash between the Union of Orthodox Banner Bearers and the performance art group Voina that took place at the Moscow Municipal Court on 12 July 2010, where the art curator Yuri Samodurov was fined 200,000 rubles for commissioning an exhibit of archly pseudo-religious paintings titled "Forbidden Art—2006" during his tenure as director of the Sakharov Museum. [19] For all of their ideological differences, Piotr Verzilov of Voina and Leonid Simonovich-Nikshich of the Union of Orthodox Banner Bearers share a keen appreciation of videography as an essential format for both performance and the expression of political dissent. [20] Anathema to both groups is the earlier counterculture notion of the "happening" as something that is only as real as its on-site participants perceive it to be. Gone too is the notion that was famously advanced by Moscow Conceptualist Andrei Monastryrsky and the Collective Actions group, of the event as something that can never be directly described, recorded or characterized in any way, but whose *effects* on people are documented with generous bureaucratic punctiliousness in the form of written logs, photographic images of seemingly ineloquent empty panoramas (*pustóty*) and post-factum interviews with "witnesses." Writing about the Collective Actions that Monastyrsky's group staged in the countryside not far from the city limits of Moscow, the art historian Ekaterina Bobrinskaya observes that the "action in the CA (Collective Actions) performances [was] [d]evoid of any symbolic meaning, and sometimes border[ed] on the absurd." She argues that the real object of the "representation"' was "the process of perception flowing through the consciousness of the spectator," and that the actions were designed to transport [the spectator] to a state of 'pure contemplation', free of continuous mental interpretation and contemplation—a state of 'emptiness' beyond the constraints of language."[21] Although the art group Voina emerged as an offshoot of the Collective Actions groups instigated by Monastyrsky—and arguably preserves some of the features of his particular brand of Moscow Conceptualism, especially in regard to the ancillary nature of the word to both the image and the action—the group's current actions have foregrounded the notion that an event becomes real only when it is recorded in a digitized format. With their newfound interest in digital image capturing as a potent materialization of the voyeuristic act, on 29 February 2008 Voina filmed and photographed "Fuck for the Bear Cub Heir!" (*Ebis' za naslednika medvezhonka!*) a simulated orgy in a stodgy natural history museum in Moscow. Among other things, the protest action was meant to draw attention to the charade of a division of power between Putin and Medvedev, and to the nationalist racism of Dmitri Medvedev's call for a higher birth rate among citizens of the Russian Federation.[22] The action could not have been further from the principles of Moscow Conceptualism. As Boris Groys puts it, the Moscow Conceptualists believed that "art documentation *is* by definition not art; it merely *refers* to art and thereby makes clear that art is no longer present and immediately visible here."[23]

The flamboyance of an all-encompassing performance esthetic that includes costumed or naked bodies in movement, captured digitally *in medias res,* is central to the public identities of Voina and the Union of Orthodox Banner Bearers. For both groups, there is no art without its digital artifact, and no public controversy without a suitable counter-event that pushes symbolic meanings fully into the realm of action and literalization. We are in a better position to understand the media logic of the Union's anti-LGBT Internet 'action' of "Spiritual Oprichnina, or DEATH TO FAGGOTS!" on 1 June 2010 once we take into account this preoccupation with videography as a form of performance art itself. The Union believes that the refulgent sexual act can only be nullified by a recorded counter-performance. Such idiosyncratic notions about media strategy also brings to our awareness the possibility that Pussy Riot may have intended—in its own public action of a "Punk Prayer" in Moscow's church of Christ the Savior two years later, conceived as being resolutely off the grid of the Internet—a rebuttal to the Union of Orthodox Banner Bearers that was both political and esthetic, asserting the primacy of performance body art over the Union's Baudrillardian obsession with the simulacra that emerge from reenactments and recordings.

NOTES

1. Irina Kislina, "Kto takie pravoslavnye khorugvenostsy?" (Who Are These Orthodox Banner Bearers?) *Pravoslavie i mir.* (11 August 2011), http://www.pravmir.ru/kto-takie-pra-

voslavnye-xorugvenoscy/, accessed 30 September 2013. All translations, unless otherwise indicated, are my own.

2. "Skinkhedy: Otkuda nogi rastut?" (Skinheads. How Do They Grow?) *Zhurnal pravoslavnoi zhizni 'Neskuchnyi sad'* (24 August 2011), http://www.nsad.ru/articles/skinhedy-otkuda-nogi-rastut, accessed 30 September 2013.

3. Masha Plotko, "Strakh drugogo. Problema gomofobii v Rossii" (Fear of the Other. The Problem of Homophobia in Russia), 12 March 2013, accessed 4 June 2013.

4. The historically revisionist view of both the Don River and the Zaporozhian Cossacks as the unyielding Praetorian guard of the Russian Tsarist empire held by virtually all contemporary Russian nationalist organizations.

5. Tat'iana Chumakova, "Novoe russkoe srednevekov'e." *Otechechestvennye zapiski.* 1:52 (2013), 229, 236–37.

6. Alexander R. Galloway, *The Interface Effect* (Cambridge, UK: Polity, 2013), 30.

7. D. S. Likhachev, *Istoricheskaia poetika russkoi literature. Smekh kak mirovozzrenie (An Historical Poetics of Russian Literature. Laughter as a World View)*, (St. Petersburg: "Aleteia," 1997), 262.

8. Catherine Goodfellow, "Videogames.ru: Constructing New Russian Identities in Virtual Worlds." https://www.academia.edu/2995258/Videogames.Ru_exploring_the_Russian_online_gaming_community, accessed 14 November 2013 (6).

9. C. J. Chivers, A6. "With Lenin's Ideas Dead, Russia Weighs What to do With His Body," *New York Times* (5 October 2005), A6.

10. Galloway, 4–5.

11. Pierre Lévy, *Collective Intelligence: Mankind's Emerging World in Cyberspace,* translated by Robert Bononno (Cambridge, MA: Perseus Books, 1997), 48.

12. "Dukhovnaya oprichnina, ili SMERT' PIDORASAM!" http://drakula.org/sv_horugv/7/29.shtml, accessed 4 October 2014.

13. The sadistic and exhibitionistic videos of the neo-Nazi Russian body builder Maksim "Tesak" (Shank) Marzinkievich provide an even starker example of such deliberate ambiguity on homophobic social media (http://vk.com/club15711409). For more on Marzinkievich, see Benjamin Bidder, "Grausame Schau der Schwulenhasser," *Spiegel Online* (12 November 2013). http://www.spiegel.de/politik/ausland/folter-videos-russische-neonazis-quaelen-schwule-a-933216.html, accessed 14 November 2013.

14. "Ne robei, zelen!'" Sorokin, *Den' oprichnika* (Moscow: Zakharov, 2009), 201; *The Day of the Oprichnik,* translated by Jamie Gambrell (New York: Farrar, Straus and Giroux, 2011), 170.

15. Eve Kosofsky Sedgwick, *The Epistemology of the Closet,* updated with a New Preface (Berkeley: University of California Press, 2008), 9.

16. "Staruskha Ciccone—ved'ma!" (The Old Crone Ciccone is a Witch!), 11 avgusta 2012 goda: Interv'iu Glavy Soiuza Pravoslavnykh Khorugvenostsev dla 'Den' TV'http://www.pycckie.org/video/video-11082012.shtml, accessed 11 July 2013.

17. Bakhtin, *Raboty 20-x godov* (*Works From the Twenties*) (Kiev: "NEXT," 1994), 139; *Art and Answerability: Early Philosophical Essays,* tr. Vadim Liapunov (Austin: University of Texas Press, 1990), 65.

18. For an incisive discussion of the evocation of the theology of icon in contemporary Russian controversies about performance art, see Bernstein, "*Caution, Religion!* Iconoclasm, Secularism, and Ways of Seeing in Post-Soviet Art Wars," *Public Culture* 26:3 (Fall 2014), 434–35. For an analysis of the significance of "reverse perspective" in Russian icon art, see B. A. Uspenskii's "K sisteme peredachi izobrazheniia v russkoi ikonopisi" (Toward an Analysis of the System for Transmitting Representation in Russian Icon Art), *Trudy po znakovym sistemam* 2 (1965), 248–57.

19. For a detailed account of Voina's protest of this legal proceeding, see Bernstein, 419–21. In her article, Bernstein reproduces a striking photograph of Verzilov and Simonovich-Nikshich in the vestibule of the building, both engaged in their signature gestures of political protest (420).

20. Less than two weeks later, the video became widely available through the news website grani-tv.ru, and was posted by a Lithuanian user on YouTube, where it elicited a wide range of

ideologically driven responses in Russian. The video can be seen at "Cockroach Court: 'Voina' and the Orthodox Brotherhood'" (Tarakanskii sud: Voina i pravoslavnoe bratstvo) http://www.youtube.com/watch?v=RPhrIvSqpyU, accessed 14 November 2013.

21. Ekaterina Bobrinskaya, "Moscow Conceptual Performance Art," in Alla Rosenfeld, ed. *Moscow Conceptualism in Context* (Munich: Prestel, 2011), 168–69.

22. Dmitrii Desiaterik, "Moskovskaya art-gruppa 'Voina' kak iskusstvo protestov v chistom vide" *Den'* [Ukraine] 132 (2009), http://www.webcitation.org/665Q2XKR8, [original URL: http://www.day.kiev.ua/290619?idsource=277850&mainlang=rus], accessed 14 November 2013. Both Verzilov and his wife Nadezhda Tolokonnikova took part in Voina's "Fuck for the Bear Cub Heir!" Certainly the singular imperative of the verb *ebis'* suggests that Voina's performance piece was meant to underscore the solipsistic autoeroticism of nationalism, which emerges more as an intersection of the personal fantasies of disparate individuals than as the communal action of orgiastic sharing and reciprocal affection that it purports to be. Tolokonnikova's refusal to participate in Voina's 2010 courthouse protest might have stemmed from her increasing interest in the concept of the non-recordable 'happening' or action (*deistvie*), away from the exhibitionism of the recorded spectacle that was coded into Voina's 2008 museum action. Arguably, this shift signals her return to the esthetics of the Moscow Conceptualists that informed the early work of Voina.

23. Boris Groys, *History Becomes Form: Moscow Conceptualism* (Cambridge, MA: MIT Press, 2010) 149–50.

REFERENCES

Bakhtin, M. M. *Art and Answerability: Early Philosophical Essays.* Translated by Vadim Liapunov. Austin: University of Texas Press, 1990.

Bakhtin, M. M. *Raboty 20-x godov* (*Works From the Twenties*). Kiev: "NEXT," 1994.

Bernstein, Anya. "*Caution, Religion!* Iconoclasm, Secularism, and Ways of Seeing in Post-Soviet Art Wars." *Public Culture* 26:3 (Fall 2014): 419–48.

Bidder, Benjamin. "Grausame Schau der Schwulenhasser." *Spiegel Online* (12 November 2013). http://www.spiegel.de/politik/ausland/folter-videos-russische-neonazis-quaelen-schwule-a-933216.html. Accessed 14 November 2013.

Bobrinskaya, Ekaterina. "Moscow Conceptual Performance Art." In Rosenfeld, Alla, ed. *Moscow Conceptualism in Context.* Munich: Prestel, 2011: 154–77.

Chivers, C. J. "With Lenin's Ideas Dead, Russia Weighs What to do With His Body," *New York Times* (5 October 2005), A6.

Chumakova, Tatiana. "Novoe russkoe srednevekov'e." *Otechechestvennye zapiski.* 1 (52) 2013: 228–38.

"Cockroach Court: 'Voina' and the Orthodox Brotherhood'" (Tarakanskii sud: Voina i pravoslavnoe bratstvo). http://www.youtube.com/watch?v=RPhrIvSqpyU. Accessed 14 November 2013.

"Dukhovnaya oprichnina, ili SMERT' PIDORASAM!" (A Spiritual Oprichnina, or a DEATH TO FAGGOTS!" http://drakula.org/sv_horugv/7/29.shtml. Accessed 4 October 2014.

Davydov, Yuri. "U istokov sotsial'noi filosofii M. M. Bakhtina" (A Consideration of the Sources of M. M. Bakhtin's Social Philosophy). *Sotsiologicheskie issledovaniia* 2 (1986): 170–81.

Davydov, Yuri and Aleksandr Arkhangel'skii. "Vse vzyvaet k postupku" (Everything Comes Back to the Act). *Literaturnoe obozrenie* 2 (1987): 102–7.

Dmitrii Desiaterik, "Moskovskaya art-gruppa 'Voina' kak iskusstvo protestov v chistom vide" (The Moscow Art Group 'Voina' as Protest Art in its Purest Form). *Den'* (Ukraine) 132 (2009). http://www.webcitation.org/665Q2XKR8 (original URL: http://www.day.kiev.ua/290619?idsource=277850&mainlang=rus). Accessed 14 November 2013.

Galloway, Alexander R. *The Interface Effect.* Cambridge, UK: Polity, 2012

Goodfellow, Catherine. "Videogames.ru: Constructing New Russian Identities in Virtual Worlds." https://www.academia.edu/2995258/Videogames.Ru_exploring_the_Russian_online_gaming_community. Accessed 14 November 2013.

Groys, Boris. *History Becomes Form: Moscow Conceptualism.* Cambridge, MA: MIT Press, 2010.

Kislina, Irina. "Kto takie pravoslavnye khorugvenostsy?" (Who Are These Orthodox Banner Bearers?). *Pravoslavie i mir.* (11 August 2011). http://www.pravmir.ru/kto-takie-pravoslav-nye-xorugvenoscy/. Accessed 30 September 2013.

Lévy, Pierre. *Collective Intelligence: Mankind's Emerging World in Cyberspace.* Translated by Robert Bononno. Cambridge, MA: Perseus Books, 1997.

Likhachev, D. S. *Istoricheskaia poetika russkoi literature. Smekh kak mirovozzrenie (An Historical Poetics of Russian Literature. Laughter as a World View).* St. Petersburg: "Aleteia," 1997.

Maksim "Tesak" (Shank) Marzinkievich. Group page. *vKontakte.* http://vk.com/club15711409. Accessed 14 November 2013.

Plotko, Masha. "Strakh drugogo. Problema gomofobii v Rossii" (Fear of the Other. The Problem of Homophobia in Russia). 12 March 2013. Accessed 4 June 2013.

Sedgwick, Eve Kosofsky. *The Epistemology of the Closet.* Updated with a New Preface. Berkeley: University of California Press, 2008.

"Skinkhedy: Otkuda nogi rastut?" (Skinheads. How Do They Grow?). *Zhurnal pravoslavnoi zhizni 'Neskuchnyi sad'* (24 August 2011). http://www.nsad.ru/articles/skinhedy-otkuda-nogi-rastut. Accessed 30 September 2013.

Sorokin, Vladimir. *Day of the Oprichnik.* Translated by Jamie Gambrell. New York: Farrar, Straus and Giroux, 2011.

Sorokin, Vladimir. *Den' oprichnika.* Moscow: Zakharov, 2009.

"Staruskha Ciccone—ved'ma!" (The Old Crone Ciccone is a Witch!). 11 avgusta 2012 goda: Interv'iu Glavy Soiuza Pravoslavnykh Khorugvenostsev dla 'Den' TV' http://www.pycckie.org/video/video-11082012.shtml. Accessed 11 July 2013.

Uspenskii, B. A. "K sisteme peredachi izobrazheniia v russkoi ikonopisi" (Toward an Analysis of the System for Transmitting Representation in Russian Icon Art). *Trudy po znakovym sistemam* 2 (1965): 248–57.

Chapter Twelve

Pure Hate

The Political Aesthetic of Prussian Blue

Patricia Anne Simpson

Twins Lynx Vaughan Gaede and Lamb Lennon Gaede enjoyed a brief period of intense, transnational popularity while they performed as the white supremacist band Prussian Blue (2003–2007). To the outside eye, it appears that the blond, blue-eyed girls were pressed into politics and service by their mother, April Gaede, who home-schooled them, promoted them, and shaped their politics in her image, according to the principles of the National Alliance—though in early interviews, the girls deny this.[1] Sometimes referred to as the "Olsen-Twins of the neo-Nazi scene,"[2] the appeal of the twins resonated from the Western part of the U.S. to the former Eastern states of the Federal Republic of Germany. Featuring songs such as "Sacrifice," a tribute to Rudolf Hess, and an unpopular cover of Bob Dylan's "Knockin' on Heaven's Door," the Gaedes toured sympathetic venues as the newest and freshest faces of hate music, referred to by supporters as "racial music"[3] and white power. There are noteworthy connections between the live-music scene, political recruitment strategies, and the virtual presence of Prussian Blue in social media and the Internet. Moreover, the resonance between German and U.S. white power scenes, exemplified by "Prussian Blue," emphasizes the pan-extremist political element as well. Understanding the interplay among the aesthetics, politics, and performance of hate is the goal of this chapter.

In *Performing Rites*, Simon Frith argues that the actual communities established by shared taste about music and musical performances inform and elevate aesthetic judgment when it comes to popular music.[4] Given this premise, hate music would seem to depart from Frith's model. The political content and commitment of the respective bands takes precedence over the quality or taste level of the music. Moreover, digital media provide an opportunity to expand that local, actual community to an "imagined" and virtual type of citizenship. The articulations of white power rely on immediate, actual communities and cultures, but in a revised political profile, they have joined forces and built alliances toward a "nation," one that eschews any sense of internationalism or diversity. These expressions generate what Simi and Futrell have called "Aryan free spaces," which, among other things, "afford racial extremists opportunities to openly express their radical ideas with likeminded comrades.[5] These political and racial identities rely in turn on a Freudian "family romance," in which the parental, familial, and sexual personae assume political dimensions. The mediation of these "Aryan free spaces" changes qualitatively and quantitatively with digital distribution. There is a progression of sorts from Walter Benjamin's "The Work of Art in the Age of Its Technical Reproducibility," with its astute attention to the linkages between technical innovation and political persuasion, to the epistemological challenges posed by digital reproduction, which provides endless access without ever exhausting the "source" of a particular utterance. In the case of the far right, the reproducibility of a specific political agenda with little accountability opens up the "free spaces" even further. These "spaces" have an afterlife.

An increased use of Internet outlets, such as MySpace and YouTube, intensifies the complicity between pre-teen-teenage pop music and transnational white supremacist politics. Still, these also depend on a variety of other media and delivery systems, from pirate radio to mail-order swag, disseminating items such as T-shirts and mouse pads. The mutual reinforcement of digital media and the reality of membership in a real existing right-wing community functions performatively to persuade and empower an audience of like-minded yet necessarily secreted identities. The Gaedes' performing rites created transnational communities, reaching audiences and hitting the mark or target audience, from Montana to Mecklenburg. In this context, Prussian Blue provides a stunning example of the white power movement's explicit and unintentional commitment to a narrowly defined aesthetic of female beauty, strength, and vulnerability. The means of persuasion are closely linked to the media of the messages.

Persuasion and recruitment form the crux of Prussian Blue's appeal. Their German heritage forges links between the U.S. and the contemporary Federal Republic of Germany. They themselves make the connection, citing the origin of the band's name as evidence. According to Lynx Gaede, "My sister and I figured out the reasons why it would connect our music and our ancestry. Our eyes are blue and some of our ancestors are from Prussia."[6] Lamb Gaede supplements her sister's comment: "And we thought it was funny because it is the name for the color of the Zyklon B residue. . . . ha! ha! We read that in a back issue of *Resistance* magazine."[7] The links between the present of their "racial music" career and the past of their ethnic genealogy are forged at least in part by the print media.

Ideology also plays a role in opening the borders between whiteness, European heritage, and contemporary transatlantic geographies of identity. For example, the Gaede sisters' compilation album, *For the Fatherland*, was released and distributed in Germany with the support and sponsorship of the Nationaldemokratische Partei Deutschlands (National Democratic Party of Germany, or NPD). The release date, 2006, coincided with the entry of the NPD into federal state assemblies in Mecklenburg-West Pomerania. [8]

In this chapter, I focus on the role of Prussian Blue in the United States, with some attention to their image in the German hate music scene. Through an examination of the various, multiple venues they access to disseminate the songs of white hate, my reading reveals the homology between the aesthetic and the political expressions of a contemporary transatlantic white-power movement. Further, this homology depends on a concept of race that exerts enormous pressure on the iconography of gender roles. Fascist and proto-fascist masculinity and bellicose yet seemingly innocent femininity align to deliver a message of white-minded political activism. Further, their early appearances provoked the protective, sentimental, and idealized "masculine" response to their youth and apparent vulnerability. According to Lynx Gaede: "At the Fall 2001 Sacramento Eurofest, they were having an inter-mission and we asked if we could sing. They let us sing and Dr. [William] Pierce [of the National Alliance] was there. We sang 'Ocean of Warriors.' Everyone liked it so much that they cried." [9] With their youth and apocalyptic rhetoric, Prussian Blue and their fans play more than a supporting role of girlish tokenism in the white music scene. While male groups unquestionably dominate hate music venues both in Germany and the United States, the case of Prussian Blue and the phenomenon of their seeming success constitute a glaring exception.

In disturbing ways, their youth, innocence, and girlishness contrast sharp-ly with the brutality of most right-wing radical music—all the more jarring is the conclusion that the message is the same. In some ways, the twins play into a Lolita-like fantasy deployed to attract a specifically adolescent audi-ence to the White Power cause. The performers also trigger the protective rhetoric of both European and American radical groups: ones that lament the death of the white race, the loss of blond, blue-eyed beauty, and the hyper-bolic commitment to fostering family, family values, and the increasingly urgent need to secure a future for white children. Their youth, appearance, and recourse to folk music, upbeat pop, and mournful ballads increased their popularity, but also had the unintentional effect of undermining their mes-sage as they matured, rejected their fame, and repudiated their past. Managed by their mother, April Gaede, the twins eventually succeeded in loosening their ties to their radicalized and adoring fans, while maintaining an aesthetic and digital commentary about their status, sustained on YouTube. To explore the nurturing of Prussian Blue's politics and aesthetics, I first outline important correspondences and differences between the German and American hate music scenes; then I locate the twins in the U.S. White Power discourses they participate in and fostered; finally, I refer to the specifics of their songs, the dissemination of their message through print media and documentaries, and their Internet presence. While the twins and their family reside in the state of Montana, their reach is global.

The debate about a potential for white power music to convert violent, racist thoughts into acts of violence attempts to explain the moment of decision in the minds and bodies of perpetrators. German scholars Christian Dornbusch and Jan Raabe foreground the role of right-wing music in regulating and disseminating the political message with pervasive practices: it permeates everyday life, from activities that involve the disciplining of the body through training to the leisure-time barbeque: ". . . die neonazistische Musik ist allgegenwärtig" (neo-Nazi music is omnipresent).[10] In their work on the shootings at a Sikh temple in Wisconsin, Robert Futrell and Pete Simi make the connection between extremist acts and the musical culture that sustains hatred, serving as a soundtrack to violence. The shooter, Wade M. Page, was part of the white power scene. The authors emphasize the music in the context of a performance community and the capacity of this environment to foster primary bonds. In concluding this disturbing piece of journalism, Futrell and Simi write: "We should not be surprised when other neo-Nazis follow suit, because potent inspiration for violence continues to percolate in white power music's hidden spaces of hate."[11] While at first it might seem impossible to imagine the twins of Prussian Blue in this scene, further examination of the shared purpose, themes, and narratives of right music in Germany and the United States resolves some of the cognitive dissonance.

It is useful to draw attention to some of the major differences between the publication and dissemination of right-wing material in Germany and the U.S. According to German law, censorship applies in the case of pro-Nazi publications or music; Holocaust denial is punishable by imprisonment. In a celebrated case from the mid-1980s, copies of *Der nette Mann* (the nice man) by the group "Böhse Onkelz" were confiscated from record stores, while the violence-inspiring and proud German music remained popular; the skinhead scene boot-leg editions of the album continued to circulate, despite the confiscation and "indexing" from a federal agency.[12] From that time on, the criminalization of right-wing OI music fed directly into an Aryan narrative of martyrdom, persecution, and victimization. At the time, many of the fanzines from this scene were in fact printed in the United States; editorials often included shout-outs to comrades in the mid-western and plain states. Imprisoned musicians assumed the attributes of cult figures. Bands attacked multiculturalism as a decadent privileging of unwholesome otherness—only to insist on the argument of inclusion and tolerance as long as it extended to German-Germans proud of their race.

The paranoia of racial extinction pervades the music and the politics. In this regard, proponents of the white-supremacist platform invoke the urgent need to secure the future of the white race. In Germany of the post-Wall era, unification and subsequent economic contraction spurred a rise in nationalism, extreme forms of which became legible in the rise of right-wing activism and proprietary claims about Germany for Germans. In skinhead scenes, demographics of the new Germany signaled cause for alarm. In a collection of interviews, two skins speak to their concern about the birth rates:

> "Sie liegt bei Türken u.ä. bei 4,0, bei Deutschen bei 1,3. Um den Fortbestand zu garantieren, benötigt man eine Geburtenrate von 2,0. Wohin diese Entwicklung in einigen Generationen führen wird, tja, dafür braucht man nicht mal Prophet zu sein, um das vorauszusehen."[13]
> [It [the birth rate] for Turks is about 4.0, and for Germans 1.3. To guarantee continued existence, you need a birth rate of 2.0. Where this development is heading in a couple of generations, well, you don't have to be a prophet to predict the outcome.]

The specter of Germans disappearing from Germany looms; it is depicted as a continuous threat in the right wing's deployment of demographics. In interviews, songs, and also in party politics, children are glorified as the future of the race under siege from reproducing immigrants. In a more recent example, the party leader of the NPD, Udo Pastörs, displays outside his office some "posters of blonde children playing on a Baltic beach" which "decry the impending 'Volkstod' of the German people—the 'death of the nation.'"[14] This platform sentimentalizes children in a way that departs significantly from general European representations of the nuclear family (Simpson 2013).

The focus on family in right-wing extremist cultures pervades the politics and the performances; these collaborate to persuade potential recruits to the respective movements. This is a common point in Germany and the United States, the countries with the greatest number of white supremacist bands. In the Federal Republic, the recruitment of young people remains a crucial NPD strategy, manifest in the distribution of free CDs, anti-immigration comic books, and the organizing of concerts directed at a young demographic.[15] The NPD website unfurls under the motto: "Arbeit, Familie, Vaterland" (work, family, fatherland).[16] The trinity of a work ethic and jobs, an ethnically specific family unit, bounded by blood, and the larger imagined community of a fatherland, forge a strong bond between the NPD's public platform and the U.S. National Alliance, an organization with which Prussian Blue was affiliated.

Growing participation of women and children in right-wing circles has attracted attention in the literature on transnational extremist movements. In an article about this growth in Germany, Anna Rieger catalogs the organizations that focus on heightening the involvement of women and children as young as seven in the project of repopulating the fatherland. She foregrounds the activities and statements of, among others, Gitta Schlüßler, founder of the "Ring nationaler Frauen" (RNF, circle of national women): "'Ziel der RNF ist vorrangig in der Öffentlichkeit auf die Anliegen weiblicher Nationalistinnen aufmerksam zu machen, . . . und auch als Sprachrohr der nationalen Frauen—nach innen und nach außen—zu dienen'" (The goal of the RNF if primarily to draw attention in the public sphere to the concerns of female nationalists, . . . and also to serve as a mouthpiece for national women— internally and externally).[17] Rieger takes note of the increase since the 1990s of nationalist women's groups, with focal points on becoming mothers in good nationalist households. Intergenerational emphasis, with an accent on maternal role, expands the more traditional, narrow definition of extremism as predominantly masculine. In this regard, the establishment of a "Heimattreue Deutsche Jugend" (HDJ; German Youth Loyal to the Homeland) for children ages seven and up provides a complete ideological package for the nationalist-oriented single-white male seeking single white women. The organization was banned in 2008.

Even with the banning and criminalizing of certain organizations and activities that target the indoctrination of children, the Internet provides ample opportunity for further connections. There is, for example, a Web presence for right-wing partner searches that reflect the movement of women past the role of mothers for the fatherland. The site "Odin Kontaktanzeigen" (Odin Contact Classifieds) is directed toward men and women who share a commitment to nationalism, family, and camaraderie. As if echoing the sentiments of Prussian Blue's mother, April Gaede, the want-ads insist on pride in heritage. This Internet presence marks a relatively new phenomenon, one that exceeds the previous and well-known use of digital dissemination for music and propaganda, according to the author Johann Osel: "Doch inzwischen suchen Neonazis dort auch gezielt Partnerschaften mit Gleichgesinnten. Und sie propagieren rechte Sprüche und krude Theorien, die beim rechten Flirt helfen sollen. Je aggressiver, desto besser."[18] (But in the mean time neo-Nazis are also there specifically seeking partnerships with the like-minded. And they are propagating rightist slogans and crude theories that should help with the right-wing flirting. The more aggressive the better). Further, Osel, whose newspaper article refers to the important research of sociologist Michaela Köttig, notes as well the platforms and influential opinions represented in the NPD's online news source, *Deutsche Stimme* (German voice): "Und falls eine Mitstreiterin den Kampf um die Straße oder die Parlamente nicht mitmachen wolle, so leiste sie doch auf ihre Art trotzdem 'einen Beitrag für das Überleben Deutschlands'—und zwar als Mutter im täglichen 'Kampf gegen die verrohte Konsumgesellschaft'" (And in case a fellow female protester may not want to join the fight for the street or parliaments, she can still, in her own way, make a 'contribution to the survival of Germany'—and indeed as a mother in the daily 'battle against the brutalized consumer society').[19] The woman warrior joins the pantheon of venerated female figures from the far right.

Women and their reproductive capacities thus assume other important ideological and political roles. Rieger engages with the sociological research on this apparent shift in the culture of familial, intergenerational extremism. She observes that the children, especially girls, are cast as the salvation of the white race. In what appears to be an extremely odd form of neo-liberal National Socialist theory, Thomas Grumke addresses the global reach of this pan-Aryanism: "Gegenwärtig ist im Rechtsextremismus eine transnational kompatible pan-arische Ideologie auf dem Vormarsch, die in der Szene selbst auch so genannt wird'" (A transnationally compatible pan-Aryan ideology is on the march, and it is even called that from within the scene).[20] Unlike the more discriminating National Socialist theory that would exclude people of Slavic descent, for example, Grumke notes that this development includes anyone in the "white race," from Russia to South America, from Australia to the United States. The rise of Prussian Blue and their political profile in the United States seem to exemplify this transnational, pan-Aryan movement, fitting into the aesthetic and political forms of a different "racial profiling."

ARYAN AESTHETICS: BLONDING INNOCENCE

The Aryan racialization of innocence legible in the portraits of blonde, blue-eyed women and children serves both to ennoble and to justify the vehemence—and even violence—of the white supremacist cause. Moreover, the strategy of claimed victimization aligns with what one analyst calls the "trick of persecuted innocence," a model in which a right-wing populist leader would regard "himself as a victim, wrongly stigmatized by the media and by the 'old parties.'"[21] Aligned with defending the fatherland, the duty to protect women and children to preserve Aryan beauty inflects the political imperative. The contemporary radical right in Germany and the United States shares this doctrine. The white supremacist David Lane (1938–2007), member of The Order and Knights of the Ku Klux Klan (Colorado), was among those who propagated this belief in the U.S. Lane, who makes a voice appearance in the Quinn documentary on the Gaede twins, stated that a commitment to this sense of beauty organized his political life. According to entry on the ADL archive website: "In retrospect, Lane says, his enchantment was an "indication of what would become my life's purpose," namely, to

advance the idea that the "beauty of the White Aryan woman must not perish
from the earth."[22] His infamous coining of the "14 words" code also reveals
his conviction, through the promotion of this citation from Hitler's *Mein
Kampf*, that the purportedly loftier purpose of the movement coincided with a
commitment to preserving the well-being of children: "We must secure the
existence of our people and a future for white children."[23]

In a poster that can be downloaded from a National Front website (as a
PDF), the German motto "Liebe deine Rasse" is inscribed above the realistic
but stylized image of a blond woman, viewed in profile. The coy command,
"love your race," is titillating and ambiguous. Is the command issued to male
viewers, whose gaze makes this woman available? Is it an articulation of the
image's desire? In 2004, this image and the slogan made their way to a
Martin Luther King, Jr., Day celebration march in Bozeman, Montana. A
small group of thirteen counter-protesters, organized by Kevin McGuire,
carried large format versions of this and other posters.[24] McGuire was running for public office. Endorsing a white-supremacist platform, neo-Nazi
McGuire was a candidate in a local school-board election. He did gain a
small percentage of the vote (157 votes or 3.6 percecnt). McGuire was openly affiliated with the National Alliance (NA). He practiced the tactics of
attracting young people to the white pride cause through the use of music in
the form of free downloads and placing ads for music in school newspapers.
With some links to Resistance Records, the NA's label, McGuire maintains a
Victory Forever Web site.[25] His activism in Montana and affiliation with the
NA, supported by music, locate him in the same sphere of influence and
geographic territory in which Prussian Blue operated.

The Gaede twins are poster girls for the neo-Nazi cause; their management and reception serve as indicators of how paternal, fraternal, and maternal bonds form and fracture in these circles. Transcending gender is the need
to protect and nourish a particular type of racial "beauty." In the documentary film, *Nazi Pop Twins*, directed by James Quinn, the audience gains
insight into this doctrine when we catch a glimpse of the twins' mother. In
this scene, April Gaede is playing with her youngest daughter, Dresden,
April wonders aloud about what a loss it would be if this type of beauty were
to disappear. In another scene with Dresden, April rehearses a highly ideological version of the ABCs, beginning with "A is for Aryan" ("B is for
blood," it continues, "N is for nation"). It is worth noting that April home-
schooled the older twins; their political change-of-heart to liberalism and an
embrace of diversity began when they started public school in Kalispell. In
the scenes described above, the maternal gaze is filtered through the lens of
an Aryan aesthetic.

The performing twins also elicit protective impulses from fellow musicians. There is an element of fraternal commitment in their reception. Director Quinn encounters this brand of Prussian Blue supporters in the more

radical group "Stormtroop 16," a band based in Sacramento. With songs such as "War Machine," they attract a small but loyal following. Many of their performances, complete with skinhead audience, are available on YouTube. In the documentary film, the band's front man asserts that the twins have "opened a whole new area of music." He continues in the determined voice of solidarity: "We'll bleed for them and we'll die for them."[26] It must be said that the girls' voices are fairly untutored, the music ability basic, and even die-hard fans in YouTube comments suggest they avail themselves of the auto-tune function. The dedication expressed by "Stormtroop 16's" front man clearly exceeds the model suggested by Frith's reading of aesthetic judgment. The fraternal bond, mediated as much by racial as musical identification, takes precedence.

In another prominent example of political loyalty, we see the potential for paternal protection, though it segues into another form of desire. In the same film, the twins' mother April puts David Lane, who at the time of his death was serving a 190-year prison sentence, on speakerphone. Lane has written lyrics for the twins. During the phone call, he describes himself as a "natural male" who has alternately thought of the girls as "daughters" and "fantasy sweethearts," relationships that leave the off-screen audience skeptical and distressed. The maternal agency reigns supreme; the daughters replicate her politics and project racist messages through the megaphone of their own vulnerability and beauty. The twins elicit and foster fraternal protective feelings and paternal custodial impulses, but not without a subtext of desire.

For all the racial politics and focus on the girlish innocence of the twins, the rhetoric of family and gender hierarchy suffuses the lyrics and performance of Prussian Blue's most popular songs. In particular, "Victory Day" (from *Fragments of the Future*), celebrates an imagined victory of the white race after an apocalyptic racial war. The lyrics reinforce the notion that proud white men are suffering now, but in this fantasy of triumph, the world will be secured so that white women can finally smile while the children can play and thrive. The twins perform this paradigm in the YouTube video version of their song. In it, they wear modified dirndls, frolic barefoot in a meadow, tease each other innocently, and play over their toddler sister, Dresden. Wearing simple frocks, their tresses swaying in the wind, the wholesome, homespun goodness of their aspect is belied by the vehemence and violence of the song itself and the lyrics, referring to a "bloody but holy day."

Other songs reinforce the idea of a recruitment and flirtation purpose of the twins' performances and recordings. Titles like "Skinhead Boy" are indicative of their outreach capabilities to a cohort interested in their political profile. In "Keepers of the Light," a more recent release that would seem to belie the newly minted and espoused liberal politics, they perform with a male band to insist on the need for permanent struggle. In general, their performance aesthetic, corroborated by their lyrics, present a family romance that uses race to suspend or render more porous any sexual taboos. There is a sense of permitted predators if the cause is deemed pure, i.e., consistent with the naturalization of whiteness and sustained genealogies of the Aryan race.

Unsurprisingly, the lyrics of "Victory Day" also convey a sense of unity and harmony between whiteness and nature. Not only will the children play and the women sing, but nature will recover. The text suggests a new kind of eco-Nazism, reminiscent of the nature poetry and symbolization of the German forest familiar from the literature and thought of Romanticism. The forest will ". . . grace the brand new dawn of our race." In addition, the sun smiles and sky shines. In an uncomplicated anthropomorphizing of the natural world, human agency is attributed to the natural world. In *Male Fantasies*, Klaus Theweleit writes: "It would be nonsense to claim that the romantics were intellectual forerunners of fascism—there are no such forerunners. And no one ever becomes a fascist on the basis of things that were thought or written earlier; he evolves out of his own circumstances."[27] Still, there is a common denominator in the type of thinking and style of representation invoked by the Romantic poet Clemens Brentano, the topic of Theweleit's assertion, and the association between male desire, female fluids, and the natural world, and I will return to this point below. In the instance of the forest cited in this lyric, the natural world assumes agency in a way that is reminiscent of the pathetic fallacy, the Romantic aesthetic in which human subjectivity and intentionality are attributed to the natural world. The forest's echo instantiates such an empowerment of nature. This naturalization of racial hierarchy simultaneously incorporates an unexamined alliance between Romantic subjectivity and Nature into eco-racism and forges blood bonds among the twins and the proud white men who fight for them.

FOUNDING (FINDING) FATHERS

In her introduction to the first volume of Klaus Theweleit's *Male Fantasies*, Barbara Ehrenreich cautions the reader: "That is, we approach the subject of fascist men with the mind-set of a public health official: We want to get near (to the toxin or the protofascists) in order to get as far away as possible."[28] In two crucial songs with music videos, Prussian Blue performs in a way that brings the audience too close for comfort. As noted above, David Lane was in contact with their family. He wrote the lyrics for the song "Lamb near the Lane," the refrain of which explicates the "daughters" and "sweethearts" dissonance in the recorded phone conversation: "Some day in Valhalla, when he's young once more. He will hold the hand of the image he adored" (YouTube). The lyrics indict the cowardice of white men who have chosen the wrong path over "white" allegiances, forcing the women and children to fight their battles. The twins, who in the video are filmed in a cell and behind bars, assume the role of partisans, Nordic maidens who have taken up arms when male valor failed. Lines from the first stanza seem self-referential: a man in a prison cell, a soldier of the people, is punished for fighting ". . . to save his own kind, an image of beauty, he sees in his mind Of a beautiful maiden, now forced to the fight." In thinly veiled sexual imagery, the lyricist challenges the "rams" to fight for the hornless "Lamb" who does not abandon the founding father: "I am the Lamb. I'll stand beside the Lane."

The capacity for fraternal bonds is present in the twins' performances as well. In the quotation from "Stormtroop 16," "we will bleed for them," the front man makes reference to a Prussian Blue song, "I'll Bleed for You." As in "Lamb near the Lane," we encounter the personae of bellicose maidens who are willing to sacrifice themselves for the cause that white men are too downtrodden to mobilize for and too timid even to acknowledge their predicament. In the music video, the girls occupy a bleak townscape; they sing before a wall covered with senseless graffiti, walk along a dusty road, pause before an electric substation, and embody the bold solitude of those who are willing to stand and fight, even if they stand alone. The refrain directly addresses the white male listener: "To every man who doesn't dream, I am the dreamer." They repeat the phrase with "believer," and suggestively, with "receiver." The passive inaction they identify escalates into an active accusation: "To every man who refuses to bleed, I will bleed for you." The conflation of politics and sexuality in the lyrics of the refrain surfaces in the first stanza as well, when the twins sing of their own activism: "while they rape your land."

MATERNAL MANAGEMENT

In Quinn's film, as in numerous YouTube comments and Internet blogs about the twins, a critique of April Gaede, their mother and manager, rises above the sounds of youthful innocence, folk pride, and hate-laced lyrics. In several scenes, the girls speak freely only when their mother is not present or assumed to be asleep. Their public conversion to liberalism elicits a plethora of comments, most congratulatory, about their emergence into adulthood, away from their mother's control. Many comment on the conviction that no child could truly believe, let alone understand, the white supremacist slogans they sang; most critical voices reached consensus that Lynx and Lamb were the mouthpieces for their mother, who now has her own weekly radio program, broadcast from her basement. The constellation of mother and daughters warrants further examination, though the twins have ostensibly distanced themselves from the scene. April Gaede, who grew up on a cattle ranch in California with her father branding cattle with swastikas, projects her voice through her daughters' folksy music—with echoes of American folk ballads.

She is in charge of the mail-order business, and one scene in the film shows her packing bags with items such as T-shirts, CDs, and mouse pads. In another scene, she shows how she could hand doctor the smiley face t-shirts that, with a bit of geometric inflection, turned the happy faces into little Hitlers. The photograph of the girls in these shirts circulated globally. In the course of their development through adolescence into young adulthood, Lynx and Lamb seemed to distance themselves from their mother's politics. The YouTube virtual public sphere reacted. In a final reading, the fans or foes also imagine Lynx and Lamb separating from the father figure and say good-bye to Hitler.

The political and personal identification between maternity and race did not recede with the independence of the twins. According to a briefing paper by the Montana Human Rights Network, Gaede channeled her maternal impulses into support for Hope Pregnancy Ministries, joining an effort "to 'help save white babies.'"[29] In her work on pro-life politics, Carol Mason connects the rhetoric of race to that of fetal protection in her chapter on the "fetal citizen" as represented by the "crack baby" and the "partially born." She continues:

> There seemed to be a link between spiritual purity or innocence and the racial purity of the unborn. The term *fetal protection*, therefore, encompasses a double meaning: protect us from the fetuses who would be born as members of degenerate races, and let us protect those fetuses who would emerge as wholly pure in the genetic sense and holy pure in the spiritual sense.[30]

Mason's analysis identifies the connection between pro-life and apocalyptic narratives that prevailed at the end of the millennium. Subsequent work foregrounds the "overlap between hardcore white supremacists and anti-choice activists in Montana."[31]

FAREWELL TO FASCISM

The morphing of a smiley face into a recognizable avatar of Adolf Hitler shocks; the description of the gesture as in any way cute or amusing defies reason. The recent spate of films and books about Hitler, both fictional and factual, situate contemporary audiences in the midst of an impossible dilemma of speaking about the history of German fascism without polemics. Yet the gaze of the "public health official" Ehrenreich so shrewdly identifies does not bring us closer to any understanding of the seemingly transhistorical attraction of this political extremism. The recent popularity of films demands closer examination. One frame in which to consider this persistence leads to the complicity of totalitarian politics and aesthetics. Susan Sontag dwells on this link in the essay "Fascinating Fascism." In that influential piece, Sontag critically explores Leni Riefenstahl's endorsement of beauty, health, vitality, arguing that it is "never witless. . . ." (1975). Riefenstahl's role as the "priest-ess" of the beautiful was the credential that enabled her possible "rehabilita-tion" in the first place. In the rise and demise of "Prussian Blue," we see something similar to the "cycles of taste," as Sontag formulated it: the exi-gencies of fashion that inform aesthetic politics. These shifted sufficiently in the mid-1970s to accommodate Riefenstahl's Nazi past. The shock-value of finding anything cute in a Hitler T-shirt highlights reinforces the radical taboo involved in any representation of the Führer without expressed abhor-rence. But it is "never witless."

In the twenty-first century, both in Germany and the United States, a series of films in which Nazi characters appear to be either sexy or sympa-thetic, from *The Reader* (2008) to *Inglorious Basterds* (2009), thus challeng-ing any absolute notions of good and evil. In Germany, the film *Der Unter-gang* (*The Downfall*, 2004), directed by Oliver Hirschbiegel, represented the demise of Hitler through the perspective of his secretary. In one dramatic scene, much parodied on YouTube, the actor Bruno Ganz rants and rages upon learning that his war is nearly lost. 555ReactionTime has uploaded seven videos in which a particular segment of film is reworked to purported-ly humorous or parodying effect with English subtitles. In this video up-loaded on 2 January 2012, 555ReactionTime subtitles the excerpt as Hitler's reaction to Lynx and Lamb's renunciation of all things Aryan. One dismayed marshal dares to ask: "Can't you just accept it? Lynx and Lamb Gaede have renounced Aryan Nations and you with it." The subtitles of Hitler's interpo-lated response point to the undertones and overt references to taboo desire in their performance history. "Hitler" screams about his "creepy obsession" with the girls, lamenting that all those years of ideological pedagogy have fallen to waste, now that they have turned eighteen. He screams: "Those hot-to-go barely legal whores!" The parody uses informed humor to articulate the unspeakable and unspoken about the charismatic, volatile, and repugnant desire that opens a portal to a virtual space in which dictators are people, too, and are entitled to their feelings. Of the seven videos, this one has the most traction, with 5,411 views, including one "like" presumably from the girls: "HAHAHAHA! Thanks for this, cracked us up." In his reply, 555Reaction-Time writes:

> Hi Lamb, let me just apologize for some of the crude subtitles, I would have tried to do a better job if I knew you guys were going to pay me the undeserved honor of watching the video, but thanks for liking :)[32]

While the twins have receded from the scene, their mother and family have pursued other ways of articulating and living their political ideology. As noted above, maternal activism in support of racial politics provides a transitional path from stage mother of a sort to selective pro-life activist. Her access to the community of like-minded activists is both local and virtual. Gaede's endorsement of the Hope Pregnancy Ministries' work in Kalispell was facilitated by posts on the Stormfront website; she encouraged her peers to send money in the expectation of preventing the abortion of "'White babies.'" Her virtual activism in the service of preserving racial supremacy extends to a proprietary sense of ownership in the separatist living community she fosters.

One of her causes involves the establishing of "Pioneer Little Europe," self-advertised as "expressly a settler styled movement or sometimes known as separatists." The description insists: "PLE *is not* about hate or racism, it is about love for one's culture, faith, and heritage of European peoples and their own diversity."[33] PLE attempts to be a movement beyond the local. In a thread on the stormfront.org site, forum moderator Haman (described as a sustaining member), writes: "PLE (Pioneer Little Europe is an advocacy for 'Stormfronts of the street,' partly visible and partly invisible, placing one foot in a local system and keeping the other foot out) is a kind of community organizer's Judo."[34] The PLE website itself warns against the Marxists who harass the membership, and also provides links to promotional videos on related topics, one of which, "Stop White Genocide," a re-upload of a video posted on and removed from YouTube and banned in eighteen countries, but that tallies 183,502 views between 29 December 2012 and 10 November 2013. By Johnny Mantraseed et al., the message of this video is "anti-racist is a code word for anti-White."[35] The slogan or "mantra" echoes and replicates the message emanating from other sources, online and otherwise. A closer examination of this mantra connects the rhetoric of the street, settlement, and sites.

The main web page for stormfront.org advertises the Annual Stormfront Summit with the same mantra appearing under the hovering cursor. The site boasts 3,607,769 visits.[36] On the masthead, a visitor can click on the "billboard" with the same message. This navigates to another site, White Rabbit Radio, on which one can learn about the racist versions of history in animations. Other videos are available with the same text as the mantra, spoken or sung with some variation.[37] A bit more linking connects the curious or committed surfer to the source, where the full actual text of the mantra appears on the website of the White GeNOcide Project.[38] Here, one may donate to the next billboard, with the updated mantra: "Diversity is a code word for White genocide."[39] The uniformity of the message travels intact from summits in Eastern Tennessee to the mountain lakes of northern Montana, where PLE disseminates the message further.

The PLE's activities and attractions share space on another site, one with "A Day on the Water—A Kalispell PLE Promotional Video." The video, directed by Father Land Descendant, includes voiceover and commentary on the group of friends and family who are enjoying a chilly day on the water at Flathead Lake. Posted by (Scott) Mjodr, the camera-man narrates the promotional prose about the "PLE experience":

> PLE is all about pioneering Little Europe, but more importantly Stormfront of the street, where we go and we participate in community events, whether we generate the event or whether we attend an event together. This is what its all about, folks. White friends and families out enjoying a day. [40]

The camera pans across the water to find April and her daughter Dresden, who are paddling in separate kayaks. He searches momentarily for the father, and when he appears, the narrator opines: "Now there, there is what White Nationalism is all about, preserving the White family. That is what it's all about folks." When the cameraman focuses on Dresden alone, he supplies a corrective: "Reality of it is, that right there is what we're protecting."[41]

The rhetoric of supremacist sites on the Internet relies on, reinforces, and inflects the messages as proponents and activists disseminate them further. In their work on persuasion and social movements, Stewart et al. analyze methods of persuasion in resistance movements; they count white supremacy in this category, defined in the following:

> A *resistance social movement* seeks to block changes in norms and values because it perceives *nothing wrong with the status quo*, at least nothing that cannot or will not be resolved in due time through established means and institutions. Resistance social movements include anti-women's liberation, anti-civil rights, antigay rights, white supremacy, and pro-choice movements. [42]

The authors contrast this type of social movement to an "*innovative social movement* [which] seeks to replace existing norms and values with *new* ones."[43] The authors further emphasize the future-oriented rhetoric deployed to persuade others to share the vision: "Social movements portray a vision of the future that instills a sense of urgency in audiences to organize and do something *now* before it is too late."[44] In the context of my analysis, the message in Prussian Blue's lyrics, undergirded by the support from rightist-white political and social groupings, such as the National Alliance, the self-definition of pristine, separatists communities, such as Pioneer Little Europe, enter into a symmetry with a discourse that advances multiculturalism and diversity. The various sites mentioned here include links to "news" articles from around the world that contribute to that sense of urgency—that something must be done to stop a genocide. With the leverage of the Internet, white supremacy transitions from a resistance to an innovative movement, one that asserts an ahistorical racial hierarchy with whites now a minority in need of protection. The racialized logic travels across town and across time.

CONCLUSION

Right-wing, white supremacist music and politics participate in a culture of recruitment and persuasion, with both aesthetics and politics enlisted in the service of racial survival and superiority. While scholars may want to assume the attitude of the public health official Ehrenreich describes, it remains imperative to look closely at the mechanics of production and dissemination of this music, the soundtrack of hate. While much of Prussian Blue's popularity, intense and short-lived, may strike us as irrational, the fact is that their fans and image survive. Their political significance far outweighs their modest musical contributions. The deployment of their physical appearance and racial attributes points to a totalizing concept of family identity and citizenship in a white "nation" that can only be achieved after an apocalyptic racial war. The presumed identity between their skin color, hair color, and innocence leaves little margin for diversity. The vehemence with which they were defended and desired remains open to mobilization by extremist ideologies and cultures that underwrite them.

NOTES

1. "Double Vision with Prussian Blue. Interview with Lynx and Lamb Gaede. *Resistance Magazine* 22 (Winter 2004): 12–14, here 13.
2. Pete Simi and Robert Futrell, *American Swastika: Inside the White Power Movement's Hidden Spaces of Hate*. Lanham, MD: Rowman & Littlefield, 2010), 63.
3. "Double Vision," 13.
4. Simon Frith, *Performing Rites: On the Value of Popular Music* (Cambridge, MA: Harvard University Press, 1996), 72.
5. Simi and Futrell, *American Swastika*, ix.
6. "Double Vision," 13.
7. "Double Vision," 13.
8. Britta Schellenberg, "Right-Wing Extremism and Terrorism in Germany: Developments and Enabling Structures," in *Right-Wing Extremism in Europe*, Ralf Melzer and Sebastian Serafin, eds. (Berlin: Friedrich Ebert Foundation, 2013), 35-74.
9. "Double Vision," 12.
10. Christian Dornbusch and Jan Raabe, "'Rechtsrock fürs Vaterland,'" in *Braune Kameradschaften: Die militanten Neonazis im Schatten der NPD*, edited by Andrea Röpke and Andreas Speit (Berlin: Christoph Links Verlag, 2005), 67-86; here 86. All translations, unless otherwise noted, are my own.
11. Simi and Futrell, *American Swastika*, 3.
12. "Böhse Onkelz. Der nette Mann." http://www.onkelzvinyl.de/onkelz-originale-schall-platten/der-nette-mann/index.htm. Accessed 25 November 2014.
13. Quoted in Klaus Farin, ed. *Skinhead—A Way of Life: Eine Jugendbewegung stellt sich vor* (Berlin: Archiv der Jugendkulturen, 1999, 2001), 120.
14. Quentin Peel, "The faces of neo-Nazism." *Financial Times.* 23 November 2012.http://www.ft.com/cms/s/2/dfda3010-3438-11e2-9ae7-00144fea, accessed 23 April 2013, 11.
15. Patricia Anne Simpson, *Cultures of Violence in the New German Street* (Lanham, MD: Rowman & Littlefield, 2011), 121–26.
16. NPD, 2013. http://www.npd.de/.
17. Quoted in Anna Rieger, "'Liebe deine Rasse.' Neonazistinnen auf dem Vormarsch." *Antifa* 7-8 (2007): 26. http://antifa.vvn-bda.de/200707/2601.php, accessed 25 April 2013.

18. Johann Osel, "Rechte Partnersuche im Netz." *Süddeutsche Zeitung* (17 May 2010). http://www.sueddeutsche.de/politik/weibliche-neonazis-rechte-partnersuche-im-netz-1. 570929, accessed 5 September 2014.

19. Osel, "Rechte Partnersuche im Netz."

20. Quoted in Rieger, "Liebe deine Rasse," 26.

21. Florian Hartleb, *After Their Establishment: Right-wing Populist Parties in Europe* (Brussels: Centre for European Studies, 2011), 45.

22. Anti-Defamation League, "David Lane. Update: David Lane, white supremacist terrorist and ideologue, dies in prison." http://archive.adl.org/learn/ext_us/lane.asp?xpicked=2& item=lane, accessed 5 September 2014.

23. ADL, "David Lane"

24. On a personal note, I was taken aback by these images when asked by fellow demonstrators to translate the German slogans into English.

25. The site, with links to NSM88 Records, describes itself as "A Social Networking Site for People of European Descent," http://newsaxon.org/angelinthewilderness/video/europe-s-fallen-tribute-to-white-victims/, accessed 26 April 2013.

26. Quoted in James Quinn, dir. *Nazi Pop Twins* (2007).

27. Klaus Theweleit, *Male Fantasies: Volume 1: Women, Floods, Bodies, History*, translated by Stephen Conway, with Erica Carter and Chris Turner. Foreword by Barbara Ehrenreich (Minneapolis: University of Minnesota Press, 1987), 361.

28. Barbara Ehrenreich, "Foreword," x.

29. Montana Human Rights Network, "'Saving White Babies': White Supremacists Raise Funds for Kalispell Crisis Pregnancy Center." Briefing paper, 25 January 2010.

30. Carol Mason, *Killing for Life: The Apocalyptic Narrative of Pro-Life Politics* (Ithaca and London: Cornell University Press, 2002), 5–6.

31. Montana Human Rights Network, "'Saving White Babies,'" no page numbers. The report discusses Shawn Stuart's 2006 candidacy for the Montana Legislature and identifies him as the state leader of the National Socialist Movement.

32. https://www.youtube.com/watch?v=PFXpTK_vn_o&lc=mb3ymdgwHYiKd1xLWp2h Z1zRJ1-Fw6okl_3YAB3dj1E, accessed 8 October 2014.

33. Pioneer Little Europe, www.pioneerlittleeurope.com, accessed 12 September 2014. Emphasis in the original.

34. "Haman," "Visual Answers About Pioneer Little Europes," https://www.stormfront. org/forum/t820125/#post9434244, posted 27 July 2011, accessed 8 October 2014.

35. Johnny Mantraseed et al., "Stop White Genocide," posted on www.pioneerlittleeurope, accessed 12 September 2014.

36. Stormfront.org, accessed 12 September 2014.

37. http://whiterabbitradio.net, accessed 12 September 2014.

38. http://whitegenocideproject.com/the-mantra/, accessed 12 September 2014.

39. http://whitegenocideproject.com, accessed 12 September 2014.

40. Father Land Descendant, "A Day on the Water—A Kalispell PLE Promotional Video," 21 May 2013, http://www.fatguyinmontana.com/2013/05/21/a-day-on-the-water-a-kalispell-ple-promotional-video/, accessed 12 September 2014.

41. "A Day on the Water."

42. Charles J. Stewart, Craig Allen Smith, and Robert E. Denton, Jr. *Persuasion and Social Movements* (Long Grove, IL: Waveland Press, 2007, fifth edition), 14.

43. Stewart et al., *Persuasion*, 14.

44. Stewart et al., *Persuasion*, 55.

REFERENCES

Anti-Defamation League. "David Lane. Update: David Lane, white supremacist terrorist and ideologue, dies in prison." http://archive.adl.org/learn/ext_us/lane.asp?xpicked=2& item=lane. Accessed 5 September 2014.

246 *Simpson*

————. "Neo-Nazi Tries to Reach Youth through Music Downloads." 17 December 2009. http://www.adl.org/combating-hate/domestic-extremism-terrorism/c/neo-nazi-tries-to-reach-youth-1.html. Accessed 26 April 2013.

"Böhse Onkelz." http://www.onkelzvinyl.de/onkelz-originale-schallplatten/der-nette-mann/index.htm. Accessed 25 November 2014.

Dornbusch, Christian and Jan Raabe. "'Rechtsrock fürs Vaterland.'" In *Braune Kameradschaften: Die militanten Neonazis im Schatten der NPD.* Edited by Andrea Röpke and Andreas Speit. Berlin: Christoph Links Verlag, 2005. 67–86.

Ehrenreich, Barbara. "Foreword." In Klaus Theweleit, *Male Fantasies.* Minneapolis: University of Minnesota Press, 1987. ix–xxii.

Farin, Klaus, ed. *Skinhead—A Way of Life: Eine Jugendbewegung stellt sich vor.* Berlin: Archiv der Jugendkulturen, 1999, 2001.

Father Land Descendant, dir. "A Day on the Water—A Kalispell PLE Promotional Video." 21 May 2013. http://www.fatguyinmontana.com/2013/05/21/a-day-on-the-water-a-kalispell-ple-promotional-video/. Accessed 12 September 2014.

Frith, Simon. *Performing Rites: On the Value of Popular Music.* Cambridge, MA: Harvard University Press, 1996.

Futrell, Robert and Pete Simi. "The Sound of Hate." *The New York Times.* 8 August 2012. http://www.nytimes.com/2012/08/09/opinion/the-sikh-temple-killers-music-of-hate.html?_r=0. Accessed 23 April 2013.

"Haman" (pseud.) "Visual Answers About Pioneer Little Europes." https://www.stormfront.org/forum/t820125/#post9434244. Posted 27 July 2011. Accessed 8 October 2014.

Hartleb, Florian. *After Their Establishment: Right-wing Populist Parties in Europe.* Brussels: Centre for European Studies, 2011.

Mantraseed, Johnny et al. "Stop White Genocide." Posted on www.pioneerlittleeurope. Accessed 12 September 2014.

Mason, Carol. *Killing for Life: The Apocalyptic Narrative of Pro-Life Politics.* Ithaca and London: Cornell University Press, 2002.

Molthagen, Dietmar. "Racist-Extremism Online—The German Link." Panel Discussion on Racist-Extremism Online and its Growing Appeal to Young Users. Friedrich Ebert Stiftung. 1 May 2006.

Montana Human Rights Network. "'Saving White Babies:' White Supremacists Raise Funds for Kallispell Crisis Pregnancy Center." Briefing Paper. 25 January 2010. http://www.mhrn.org/publications/specialresearchreports/AprilGaede.pdf. Accessed 10 September 2014.

National Alliance. "Liebe deine Rasse." http://www.natvan.com/leaflets/LoveDE.pdf. Accessed 26 April 2013.

Osel, Johann. "Rechte Partnersuche im Netz." *Süddeutsche Zeitung.* 17 May 2010. http://www.sueddeutsche.de/politik/weibliche-neonazis-rechte-partnersuche-im-netz-1.570929. Accessed 5 September 2014.

Peel, Quentin. "The faces of neo-Nazism." *Financial Times.* 23 November 2012. http://www.ft.com/cms/s/2/dfda3010-3438-11e2-9ae7-00144fea. Access 23 April 2013.

Quinn, James, dir. *Nazi Pop Twins.* 2007.

Resistance Staff. "Double Vision with Prussian Blue. Interview with Lynx and Lamb Gaede." *Resistance Magazine* 22 (Winter 2004): 12–14.

Rieger, Anna. "Liebe deine Rasse". Neonazistinnen auf dem Vormarsch. *Antifa* 7-8 (2007): 26. http://antifa.vvn-bda.de/200707/2601.php. Accessed 25 April 2013.

Schellenberg, Britta. "Right-Wing Extremism and Terrorism in Germany: Developments and Enabling Structures," in *Right-Wing Extremism in Europe.* Edited by Ralf Melzer and Sebastian Serafin. Friedrich Ebert Foundation, 2013. 35–74.

Schlatter, Evelyn A. *Aryan Cowboys: White Supremacists and the Search for a New Frontier 1970-2000.* Austin, TX: University of Texas Press, 2006.

Simi, Pete and Robert Futrell. *American Swastika: Inside the White Power Movement's Hidden Spaces of Hate.* Lanham, MD: Rowman & Littlefield, 2010.

Simpson, Patricia Anne. *Cultures of Violence in the New German Street*. Lanham, MD: Rowman & Littlefield, 2011.

Sontag, Susan. "Fascinating Fascism." *The New York Review of Books*. 6 February 1975. http://www.nybooks.com/articles/archives/1975/feb/06/fascinating-fascism/?page=1. Accessed 20 March 2013.

Stewart, Charles J., Craig Allen Smith, and Robert E. Denton, Jr. *Persuasion and Social Movements*. Long Grove, IL: Waveland Press, 2007, fifth edition.

Theweleit, Klaus. *Male Fantasies: Volume 1: Women, Floods, Bodies, History*. Translated by Stephen Conway, with Erica Carter and Chris Turner. Foreword by Barbara Ehrenreich. Minneapolis: University of Minnesota Press, 1987.

555ReactionTime. "Hitler Reacts To Being Dumped By Lynx and Lamb Gaede (Prussian Blue)." YouTube. Uploaded 2 January 2012. http://www.youtube.com/watch?v=PFXpTK_vn_o. Accessed 8 October 2014. 2013.

Chapter Thirteen

The New "Great White Hope?"

White Nationalist Discourses of Race, Color, and Country in the Career of Mexican Boxer Saúl "Canelo" Álvarez

Justin D. García

This chapter focuses on the competing white nationalist reactions to popular Mexican professional boxer Saúl "Canelo" Álvarez. Specifically, it examines how members of the white nationalist website Stormfront.org have responded to Álvarez's rapid rise to boxing fame and, for the most part, have attempted to appropriate the young pugilist as a contemporary symbol of "white pride" and "white supremacy" despite Canelo's proud Mexican heritage, which white supremacists customarily exclude from their constructed notions of whiteness. This seemingly contradictory embracing of Álvarez is all the more perplexing given that smoldering anti-Mexican and anti-Latino sentiments helped fuel a resurgence of white supremacist organizations in the United States during the first decade of the twenty-first century.

FBI statistics indicate a steady rise in the number of hate crimes committed annually against Latin American immigrants between 2003 and 2007, despite the fact that hate crimes against other groups either declined or showed no noticeable increase during this period.[1] For example, in April 2006 two neo-Nazi skinheads nearly fatally tortured and beat a 16-year-old Mexican American high-school football star in Texas.[2] Meanwhile former White Knights of the Ku Klux Klan member Daniel Schertz was arrested in May 2005 for a plot to blow up buses carrying migrant Mexican agricultural workers to Florida.[3] White supremacist backlash against Mexican immigration, both legal and illegal, has also filtered into mainstream politics. A California State Senator with connections to the Christian Identity movement was one of the leading funders of Proposition 187,[4] a 1994 anti-illegal immigration ballot referendum, and Arizona State Senator Russell Pearce, chief sponsor of the controversial bill SB 1070 (which would have granted law enforcement agents broad powers to question suspected undocumented immigrants of their citizenship status) garnered scrutiny for his close personal connection to an anti-immigrant activist who appeared at Neo-Nazi rallies.[5] Thus, Canelo Álvarez's appropriation by online white nationalists and supremacists has occurred at a critical juncture in the nation's history when the Mexican/Latino population has increased substantially and surpassed the African American population. Immigration has reemerged as a contentious social and political issue, Mexicans/Latinos have come to dominate much of professional boxing (particularly within the lower weight divisions), and white supremacist organizations have grown in number.

BOXING, RACE, AND RACISM

Sports represent a social site at which racial ideologies may be either reinforced or challenged and transformed. This phenomenon has persisted for years in both the United States and Europe, producing some highly notable socio-historical moments, in addition to reflecting the tense racial atmospheres of the respective society during the respective era. Prominent examples include Hitler's failed attempt to use the 1936 Summer Olympics in Berlin to demonstrate the alleged "Aryan supremacy" of his nation's athletes before a global audience (which backfired when black American sprinter Jesse Owens captured four gold medals) and Jackie Robinson's historic integration of professional baseball when he became the first black player in Major League history after signing with the Brooklyn Dodgers in 1947.

Perhaps no sport generates more rifts along racial fault lines than boxing, a dubious distinction that has persisted for more than a century. During the early twentieth century, Jack Johnson, the first African American boxer to win the heavyweight championship, sparked outrage among white society with his in-ring success and out-of-the-ring antics. Johnson captured the heavyweight crown in 1908, despite a general tendency at the time for white champions and promoters to avoid granting title matches to black fighters. During his impressive seven-year title reign, the American public and press openly pressed for a "great white hope," in the form of a white fighter with enough talent, to dethrone the black champion. The "great white hope" trope is still occasionally invoked by boxing insiders and sports journalists to this day, albeit primarily in a joking manner, to refer to the lack of quality among white American pugilists in a sport that is now dominated by black, Latino, and, increasingly, Eastern European/Central Asian fighters. Johnson also delighted in stoking white America's fears of interracial sex by publicly flaunting his various relationships with white women during an era in which black-white intermarriages were illegal in numerous states. Fearful that footage of Johnson pummeling his white opponents might spark race riots, Congress passed legislation outlawing the transportation of filmed boxing matches across state lines.[6]

During the 1930s and 1940s, Joe Louis emerged as a pop culture symbol of American patriotism and democracy, despite his blackness. Louis, in fact, conducted his professional career as the anti-Johnson; after capturing the heavyweight title in 1937, "The Brown Bomber" knocked out several white challengers but deliberately refrained from taunting his opponents or cele-brating excessively, so as not to infuriate the masses. However, Louis's bout with Germany's Max Schmeling on the eve of World War II in June 1938 cemented his legacy as a crossover racial star. Hitler touted Schmeling as an "Aryan superman" and emblem of Nazi supremacy prior to the bout, while President Franklin D. Roosevelt praised Louis as a symbol of American muscle and hard work. Louis knocked out Schmeling within one round at Yankee Stadium, and his non-threatening, conformist demeanor enabled Louis to become the first black athlete to achieve mainstream popularity among whites in the United States.

The most famous prizefighter of all-time, Muhammad Ali, emerged as one of the nation's most polarizing figures of the 1960s and early 1970s as a result of his outspoken criticism of societal racism and U.S. foreign policy, as well as affiliation with the Nation of Islam and his refusal to serve in the army after being drafted in 1967. One of the iconic figures of the Black Power movement, Ali openly criticized his boxing rival Joe Frazier as an "Uncle Tom" and a "white man's champion" for Frazier's alleged docile personality and his reluctance to publicly condemn white supremacy and anti-black racism.[7]

No other match in recent decades more vividly illustrates boxing's poten-tially contentious racial overtones than the June 1982 heavyweight title bout between undefeated champion Larry Holmes, an African American, and his undefeated white challenger Gerry Cooney, an Irish American, at Caesar's Palace in Las Vegas. One of the most highly anticipated bouts of the late twentieth century, the Holmes-Cooney match occurred during an era in which boxing (and other major sports in the United States, such as football and basketball) had increasingly become dominated by black athletes. A victory by Cooney would have made him the first white American heavy-weight champion since Rocky Marciano in the mid-1950s. As such, boxing promoter Don King, along with the media, presented Cooney as a "white hope" and portrayed the fight as a racial confrontation.[8] White supremacists threatened to shoot Holmes as he entered Caesar's Palace, while black acti-vists promised to return fire if Holmes was attacked.[9] Even President Ronald Reagan delved into the racial fracas. Cooney's dressing room included a telephone that had been specially placed to receive a congratulatory call from Reagan in the event Cooney won, although no such phone had been placed in Holmes's dressing room.[10] Holmes dominated Cooney throughout the fight, knocking him down in the second round and ultimately scoring a thirteenth round technical knockout. Holmes's thorough beating of Cooney greatly subsided talk of a "white hope" in heavyweight boxing over the next two decades, as black American and British champions such as Mike Tyson, Evander Holyfield, and Lennox Lewis continued to dominate the division throughout the 1980s and 1990s. Cooney's fan base shrunk considerably after this defeat, and he did not fight again until more than two years later. Despite the intense black-white dynamics surrounding their title bout, Holmes and Cooney actually became friends and consider the media, rather than one another, as the ultimate culprits for the racial animosity stoked by this match.

Long-time boxing analyst and former *Ring* magazine editor Nigel Collins attributes boxing's penchant for arousing racial passions to the inherently confrontational and combative aspect of the sport. Collins notes: "[P]erhaps the most politically incorrect aspect of boxing is that it's OK to identify with a nation or race and openly root for your own . . . no other athletic endeavor cuts closer to the bone of mortal combat than boxing."[11] Collins further points out that the emotionally charged racial nature of boxing derives from the fact that the sport's objective is to administer physical violence to an opponent:

> An activity in which human beings willingly sacrifice their bodies for the entertainment of others has created a primordial petri dish in which extreme behavior of all kinds flourishes. Similar emotions are at play in other sports, of course, but no other athletic competition lights a fuse quite like boxing. . . . That's partly because there are no buffers between action and intent. It's a fight—a common denominator that all living creatures understand and respond to in predictable ways.[12]

While Collins's basic assessment may be true, it is important to bear in mind that tense racial atmospheres surrounding boxing matches (or other sporting events) do not arise spontaneously; rather, they stem from larger societal dynamics of inequality, competition, and conflict.

THE RISE OF A NEW CHAMPION

Just twenty-four years old, Álvarez has already emerged as one of the "dynamic young stars of boxing today," according to Showtime's legendary boxing ring announcer Jimmy Lennon, Jr. Álvarez has compiled an impressive record of forty-three wins, one loss, one draw, including thirty-one victories by knockout. In January 2013, readers of *ESPN the Magazine* voted Álvarez their favorite star in professional boxing. He formerly held the World Boxing Council's light middleweight championship, is already regarded as one of the elite pound-for-pound fighters active in the sport today, and his only defeat as a professional fighter came against Floyd "Money" Mayweather, widely considered by boxing experts to be the greatest prizefighter of this generation, in September 2013.

Despite his impressive athletic talents and his accomplishments in the ring, however, Alvarez generates as much, if not more, attention for his physical appearance, which many boxing fans and casual observers alike seem to feel is at odds with his ethno-national ancestry. Santos Sául Álvarez Barragán was born 18 July 1990 in Tlajomulco de Zuñiga, Jalisco, Mexico (near the outskirts of Guadalajara) and spent his youth growing up on his family's farm in the central Mexican province of Jalisco. Although his father and three brothers all have darker skin and black hair, Sául shares his mother's phenotype of fairer skin and reddish hair. In fact, his nickname, "Canelo," is Spanish for "cinnamon" and is used to highlight his fiery-colored mane.

Today Álvarez has impressed the global boxing community with his ring credentials, although during the early months of his exposure to boxing fans in the United States, much of the reaction to "Canelo" centered on his allegedly "un-Mexican" appearance, which includes his famous redhead, creamy complexion, and freckled face. Having taken up boxing in the gyms of Jalisco during his childhood, Álvarez rose rapidly through the Mexican amateur ranks and by the age of fourteen, he was used as a sparring partner for Mexican world bantamweight and featherweight champion Oscar Larios. Canelo amassed an amateur boxing record of forty-four wins and two losses, and turned professional at fifteen years old. By the time he was eighteen, Álvarez boasted an undefeated professional record of twenty-one wins and one draw, but he was still relatively unknown to most boxing fans outside of Jalisco and unheard of in the United States. In 2008, a scout for the U.S.-based boxing promotion company Golden Boy Promotions, founded by former Olympic gold medalist and professional boxing superstar Oscar De La Hoya, discovered Álvarez and began to keep a close eye on his professional potential and development. In January 2010, De La Hoya himself flew to Mexico to personally sign Álvarez to a contract, convinced that he was a major rising star within the sport. Sensing that something big was on the horizon, De La Hoya declared that his company's signing of Álvarez marked, "a historical day for Golden Boy."[13] Shortly thereafter, Golden Boy Promotions began to sponsor boxing matches for Canelo on the undercards of main events featuring more established fighters, which granted Canelo new exposure to audiences in the United States, Canada, and Europe.

Álvarez's 1 May 2010 bout with Puerto Rican welterweight José Miguel Cotto, the older brother of four-time world champion Miguel Cotto, marked Canelo's breakthrough to spectators outside of his native Mexico. Featured on the undercard of the Floyd Mayweather-"Sugar" Shane Moseley fight at the MGM Grand in Las Vegas, this pay-per-view event was purchased by 1.4 million buyers who witnessed a thrilling match that showcased Álvarez's ability to overcome adversity. Cotto staggered Álvarez with devastating combinations within the first minute of the fight, sending Canelo careening into the ropes as he absorbed flurries of hooks and uppercuts in his first match against a name-brand opponent. Miraculously, Canelo remained on his feet and demonstrated enough fighting spirit to discourage referee Tony Weeks from stopping the contest. Álvarez regrouped after making it out of the first round and steadily took control of the fight, ultimately stopping Cotto in the ninth round with a barrage of right hand shots that prompted the referee to call a halt to the bout in order to spare Cotto from taking additional punishment.

In several respects, Canelo Álvarez's rise to stardom illustrates several important dynamics and developments regarding the positionality and cultural influences of ethnic Mexicans within the United States during the early twenty-first century. One facet of these dynamics is the highly emotional yet seemingly contradictory discourses of race and ethnicity that Mexicans have evoked in American society and, to a lesser extent, other Western nations. On one hand, Álvarez is extremely popular in his homeland and has likewise emerged as a source of ethnic-cultural pride among Mexican American boxing fans in the United States. At the same time, his physical appearance, often deemed as "not looking Mexican," has often resulted in boxing commentators remarking upon his phenotype during his fights. For example, during his world title fight against Ryan Rhodes in June 2011, HBO boxing commentator Max Kellerman declared of Canelo: "He *is* Mexican; *looks* Irish; and *fights* [like] George Foreman."[14] Another example of the color (pun intended) commentary aimed at Álvarez's complexion arose during his match against Shane Moseley on Cinco De Mayo 2012, in which longtime HBO boxing analyst Larry Merchant discussed Canelo's looks during the pre-fight introductions by mentioning that Álvarez's light complexion and reddish hair contrast with the physical appearance shared by most of his relatives. Merchant declared on air that "all of his brothers and the rest of his family are 'Mexican-looking Mexicans,' in one way or another."[15] Perhaps realizing the awkward nature of this statement, Merchant quickly followed up with a clarification of, "if there is such a thing."[16]

Merchant had previously established a record of questionable statements pertaining to ethnic Mexican fighters. While his statement about "Mexican-looking Mexicans" may have been more misinformed than malicious, Merchant received heavy criticism and prompted calls for his firing from HBO after he chastised Oscar De La Hoya, a second-generation Mexican American, on air during a 1997 bout. He complained of De La Hoya's expression of pride in his Mexican heritage by declaring that De La Hoya is "not Mexican, but a born-and-bred American"; and Merchant also commented that De La Hoya's selection of mariachi music to play as he entered the ring "sucks."[17] Merchant, a white middle-aged male, issued an on-air apology to De La Hoya and boxing fans the following week, and was punished with a one-fight suspension from HBO.[18]

While Kellerman, Merchant, and other media personalities may question Canelo's authenticity as a "Mexican-looking Mexican," Álvarez himself is fully embraced as an icon and hero by his fellow Mexican nationals south of the border and Mexican American fans in the United States. Neither skin color nor hair color has hurt his standing among ethnic Mexicans on either side of the border, as his fights consistently sell out and are marked by loud chorus chants among the audience of "Ca-ne-lo!, Ca-ne-lo!" Further alluding to his stature as a key ethno-cultural icon among the Mexican/Chicano community is the fact that over the past four years, Oscar De La Hoya and other executives at Golden Boy Promotions have consistently scheduled title matches for Álvarez on Cinco De Mayo (early May) and Mexican Independence Day (mid-September) weekends. Such was the case on 16 September 2012, when Álvarez headlined the main event against Mexican American prospect Josesito Lopez at the MGM Grand in Las Vegas. Golden Boy Promotions used Álvarez's growing stature within the Mexican and Mexican American communities to transform this fight into a full-blown, weekend-long, ethno-cultural pride festival that featured prominent displays of Mexican flags, advertising campaigns for the Mexican beer Corona, and several meet-and-greet autograph sessions with Oscar De La Hoya and other Mexican and Mexican American boxing champions.

Canelo's international fame has only grown with time. Álvarez's promoter, De La Hoya, intended to market Canelo to both Mexican fans in Mexico and Mexican American fans inside the United States, and as such, Álvarez's matches since 2010 have been staged in Los Angeles, Las Vegas, Mexico City, Guadalajara, and Veracruz. De La Hoya revealed to the *Los Angeles Times* that thousands of Mexican fans enter the United States to attend each Álvarez fight scheduled on U.S. soil,[19] and ticket demand for Alvarez's bout with Lopez was so phenomenal that it prompted the MGM Grand to add 2,000 extra seats to its arena.[20] The website Brown Planet, which describes itself as a "Música Latina Fansite" but in reality is a collective, pan-ethnic Latino pride website devoted to various aspects of Latino popular culture, such as music, film, television, and sports, has even established a Saúl Álvarez fan club on its site.[21]

While Mexican and Mexican American fans express little-to-no doubt as to Canelo's ethnic authenticity, the discourses surrounding Álvarez on online boxing forums have been different, sparking debate as to where his appearance comes from and why, if he is Mexican, does he not (in the words of Larry Merchant) look like the other "Mexican-looking Mexicans?" One question, posted by username Cellz831 from Los Angeles on Eastside Boxing Forum asked, "Why do Canelo Alvarez fans . . . get mad when people call him white? . . . they get hurt and try really hard to prove hes [*sic*] not white. U have to be blind to not notice that he looks irish or somethin[*sic*]."[22] This question prompted several responses from other boxing fans, most of whom took exception with the idea that Álvarez be identified as "white" over "Mexican." One fan, going by the username HellSpawn86, felt that the move among U.S.-born white and black Americans to appropriate Latino fighters as their own was relatively commonplace:

> . . . what I do notice is that many U.S. whites would like to claim Alvarez or [Sergio] Martinez for their own, similar to blacks claiming "Tito" Trinidad in his heyday. In their respective backgrounds, they maybe white or black, but they are also Latinos and very proud of their countries and culture. Very different than white or black U.S. culture.[23]

Another boxing fan, named saul_ir34, took great exception to the "ignorance" displayed by this question, as well as some of the other respondents. Saul_ir34 provided the forum's participants with a basic overview of Mexican history, chronicling the Spanish conquest of indigenous peoples and the subsequent interactions that occurred over successive generations that produced the blended and phenotypically diverse Mexican society of today.[24]

While discussions of Canelo Álvarez's position within the socially constructed American racial categories remained relatively civil and devoid of overtly racist rhetoric within online *boxing* forums, these topics are also discussed in online *white supremacist* forums—where they take a much more hostile and malicious tone. What is most interesting about Álvarez's meteoric rise to fame is that while, on one hand, he has emerged as the current face of Mexican boxing and is the biggest fan favorite among Mexican and Mexican American boxing aficionados today, proponents of white supremacy have simultaneously attempted to appropriate Canelo as an alleged symbol of white racial superiority. The website Stormfront.org, an international white supremacist website, contains several threads on its online forums section that are devoted to discussions of Canelo Álvarez and his presumed or contested whiteness. These forums, ironically, invoke Canelo's athletic talents and his success in boxing as alleged "proof" of white racial supremacy over Mexicans, other Latinos, and African Americans in the boxing ring. Analysis of these racialized discourses of Canelo Álvarez among individuals with registered accounts at Stormfront.org reveals how those espousing white supremacist ideologies have, seemingly contradictorily, embraced a Mexican national as one of their own. Prior to examining the specific comments posted about Canelo on Stormfront.org, however, it is worthwhile to recount the general white supremacist movement in the United States and Europe, as well as the specific history and agenda of Stormfront.org.

WHITE SUPREMACY, WHITE NATIONALISM, AND STORMFRONT.ORG

A precise count of the number of persons aligned with white supremacist organizations in either the United States or Europe is difficult to enumerate, given that such groups generally prefer to maintain a low profile, and members do not always openly and publicly identify with, given the strong social stigma against white supremacist organizations among the general public. Nevertheless, social scientists and anti-extremist activists contend that the number of organized racist, extremist, and white supremacist groups has dramatically increased over the past two decades. In the mid-1990s, researchers identified 329 white supremacist organizations active in the United States and estimated that approximately 150,000 Americans either were members of white supremacist organizations or had links to white supremacist groups through regularly reading such groups' literature or participating in such groups' activities.[25] By 2011, however, civil rights and human relations monitoring groups estimated that the number of extremist organizations espousing white supremacist agendas had sharply increased to more than 1,200 groups,[26] primarily attributed to increased levels of immigration from Mexico and Latin America, the election of Barack Obama as the nation's first black president, and a press release by the U.S. Census Bureau in the spring of 2012 that 2011 marked the first year in American history in which the number of black, Asian, and Latino children born in the United States outnumbered the births of white children,[27] suggesting a profound demographic transition in the coming years.

Mark Potok, director of the Southern Poverty Law Center, an anti-racist human relations group that monitors hate group activities, responding to the rising number of hate groups in early twenty-first century American society, declaring that: "White supremacist groups have been having a meltdown ever since the census bureau predicted that non-Hispanic whites would lose the majority by 2050. The demographic change in this country is the single most important driver in hate groups and extremist groups over the last few years."[28] Immigration from Latin America, particularly Mexico, has played a profound role in this demographic shift, as the Latino population of the United States has more than tripled from 14.6 million in 1980 to more than 52 million by 2011.[29] Mexico remains the largest source of both legal and undocumented immigrants to the United States, and the younger median age of the Latino population, relative to the median age of the non-Hispanic white population, indicates that a greater portion of Latinos are in their prime child-bearing years than non-Hispanic whites, accounting for the birth rate differences between the two groups. As such, white supremacist rhetoric in the United States, which historically targeted primarily African Americans and Jews, today increasingly channels its vitriol towards Mexicans/Latinos and the alleged negative repercussions on American society and American whiteness.

Since the 1980s, sociologists have identified four major branches of the white supremacist movement in the United States; these include the Ku Klux Klan, the neo-Nazis, the Christian Identity movement, and the militia, or patriot, movement.[30] Of these four branches, the Ku Klux Klan is the oldest, most well-known, and identifiable, with its origins dating to shortly after the conclusion of the Civil War. The Neo-Nazi movement originated in 1958;[31] Neo-Nazis openly express admiration for Adolf Hitler and the Holocaust, and members often shave their heads and sport various tattoos depicting racist or Third Reich imagery. Experts regard Neo-Nazis the most violent wing of American white supremacy,[32] given that the vast majority of Neo-Nazis are working-class white males in their teens and early-to-mid twenties whose teenage angst, youthful rebelliousness, and impressionable age have inspired various incidents of violence over the years, such as the murder of a twenty-eight-year-old Ethiopian immigrant in Portland, Oregon, in November 1988[33] and the double murder and rape of three Cape Verdean immigrants in Brockton, Massachusetts, in January 2009.[34] Neo-Nazi violence gained additional awareness through the 1998 Academy Award-nominated film *American History X*, in which Edward Norton portrays an incarcerated neo-Nazi leader from southern California who renounces white supremacy while in prison and struggles to dissuade his younger brother from harboring racial prejudices. While neo-Nazis are known for a penchant towards violence, other wings of the white supremacist movement incorporate religious imagery into their ideology, such as the Christian Identity movement. The Idaho-based Aryan Nations constitute the best-known example of the Christian Identity movement, which engages in Biblical distortion to claim that white Anglo-Saxons are God's true "chosen people" and that Jews are the alleged "children of Satan" and, consequently, the ultimate enemy of white Christians.[35] The militia movement, also known as the "patriot movement," generally invokes racialized rhetoric to a much lesser degree than the other three branches, although its ideology, which envisions disgruntled patriotic citizens victimized by an overreaching federal government, does not entirely refrain from racist discourses[36] that mirror the other three branches, such as allegations that Jews secretly control the U.S. government and economy or that non-white immigrants are overrunning the nation.

   The advent of the Internet in the mid-1990s provided white supremacists with a new vehicle to bypass mainstream media outlets and directly reach the general public in effort to attract new members.[37] Additionally, the Internet and e-mail allowed persons who were curious about white supremacist groups and their beliefs, or who harbored such beliefs themselves, with new opportunities to discreetly access such materials in the privacy of their homes. Don Black, former Grand Wizard of the Alabama chapter of the Knights of the Ku Klux Klan in the 1970s, launched the Internet's first white supremacist website, Stormfront.org, in March 1995.[38] Black's goal in establishing Stormfront.org was to create an online community of white supremacists, facilitated by the site's message board forums, which first appeared in 1996.[39] In addition to the forums, which allowed registered users to post messages and ask questions, members could create personal profiles, post pictures, and directly contact one another. The site also contained a list of registered members' birthdays. Black also sponsored essay contests pertaining to race on his site, which awarded $2,000 university scholarships for white students.[40] Additionally, Black's teenage son Derek hosted a "white pride" radio program broadcast on Stormfront.org[41] and maintained a children's page on the site. Stormfront.org's pioneering status as the first-ever white supremacist website garnered significant media attention, and Black conducted several interviews with nationally televised news programs regarding his website and its ideology in the mid-to-late 1990s, which only served to increase traffic on the site.[42]

   By the early twenty-first century, Stormfront.org had achieved tremendous online success, and it remains the largest and most active white supremacist website to this day. Its registered membership increased exponentially from approximately 5,000 in 2002 to more than 130,000 by 2008.[43] In 2005, Stormfront.org was ranked as the "338th largest electronic forum on the Internet, putting it easily into the top one percent of all sites on the World Wide Web."[44] Don Black attributed the meteoric rise in his website's membership during 2008 to Barack Obama's presidential candidacy in an interview with *The Washington Post*:

> I get nonstop E-mails and private messages from new people who are mad as hell about the possibility of Obama being elected [president]. White people, for a long time, have thought of our government as being for us, and Obama is the best possible evidence that we've lost that. This is scaring a lot of people who maybe never considered themselves racists, and it's bringing them over to our side.[45]

In effort to attract more visitors to his site, in late 2008 Black attempted to "mainstream" Stormfront.org by implementing new guidelines that prohibited registered members from posting messages containing slurs such as "nigger" and "kike," while removing swastikas, pictures of Adolf Hitler, and other Nazi imagery from Stormfront's pages. Black also attempted to increase appeal by transforming his site from one that espoused explicit white *supremacy* to one that articulated white *nationalism*. Although obvious similarities persist between these two ideologies, white nationalism differs somewhat from classic white supremacy in that it eschews racial slurs and explicit expressions of racial hatred and calls for non-white genocide in exchange for a toned-down message of racial realism centered around notions of white victimization at the hands of non-whites.

Despite its revamped image, however, relatively little has substantively changed at Stormfront.org, and direct references to race remain commonplace on the site, including the use of antiquated pseudoscientific terms like "mulatto" and "mestizo."[46] The hallmark of white nationalist ideology is its insistence that white racial identity in North America and Europe is jeopardized by, and in dire need of defense against, multiculturalism, immigration from non-white and non-Western nations, crimes against whites committed by non-whites, and intermarriage and "interbreeding" between whites and non-whites. In fact, the boundary line between white nationalism and white supremacy is a blurry one, as "[w]hite nationalist groups espouse white supremacist or white separatist ideologies, often focusing on the alleged inferiority of non-whites," with the only significant distinction that white nationalist groups often "present themselves as serious, non-violent organizations and employ the language of academe."[47] Stormfront.org's homepage displays its logo consisting of a white Celtic cross encircled by the phrase, "White Pride World Wide," and another graphic appearing on its homepage proudly boasts that Stormfront is the "Voice of the new embattled *White* minority!"[48]

WHITE NATIONALISTS APPROPRIATE CANELO ÁLVAREZ

The forums on Stormfront.org discuss a wide range of social, political, and cultural issues, including contemporary pop culture. Members post thoughts and pose questions regarding various dimensions of pop culture, such as music, television, movies, and sports. These pop culture forums frequently criticize the perceived anti-white bias and pro-multiculturalism agendas of the arts and entertainment industries or praise white athletes who excel in sports usually dominated by non-whites. For example, discourses of Canelo Álvarez on Stormfront's forums frequently discuss the red-headed Mexican pugilist in a variety of racial taxonomic terms, including "white," "Celtic," "Aryan," "Nordic," etc. Similar discourses regarding former middleweight champion Sergio Martinez, an olive-complexioned Argentine prizefighter with jet-black hair and blue eyes, but whom white supremacists still consider "white enough" to count as one of their own, also exist on the Stormfront site. This trumpeting of white athletes' accomplishments on Stormfront.org dually serves as a means of expressing white racial pride and showcasing "evidence" of innate white superiority over black, Jewish, Latino, and other minority communities.

Following Álvarez's victory over British contender Matthew Hatton to capture the World Boxing Council's light middleweight title in March 2011, Stormfront's message board erupted with a thread triumphing Canelo's win. Despite the white nationalist and white supremacist nature of Stormfront, some comments refrained from explicit racism and instead expressed a degree of pride in Álvarez as allegedly of Irish/Celtic stock. One commenter, named LeoMcCarey, gleefully declared, "Saul looks like a son of Erin!,"[49] while another user, EuroVision, followed up this post by attempting to educate fellow white supremacists that approximately half a million Mexicans of Irish descent live in Mexico, particularly within Mexico City and the nation's northern provinces.[50] One user, going by the moniker Deer, posted, "His mother is of Irish descent; and his father is of Spanish descent. Great that there is 9 of them!"[51] This comment alludes to common constructions of gender roles within white supremacist discourses, discussed by sociologist Abby Ferber and others, in which the ultimate purpose of white womanhood is believed to be reproduction to continually populate the world with a new supply of white bodies.[52]

Other Stormfront subscribers invoked Canelo Álvarez for more sinister and hostile purposes by citing his championship credentials as evidence of white racial superiority, in discourses not unlike those that Adolf Hitler and the Third Reich invoked in claiming presumed Aryan racial athletic supremacy in the lead-up to the 1936 Olympics in Berlin. One Stormfront member, named latiniseurope, lauded Canelo on both sporting and racial grounds:

I am glad to hear Stormfront is hearing of Saul. Maybe like most whites of Mexican nationality, he is influenced by the media into not knowing much of his European roots, but I feel proud to have someone as him as a good athlete of Mexican nationality. I hope he beats that arrogant mestizo Julio Cesar Chavez, Jr. and maybe he can beat [Manny] Pacquiao ... Best wishes Saul![53]

This comment is particularly interesting in that latiniseurope pits Canelo Álvarez against his contemporary and co-national prizefighter Julio César Chávez, Jr. Chávez, Jr. and Canelo Álvarez are dually considered the best Mexican fighters in the sport today, as each has won world titles during their professional careers. Chávez, Jr. is the son of legendary six-time world champion Julio César Chávez, who most boxing experts regarding as one of the greatest pound-for-pound fighters in the sport's history. Latiniseurope's comment clearly elaborates that he does not see Álvarez and Chávez Jr. as simply *Mexican* nationals, but rather that he further divides Mexicans into "whites" and "mestizos"—with his admiration for Canelo stemming from his strong degree of European heritage and phenotypic features. The irony of discourses such as this, as revealed by numerous comments on Stormfront.org that elaborated upon or praised the European roots of Mexican society, is that the nativist rhetoric invoked in right-wing anti-immigration discourses in the United States over the past decade (which scholars credit heavily with reviving the organized white supremacist movement across the nation) have decried the influx of Mexicans for posing an alleged "threat" to whiteness in American society.

In heaping praise upon Canelo's proclaimed whiteness, the user Pinpoint declared, "At Stormfront, we tend to celebrate any White man triumphing in an important boxing bout. In fact we highlight almost any important White sporting victory."[54] Still, other Stormfront members (albeit a small minority of commenters) questioned or flat-out rejected the idea of Saúl Álvarez as belonging to the "white race" or extending white racial pride to Canelo. A user named MVSN fumed, "We are reduced to trumpeting white male prowess (to all those white women that lust after brown skin) by a white Mexican? What the hell is that? No such thing. He's either Spanish or he's an Indian."[55]

Stormfront.org's message board again lit up with postings pertaining to Canelo Álvarez on 31 May 2013, just a few weeks after boxing promoters announced that Canelo would face undefeated ten-time world champion Floyd Mayweather, Jr., an African American, in a bout scheduled to be held on Mexican Independence Day Weekend 2013. Mayweather's undefeated record, his reputation as the greatest pound-for-pound fighter in boxing today, and his outspokenly arrogant demeanor have made Mayweather both loved and hated by ardent boxing fans and the general public for years, and at times, Mayweather's detractors have invoked racist, anti-black slurs and insults to express their opposition to him. Rather than use the opportunity to denigrate Mayweather, however, Stormfront's members primarily revisited the debate over Canelo's racial identity, with most members expressing support for the Mexican slugger and arguing for him to be accepted as a fellow white man. For example, one member named Xizor commented, "Well he sure as hell isn't brown. Looks White to me! I hope he kicks Mayweather's Black ass."[56] A different user named yelnatSSyerhpmuh shared similar views and posted "Yes he is definitely white. Only Europeans carry the genes for red or blonde hair."[57] Another Stormfront member, Redarrowhead, asserted: "Hispanics have a lot of white blood in them. My rule is if he looks white he is. I consider many white Hispanics white or heavily white."[58]

Some Stormfront members took contrarian views, however. One member, username Coldstar whose profile identifies him as a "Stormfront Regular," declared, "Red hair is not a sign of people being Whites at all. Mixed races also sometimes have red hair. Also, many Jews are Caucasians but that does not make them of a Northern White ancient native European line."[59] Another member, going by the username Analyst, objected to Canelo being considered white:

> Mestizos sometimes have freckles. Many whites from the Americas (USA included) are actually predominantly Caucasoid with minor Amerindian. People from USA, Argentina, etc who claim to be white cannot be automatically assumed to be white even if the Amerindian is not apparent to most people. Most people would not see the Amerindian in Brad Pitt, for example, but it is there. A close analysis is always due. To answer the [Original Poster's] question: no, [Canelo Álvarez] is not white.[60]

These last two postings are interesting because, while in the minority on Stormfront.org, they reject the most commonly cited alleged physical "proofs" of Canelo Álvarez's whiteness, his reddish hair and freckled face. Analyst's post alludes to the fact that race is not necessarily clear-cut, and a person's racial identity is not always easily identifiable—points that fly in the face of customary white supremacist ideology, which is based on biological racial essentialism,[61] that is, the idea that "races" are biologically real and mutually exclusive, self-evident, and easily distinguishable from one another. To take this point further, Coldstar's post alludes to a fundamental philosophical problem that has troubled white supremacists for decades, namely the question of who is "white" and just what, exactly, constitutes whiteness? White supremacists disagree on this topic, with some utilizing a relatively loose and inclusive definition of whiteness (whereby any person of alleged "pure" European, Middle Eastern, or Arab ancestry is deemed "white"), while others invoke a much more limited and exclusionary definition of whiteness (restricting "white" identity only to persons of Northern European extraction). Of course, biologists and physical anthropologists have long noted that biologically-distinct human races do not exist within the human species, and any attempts at categorizing people into races is ultimately a social project, rather than a biological or scientific one.[62] Distinct racial blood types do not exist, and contrary to popular misconception, physical traits such as freckles and reddish or blondish hair are not exclusive to persons of Northern European ancestry.

CONCLUSION

Critical analysis of Canelo Álvarez's fanfare thus reveals that he is dually embraced as an icon, a sports hero, and a symbol of pride among two segments of society that are otherwise antithetical to one another, that is, the Mexican/Mexican American community and white nationalists/supremacists. Canelo's standing among Mexican and Mexican American boxing fans is relatively clear-cut and understandable; after all, he is the latest in a long line of outstanding, fan-favorite ethnic Mexican boxing champions that include Bobby Chacón, Salvador Sánchez, Julio César Chávez, Oscar De La Hoya, Marco Antonio Barrera, and Erik Morales. Among white nationalists and supremacists, the fascination with Canelo Álvarez is a much more complex and contradictory story. One on hand, professional boxing in the United States has long been marked by the periodic emergence of the "great white hope" dating to the days of Jack Johnson, that is, the rise of a white champion who achieves boxing success by triumphing against the black and Latino masses who have dominated the sport since World War II. On the other hand, white nationalists/supremacists have vehemently condemned Mexicans (along with Mexican culture, the Spanish language, and Mexico in general) as constituting a "danger" to American society, in general, and American whiteness, in particular, in recent years.

Of course, this seemingly schizophrenic reaction to Saúl "Canelo" Álvarez among white nationalists/supremacists is just one small example of the larger and much more complex history of the contradictory social positioning of Mexicans within the socially constructed hierarchy of racial categories in the United States. Since the annexation of Texas and the other present-day southwestern states at the conclusion of the U.S.-Mexico War in 1848, Mexicans have occupied an ambiguous status within American constructions of race. Although some lawmakers in the nineteenth and early twentieth centuries considered Mexicans to be "racially inferior" and "biologically tainted by Indian blood,"[63] Mexicans were officially considered as "white" by the federal government and were exempt from racially restrictive immigration policies enacted in 1921 and 1924. Nevertheless, anti-Mexican prejudice remained strong throughout the southwest, as the larger American public tended to socially regard Mexicans as "non-white," and in 1930, the U.S. Census Bureau even established "Mexican" as its own distinct racial category, although this Mexican racial category was rescinded a decade later.[64] Skin color and physical appearance differs widely in Mexico and among Mexican Americans, but this fact is generally not well-known among non-Mexicans—which helps fuel the public fascination surrounding Canelo Álvarez's phenotype.

NOTES

1. The Leadership Conference, "The State of Hate: Escalating Violence Against Immigrants," *Civilrights.org*, 2014, http://www.civilrights.org/publications/hatecrimes/escalating-violence.html, accessed 30 July 2014.

2. Jim Avila, Elizabeth Tribolet, and Chris Francescani, "Hate Makes a Comeback," *ABC News*, 1 May 2007, http://abcnews.go.com/TheLaw/story?id=3104860, accessed 5 July 2014.

3. Southern Poverty Law Center, "Former Klansman Admits Plot to Bomb Migrants," *SPLC.org*, Fall 2005, http://www.splcenter.org/get-informed/intelligence-report/browse-all-issues/2005/fall/domestic-terrorism, accessed 5 July 2014.

4. Elizabeth Kadetsky, "Bashing Illegals in California," *The Nation*, 17 October 1994, 418.

5. Nelson, Leah, "The Astonishing Bigotry and Paranoia of Russell Pearce," *Hatewatch*, 18 July 2012, http://www.splcenter.org/blog/2012/07/18/the-astonishing-bigotry-and-paranoia-of-russell-pearce/, accessed 2 July 2014.

6. "*Unforgiveable Blackness*: About the Film," *PBS.org*, January 2005, http://www.pbs.org/unforgivableblackness/about/, accessed 2 July 2014.

7. Justin D. García, "Boxing, Masculinity, and *Latinidad*: Oscar De La Hoya, Fernando Vargas, and *Raza* Representations," *The Journal of American Culture*, Vol. 36, No. 4 (2013): 335.

8. "Larry Holmes vs. Gerry Cooney," *Boxrec.com*, 10 June 2014, http://boxrec.com/media/index.php/Larry_Holmes_vs._Gerry_Cooney, accessed 2 July 2014.

9. "Holmes vs. Cooney," 2014.

10. "Holmes vs. Cooney," 2014.

11. Nigel Collins, "Another Colorful Boxing Incongruity," *ESPN.com*, 17 July 2013, http://www.chicagomanualofstyle.org/tools_citationguide.html, accessed 30 June 2014.

12. Collins, "Another Colorful Boxing Incongruity," 2013.

13. Dan Rafael, "Saul Alvarez is Prospect of the Year," *ESPN.com*, 29 December 2010, http://sports.espn.go.com/sports/boxing/columns/story?id=5962041, accessed 5 July 2014.

14. "Sául 'Canelo' Álvarez vs. Ryan Rhodes." *HBO Boxing After Dark*. Home Box Office, 18 June 2011.

15. "Mexican looking Mexican," *Youtube.com*, 5 May 2012, https://www.youtube.com/watch?v=5XWBpZlpt5Q, accessed 2 July 2014.

16. "Mexican looking Mexican."

17. García, Justin D., "Boxing, Masculinity, and *Latinidad*," 335.

18. Garcia, "Boxing, Masculinity, and *Latinidad*," 335.

19. Bill Dwyre, "Canelo Alvarez Does His Fighting in the Ring Now," *Los Angeles Times*, 12 September 2012, http://articles.latimes.com/2012/sep/12/sports/la-sp-0913-dwyre-boxing-20120913, accessed 2 July 2014.

20. Dwyre, "Canelo Alvarez Does His Fighting in the Ring Now."

21. "100% Saul Alvarez Fan Club," *Brownplanet.com*, 28 December 2011, http://www.brownplanet.com/saul-alvarez/, accessed 2 July 2014.

22. "Why Do Canelo Alvarez Fans...," *Boxing News 24*, 31 January 2012, http://www.boxingforum24.com/showthread.php?t=377803, accessed 2 July 2014.

23. "Why Do Canelo Alvarez Fans.".

24. "RE: Why Do Canelo Alvarez Fans...," *Boxing News 24*, 31 January 2012, http://www.boxingforum24.com/showthread.php?t=377803&page=2, accessed 2 July 2014.

25. Abby L. Ferber, "The White Supremacist Movement in the United States Today," in *Race and Ethnic Conflict: Contending Views on Prejudice, Discrimination, and Ethnoviolence*, 2nd edition, ed. Fred L. Pincus and Howard J. Ehrlich (Boulder, CO: Westview Press, 1999), 346.

26. Kim Severson, "Number of U.S. Hate Groups is Rising, Report Says," *New York Times*, 7 March 2012, http://www.nytimes.com/2012/03/08/us/number-of-us-hate-groups-on-the-rise-report-says.html?_r=1&, accessed 2 July 2014.

27. Colleen Curry, "Hate Groups Grow as Racial Tipping Point Changes Demographics," *ABC News*, 18 May 2012, http://abcnews.go.com/US/militias-hate-groups-grow-response-minority-population-boom/story?id=16370136, accessed 2 July 2014.

28. Curry, "Hate Groups," 2012.

29. Emily Badger, "The Extraordinary 30-Year Growth of the U.S. Hispanic Population," *Citylab.com*, 30 August 2013, http://www.citylab.com/politics/2013/08/extraordinary-growth-americas-hispanic-population/6733/, accessed 2 July 2014.

30. Abby L. Ferber, "The White Supremacist Movement in the United States Today," 348–50.

31. Ferber, "The White Supremacist Movement," 348–49.

32. Ferber, "The White Supremacist Movement," 349.

33. Ravleen Kaur, "The Mulugeta Seraw Murder: 25 Years Later," *Wilmette Week*, 21 November 2013, http://www.wweek.com/portland/blog-30937 the_mulugeta_seraw_murder_ 25_years _later.html, accessed 30 July 2014.

34. Brian Ballou, "Self-Described Neo-Nazi Guilty of 2009 Brockton Murders, Rape," *The Boston Globe*, 30 May 2013, http://www.bostonglobe.com/metro/2013/05/30/self-described-white-supremacist-keith-luke-convicted-first-degree-murder-for-rampage/UOI1ACrfLJg Gbny2QluitI/story.html, accessed 30 July 2014.

35. Ferber, "The White Supremacist Movement," 349.

36. Ferber, "The White Supremacist Movement," 349–50.

37. Ferber, "The White Supremacist Movement," 346.

38. Southern Poverty Law Center, "Stormfront," *SPLC.org*, 2014, http://www.splcenter.org/get-informed/intelligence-files/groups/stormfront, accessed 2 July 2014.

39. Southern Poverty Law Center, "The Forums," *SPLC.org*, Summer 2005, http://www.splcenter.org/get-informed/intelligence-report/browse-all-issues/2005/ summer/electronic-storm/the-forums, accessed 2 July 2014.

40. "Stormfront," accessed 2 July 2014.

41. Caitlin Dickson, "Derek Black, the Reluctant Racist, and His Exist from White Nationalism," *The Daily Beast*, 29 July 2013, http://www.thedailybeast.com/articles/2013/07/29/derek-black-the-reluctant-racist-and-his-exit-from-white-nationalism.html, accessed 5 July 2014.

42. "Stormfront," accessed 2 July 2014.

43. Southern Poverty Law Center, "Don Black," *SPLC.org*, 2014, http://www.splcenter.org/get-informed/intelligence-files/profiles/don-black, accessed 2 July 2014.

44. T.K. Kim, "Hate Website Stormfront Sees Rapid Growth of Neo-Nazi Community," *SPLC.org*, Summer 2005, http://www.splcenter.org/get-informed/intelligence-report/browse-all-issues/2005/summer/electronic-storm, accessed 2 July 2014.

45. "Don Black," accessed 2 July 2014.

46. Although not used in scientific or medical research today, white supremacists still frequently use these terms in their racial rhetoric. Both terms derive from 16th and 17th century Spanish and Portuguese colonial practices of attempting to racially classify the peoples inhabiting the territories they conquered. "Mulatto," stemming from "mule," was used to describe a person of both African and European ancestry, while "mestizo," Spanish for "mixed," was used in reference to an individual of both indigenous and European ancestry.

47. Southern Poverty Law Center, "White Nationalist," *SPLC.org*, 2014, http://www.splcenter.org/get-informed/intelligence-files/ideology/white-nationalist, accessed 2 July 2014.

48. "Introduction," *Stormfront.org*, 2014, https://www.stormfront.org/forum/t538924/, accessed 5 July 2014.

49. "White Mexican boxer Saul Alvarez (aged 21) wins WBC title against Ricky Hattons [sic] brother," *Stormfront.org*, 7 March 2011, https://www.stormfront.org/forum/t785086/, accessed 2 July 2014.

50. "White Mexican boxer," 2011.

51. "White Mexican boxer Saul Alvarez (aged 21) wins WBC title against Ricky Hattons [sic] brother," *Stormfront.org*, 8 March 2011, https://www.stormfront.org/forum/t785086-2/, accessed 2 July 2014.

52. Ferber, "The White Supremacist Movement," 352–53.

53. "White Mexican boxer Saul Alvarez (aged 21) wins WBC title against Ricky Hattons [*sic*] brother," *Stormfront.org*, 8 March 2011, https://www.stormfront.org/forum/t785086-2/, accessed 2 July 2014.

54. "White Mexican boxer," 2011.

55. "White Mexican boxer Saul Alvarez (aged 21) wins WBC title against Ricky Hattons [*sic*] brother," *Stormfront.org*, 7 March 2011, https://www.stormfront.org/forum/t785086/, accessed 2 July 2014.

56. "Is Saul Alvarez White (Caucasian)?," *Stormfront.org*, 31 May 2013, https://www.stormfront.org/forum/t848297-3/, accessed 5 July 2014.

57. "Is Saul Alvarez White (Caucasian)?," *Stormfront.org*, 22 July 2013, https://www.stormfront.org/forum/t848297-7/, accessed 5 July 2014.

58. "Is Saul Alvarez White (Caucasian)?," *Stormfront.org*, 31 May 2013, https://www.stormfront.org/forum/t848297-3/, accessed 5 July 2014.

59. "Is Saul Alvarez White (Caucasian)?," *Stormfront.org*, 31 May 2013, https://www.stormfront.org/forum/t848297-5/, accessed 5 July 2014.

60. "Is Saul Alvarez White," 2013.

61. Ferber, "The White Supremacist Movement," 350-351.

62. Jonathan Marks, "Black, White, Other: Racial Categories are Cultural Constructs Masquerading as Biology," *Natural History*, December 1994, 33–35.

63. Adalberto Aguirre Jr. and Jonathan H. Turner, *American Ethnicity: The Dynamics and Consequences of Discrimination,* 7th ed., (New York: McGraw-Hill, 2009), 205–6.

64. Neil Foley, "Becoming Hispanic: Mexicans Americans and Whiteness," in *White Privilege: Essential Readings on the Other Side of Racism*, 3rd edition, ed. Paula S. Rothenberg (New York: Worth Publishers, 2008), 59–60.

REFERENCES

Adalberto Aguirre Jr. and Jonathan H. Turner. *American Ethnicity: The Dynamics and Consequences of Discrimination,* 7th ed. New York: McGraw-Hill, 2009.

Avila, Jim, Elizabeth Tribolet, and Chris Francescani. "Hate Makes a Comeback." *ABC News*, 1 May 2007. http://abcnews.go.com/TheLaw/story?id=3104860. Accessed 5 July 2014.

Badger, Emily. "The Extraordinary 30-Year Growth of the U.S. Hispanic Population." *Citylab.com*, 30 August 2013. http://www.citylab.com/politics/2013/08/extraordinary-growth-americas-hispanic-population/6733/. Accessed 2 July 2014.

Ballou, Brian. "Self-Described Neo-Nazi Guilty of 2009 Brockton Murders, Rape." *The Boston Globe*, 30 May 2013. http://www.bostonglobe.com/metro/2013/05/30/self-described-white-supremacist-keith-luke-convicted-first-degree-murder forrampage/UOI1ACrfLJgGbny2QluitI/story.html. Accessed 30 July 2014.

Collins, Nigel. "Another Colorful Boxing Incongruity." *ESPN.com*, 17 July 2013. http://espn.go.com/boxing/story/_/id/9485865/why-boxing-only-sport-left-which-ok-root-your-guy. Accessed 30 June 2014.

Curry, Colleen. "Hate Groups Grow as Racial Tipping Point Changes Demographics." *ABC News*, 18 May 2012. http://abcnews.go.com/US/militias-hate-groups-grow-response-minority-population-boom/story?id=16370136. Accessed 2 July 2014.

Dickson, Caitlin. "Derek Black, the Reluctant Racist, and His Exist from White Nationalism." *The Daily Beast*, 29 July 2013. http://www.thedailybeast.com/articles/2013/07/29/derek-black-the-reluctant-racist-and-his-exit-from-white-nationalism.html. Accessed 5 July 2014.

"Don Black." Southern Poverty Law Center. *SPLC.org*, 2014. http://www.splcenter.org/get-informed/intelligence-files/profiles/don-black. Accessed 2 July 2014.

Dwyre, Bill. "Canelo Alvarez Does His Fighting in the Ring Now." *Los Angeles Times*, 12 September 2012. http://articles.latimes.com/2012/sep/12/sports/la-sp-0913-dwyre-boxing-20120913. Accessed 2 July 2014.

Ferber, Abby L. "The White Supremacist Movement in the United States Today." In *Race and Ethnic Conflict: Contending Views on Prejudice, Discrimination, and Ethnoviolence*, 2nd edition, ed. Fred L. Pincus and Howard J. Ehrlich. Boulder, CO: Westview Press, 1999. 346-354.

Foley, Neil. "Becoming Hispanic: Mexicans Americans and Whiteness." In *White Privilege: Essential Readings on the Other Side of Racism*, 3rd edition, ed. Paula S. Rothenberg. New York: Worth Publishers, 2008. 59–60.

"Former Klansman Admits Plot to Bomb Migrants." Southern Poverty Law Center. *SPLC.org*, Fall 2005. http://www.splcenter.org/getinformed/intelligence-report/browse-all-issues/2005/fall/domestic-terrorism. Accessed 5 July 2014.

"The Forums." Southern Poverty Law Center, *SPLC.org*, Summer 2005. http://www.splcenter.org/get-informed/intelligence-report/browse-all-issues/2005/summer/electronic-storm/the-forums. Accessed 2 July 2014.

García, Justin D. "Boxing, Masculinity, and *Latinidad*: Oscar De La Hoya, Fernando Vargas, and *Raza* Representations." In *The Journal of American Culture*, 2013: Vol. 36, No. 4: 323–41.

"Is Saul Alvarez White (Caucasian)?" *Stormfront.org*, 22 July 2013. https://www.stormfront. org/forum/t848297-7/. Accessed 5 July 2014.

Kadetsky, Elizabeth. "Bashing Illegals in California." *The Nation*, 17 October 1994, 418.

Kaur, Ravleen. "The Mulugeta Seraw Murder: 25 Years Later." *Wilmette Week*, 21 November 2013.   http://www.wweek.com/portland/blog-30937-the_mulugeta_seraw_murder_25_ years_later.html. Accessed 30 July 2014.

Kim, T. K. "Hate Website Stormfront Sees Rapid Growth of Neo-Nazi Community," *SPLC.org*,   Summer   2005.   http://www.splcenter.org/get-informed/intelligence-report/ browse-all-issues/2005/summer/electronic-storm. Accessed 2 July 2014.

The Leadership Conference. "The State of Hate: Escalating Violence Against Immigrants," *Civilrights.org* 2014. http://www.civilrights.org/publications/hatecrimes/escalating-vio- lence.html. Accessed 30 July 2014.

"Larry Holmes vs. Gerry Cooney." *Boxrec.com*, 10 June 2014. http://boxrec.com/media/in- dex.php/Larry_Holmes_vs._Gerry_Cooney. Accessed 2 July 2014.

Marks, Jonathan. "Black, White, Other: Racial Categories are Cultural Constructs Masquerad- ing as Biology." *Natural History*, December 1994: 33–35.

"Mexican looking Mexican." *Youtube.com*, 5 May 2012. https://www.youtube.com/watch?v= 5XWBpZlpt5Q. Accessed 2 July 2014.

Nelson, Leah. "The Astonishing Bigotry and Paranoia of Russell Pearce." *Hatewatch*, 18 July 2012.   http://www.splcenter.org/blog/2012/07/18/the-astonishing-bigotry-and-paranoiaof- russell-pearce/. Accessed 2 July 2014.

"100% Saul Alvarez Fan Club." *Brownplanet.com*, 28 December 2011. http://www. brownplanet.com/saul-alvarez/. Accessed 2 July 2014.

Rafael, Dan. "Saul Alvarez is Prospect of the Year," *ESPN.com*, 29 December 2010. http:// sports.espn.go.com/sports/boxing/columns/story?id=5962041. Accessed 5 July 2014.

"Sául 'Canelo' Álvarez vs. Ryan Rhodes." *HBO Boxing After Dark*. Home Box Office, 18 June 2011.

Severson, Kim. "Number of U.S. Hate Groups is Rising, Report Says." *New York Times*, 7 March 2012. http://www.nytimes.com/2012/03/08/us/number-of-us-hate-groups-on-the- rise-report-says.html?_r=1&. Accessed 2 July 2014.

"Stormfront." Southern Poverty Law Center. *PLC.org*, 2014. http://www.splcenter.org/get-in- formed/intelligence-files/groups/stormfront. Accessed 2 July 2014,

"*Unforgiveable Blackness*: About the Film." *PBS.org*, January 2005. http://www.pbs.org/un- forgivableblackness/about/. Accessed 2 July 2014.

"White Mexican boxer Saul Alvarez (aged 21) wins WBC title against Ricky Hattons [*sic*] brother." *Stormfront.org*, 7 March 2011. https://www.stormfront.org/forum/t785086/. Ac- cessed 2 July 2014.

"White Nationalist." Southern Poverty Law Center. *SPLC.org*, 2014.http://www.splcenter.org/ get-informed/intelligence-files/ideology/white-nationalist. Accessed 2 July 2014.

"Why Do Canelo Alvarez Fans...," *Boxing News 24*, 31 January 2012. http://www. boxingforum24.com/showthread.php?t=377803. Accessed 2 July 2014.

Chapter Fourteen

The Roots of East German Xenophobia

Freya Klier

In April 2013, Beate Zschäpe, the last surviving member of the right-wing extremist terror cell the National Socialist Underground (NSU) was brought to trial in Munich. Along with her, four neo-Nazi supporters are being tried.[1] Since Zschäpe's arrest, 1,200 witnesses have been deposed and more than 6,000 documents were amassed and entered into evidence. This trial puts the victims' families through emotional trauma one more time, but hopefully it will also constitute an enduring history lesson for all of us. Three young men and women from the former German Democratic Republic (GDR) embarked on a multi-year rampage in the West to kill. Nine of the victims hailed from a "migrant background—they were German Turks, or more recent Turkish immigrants, one German policewoman was also killed. In addition to these murders, the perpetrators also carried out bombings, bank robberies, and aggravated arson. After the arrest and the onset of the trial, in the spring of 2013, topics such as "the terror cell from Zwickau," "the Thuringian home-land protectors," "the Nazi bride," and "the Jena brigade" once again domi-nate the media—and so does the shocking failure of national security. The euphemism "döner killings" was the label under which the search for the perpetrators began, and in 2011, this moniker was declared "worst misnomer of the year." This is a good sign. But it begs the question: Will we now look more closely at the causes of such crimes, this time beginning with the question of origin: What kind of environment, what type of social formation, produced the murderers?

After all, the former GDR is a region where crimes of xenophobic vio-lence—seen in relation to its population rate—are twice as high as in the West even today . . . which of course does not render those crimes less horrible. There was a time when the ratio of xenophobic violent crime in the East versus the West was eight to one. That was roughly in the mid-nineties.[2]

At that time, in February 1995, Beate Zschäpe registered a planned demonstration of the "interest group Thuringian Homeland Protection" with the motto "For the preservation of Thuringian identity, against internationalization by the European Community" (emphasis in the original). The following year, Uwe Böhnhardt—one of the NSU murderers—hung a doll bearing a yellow star from a highway bridge in Jena, and in addition, he rigged up a fake bomb.[3]

Two young men, educated as children and young adults in the GDR, take to the road, traveling to Nuremberg, Kassel, Dortmund, Hamburg, Cologne, and Munich—they will attack more than once in some cities—on a mission to kill others who do not look as German as they do. It is remarkable that these "murderous homeland protectors" emerged from an area where foreign cultures are virtually absent.[4] So then was the single killing they committed in the East—the one in Rostock—for them a test of courage similar to the one in which they killed the young policewoman in Heilbronn?

Or was it an allusion to the xenophobic pogrom atmosphere of Rostock-Lichtenhagen? In 1992, this city witnessed the most massive xenophobic attacks in postwar German history. In front of a dormitory for former Vietnamese contract laborers who wanted to remain in Germany, several hundred agitators, mostly right-wing extremists, had gathered and were making trouble, and then they firebombed the dwelling which, at that moment, was home to more than 100 Vietnamese men, women, and children. At the scene, 3,000 bystanders were watching and fiercely applauding—mostly locals from the neighboring apartment blocs, who also obstructed the work of the police and the fire department. At times the police withdrew from the area completely and abandoned the people who were trapped in the burning building. We all remember the TV images, which showed desperate people trying to save themselves by climbing onto the roof of the high rise, helped up by a social worker.

Such horrific incidents were not the exception. Directly following the Fall of the Wall, some skins in Dresden attacked a contract laborer from Mozambique and threw him out of a moving tram. Shortly afterwards, he died of his injuries. At this point, there were already a few comrades from the West involved.

In Wittenberg, young men throw a man from Namibia from the fourth floor of a building; in Eberswalde, east of Berlin, they hunt down an asylum seeker until he is killed. In 1991, in an elevated train near Berlin, twelve power-drunk youths yell: "Nigger, get down on your knees!" as they beat up a man from Sudan, with several girls egging them on. The man ends up in hospital because he had ignored the unwritten law for those who look different not to be out and about on Eastern subways or trams after 6:00 pm. Once the train makes a stop in Berlin-Karow that night, they throw the African man—a father of a toddler—from the car like a piece of meat. He is still able to speak and asks the female train conductor to stop the train so that he might call the police. The woman replies: "I am not allowed to stop the train and anyway, this kind of thing happens here all the time."[5] How do people become so dehumanized after spending their lives in a dictatorship?

But this case also demonstrates a different viewpoint. For once he arrives back at his residence in Berlin-Schöneberg, the injured Sudanese man drags himself to the police station. A police officer makes note of the incident—he does it correctly and even with some engagement. But the actual report has to be sent to his colleagues in Berlin-Pankow in the East, and "the time it'll take until your case file returns from there to here," he warns the Sudanese man, "that'll be three weeks from now."

Now this is an experience I encountered myself for many years in the GDR: the police were in league with right-wing extremists! I vividly remember the Fascist mob in October 1987, attacking my neighborhood church, screaming "Sieg Heil" and "Jews get out of German churches!" I remember how they lashed out with broken bottles at fleeing punks. The police, who were called to the scene by myself and some others, seemed less than motivated to stop them. "Jews get out of German churches?" I wondered, "Are there any Jews left in the GDR?" The few, tiny Jewish communities were literally never in the news, and just one year earlier, I had been collecting signatures with a few friends to stop the destruction of the Jewish cemetery in Berlin-Weißensee that had been ordered by the leadership of the Socialist Unity Party (SED). Jewishness came up prior to 1987 only in the context of a remark that was often heard and did not seem to bother many: "They must have forgotten to send you to the gas chamber?!" . . .

The masters were always referring to "anti-Fascism" as their propaganda tool, which they clubbed over people's heads relentlessly. But de facto the GDR was turning into an increasingly right-wing extremist state. The behavioral patterns acquired and inculcated during the Nazi period also served their purpose during the second German dictatorship. We in the GDR had no 1968, quite the contrary: the responsibility for World War II was delegated wholesale to the West Germans ". . . the place where all the Nazis fled to and are now being harbored," that was the received wisdom every child of school-age would be told for forty years. Consequently, obsequiousness, obedience to authority, and lack of everyday oppositional spirit remained popular—those who opposed living this way were punished.

ONE INDIVIDUAL FROM WEST GERMANY DID SEIZE ON THIS WITH ALACRITY: FRANZ SCHÖNHUBER

Beginning in 1991, Franz Schönhuber, former member of the NSDAP, now party rep of the right-wing extremist "Republicans," makes several recruiting trips to the East. Here he replenishes the scanty Western ranks of his party with old communist party cadres. He selects, by the way, an army sergeant from Berlin-Strausberg. But even more promising is a professor from Leipzig, a long-time SED member and program chair of Sociology in the department of "Scientific Communism" at Leipzig's Karl-Marx-University. This man is promoted to the role of Saxony's regional representative for the right-wing Republicans.

Schönhuber loves the GDR. Sometimes, he opines: "The GDR was much more German than the Federal Republic of Germany (FRG). Here they still had family values and not that society of every man for himself,"—other times, he praises the "orderly goosestep" of the army, or the "almost complete freedom from the foreign element." . . . This right-wing politician hits the nail on the head.

Then, he had not yet realized what else his socialist comrades in the East would be offering him: a strong, barely disguised anti-Semitism that had been nurtured for 40 years (there, where no Jews were visible in the public sphere) as well as a coercive approach towards the very small minority of foreigners, who were only allowed temporary sojourn in the isolationist GDR. They were not liked: however, after the mass flight of millions of GDR citizens, such a profound shortage of qualified workers occurred—that the GDR Leadership decided against their better judgment to admit some contingents of Vietnamese and Mozambicans.—"Alien workers," as Oskar Lafontaine would call them.[6] They would stay for three years—then they would be swapped out.

How did they fare? "Fidschis and Mocis," as they were called, were housed in segregated living quarters; the regular pubs were off-limits for them. They were forbidden to leave the city precincts, and the German language—they were not supposed to learn any at all. Most importantly, and this still has the power to render far right extremists misty-eyed—Vietnamese women were forced to have abortions. On this point, a government treaty between the GDR and the Socialist Republic of Vietnam dating back to 1980 and renewed in 1987, entitled "Agreement about Protocol in Case of Pregnancy of Vietnamese Female Workers," reads as follows;

> "Pregnancy and motherhood change the personal situation of those women of working age so profoundly that the ensuing demands of part-time labor and qualification cannot be realized. Those Vietnamese women who will not resort to available pregnancy prevention methods or abortion, must be sent home early after a doctor attest to their ability to travel." That trip home had to be paid for by the worker herself.[7]

Could there be a more far-right program? Those who enacted these policies have since renamed themselves a few times and are now performing a show they call "Die Linke"—"The Left." Right after the fall of the Wall, they began to scapegoat the West for their own failings and dodgy machinations.

GDR propaganda would sonorously intone: "Solidarity with the Peoples of the World," but in practice, they were not allowed entry. The policies of the reigning socialists were grist for the mill for those who resented anything that deviated from the norm. Never did the homeless taint the grey streetscape of the GDR—those who were not invested in work would find themselves behind bars labeled "asocial," where they would be put to work, but for slave wages. For the handicapped, there were no ramps; integrated schools were unknown.

And I will never forget Leipzig, where I was a theater student in the 1970s. My fellow student Angela had begun a liaison with a Nigerian student (who of course was sent home immediately after he finished his studies). One day, she showed up in class with a black eye. Her dad, a Socialist Unity Party secretary, had hit her saying: "Over my dead body, you are not going out with a nigger, Geli—your mission is to be a role model!"

Most functionaries and most GDR citizens were uncomfortable with any deviation from the norm—whether it was the vivid hair color sported by punks or "Negroes" or "Fidschis," or the handicapped or even just people with unusual headgear.

It would be fatal to omit that even under GDR-conditions there were always those who fought for tolerance and public spiritedness. Those for whom such notions were not just words. Even in the East, after the Fall of the Wall, citizens placed themselves in a protective cordon around the dorms of asylum seekers, ducking rocks when the local police force was nowhere to be seen.

But these people were never the norm. The norm was the attitude of the citizens of Hoyerswerda, where in 1991, thirty Skinheads managed by a barrage of violence to drive out all foreigners from their city. Here again, workers and employees, the next-door neighbors, applauded frenetically,— the Press called them "curious rubberneckers"—a euphemism—when the dormitory for the traumatized asylum seekers had to be evacuated.[8] How many decades will a society function according to these deeply internalized behavioral patterns?

In September 1990, I published an essay in the "Jewish Weekly" about anti-Semitism and xenophobia that I had written long ago, back in the time of the GDR. That netted me spot number eight on the kill list of GDR neo-Nazis, as a renegade neo-Nazi was to tell me years later. I had written up what was going on in our German organized bloc supervisor system, back then when the Federal Republic was not even present in the East.

I wrote about the Vietnamese women and my old Jewish friend Johanna. She faced the same Nazi who had raped her in 1935 and had pushed her into the Elbe River to drown,—now as party Secretary of the SED.[9] I wrote about the agricultural production society (*Landesproduktionsgenossenschaft*) where I was invited and where the drunk farmers danced a conga line out-doors squeezing by the lawn furniture—all of them belting out the Nazi song about "the little Polish town"—every last one—from the lowest farmhand right up to the SED-Party Secretary. I wrote about our short theater play against racism, that I had rehearsed with two Berlin youths who had been born as offspring of a German-Sudanese student love affair. Those boys grew up being called "nigger" and "coal" (their father was not granted the right to remain in the GDR) and finally, they had to be placed in a special platoon in the GDR army, so that they had a shot at surviving mandatory army service. As I was saying—we were rehearsing this theater play in an era when the "antifascist protection wall" was still protecting us from the Western Nazis.

Respect for human life—for every human life—was not part of the educa-tional program in the GDR's daily practice. Respect was only afforded those who conformed to the political agenda of the socialists and who met their expectations of a certain outward appearance. Many failed, and it was no accident that for many years, the East German suicide rate was the second highest in the world. The skins, by contrast, did meet the visual norms. This is why I raise the question once again: did the ideation of the Böhnhardts, Mundlos, and Zschäpes—and the many other neo-Nazis—develop in a vacu-um?

In 1993, I was present at a citizens' gathering in Berlin-Köpenick, where the residents of a development of single-family homes were informed that soon a transitional dormitory for Bosnian war refugees would be built in their neighborhood. In 1993, these former GDR-citizens had not yet adopted polit-ical correctness, and so 300 residents of Köpenick reacted with unrestrained fury to the city council's announcement. At first, uncoordinated shouting broke out, but then one loud voice established the tenor: "People in the new Germany were already financially struggling." They would categorically op-pose letting in "those pigs"—a reference to the war refugees. That man received rousing applause, and then the next one wanted to know, down to the last dime, what all this was going to cost. When the city councilor ob-jected that, after all, it was a question of human beings in dire need, his words were drowned out by loud noise.

Around the same time, in Brandenburg half a village raised money to encourage one young man's self-styled mission to torch the newly renovated home for asylum seekers.[10] A neighbor commented: "Better he does it now, than when there are people inside." . . . It was around then that I felt the urgent need to develop an eleventh commandment: *"Thou shalt remember!"*

Today, many former GDR citizens will still subscribe to such views, but they are no longer untutored enough to be caught saying them openly in public. The wagging tongues have retreated into the private sphere, but there they do reach today's youths at the dinner table. Many children grew up after unification in the East being told: "Those foreigners are taking away our jobs." And they were also raised with behavioral conditioning that did not exclusively target foreigners: even when a "retard is smashed up" or when a homeless person is kicked down, there will only be a feeble outcry of protest heard in the rows of houses between Frankfurt/Oder and Magdeburg, Rostock and Gera.

Of course, there are courageous and credible people even in those places, but: they are too few to oppose narrow-mindedness and brutality with education and broad-based resistance. Almost always ministers, social workers, and small grassroots initiatives are fighting on their own—up against secret enjoyment at the misfortune of the other guy, and up against a vicious circle of silence. Their small number indicates a further problem in the East—the many years during which the country became drained of people with substance who left for the West. For it is really a pernicious aftereffect of these departures that a majority of our own critical intellectuals, and a majority of real-life mentors and role models, were among those four million GDR citizens who were chased away. Generations were displaced and disconnected this way. It goes without saying that of those who remained behind, some of the more alert members of the younger generation are now also choosing to escape such a stagnant social climate.

Since the nineties, I have been visiting East German schools to discuss dictatorship and democracy, tolerance and xenophobia—in those few schools where one may possibly introduce such topics. Such a meeting in a vocational school in Neuruppin ended at some point with the claim: *"We're outnumbered by foreigners here"* In response, I asked the approximately sixty vocational trainees to raise their hand if they were not born in Germany—not a single arm went up. *"Well, your group does not seem to be outnumbered."* I observed laconically, expecting the rote answer: *"Well, not us, but in general . . . "* Then the usual complaints followed about the East having enough problems of its own, no apprentice slots and so on . . . After school, quite a few of these apprentices got into their own cars and zoomed off.

Most likely none of those youths I met had ever participated in an attack on defenseless people. But might they belong among the group of bystanders who applaud such acts? And, in the end, how much more would it take for that last step—to trample people to death, to throw them out of moving trains, or to shoot them execution-style?

Will we East Germans, now that the showy NSU- trial has begun, repress our past a second time? Will we act like all those jurists, former party secretaries and pioneer leaders, not to mention the children of Stasi staff—who became quick-change artists and reinvented themselves as "The New Left" ("Die Linke")? So that they would avoid any accountability for that GDR that had been permeated by right-wing extremism?

Even now, foreign residents only feel at ease in Berlin, our invisibly divided capital, when they return from the East to West Berlin.

I, too, feel this way.

We are facing a broken country, I wrote in 1990, *and it is our job to be accountable, accountable for a fraudulent society. In the cities of the disintegrating GDR there reigns a climate of open violence. . . .*

A short time before, I had a scary encounter late one evening: in Königs-Wusterhausen, I had to escape from a compartment in the elevated train to hide out in the caboose, because a rabble dressed in combat boots and bomber jackets had mistaken me because of my dark hair for a "Jewish cunt." I only felt safe again once I reached West Berlin territory.

Well, that was back in 1990. But have we overcome such attitudes twenty-three years later? Two days ago, a friend of mine dared to travel deep into the East—to Hellersdorf: there a group called *Engerling* (slug) were performing, a blues band that had been a longtime favorite of his. My friend is more than fifty years old and his looks do not attract attention. Nonetheless, he almost bought it on the way home—in the subway, still deep in the East, two girls began to goad him with insults. They were part of a group of drunken twenty-somethings, most of them male knuckleheads. When he did not rise to the bait, they confronted him: "What's your problem? Don't you understand German, you must be a foreigner?" Of all people it was a punk who came to his aid, and fortunately, the group exited the train soon afterwards. But my friend, like me, only felt safe when he had reached West Berlin.

My non-white friend Harry, who is from Guadeloupe, entirely avoids traveling far into the East.

BERLIN, AUGUST 2014

At the time of writing, the NSU-trial at Munich District Court has been ongoing for more than one hundred and thirty days. The scope of this trial is massive: there are ninety accessory plaintiffs and an estimated six hundred or more witnesses. It is an important moment for Germany, because in addition to the ten murders, two bomb attacks and fifteen armed robberies, also at stake are investigative failures, and the Federal Intelligence Office's and the government's underestimation of right-wing terrorism,

Beate Zschäpe is the sole survivor of the trio of self-styled terrorists of the National Socialist Underground—she is the main defendant in this trial. She is charged with ten murders, attempted murder and aggravated arson. Besides Zschäpe, four additional defendants are charged with supplying weapons or residences to the murderous trio: these defendants also emerged from the far-right scene.

The entire time, we have only been seeing the main defendant Zschäpe with her back turned to the audience. Each and every day, she enters the courtroom in nice, but not too provocative outfits, she varies her hair style and hair ornaments—quite as if what was at stake was not murder, but a hair-styling competition. . . .

We feel shame for this woman, and we wish she would finally turn around to face the wives and children of the murder victims and ask them for forgiveness.

Instead, Ms. Zschäpe suddenly attempted to dismiss her defense counsel after a whole year had passed. The court did not accept her petition, it was unwarranted. Two weeks later, she filed a challenge on grounds of bias against all the judges on the State Security Senate tribunal. The federal prosecutor and secondary plaintiffs called her challenge absurd, and they assumed that she was trying to delay the trial. This second petition was also rejected.

Might we still hope for Beate Zschäpe to show some shame and remorse? Probably not. But no matter what the result of the present long trial may be, by now, we can already note one positive outcome. The suffering families of the murder victims, mostly of Turkish ethnic background, are no longer treated as foreigners and placed under suspicion. They are now included in the German mainstream. They experience a warmth they had been missing for a long time, as well as broad-based support.

NOTES

1. Translation from the German by Helga Druxes.
2. Richard Stöss, "Rechtsextremismus in West- und Ostdeutschland," Forschungsinstitut der Friedrich-Ebert-Stiftung, eds. *Rechtsextremismus und Fremdenfeindlichkeit im vereinten Deutschland: Erscheinungsformen und Gegenstrategien* (Bonn, 1999), 33–42. See also Olaf Sundermeyer, *Rechter Terror in Deutschland: Eine Geschichte der Gewalt* (München: Beck, 2012), 85–86.
3. Christian Fuchs and John Goetz, *Die Zelle: Rechter Terror in Deutschland* (Reinbek bei Hamburg: Rowohlt, 2012), 85–86; 97.
4. Klaus Bade, and Jochen Oltmer: *Normalfall Migration*, ZeitBilder, Bd. 15 (Bonn: Bundeszentrale für politische Bildung: 2004), 90–96.
5. Andrea Böhm, "Der Nigger soll auf die Knie: Rassismus in Ostdeutschland," *taz* 10 May 1991, accessed 28 September 2014.
6. Jörg Lau, "Oskar Haider," *Die Zeit* 23 June 2005, http://www.zeit.de/2005/26/Spr_9fche, accessed 29 September 2014.
7. Freya Klier, "Wir müssen ja jetzt Westen sein," Berlin: Sender Freies Berlin: 2000, 8. http://www.freya-klier.de/texte/6_wirmuessenjajetztwesten.pdf, accessed 29 September 2014.
8. Tja, "Stadt ist mit rechten Vorfällen von 1991 längst nicht fertig," 15 January 2014, Freiburg: *Badische Zeitung*, http://www.badische-zeitung.de/deutschland-1/stadt-ist-mit-rechten-vorfaellen-von-1991-laengst-nicht-fertig--79646507.html, accessed 29 September 2014.
9. Freya Klier, *Johanna: Eine Dresdner Ballade*, Leipzig: Mitteldeutscher Rundfunk, 1996. Film.

10. Constanze Stelzenmüller, "Wir sind ein ganz normales Dorf," 17 June 1994, *Die Zeit* No. 25 (Hamburg: Die Zeit, 1994), http://www.zeit.de/1994/25/wir-sind-ein-ganz-normales-dorf, accessed 29 September 2014.

REFERENCES

Bade, Klaus and J. Oltmer. *Normalfall Migration.* Bonn: Bundeszentrale für politische Bildung, 2004.

Fuchs, Christian and J. Goetz. *Die Zelle: Rechter Terror in Deutschland.* Reinbek bei Hamburg: Rowohlt, 2012.

Lau, Jörg. "Oskar Haider." *Die Zeit* 23 June 2005. http://www.zeit.de/2005/26/Spr_9fche. Accessed 29 September 2014.

Klier, Freya. *Johanna: Eine Dresdner Ballade.* Leipzig: Mitteldeutscher Rundfunk, 1996. Film.

Klier, Freya. "Wir müssen ja jetzt Westen sein." Berlin: Sender Freies Berlin: 2000, 8. http://www.freya-klier.de/texte/6_wirmuessenjajetztwesten.pdf. Accessed 29 September 2014.

Tja. "Stadt ist mit rechten Vorfällen von 1991 längst nicht fertig." Freiburg: *Badische Zeitung* 15 Januar 2014. http://www.badische-zeitung.de/deutschland-1/stadt-ist-mit-rechten-vorfaellen-von-1991-laengst-nicht-fertig--79646507.html. Accessed 29 September 2014.

Stelzenmüller, Constanze. "Wir sind ein ganz normales Dorf." *Die Zeit* No. 25 17 June 1994. Hamburg: Die Zeit, 1994. http://www.zeit.de/1994/25/wir-sind-ein-ganz-normales-dorf. Accessed 29 September 2014.

Stöss, Richard."Rechtsextremismus in West- und Ostdeutschland." Forschungsinstitut der Friedrich-Ebert-Stiftung, eds. *Rechtsextremismus und Fremdenfeindlichkeit im vereinten Deutschland: Erscheinungsformen und Gegenstrategien.* Bonn, 1999.

Sundermeyer, Olaf. *Rechter Terror in Deutschland: Eine Geschichte der Gewalt.* München: Beck, 2012.

Index

About the Contributors

Chip Berlet, an investigative journalist and independent scholar, co-authored the book *Right-Wing Populism in America: Too Close for Comfort* (Guilford 2000), and co-authored the revised entry on "Neo-Nazism" in the new second edition of the *Encyclopaedia Judaica*. He has written for the journals *Totalitarian Movements and Political Religions, Contemporary Sociology, American Anthropologist, Critical Sociology, Criminology and Public Policy*, and *Research in Political Sociology*. His chapter on U.S. neo-fascist groups, "The United States: Messianism, Apocalypticism, and Political Religion," appeared in *The Sacred in Twentieth Century Politics: Essays in Honour of Professor Stanley G. Payne* (Palgrave Macmillan 2007).

Kyle Christensen is an associate professor of Political Science and Public Administration at Columbus State University. He also serves as the director of the Social Research Center at Columbus State University. Christensen's research interests include comparative public policy, international security, and European Union politics. He has previously published work in *PS: Political Science and Politics, the European Journal of Public Policy*, and in various edited volumes.

Helga Druxes is professor of German at Williams College where she teaches twentieth- and twenty-first century German Studies. She is the author of two monographs: *The Feminization of Dr. Faustus* (1993) and *Resisting Bodies: The Negotiation of Female Agency in Twentieth-Century Women's Fiction* (1996) and of numerous articles in German Studies, on critiques of neoliberalism, and on migration film. Her current project is an edited volume on German writer Navid Kermani, in the series *Contemporary German Writers and Filmmakers*, forthcoming with Peter Lang Oxford.

Glen M. E. Duerr is assistant professor of International Studies at Cedarville University in Cedarville, Ohio. His teaching and research interests include nationalism and secession, comparative politics, international relations theory, sports and politics, and Christianity and politics. He has published numerous refereed journal articles, book chapters, encyclopedia entries, and book reviews.

Robert D. Duval is an associate professor in the Department of Political Science at West Virginia University and has teaching and research interests in statistical methods, international politics, environmental policy, and national security policy. His published research is in the areas of international relations, public policy, and statistical methodology. His more recent funded research has been in the areas of health policy, the applications of statistical methods in health care and data fusion for intelligence analysis. Professor Duval is also the Interim Chair for the Department of Health Policy, Management, and Leadership in the WVU School of Public Health.

Justin D. García is assistant professor of Anthropology at Millersville University in Millersville, Pennsylvania, where he teaches a range of courses on topics such as Latino Issues of Identity and Culture through Film. Having earned his PhD at Temple (2011), García's research interests include social constructions of race and ethnicity, U.S. immigration, urban anthropology, the anthropology of sport(s). Recent articles include: "'You Don't Look Mexican!': Life in Ethnic Ambiguity and What It Says About the Construction of Race in America" (Multicultural Perspectives, forthcoming) and "Stuck Between Barack and a Hard Place: Obama's Impact on Race Relations in the 21st Century" (Idea Exchange ABC-CLIO, 2013).

Freya Klier is a writer, documentary filmmaker, and German political activist. Prior to 1989, Klier was a high-profile East German dissident and theater director. Selected publications include: *Promised New Zealand: Escapes to the Ends of the Earth* (2009; *Lüg Vaterland—Erziehung in der DDR* (*Lying Fatherland—The GDR Education System*, 2001); and *Verschleppt ans Ende der Welt: Schicksale deutscher Frauen in sowjetischen Arbeitslagern* (*Deported to the Ends of the Earth: Fates of German Women in Soviet Labor Camps*, 1998). Her films include: *We want to be free: East Germans Rise Up: June 17, 1953* (2013); *Die Vergessenen: Tod, wo andere Urlaub machen* (The Forgotten Ones: Death where Others Vacationed, 2011); *Flucht mit dem Moskau-Paris-Express* (Escape by Moscow-Paris Express, 2001); and *Die Odyssee der Anja Lundholm* (The Odyssey of Anja Lundholm, 1998).

Alexandra Koronaiou is professor of Sociology at Panteion University of Social and Political Sciences, at the University of Athens, and at the Greek Open University. Since June 2011, she has been responsible for the Panteion University MYPLACE research team, coordinating and conducting research on youth political activity and civic engagement. She has directed and conducted research on sociology of work and free time, education, youth sociopolitical participation and engagement, and the media impact on youth and gender issues. She is a member of the Scientific Committee of the "Observatory on Gender Equality in Education" and of KETHI (Research Centre for Women's Equality). She is the author of more than fifty articles and book chapters, and several books including: *Youth and Media of Mass Communication* (1995); *Sociology of leisure time* (1996); *Educating outside school* (2002); *The role of fathers in balancing Professional and Family-Private Life* (2007); and *When Work Becomes Illness* (2010).

Evangelos Lagos is sociologist-researcher and a member of the Panteion University of Social and Political Sciences research team for the FP7-MY-PLACE research program. He is currently doing research on youth political activity and civic engagement focusing on youth political activism, young people's receptivity toward far-right and fascist ideology and political agenda, and young people's participation in the 2011 Greek Indignant movement. He has done research on immigration, unemployment and job training, youth subcultures, youth radicalism, cultural politics and policy, social policy and free time, and modernization processes of the Greek society. He has published and presented papers on youth radicalism, contemporary neo-fascist ideology and cultural politics, youth's receptivity toward far right and fascism, social policy and culture, and modernization processes and social policy.

Carol Mason, PhD, is professor of Gender and Women's Studies at University of Kentucky. She is the author of three books detailing the rise of the right in different contexts. They are: *Killing for Life: The Apocalyptic Narrative of Pro-life Politics* (Cornell 2002); *Reading Appalachia from Left to Right: Conservatives and the 1974 Kanawha County Textbook Controversy* (Cornell 2009); and *Oklahomo: Lessons in Unqueering America* (SUNY Press 2015).

Lara Mazurski is a doctoral candidate in the Literary Studies department at the University of Amsterdam, Netherlands, and an affiliate of the Amsterdam School for Cultural Analysis. Her research and teaching interests include gender theory, critical race theory, post-colonial studies, Islamic feminism, and Muslim women's studies.

Alexandar Mihailovic is Professor Emeritus of Russian and Comparative Literature at Hofstra University and currently Visiting Professor of Russian at Brown University where he teaches courses on Russian film, Bakhtin, and on the Black Experience and Russian Culture. He is the author of *Corporeal Words: Mikhail Bakhtin's Theology of Discourse* (Northwestern 1997), and the editor of *Tchaikovsky and His Contemporaries: A Centenary Symposium* (Greenwood 1999). His recent articles include: "Desensitized Migrants: Organized Crime Workers in Cronenberg's *Eastern Promises* and Balabanov's *Stoker*." Work in Cinema: Labour and the Human Condition. Ed. Ewa Mazierska (Palgrave 2013), "Wings of a Dove: The Shifting Language for Same-Sex Desire in Putin and Medvedev's Russia." *The Meanings of Sexual Identity in the 21st Century.* Eds. David A. Powell and Judith Kaufman (Cambridge Scholars Press 2014), "Globalist Gangsters: Reading Mexican Drug Cartels and Russian Organized Crime." *The International Journal of the Humanities* Volume 9, Number 6 (2011): 153–64.

Alexandros Sakellariou holds a PhD on Sociology from the Department of Sociology of Panteion University of Social and Political Sciences of Athens. He studied at the School of Philosophy of the University of Athens and he obtained his M.A. from the Department of Sociology of Panteion University. He is currently a researcher in the 4-year FP7-European Commission Research Project entitled MYPLACE, *Memory, Youth, Political Legacy and Civic Engagement* and he is a post-doctoral researcher at Panteion University at the Department of Sociology, studying the forms of atheism in contemporary Greek society. He has conducted research on young people's civic and political engagement, on the rise and receptivity of neo-Nazi ideology, on racist speech, on religious communities, and on the relations between religion and politics. His scientific interests include sociology of religion, sociology of youth, political sociology, and the study of right-wing extremism. He has presented papers and published on these topics in Greece and abroad.

Domonkos Sik is a sociologist and philosopher, currently working at the University Eötvös Loránd as an assistant professor in Budapest. His research focuses on critical theories of modernization in post-transition countries, with special attention to the political formation of youth. Currently he is participating in the project MYPLACE (FP7-266831). Among his most important publications are: "A modernizáció ingája" (The pendulum of modernization, Eötvös Kiadó 2012); "Demokratikus kultúra és modernizáció" (Democratic culture and modernization, L'Harmattan 2014); "Civic socialization in post-transition condition" (In *Politics, Culture and Socialization*, 2. Vol., No. 3/2011, 257–71); "The Transformation of Action coordination?— A Critical Interpretation of the Hungarian Transition" (In *Review of Sociology of the Hungarian Academy of Science* 2010/2).

Patricia Anne Simpson is Professor of German Studies at Montana State University in Bozeman. The author of *The Erotics of War in German Romanticism* (Bucknell 2006) and *Cultures of Violence in the New German Street* (Rowman & Littlefield 2011), her monograph, *Reimagining the European Family: Cultures of Immigration*, appeared in 2013 with Palgrave Macmillan. Recipient of the Goethe Society of North America's Essay Prize (2013), Simpson has co-edited several volumes on culture in the Age of Goethe and is currently completing a project on theories and practices of play in transatlantic modernity.

Arian Spahiu is an Associate with BayFirst Solutions LLC, a Security and Risk Management and Consulting firm. Prior to joining BayFirst Solutions LLC, he was a risk consultant with ABS consulting, a Safety and Risk Management consulting firm, and a Social Scientist with the United States Department of the Army. Spahiu received his PhD in Political Science from

West Virginia University with topical emphasis in national security and terrorism studies.

Kjetil Stormark is an award-winning reporter and author, as well as the editor-in-chief of Hate Speech International, an investigative center monitoring extremist groups in Europe, North Africa, and the Middle East. He has published two books on the 2011 terror attacks in Norway. Stormark is a former editor-in-chief and managing editor of several Norwegian newspapers. Stormark is also a former PR consultant and press counselor at the Norwegian Mission to the UN in New York in 2001–2002, when Norway was a member of the Security Council.

Øyvind Strømmen is a Norwegian journalist who has written extensively on extremist movements. He has published three books on the radical and extreme right, *Det mørke nettet* (Cappelen Damm 2011); *Den sorte tråden* (Cappelen Damm 2013); and *I hatets fotspor* (Cappelen Damm, 2014); the first of which was also translated into Swedish, Finnish, and French.

Fabian Virchow is Professor of Political Science at University of Applied Sciences Düsseldorf, Germany. His research focuses on the extreme right in Europe. He is the editor of *Visual Politics of the Far Right* (Springer VS 2015), and, with Gideon Botsch and Christoph Kopke: *Verbote extrem rechter Parteien und Organisationen, 1951–2012* (Making Extreme Right Parties and Organizations Illegal, Verlag für Sozialwissenschaften 2013). With Martina Thiele and Tanja Thomas, Virchow co-edited *Medien—Krieg—Geschlecht* (Media—War—Gender, Verlag für Sozialwissenschaften 2010); *War isn't Hell, it's Entertainment: War in Modern Culture and Visual Media*, co-edited with Rikke Schubart, Debra White-Stanley, and Tanja Thomas, appeared in 2009 (McFarland). He has also co-edited two other volumes on the Far Right in Germany.

Bret Wilson is the Data Analyst for the Office for Equity and Diversity at East Carolina University. His research interests include Policy Analysis, Political Behavior, and the Presidency. Wilson's research and career are focused on how empirical research can tell compelling and meaningful stories.

www.ingramcontent.com/pod-product-compliance
Lightning Source LLC
Chambersburg PA
CBHW051225050326
40689CB00007B/803